Gender, Emotions and Power, 1750–2020

 New Historical PERSPECTIVES

New Historical Perspectives is a book series for early career scholars within the UK and the Republic of Ireland. Books in the series are overseen by an expert editorial board to ensure the highest standards of peer-reviewed scholarship. Commissioning and editing is undertaken by the Royal Historical Society, and the series is published by the University of London Press in association with the Institute of Historical Research.

The series is supported by the Economic History Society and the Past and Present Society.

Series co-editors: Professor Elizabeth Hurren (University of Leicester) and Professor Heather Shore (Manchester Metropolitan University)

Founding co-editors: Simon Newman (University of Glasgow) and Penny Summerfield (University of Manchester)

Editorial board: Professor Charlotte Alston (Northumbria University); Professor David Andress (University of Portsmouth); Dr Christopher Bahl (Durham University); Dr Milinda Banerjee (University of St Andrews); Dr Robert Barnes (York St John University); Dr Karin Bowie (University of Glasgow); Professor Catherine Clarke (Institute of Historical Research, University of London); Professor Neil Fleming (University of Worcester); Professor Ian Forrest (University of Oxford); Dr Emma Gallon (University of London Press); Dr Sarah Longair (University of Lincoln); Professor Jane Whittle (University of Exeter); Dr Charlotte Wildman (University of Manchester); Dr Nick Witham (University College London)

Recently published

Anti-Communism in Britain During the Early Cold War: A Very British Witch Hunt, by Matthew Gerth (April 2023)
The Glasgow Sugar Aristocracy: Scotland and Caribbean Slavery, 1775–1838, by Stephen Mullen (November 2022)

Gender, Emotions and Power, 1750–2020

Edited by
Hannah Parker and Josh Doble

Available to purchase in print or download
for free at https://uolpress.co.uk

First published 2023 by
University of London Press
Senate House, Malet St, London WC1E 7HU

© Authors, 2023

The right of the Authors to be identified as authors of
this Work has been asserted by them in accordance
with sections 77 and 78 of the Copyright, Designs and
Patents Act 1988.

This book is published under a Creative Commons
Attribution-NonCommercial-NoDerivatives 4.0
International (CC BY-NC-ND 4.0) license.

Please note that third-party material reproduced here may
not be published under the same license as the rest of this
book. If you would like to reuse any third-party material
not covered by the book's Creative Commons license, you
will need to obtain permission from the copyright holder.

A CIP catalogue record for this book is
available from The British Library.

ISBN 978-1-915249-15-9 (hardback)
ISBN 978-1-915249-16-6 (paperback)
ISBN 978-1-915249-17-3 (.epub)
ISBN 978-1-915249-19-7 (.pdf)

DOI https://doi.org/10.14296/cwfb4352

Cover image: Edvard Munch, *Jealousy*, 1907? Oil on canvas.
75.5 × 98cm. MM.M.00447 © Munchmuseet.
Photo: Munchmuseet / Jori Kobayashi. All rights reserved,
used with permission.

Cover design for the University of London Press
by Hayley Warnham.
Book design by Nigel French.
Text set by Westchester Publishing Services in
Meta Serif and Meta, designed by Erik Spiekermann.

Contents

Notes on contributors	vii
Acknowledgements	xi
Introduction *Hannah Parker and Josh Doble*	1

Part I Gender, class and sexuality in the negotiation of political power

1. 'My old eyes weep but I am proud of my own children': grief and revolutionary motherhood in the Soviet 1920s   31
   Hannah Parker

2. Emotion as a tool of Russian bisexual and transgender women's online activism: a case study   55
   Olga Andreevskikh

3. Sounding the socialist heroine: gender, revolutionary lyricism and Korean war films   77
   Yucong Hao

4. Emotions at work: solidarity in the Liverpool dock dispute, 1995–8   95
   Emma Copestake

Part II Power and place-making: class, hygiene and race in the British Empire

5. White pride, male anger and the shame of poverty: gendered emotions and the construction of white working-class identity in interwar Southern Rhodesia   121
   Nicola Ginsburgh

6. 'Africans smell different': disgust, fear and the gendering of interracial intimacy in Kenya and Zambia   145
   Josh Doble

7. Gender, mission, emotion: building hospitals for women in northwestern British India   169
   Sara Honarmand Ebrahimi

vi   CONTENTS

Part III Modern Europe's public sphere and the policing of the gendered body

8. 'The sap that runs in it is the same': how the ideal of romantic love challenged the myth of 'primitive' polygamy in Paolo Mantegazza's sexual science   195
Francesca Campani

9. Writing the man of politeness: the hidden importance of shame in eighteenth-century masculinity   217
Michael Rowland

10. 'At nature's mighty feast there is no vacant cover for him': suicide, masculine shame and the language of burden in nineteenth-century Britain   239
Lyndsay Galpin

11. 'Sadistic, grinning rifle-women': gender, emotions and politics in representations of militant leftist women   261
Hannah Proctor

Index   285

Notes on contributors

Olga Andreevskikh is a senior lecturer in Russian Language and Culture at Tampere University, Finland. Her research focuses on queer media and culture, in particular on mediated non-heteronormative masculinities.

Francesca Campani (she/her) received her PhD in Modern History from the University of Padua in co-tutorship with the University of Lincoln, with research on the anthropologist Paolo Mantegazza and his contribution to the emergence of sexual science in the second half of the nineteenth century. She is currently a postdoctoral researcher at the University of Padua with a research project on the role of anthropological visual and material culture in the construction of scientific discourses on sexuality between the nineteenth and twentieth centuries.

Emma Copestake (she/her) completed her PhD at the University of Liverpool in 2022 with the support of the Arts and Humanities Research Council and the Institute of Historical Research. Her thesis examines the emotional history and cultural memory of dock work in Liverpool from the 1960s. Emma's broader research interests include oral history, modern British history, the history of work, deindustrialization and public history.

Josh Doble is the policy manager at Community Land Scotland and an honorary fellow at the University of Edinburgh. He is a historian of twentieth-century colonialism who has previously worked at the University of Edinburgh, the University of Leeds and the Institute of Historical Research. His research focuses on histories of emotions, settler colonialism and race, largely within the decolonizing territories of East and Central Africa. His recent articles have focused on 'racist dogs' in *History Workshop Journal* and colonial pidgin languages in the *Journal of Southern African Studies* and he has recently co-edited a collection, *British Culture after Empire*, with Manchester University Press (published in 2023).

Lyndsay Galpin completed her PhD, funded by the Friendly Hand, at Royal Holloway, University of London in 2019, with a thesis exploring the cultural narratives of male suicide through nineteenth-century newspaper reports. Her book, which is based on her thesis and titled *Male Suicide and Masculinity in 19th-Century Britain: Stories of Self-Destruction*, was published by Bloomsbury in 2022.

Nicola Ginsburgh is a research fellow at the International Studies Group based at the University of the Free State in South Africa. Her monograph, *Class, Work and Whiteness: Race and Settler Colonialism in Southern Rhodesia, 1919–79*, was published in 2020 with Manchester University Press.

Yucong Hao received her PhD from the University of Michigan. Her research interests include Chinese socialist culture, media theory and performance studies. She is completing a dissertation on the intersection of political revolutions and media revolutions in modern China.

Sara Honarmand Ebrahimi is a Humboldt research fellow at Goethe University Frankfurt. Her research interests span the history of emotions, hospital architecture and internationalism. Her first book, *Emotion, Mission, Architecture: Building Hospitals in Persia and British India, 1865–1914*, was published by Edinburgh University Press in 2022. She is also the editor of the special section of *Emotions: History, Culture, Society* on 'Exploring Architecture and Emotions through Space and Place'. She is currently co-writing (with Padma Maitland) a book, *Feeling Modern European Imperial Architecture*, for the Cambridge Elements series on Histories of Emotions and the Senses.

Hannah Parker (she/her) is a historian of the Soviet Union. She holds a PhD from the University of Sheffield, and works at the Open University. Her recent publications have pursued interests in the emotions of female librarians in the Soviet 1920s, gender, loyalty and gratitude in letters to Soviet authorities during Stalin's Terror, and she is currently working on her first monograph, on letter-writing, emotion and 'emancipation' among women in the Soviet Union. She is an organizer with the Sheffield Feminist Archive.

Hannah Proctor is a historian of the human sciences based at the Centre for the Social History of Health and Healthcare at the University of Strathclyde, Glasgow currently working on a Wellcome Trust-funded project called 'De-pathologising dissent'. Her first monograph, *Psychologies in Revolution: Alexander Luria's 'Romantic Science' and Soviet Social History*, was published as part of the Palgrave Macmillan series 'Mental Health in Historical Perspective' in 2020. Her second book, *Burnout: The Psychic Life of Political Defeat*, will be published by Verso in 2024. She is a member of the editorial collective of *Radical Philosophy*, a contributing editor to *Parapraxis* magazine and reviews/web/social media editor of *History of the Human Sciences*.

Michael Rowland holds a PhD in Eighteenth-Century Literature from the University of Sussex, which was funded by the Arts and Humanities Research Council. His research interests focus on the influence of individual and collective emotional experiences on structures of masculinity in the eighteenth century. He has previously published in *Eighteenth-Century Fiction* and the *European Journal of English Studies*. He works at the University of Sussex.

Acknowledgements

We would like to thank each of the contributors to this book who have patiently and diligently worked with the editorial team for almost four years, under some very challenging personal and collective circumstances – not least the ongoing pandemic. We thank each of them for their good humour, intellectual engagement and perseverance! It has been a genuine pleasure to be able to read such lively and insightful research, and we have sought to emphasize the unique and captivating voices of each of the authors in our editorial work. We hope that this has been successful.

This book began as a series of conversations in seminars at the University of Sheffield and pubs around the city between Hannah Parker, Dr Becca Mytton and Dr Elizabeth Goodwin. These informal chats later became the Gendered Emotions in History conference, hosted at the university in June 2018, which sought to bring wider perspectives to bear on the questions we had raised about the troubling intersections of gender and emotion. The conference featured a wide range of submissions and disciplines, all of which spoke to the ongoing political and social urgency of the theme, and whose ambition and interdisciplinarity served to drive this volume. We want to start by thanking all those who attended and presented at Gendered Emotions, including the keynote addresses from Thomas Dixon and Hannah Proctor. Your interventions and participation at that event laid the foundations for the work in this book. We are also grateful to the institutions and bodies who provided generous funding and support for this project, and in particular the funding provided for childcare and children's items to make the conference 'child-friendly': the White Rose College of the Arts and Humanities, the Social History Society and the Royal Historical Society.

Finally, our thanks to University of London Press and in particular to our mentor Nick Witham and Books Manager Emma Gallon, whose support and guidance has made the sometimes lengthy editorial process enjoyable. We would also like to thank the editors, Elizabeth Hurren and Heather Shore, who have supported this project since first seeing it. Thank you too to our anonymous reviewers for their clear, engaged and supportive feedback, which helped shape the book into its final form.

Olga Andreevskikh: This work is dedicated to the brave women who kindly agreed to share their experiences for my case study and all the other courageous bisexual and transgender activists fighting for equal rights in Russia.

Emma Copestake: My work would not be possible without the generosity of the dock workers and their family members in Liverpool who helped me to understand the meaning of solidarity in new ways. My contribution here is also indebted to the kind academics and archivists who have encouraged me to keep going over the last few years, including both Hannah and Josh. My final thank you goes to my husband, family and friends for their endless love, support and reminders that life exists outside of research.

Josh Doble: My research is indebted to the generosity of many people in Kenya and Zambia. The staff at the National Archives of both countries must be given special mention for their patience with my relentless requests and their dedication to finding obscure records. A particular thanks has to go to the participants in this research, whose testimonies, photos, private archival material and open address books are what made this research possible. The distinct direction this research took was a direct result of my participants' hospitality and willingness to engage. I cannot name specific individuals or family collections but there are key interlocutors in both countries who deserve special mention. I would like to think they know who they are.

Hannah Parker: I owe a debt of gratitude to friends, family and a number of academics, though there are two named dedications I'd like to make here. First, given the subject of my research, to the victims of the full-scale Russian military invasion of Ukraine. Second, to the contributors to this collection, for entrusting us with their excellent research.

Michael Rowland: This chapter is for Yousif Ali: the accelerator to my brake; the joy to my sadness. And for Lesley Rowland, my mother and very first role model.

Introduction

Hannah Parker and Josh Doble

The weather was calm and pleasant. But the waves, in excited confusion, were washing new shores that had never before met the sea. The volcano that had started all the fuss had calmed down. It sighed wearily now and then, and breathed a little ash towards the sky.

—Tove Jansson, *Moominsummer Madness*

The essential, or naturalized, qualities of gendered emotion can be found in the discursive engagement with our natural environment, as Tove Jansson neatly encapsulates above. Our environments often appear to be in possession of their own 'moods', and emotions' metaphysical qualities find comfortable companion in metaphors from the natural world. Landscapes, natural environments or phenomena are frequent metaphors in both literary and academic discussions of the emotions.[1] In English, one can have a sunny disposition; a volcanic temper; be ablaze with fury, lust, love or torment; remain stony-faced and stoical; be petrified by fear; or have a face like thunder.[2] Relationships can be rocky or frosty, grief can be said to hit one like a tsunami and while we are all prone to sudden waves of any given feeling, like tides, feelings can ebb or flow. Clouds can blight us with confusion or depression. Unwanted emotions are 'buried' until they can no longer be suppressed, when they 'erupt', and emotional distance between people is considered a 'chasm' to bridge. In Russian, nervousness – *volnenie* – is related to the word 'wave' (*volna*) and to hold unrealistic hopes is to 'build castles in the sand' (*stroit' zamki iz peska*).[3] As in the English language, both love and hope can be described as fires or flames in French, Spanish and Dutch.[4]

Women who are considered less than forthcoming with their affections are described as icy or glacial; women thought to display too much emotion are said to have fiery tempers, referred to as 'forces of nature'. Historical accounts of women's political activity – and crucially their anger – have a tendency to characterize it as 'elemental', rooted in 'basic' demands such as 'hunger' – so aptly demonstrated by the 'wild furies' of Hannah Proctor's Chapter 11 in this volume. Highly gendered notions of fertility often accompany similar statements about emotionality, landscape and the 'warmth' of individuals' feelings or demeanours. Mirroring descriptors of female fertility, biological infertility is described through the pseudo-agricultural discourse of 'barren' earth and the insinuated notions of drought and unproductiveness.[5] Although far from the only common allegory used to comprehend human feeling, metaphors and similes of landscapes and the natural world are undeniably evocative, raising the question of why they are so pervasive and why the connection of emotions to nature seems so instinctive. According to the 'Mapping Metaphor' project based at the University of Glasgow, strong metaphorical connections between land and water, landscape, and atmosphere, and what we now refer to as 'the emotions', have existed in the English language since as early as the eleventh century.[6]

While the emotional poetics of meteorological prose may seem a far cry from the attacks on forced migrants in twenty-first-century 'Fortress Europe', both examples rely upon recalcitrant notions of naturalness and fixity to justify relatively recent social constructions: on the one hand, the innate and therefore supposedly unchanging forces of the natural world placed onto gendered emotions, and on the other the inherited and supposedly pre-ordained borders of contemporary nation states. Borders, emotions and gender are uncritically considered to be natural and therefore fixed, as though as much a part of the natural world as the landscape or weather which surrounds us. These notions of inevitability work to justify interconnected power structures of patriarchy and racially minded European nation states, making clear the urgency of thoroughly historicizing and analysing the means through which supposedly natural categories of organization and classification are constructed. The ways in which gender, and connectedly class, race and sexuality, has been constructed, contoured and naturalized by prevailing power structures are at the heart of our analysis, encouraging future emotional analysis of the imagined nation states of Europe.[7]

The chapters presented in *Gender, Emotions and Power, 1750–2020* explore the social, political and cultural pressures upon subjects and societies in different historical locations and scrutinize the relationship between power, emotions and gender through a global comparative and contemporary lens. While contingent upon the socio-cultural context of the subject-society, both emotions and gender, and their interactions with each other and intersections of race, class and sexuality, appear to be naturalized by constructions and orientations of selfhood. Disaggregating this fixity of gender and emotion stands as the key aim of this collection. From this basis the volume makes four interventions. In the first instance, it aims to interrogate the essentialization of emotion and feeling through a sustained focus on the social and cultural construction of gender. This focus is expanded to consider, second, explicitly how power relations shape the normative expression of both categories and in turn play a role in shaping (although not dominating) what emotions are, and how they 'work' in society. The third contribution is the collective impact of the chapters to identify, destabilize and denaturalize the power relations which underpin emotion and gender in all of these case studies. While the social and cultural formulations of emotions are fundamentally and intrinsically gendered, the underexplored interaction of this vector with other social categories forms a key contribution of this collection. Finally, the collection of essays brings the history of emotions into time periods and area studies beyond the typical geographic remit of the field, and so explores the merits of approaching 'regular' histories through an emotional lens.[8] This book's focus on histories of Africa, China, India and Russia alongside those of modern Europe uncovers the role of emotions in colonialism, anti-imperialism and communism: areas for the historian of emotions that have not yet been fully interrogated. The geographical and methodological scope offered by the chapters as a collective provides a set of heuristic tools for further use by the field and encourages other scholars to think expansively about varying contexts and sources which can be used to interrogate the entangled histories of gender, emotion and power.

In the time that has elapsed since this book was initially conceived, the ubiquity of emotional rhetoric in global politics seems to have reached the point of oversaturation. In its early iterations – as plans for the 2018 conference Gendered Emotions in History – we as organizers had, in pub chats and department seminars, been interested in the parallels between our then doctoral research and currents in our own lives: that certain emotions were deemed more or less natural, based on gendered or sexed bodies, be they in the new society of the Soviet Union, late medieval English convents, among Irish Republican men after the Easter Rising, in academic workplaces or in our friendships.[9] Plans were driven by the selective media appetite for women's emotions in response to long-overdue and highly publicized criticisms of institutionalized sexual harassment and assault in the entertainment industry and beyond. Misogynistic and racist attacks in the media on Serena Williams for the emotions she displayed at the US Open umpire's decision against her provided a jarring counterpoint following the outpourings of public praise for emotionally charged denunciations of routine sexual harassment and assault by stars such as Uma Thurman earlier in the same year.[10] Common to these discussions was the significance of emotions as 'naturally' gendered qualities, with the consequence of regulating or maintaining existing hierarchies of power.

Since then, the power dimensions and consequences of these emotional themes have become ever starker. We have been struck in particular by the escalating media rhetoric about the crisis facing forced migrants since 2014, and the media's frequently false allegations about sexual violence against western European populations. These emotionally charged and dishonest accounts have been a key part of the corresponding attempts – rooted in emotive language – to justify border regimes and solidify the territoriality and political status quo of nations throughout Europe and the United States. Using fear, confusion and anger to subdue critical voices and resistance to the UK border regime, the UK's former home secretary Priti Patel labelled the victims of the Home Office's forced deportation schemes as 'foreign criminals' in order to emotionally – and consequently morally – 'justify' their severance from their families, communities and lives in the UK to the electorate.[11] German (and British) mass media coverage of the arrival of refugees in Europe between 2014 and 2016 has reproduced 'age-old stereotypes of "coloured men" as ... dangerous sexual predators, targeting European "white women" with their allegedly untamed sexual desires', despite research clearly and consistently finding that migrants 'face heightened threats of sexual and gender based violence as they seek refuge in other countries', often as a result of the hostile environments and their emotional discontents already described.[12] Casting light on the emotional, rather than legal or moral, foundations of such policy, deportations have even been cancelled because of the danger to life the destinations pose to officials, let alone to deported persons.[13]

While far-right targets of ire amplify one set of power relations shaped by emotional and gender norms, emotions have also been identified with power and the 'personal political'. The identification of extreme manifestations of normative masculinities as 'toxic masculinity' has been employed to divert sustained criticism of systemic injustice, part of the same conservative appropriation of the emotional rhetoric of social justice that has led to action *against* the accommodation of migrants in Germany, in the name of feminism. The most recent iteration of this tendency was the former UK prime minister Boris Johnson's baffling claim in 2022 that Russia's reinvasion of Ukraine – which he labelled a 'crazy, macho war of invasion and violence' – would not have happened were its president Vladimir Putin a woman.[14] At the same time as Johnson claimed that education and gender equality were the real solution to the conflict, G7 leaders joked that it was necessary for them to 'show their pecs' to prove they were 'tougher than Putin', and real-terms investment in school education per pupil, and in adult education overall, reached a nadir in the UK in 2021. Despite his critique of Putin's 'toxic masculinity', Johnson is well known for casual misogyny in government, and his government excluded trans people from legal protection by the Conversion Therapy Ban in May 2022.[15]

Similarly, Arlie Russell Hochschild's concept of emotional labour has been evoked as a critique of interpersonal relations and workplace burnout, and in particular in criticism of the identification of women with pastoral roles in workplaces on an individual basis.[16] Hochschild herself reported feeling 'horrified' by the 'concept creep' of the term to describe things such as housework and 'the enacting of to-do lists in daily life,' which are less emotional labour than simply domestic labour.[17] Hochschild's disdain for the co-optation of emotional labour has illuminated the atomizing tendencies of mainstream critiques of the gender and emotional iniquities within workplaces, the dimensions of power resulting and the solutions presented.[18] This tendency to atomize has consequences: the individualization of responsibility for misuses and imbalances of power, and the micro-solutions posed, stand in stark contrast to the collective efforts and results Emma Copestake identifies in her analysis of the Liverpool dock strike in Chapter 4 of this volume. The atomization of injustice obscures more than it illuminates. As this book argues, gender, emotions and power should properly be considered as interconnected social co-constructions: an overemphasis upon individual 'emotional labour' denies the potential for transnational, translocal solidarities among marginalized groups – such as the bisexual and trans women upon whom Olga Andreevskikh focuses her interventions on digital spaces for activism among Russian LGBTQI+ groups in Chapter 2 of this volume.[19]

The contributions to this book illuminate the need for focused discussion of emotion as a dimension of power, but also call for collective focus on how emotions – shared and individual – play a central role in contesting and redefining social categorizations such as gender. In this sense, the volume's primary intervention is to identify how social stratifications according to gender, class, race and sexuality have justified and maintained the status quo, yet also how the emotional politics of these intersections of identity have been central to galvanizing individual and collective consciousness which have challenged established power structures. While this book aims to contribute to the field of emotion and gender history in general, the chapters themselves are rooted in the historical and cultural contexts of their case studies, enabling a more precise historicization of what the casual observer may recognize as the entanglements of gender, politics and emotion in a historically male-dominated and increasingly populist political scene around the world.

Gender, power and emotion

This volume's intention is not to re-theorize the history of emotions but to explore the entangled relationships of gender, emotion and power by drawing on a multitude of case studies worldwide. Thus far, the accomplishments of studies of gender within the history of emotion have been extensive, far exceeding emotion history's recognition within the discipline. Historians of love and marriage in particular have skilfully interrogated historical interactions between the self and others in public and private life in emotional vocabularies and behaviours.[20] They have illuminated the links between emotion, selfhood and subjectivity in historical performances of gender roles through emotional behaviours.[21] Scholarship has also historicized, and mapped a future for, the integration of scientific and historical inquiry into the emotions.[22] Recent studies have also established sophisticated integrations of the history of emotions into what Rosenwein calls 'regular' histories, employing emotions as a lens through which to reconsider, for example, work, family, war and generational cohorts.[23] This volume attends to the questions generated by this body of work and scrutinizes the constructions of these roles and vocabularies from the bottom up, interrogating the political implications of those intersections of gender, emotion and power.

An explicit consideration of power relations in connection with emotions history illuminates the work done by emotions to stratify populations, without aligning social groups with particular emotions. By identifying diverse emotional responses within groups, we can complicate perceptions of social groups, as well as stepping back to identify the emotional exchanges present in their categorization, or to consciously perform or subvert anticipated emotional expression, as the activists in Olga Andreevskikh's study in Chapter 2 demonstrate. In this sense, 'emotions can create or reproduce subordination, but can also unravel it'.[24] Of course, power has been conceived of in myriad ways. Power, as the capacity to dominate through means such as ideology, religion, race, gender, sexuality or class, is often connected largely to its institutional capacities and embodiment: in broad or narrow terms, by members of a ruling class, such as owners of the means of production, a patriarchy, families or courts.[25] As recent scholarship has acknowledged, to impose a totalizing model for the operation of power draws attention from the analysis of its diffuse nature as it operates within, between and across social and political structures in different contexts. Nor, for this reason, is it useful to subscribe to a single theorization, and this volume is less concerned with conceptualizing power than with the significance of emotions for the creation and negotiation of emotional subjectivities within dominant discourses.

The collection of essays to follow draw upon a diverse range of contexts and methodological approaches to power, to explore how the cultivation, regulation and negotiation of emotional norms interact with relations of power. While broad consensus can be found across the field of emotions history that emotions function both as an instrument of self-identification and expression of power, social categories of class or gender are often accepted as given, with emotions discussed within or attributed to such groups. Heeding Joanna Bourke's astute critique of the reduction of fear to a phenomenon 'spawned within individual psyches before stretching outwards', this collection seeks to counteract the individualization of categories of oppression by attending closely to the work done by emotion to mediate relations of power and 'fix' otherwise nebulous social categories, as Michael Rowland's interrogation of the engagement with shame required for the performance of 'polite' eighteenth-century masculinity demonstrates in Chapter 9 of this volume.[26] Ultimately, the case studies within this collection provide a means by which we can root the naturalization of power relations in the concomitant constructions of gender and emotion in historical contexts and traced across time and space. The chapters included here actively intervene in, and consequently destabilize, the essential qualities afforded to gendered emotion.

The naturalization, and therefore fixity, of emotions and gender within the territories and colonies of Europe since the Enlightenment has been an essential part of obscuring the continual shaping of gendered emotional norms by dominant structures. As the cases opening this Introduction and constituting this volume show, this is key to understanding how gender and emotional norms, once established, serve to embed and police the power structures which generated them. Focusing on the power relations which infuse the connections of social life, this volume interrogates what Emma Copestake in Chapter 4 terms 'the ebb and flow of power [that] has defined who could act, and how'. A focus upon power, and the contexts and dynamics which shape both gender and emotion, does not mean an uncritical acceptance of emotions as social constructions. Instead, we approach embodied, as well as cultural, histories to understand the dynamic relationship between the ways in which people and communities have emotionally responded to normative expressions, or societal expectations of emotional response. The histories within this book are situated within this dynamic relationship but also work to historicize and interrogate the power structures which shape normative expressions and give both gender and emotion a seemingly fixed status.

Situating class, race and sexuality in the history of emotions

The history of emotions as a field of historiography has had a particularly strong focus upon European cultural histories, which have provided apt foundations for this collection, and the methodologies historians might use to engage with the embodied and political aspects of emotions have been adeptly mapped.[27] Our focus on everyday power structures and the people who have sought to challenge them has naturally led to an intersectional approach to understanding gender and emotion. The practice of power in a given cultural or historical context carves out a society's predominant emotional styles or regimes, and the manner in which these styles and practices are delineated by categories of gender, race, class and sexuality.[28] As emotional subjects, our ways of navigating our communities and making our feelings understood are along 'well-worn paths that all of us are familiar with'.[29] As Rosenwein suggests, 'even our most "sincere" and "unpremeditated" expressions are constrained by our emotional vocabulary and gestures'.[30] Worn into shape by relational sets of values and social convention, not to mention the dominant theorization of what they 'really are', emotions as a category of feeling are perhaps best, if broadly, considered as a means of interaction.[31]

The analogous ways in which emotions are worked upon and contoured by exposure to social, political, cultural and economic 'elements' of power have seen relatively limited exploration. Emotional experiences are about encounters, and Sara Ahmed has made the case perhaps most persuasively for the rejection of emotions as private matters, arguing that emotions play a critical role in the 'surfacing of individual and collective bodies' and that the affective orientations of individual and collective bodies towards or against one another are instrumental in the construction of the everyday.[32] These everyday environments are carved out by collective imprints upon one another, cultural productions and historical processes, all of which govern the 'stage' for the performance of emotions. Relating the individual to the social, emotions are at the heart of power relations, as what sociologist Jonathan Heaney has described as 'conceptual twins': 'if social relations are seen to imply relations of power then ... they should also be seen to imply relations of emotion'.[33] Emotions are mobilized to generate profit; like land, labour or persons, they can be (de)valued as 'excessive' or 'wasteful' and controlled as consequence; they are co-opted to (re)produce power and are the primary mechanisms of social interaction and function. Scholars have worked across and against disciplines to trace the relationship between power, emotion and inequality. While the history of emotions has been dominated by studies of Europe and the West, scholars have made clear the importance of emotion and emotional regulation and redefinition in the establishment of colonial power, and resistance to it.[34] The roles of emotions in protest and social movements – and, in particular, the correlation between irrationality and emotion – have seen substantial critical revision by sociologists and historians, who have identified emotions (such as hope, resentment and solidarity) as key strategic components in social movement cohesion and mobilization.[35]

The role of emotions in resistance and for communal mobilization is a particularly compelling theme throughout this book. This intervention develops Frantz Fanon's call in the 1960s for a more thorough interrogation of the emotional dynamics of racialization and empire, and the equally important emotional dynamics of decolonization. Fanon argued that 'it is not possible to enslave men without logically making them inferior through and through. And racism is only the emotional, affective, sometimes intellectual explanation of this inferiorization'.[36] The construction of race, and its policing through racism, is an emotive exercise, as the contributions on settler colonialism and whiteness by Ginsburgh (Chapter 5) and Doble (Chapter 6) demonstrate. Racism requires the rallying and performance of certain emotions to 'build' the racialized other and then confine and define them through the learned behaviours and emotions of racism.[37] These patterns of identity construction and social policing also resonate with social categories of class and sexuality, and struggles against their subordination. Homophobia, transphobia and class struggle resound throughout Olga Andreevskikh's and Emma Copestake's chapters, in which Russian bisexual and transgender activists and Liverpool's striking dock workers push back against oppressive power structures and their prevailing emotional forces.

When Fanon critiqued the colonial logics that had imagined the 'emotional instability of the Negro', he elucidated the ideological entanglements of race and emotion within the makings of colonial power, and their inseparability from the construction of race. For Fanon, colonialism was 'too affective and too emotional'; it displaced the reality of oppression and the need for self-determination by focusing on the necessity for individual behaviours to be 'more liberal' and less 'racist'.[38] This book too looks beyond the individual to the structural and the collective, and to the 'racial edifices' of society, as Bonilla-Silva would term them, which shape the modes of classification inherent to how power 'works'.[39] However, attention to the individual's absorption of the predominant emotional norms of their given emotional regime and vocabulary – critical to understanding how power shapes emotions and subjectivities – is not lost.[40] Fanon and many since have interrogated the intersection of emotions with the potential violence of social categorizations; yet in the field of history, questions remain.[41] Our focus upon intersectional identities addresses how they are constructed and naturalized within specific historical settings, but also how these identities take on emotive power of their own, acting as sources of empowerment and resistance. This approach illuminates how power shapes the social categorizations and emotional communities of our various case studies, while also demonstrating the power of social groups – empowered by their identities – to contest, resist and redefine the power structures from which they spring.

The social identities formed by emotions are not only racialized, classed and sexualized but are also well known to be gendered by culturally specific and colonial notions of sexual difference. A great deal of careful attention has been paid to the ways in which emotional expectations, practices, behaviours and experiences have been delineated by gender in different historical spaces and cultures.[42] Accounts of gender and social change over time have successfully destabilized notions of emotional 'watersheds', while detailed studies of historical events such as early modern witch trials, criminal cases and war have reached critical conclusions about the relationships between individual selfhood and communal identities.[43] Scholars working in the field of gender and sexuality have powerfully demonstrated the emotional histories of their subjects to be fluid and multifaceted.[44]

Nevertheless, there remains a need to interrogate the intertwined construction and naturalization of gender and emotion with power. Emotions have been shaped through gendered language and expression, while gender has been codified and policed through emotional expression.[45] Revising her influential 1986 thesis, Joan Scott warned that gender 'too often connotes a programmatic or methodological approach in which the meanings of "men" and "women" are taken as fixed; the point is to describe differing roles, not to interrogate them'.[46] Likewise, in her study of fear in modern history, Joanna Bourke argued that, despite our temptation as historians to 'disembody' emotions, treating them as 'by-products of rational class-based responses to material interests', one cannot deny that emotions are felt physiologically, that bodies and discourse shape one another and that '[a]lthough there is a theatre to the physiology of fear ... it is not always choreographed according to any pre-determined schema of class, gender or ethnicity'.[47] Indeed, emotional responses and experiences are frequently shared across social hierarchies, and can transgress or shrink from the boundaries of emotional communities and regimes.[48] Rob Boddice, in discussion of the brain as a cultural artefact, lamented the reduction of culture to an exterior process, calling for a complication of culture as a concept to account for the unstable boundary between interior and exterior worlds, and for the role of 'historical brains forming historical cultures, and vice-versa'.[49] Rather than using emotions to define specific groups, the chapters in this volume explore the myriad ways in which emotional states have been induced and put to work to 'align people with others and [subject] them to power relations', and how these relations are maintained.[50] As Joan Scott has explained, centring experience takes 'as self-evident the identities of those whose experience is being documented and thus naturalizes their difference', locating 'resistance outside its discursive construction'.[51] As such, the volume avoids centring the *experience* of emotion in favour of examining what those emotions *do*: the rules of their performance and alignment with gender norms.

Subjectivity and performance have been key to understanding the dynamic processes through which emotions are constituted from physiology and culture.[52] Scholars such as Michael Roper have explored subjectivity as the site for the 'constant mediation between unconscious motivations and languages of the self' and negotiations between 'experience, internal states and the cultural forms through which those states are rendered'.[53] In her study of witchcraft trials in early modern Germany, Laura Kounine identifies how, by acting as a 'site' for the construction of the self, witch trials occurred almost as 'collisions' whereby the confluence of relational concepts such as class, generation and marital status interact with notions of gender to determine the 'rules' of emotional performance. Pointing to the tensions between the fluidity of the individual emotional worlds of accused witches and the binary approach to communal identities prevalent in authoritative scripts such as church texts, Kounine demonstrates precisely why 'any historical study of emotions must also be a study of selfhood'.[54] Likewise, as Katie Barclay has shown, the politics of respectability have frequently been policed through gendered bodily performances and emotions. In eighteenth-century Ireland, 'performances of masculinity became implicated in the making of justice, as it was through recognition of the multiple possibilities for manly identity that sympathetic exchange was enabled'.[55] It is here – in the cross-section between gendered and emotional selves, amid the 'rules of performance' within the collective – that this volume lies.

Inherent to the performance or practice of emotion is the performance or practice of gender identity, and consequently, as Peta Tait has shown in her examination of gendered bodies in Chekhov's and Stanislavski's theatre, emotions can not only sustain but also resist gender identity.[56] Ideas of performance have proven to be crucial to understanding and historicizing selfhood. Goffman's and Hochschild's metaphors of performance, employed also by Judith Butler, while intrinsic to our knowledge of selfhood and feelings as culturally constructed and temporally specific, presuppose an ability to self-induce or subconsciously manage 'genuine' feelings.[57] Critical revisions of the dramaturgical metaphor have problematized its dichotomy between public and private self, pointing out the metaphor's reliance upon historically specific nineteenth-century assumptions about the liberal rational self – reflected in the realist methods emerging in contemporary theatre.[58] Consciousness of the construction and stratification of gender normativities and the ambiguities and porousness of the enduring dichotomy between body and mind is crucial for any study of the structures of power which 'gender' emotions. As Barclay, Kounine and Roper have all shown, careful attention to the historical circumstances of the performance of gender and emotion can illuminate these power structures, and correspondingly the mediations between individual and the social.[59] Revealing the relationship between gender and emotion in this way centres the temporal and cultural contingency of the volume's chapters, and critically examines the cultural contingency of both emotions and gender and their situatedness in space and time.

Scope and parameters

With the intention of historicizing how gendered practices and emotional norms are formed in dynamic relationships with structures of power, the chapters in this collection range in their chronological focus from the early modern to contemporary world. Applying a keen eye to how gender and emotion have been co-constituted across this broad span of time, the authors involved employ a variety of disciplinary tools to produce a collective insight into how the concomitance of these dynamics has been afforded the appearance of fixity across what might quite broadly be termed 'modernities'.[60] As editors whose own work has drawn upon and benefited from research across the boundaries of disciplines such as history, anthropology, area studies and sociology, we felt this approach was vital. Drawing upon backgrounds in sociology, literary studies, activism and psychology in addition to those similar to our own, the authors who produced this collection with us are able to bring an interdisciplinary richness to their analysis and trace their (re)configurations to the present day.

Despite the disciplinary diversity brought to this volume by its authors, Barbara Rosenwein's theorization of 'emotional communities' is a common feature among the case studies, as it accounts for power, politics and complexity as well as for a multiplicity of communities within each historical case study.[61] Members of emotional communities move within and between places, where individual and collective practices of emotions are 'shaped' by the emotives of official or known representations in a given environment.[62] This broad understanding of emotional multiplicity being shaped by dominant power structures and underpinned by an emphasis upon certain modes of emotionality within given communities is a consistent theme within the chapters and facilitates the volume's chronological breadth. The collection of chapters spans the early modern to contemporary world, and many of the chapters use their case studies to draw transhistorical links, clearly stating the influences of their area studies on contemporary matters. Lyndsay Galpin in Chapter 10, for example, considers the contemporary enactment of nineteenth-century Malthusian values in British attitudes to unemployment and men's mental health, while Olga Andreevskikh in Chapter 2 roots joint reflections on the online activism of bisexual and transgender women in the Russian Federation in the Soviet Union's unsuccessful attempts to revolutionize binary gender roles. Despite the considerable chronological scope offered by the volume, it is not possible for one volume to address every possible period or context, and so it is hoped that scholars will continue this line of inquiry in the future.

In compiling the volume, we sought a geographic as well as chronological breadth in order to expand the traditional geographic scope of studies of gender and emotion, and to encourage the interrogation of historical continuities and ruptures across time and space. The chapters in this volume discuss France, India, Indonesia, Italy, Kenya, the People's Republic of China, the Russian Federation, Southern Rhodesia (now Zimbabwe), the Soviet Union, the United Kingdom, the United States and Zambia, and pay sustained attention to specific cultural contexts and transnational and translocal connections on a global scale. Emma Copestake's close focus on the Liverpool dock workers' strike in the 1990s in Chapter 4 illuminates the bonds of solidarity cemented by shared struggle, while Hannah Proctor's re-evaluation in Chapter 11 of the gender binaries upon which political opposition tends to rest brings women in Indonesia, France and the United States and beyond shoulder to shoulder. Josh Doble's interrogation in Chapter 6 of the racialized gender politics inherent to settler colonialism in Africa unearths the centrality of sensory emotions to the tenuous belonging of white settlers who have remained in post-colonial Kenya and Zambia. Belonging – to the community and the territory – is revealed as an ongoing emotional endeavour, one which requires constant maintenance and reinforcement, not least in the racially fraught environment of post-colonial Africa. Nonetheless, it is imperative to note that the focus taken by this volume inevitably remains incomplete. As editors, we decided to structure the collection thematically rather than chronologically, dividing the chapters into three parts: 'Gender, class and sexuality in the negotiation of political power'; 'Power and place-making: class, hygiene and race in the British Empire'; and 'Modern Europe's public sphere and the policing of the gendered body'. Grouping the chapters along these lines highlights the potential for collective empowerment through attention to and engagement with gendered emotional norms, as well as emphasizing the dominant themes which run through them.

Among the chapters in Part I, attention is paid to the interests and influences at play in shaping emotional communities, and their capacity to act as such. Paper, fax, internet, film and social media all constitute means by which gendered emotions are performed and manifested: testing, negotiating and consolidating boundaries of political belonging. Hannah Parker's analysis in Chapter 1 of women's discussions of private grief in letters to Soviet authorities expands the conventional significance of letters as textual sources for emotional vocabulary. Parker argues that while gendered notions of revolutionary motherhood served to validate highly individual feelings of grief for the loss of the mother–child bond, the physical-mental ritual of letter-writing and the mobile object created work to reify these now politically legitimate emotions. The theme of the sublimation of interiority to collective struggle is continued in Yucong Hao's Chapter 3, which explores the changing politics of gender in Maoist China through the representation of singing women, and the cultivation of an emotional culture of revolutionary lyricism, in two Chinese feature films about the Korean War, *Shanggan Ridge* (1956) and *Heroic Sons and Daughters* (1964). While gender was meaningfully engaged in the earlier period, it was abstracted by the mid-1960s with Jiang Qing's rise to power and the implementation of the 'two-line struggle' in the film industry. This shift epitomized how the politics of socialist feminism surrendered to that of class struggle on the eve of the Cultural Revolution, when class feeling (*jieji ganqing*) was elevated as the sole 'socialist grammar of emotion', erasing gender, family and interiority from the radical politics of 'continuous revolution'.

Conscious attention to gender roles by members of an emotional community is evident in Chapter 4, where Copestake's analysis of interviews with and sources produced by striking dockers and their families highlights the ways striking families built and reinforced bonds of solidarity by adapting emotional and social expectations of gender roles to the conditions of industrial action. Social media provides a comparable venue for the performance of gendered emotions in Andreevskikh's Chapter 2. In conversation with the LGBTQ activists upon whom Andreevskikh's research has focused, her chapter reflects upon the ways in which emotions both congruous and incongruous with gender norms are consciously performed in online spaces 'to transgress binary monosexist and cisnormative discourses, and to produce mediations and self-mediations of non-binary gender and sexual identities'. Together, the chapters advance our understanding of the importance of emotional language to power and how – as Proctor's chapter at the end of this volume so clearly argues – this lends gender, emotions and gendered emotions their appearance of fixity, subsequently enacting power through usage and perpetuating the hierarchies of power they cloak. Their collective analysis draws attention to the importance of grounding histories of experience and restoring voice to historical actors – particularly those most marginalized or disempowered.[63]

The volume proceeds to examine the roles played by emotion and gender in shaping the contours of colonial power and the boundaries of whiteness, while also demonstrating the uses of 'gendered emotion' in maintaining and reproducing colonial power, across three planes of emotional experience: the social, the sensory and the spatial. Nicola Ginsburgh's Chapter 5 sheds light upon the roles emotion played in projecting racial difference in Southern Rhodesia, interrogating the intersecting stratifications maintained by colonial capitalism. Ginsburgh's analysis of Rhodesian Railway publications highlights the mental contradictions the tensions between presumed racial superiority and relative poverty caused working-class whites in Rhodesia, and the anger at and emotional projections upon Africans and white women consequently. The case study of white working-class Rhodesians establishes a key strand in the grouping of chapters: the uses and justifications of gendered emotional norms to reassert established hierarchies of racialized, classed and gendered people. Doble's Chapter 6 develops Ginsburgh's arguments about the emotional policing of whiteness for post-colonial Kenya and Zambia. Using archival and oral history sources, the chapter develops the notion of 'sensory knowledge' as an embodied, emotional tool which post-colonial white communities have used to stress their belonging in Africa, while also reinforcing their emotional distance and separation from Africans. The sensory, and connectedly emotional, experience of physical and social proximity to Africans has resulted in sensory knowledge being used to police interracial intimacy, most notably between white women and African men. Sara Honarmand Ebrahimi in Chapter 7 maps how medical missionaries in northwestern India during British colonialism sought to overcome distrust of the local people through hospital building practices. Excavating the contributions female missionaries made to 'Purdah hospitals' in the built environments of northwestern India – contributions buried in official sources – Honarmand Ebrahimi clearly demonstrates their importance in seeking the trust and friendship of local women with the mission. Honarmand Ebrahimi's chapter expertly lays bare the social stratifications and hierarchies of power inherent to colonialism, and in particular how the subjugation of European women in imperial centres not only facilitated but also encouraged their own subjugation of colonized communities, through assumptions about the moral and emotional qualities inherent to (European) women.

The collection of chapters closing the book explore understandings of society and class in Britain and Italy with a sustained focus on the purposes of shame and pleasure in the eighteenth and nineteenth centuries. Through the case study of the Italian middle class in the nineteenth century, Francesca Campani shows in Chapter 8 how discourses of romantic love in physiologist and author Paolo Mantegazza's sexual science reveal the adaptability and insidiousness of colonial logics, which simultaneously shaped Italian society and its emerging imperialist thought. The shifting emotional paradigm of the Italian middle class towards love marriages mirrored in Mantegazza's work both challenged notions that polygamy was somehow 'inherent' to colonized people and ensured the adaptability of colonial pseudo-sciences to changing social and emotional mores in the colonizing population. Campani's illustration of the nebular shifts in Italian colonial discourse provides a key intervention in post-unification Italian social history and sheds light on the substance and significance of Italy's colonial ambitions, despite its limited expansion when compared to the empires of its Western neighbours. The significance of resilient emotional paradigms in ensuring the continuation of class structures resonates in Chapter 9, where Michael Rowland identifies the eighteenth century as a 'hinge' in the West's relationship to shame due to the Enlightenment's expansion of notions of individualism, with 'privacy and dignity' providing 'new routes for shame's influence'. Through the analysis of men's letters and periodicals from the first half of the eighteenth century – 'a point at which the emotional community of politeness [was] emerging' – Rowland considers how shame played a central role in attempts to construct ideal selves, and to debate infractions of these selves, among men. The literary form and its materiality offered a space key to perceptions of the stability of 'the discursive foundations of polite culture'. Rowland's chapter accommodates the 'subtleties' of emotional experience in the eighteenth century, employing insight from affect theory to reconcile the influence of affect theory in the history of emotions with the flourishing of recent historical work on sensory experience.[64]

In this vein, Galpin in Chapter 10 explores the weight that notions of productivity and its counterpart burden levied upon the embodied experiences of working-class men in nineteenth-century Britain, and the role they played in deaths by suicide among them. The chapter illuminates how shame was deployed beyond the polite culture of eighteenth-century men to regulate working-class behaviours through the individualization of responsibility for poverty, and demonstrates the continuities in these trends in the practice of power with contemporary British austerity politics. Proctor's Chapter 11, through a transhistorical and transnational account of the *pétroleuses* of the Paris Commune, the *Gerwani* of Indonesia, the violent misogyny of the *Freikorps* of Weimar Germany and Klaus Theweleit's *Male Fantasies*, offers a stark perspective on the significance of the literary and linguistic gendering of emotion for constructing a sense of their 'natural order'. Proctor's intervention possesses a clear and excoriating vision of how, through language, it might be possible to move beyond the trappings of the binaries that have dominated efforts to both consolidate and defend configurations of power and nation, and attempts to subvert them. Evident throughout these chapters are the gender roles defining respectable European society and the emotions that regulated them, which ensured the reproduction of hereditary power and privilege amidst a changing cultural landscape, and which in this period were being exported and reimagined alongside race within European colonies.

Collectively, the authors broaden the scope of emotions history to attend to areas and perspectives not often addressed within the field, but more importantly they consciously encourage further expansion, diversification and attention. Most evident throughout the contribution to this work is a clear confrontation of the gendered emotional dimensions of power relations that have dominated societies since 1750. Despite the volume's historicizations of gendered emotions, its contributions – both individually and collectively – offer the possibility of what collective interventions can achieve, and how precise, context-specific histories can speak to one another across space and time.

Notes

1. M. Smith and others, 'Introduction: Geography and Emotion – Emerging Constellations', in *Emotion, Place and Culture* (London: Ashgate, 2016), pp. 17–34; M.J. Borges, S. Cancian and L. Reeder (eds.), *Emotional Landscapes: Love, Gender and Migration* (Champaign, IL: University of Illinois Press, 2021); Björk also uses the term 'emotional landscapes' in a song by the same name on her 1997 'Jóga': Björk, 'Jóga' (music recording), *Homogenic* (One Little Indian, 1997).

2. In Spanish, *atormentado/a* ('tormented') is also etymologically related to *tormenta* ('storm').

3. *Stroit' zamki iz peska* could alternatively be translated as 'to build sandcastles'. Many Russian emotional idioms relate to notions of body and soul, another prevalent analogy in discussions of emotions.

4. Love is described in Spanish as *ardiente* ('burning' – a cognate of 'ardent' in English), and *llamas de amor* ('flames of love') is a similarly well-worn cliché. In Dutch, *vurige liefde* describes 'fiery love'.

5. See G.R. Johnson, 'In the Name of the Fatherland: An Analysis of Kin Term Usage in Patriotic Speech and Literature', *International Political Science Review*, 8, 2 (1987), 165–74; C. Delaney, 'Father State, Motherland, and the Birth of Modern Turkey', in S. Yanagisako and C. Delaney (eds.), *Naturalizing Power: Essays in Feminist Cultural Analysis* (London: Routledge, 1995), pp. 177–99; M.K. Stockdale, '"My Death for the Motherland Is Happiness": Women, Patriotism, and Soldiering in Russia's Great War, 1914–1917', *The American Historical Review*, 109, 1 (2004), 78–116; R. Boddice, *The History of Emotions* (Manchester: Manchester University Press, 2018).

6. 'Visualisation: Connections between "1A" and "2D", Strength: Strong', *Mapping Metaphor with the Historical Thesaurus* (Glasgow: University of Glasgow, 2020), https://mappingmetaphor.arts.gla.ac.uk/drilldown/?letter1=1A&letter2 =2D&viewChange=y&strength=strong&changeViewOpt=changeVis (accessed 26 August 2020). Many thanks to Dr James Chetwood for directing us to this resource. See also Carole Hough, 'The Metaphorical Landscape', in W. Anderson, E. Bramwell and C. Hough (eds.), *Mapping English Metaphor through Time* (Oxford: Oxford University Press, 2016), pp. 13–31. For more on the emergence of 'emotion' as a conceptual category, see T. Dixon, *From Passions to Emotions: The Creation of a Secular Psychological Category* (Cambridge: Cambridge University Press, 2003).

7. For the emotional power of imagined nation states, see B. Anderson, *Imagined Communities: Reflections on the Origin and Spread of Nationalism* (London: Verso Books, 2006).

8. A. Arnold-Forster and A. Moulds, 'Introduction', in A. Arnold-Forster and A. Moulds (eds.), *Feelings and Work in Modern History: Emotional Labour and Emotions about Labour* (London: Bloomsbury, 2022), p. 3.

9. 'About the Organisers', *Gendered Emotions in History*, https://genderedemotions .wordpress.com/about-us (accessed 29 June 2022).

10. B. Newman, 'The Long History behind the Racist Attacks on Serena Williams', *Washington Post*, 11 September 2018, www.washingtonpost.com/outlook/2018/09/11 /long-history-behind-racist-attacks-serena-williams (accessed 1 July 2022).

11. The use of the word 'criminals' recalls nineteenth-century beliefs about a subset of the population – 'criminal classes' – who were criminal by nature, and under which label racialized groups were included. For more on this, see P. Nijhar, 'Imperial Violence: The "Ethnic" as a Component of the "Criminal" Class in Victorian England', *Liverpool Law Review*, 27 (2006), 337–60; V. Bailey, 'The Fabrication of Deviance: "Dangerous Classes" and "Criminal Classes" in Victorian England', in J. Rule and R. Malcolmson (eds.), *Protest and Survival: The Historical*

Experience – Essays for E.P. Thompson (London: Merlin, 1993), pp. 221–56; and H. Churcher, 'Understandings of Habitual Criminality in England from 1770 to 1870', unpublished PhD thesis, University of Sheffield (2017).

12. I. Wigger, 'Anti-Muslim Racism and the Racialisation of Sexual Violence: "Intersectional Stereotyping" in Mass Media Representations of Male Muslim Migrants in Germany', *Culture and Religion*, 20 (2019), 248–71, at p. 254. For the 'multiple bordering functions' of mass media coverage, see E. Edenborg, 'Saving Women and Bordering Europe: Narratives of "Migrants' Sexual Violence" and Geopolitical Imaginaries in Russia and Sweden', *Geopolitics*, 25 (2020), 780–801; 'Threat of Sexual Violence Continues for Forced Migrants in Search of Refuge', 29 March 2022, www.birmingham.ac.uk/news/2022/threat-of-sexual-violence -continues-for-forced-migrants-in-search-of-refuge (accessed 28 June 2022).

13. D. Taylor and M. Chulov, 'Home Office Cancels Flight to Deport Kurdish Failed Asylum Seekers to Iraq', *The Guardian*, 31 May 2022, www.theguardian.com/uk-news /2022/may/31/home-office-cancels-flight-to-deport-kurdish-asylum-seekers-to-iraq (accessed 28 June 2022); www.bbc.co.uk/news/uk-60947028 (accessed 5 July 2022); www.theguardian.com/politics/2022/apr/29/boris-johnson-misogyny-parliament -tracy-brabin-labour (accessed 5 July 2022).

14. A. Durbin, 'Ukraine War: Johnson Says If Putin Were a Woman He Would Not Have Invaded', *BBC*, 29 June 2022, www.bbc.co.uk/news/uk-61976526 (accessed 1 July 2022).

15. S. O'Connor, 'What a Lost Decade of Education Spending Means for the Economy', *Financial Times*, 6 December 2021, www.ft.com/content/3dbbc60e-015d -45ff-8c9f-bf06515af929 (accessed 1 July 2022); J. Halliday, 'Boris Johnson Allowing "Wild West" of Misogyny in Parliament, Tracy Brabin Says', *The Guardian*, 29 April 2022, www.theguardian.com/politics/2022/apr/29/boris-johnson-misogyny -parliament-tracy-brabin-labour (accessed 1 July 2022).

16. A.R. Hochschild, *The Managed Heart: The Commercialization of Human Feeling* (Oakland, CA: University of California Press, 2012).

17. J. Beck, 'The Concept Creep of Emotional Labor', *The Atlantic*, 26 November 2018, www.theatlantic.com/family/archive/2018/11/arlie-hochschild-housework-isnt -emotional-labor/576637 (accessed 28 June 2022).

18. Recent historical appraisals of the relationships between feelings and work include Arnold-Forster and Moulds (eds.), *Feelings and Work in Modern History* and C. Langhamer, 'Feelings, Women and Work in the Long 1950s', *Women's History Review*, 26 (2017), 77–91. Nonetheless, the influences of power imbalances in the workplace are frequently posited as something to be mitigated, for example B.R. Ragins and D.E. Winkel, 'Gender, Emotion and Power in Work Relationships', *Human Resource Management Review*, 21 (2011), 377–93, which identifies 'cycles of powerlessness' to which women often fall victim.

19. The case for consideration of translocal connections over transnational is laid out in C. Greiner and P. Sakdapolrak, 'Translocality: Concepts, Applications and Emerging Research Perspectives', *Geography Compass*, 7, 5 (2013), 373–84, and developed further in James Michael Yeoman's *Print Culture and the Formation of the Anarchist Movement in Spain, 1890–1915* (Edinburgh: AK Press, 2022).

20. H. Charnock, '"A Million Little Bonds": Infidelity, Divorce and the Emotional Worlds of Marriage in British Women's Magazines of the 1930s', *Cultural and Social History*, 14 (2017), 363–79; C. Langhamer and D. Vassiliadou, 'The Idiom of Love and Sacrifice: Emotional Vocabularies of Motherhood in Nineteenth Century Greece', *Cultural and Social History*, 14 (2017), 283–300.

21. See, for example, K. Barclay, *Men on Trial: Performing Emotion, Embodiment and Identity in Ireland, 1800–45* (Manchester: Manchester University Press, 2018);

L. Kounine, *Imagining the Witch: Emotions, Gender, and Selfhood in Early Modern Germany* (Oxford: Oxford University Press, 2018).

22. Dixon, *From Passions to Emotions* and R. Boddice, 'Cultural Brain as Historical Artifact', in L.J. Kirmayer et al. (eds.), *Culture, Mind, and Brain: Emerging Concepts, Models, and Applications* (Cambridge: Cambridge University Press, 2020), pp. 367–74.

23. For example, Arnold-Forster and Moulds, 'Introduction', p. 3; M.L. Bailey and K. Barclay (eds.), *Emotion, Ritual and Power in Europe, 1200–1920: Family, State and Church* (Basingstoke: Palgrave Macmillan, 2017); C. Langhamer, *The English in Love: The Intimate Story of an Emotional Revolution* (Oxford: Oxford University Press, 2013); L. Noakes, C. Langhamer and C. Siebrecht (eds.), *Total War: An Emotional History* (Oxford: Oxford University Press, 2020).

24. J. Bourke, 'Fear and Anxiety: Writing about Emotion in Modern History', *History Workshop Journal*, 55 (2003), 125.

25. A. Moreton-Robinson, 'Subduing Power: Indigenous Sovereignty Matters', in T. Neale, C. McKinnon and E. Vincent (eds.), *History, Power, Text* (Sydney: UTS ePRESS, 2014), p. 189.

26. Bourke, 'Fear and Anxiety', p. 123.

27. Boddice, *The History of Emotions*; R. Boddice, *A History of Feelings* (London: Reaktion, 2019); J. Plamper, *The History of Emotions: An Introduction* (Oxford: Oxford University Press, 2015); S. Broomhall and A. Lynch (eds.), *The Routledge History of Emotions in Europe: 1100–1700* (London: Routledge, 2019).

28. B. Gammerl, 'Emotional Styles: Concepts and Challenges', *Rethinking History*, 16 (2012), 161–75; W.M. Reddy, *The Navigation of Feeling: A Framework for the History of Emotions* (Cambridge: Cambridge University Press, 2001), which provides an excellent overview of the theorizations that have recently dominated the history of emotions.

29. B.H. Rosenwein, in Nicole Eustace and others, 'AHR Conversation: The Historical Study of Emotions', *The American Historical Review*, 117 (2012), 1487–1531, at p. 1496.

30. Rosenwein, 'AHR Conversation', p. 1496.

31. Rosenwein, 'AHR Conversation', p. 1496.

32. For emotional experiences as 'encounters', see Bourke, 'Fear and Anxiety', at p. 129. S. Ahmed, 'Collective Feelings: Or, the Impressions Left by Others', *Theory, Culture and Society*, 21 (2004), 25–42, at p. 25.

33. J. Heaney, 'Emotions and Power: Reconciling Conceptual Twins', *Journal of Political Power*, 4 (2011), 259–77, at p. 259. For the historical relationship between emotion and power, see Bourke, 'Fear and Anxiety' at p. 113.

34. See S. Honarmand Ebrahimi, '"Plowing before Sowing": Trust and the Architecture of the Church Missionary Society (CMS) Medical Missions', *Architecture and Culture*, 7 (2019), 197–217; for scholarship on emotions in nineteenth-century Asia and Europe, M. Pernau and H. Jordheim (eds.), *Civilising Emotions: Concepts in Nineteenth-Century Asia and Europe* (Oxford: Oxford University Press, 2015) demonstrates clearly the colonial implications of concepts of civilization and emotion.

35. Eduardo Romanos, for example, has explored how the false opposition between rationality and emotion has been used to define social movements and their activists as 'psychologically unstable and emotionally overwrought individuals' (p. 547) in 'Emotions, Moral Batteries and High-Risk Activism: Understanding the Emotional Practices of the Spanish Activists under Franco's Dictatorship', *Contemporary European History*, 23 (2014), 545–64; see also J. Reed, 'Emotions in Context: Revolutionary Accelerators, Hope, Moral Outrage, and Other Emotions in the Making

of Nicaragua's Revolution', *Theory and Society*, 33 (2004), pp. 653–703 and J.C. Häberlen and R.A. Spinney's introduction to the special issue 'Emotions and Protest Movements in Europe since 1917', *Contemporary European History*, 23 (2014), 489–503.

36. F. Fanon, *Toward the African Revolution*, translated by H. Chevalier (London: Penguin, 1970), p. 40.

37. For the idea of the intersectional socialization of behaviour, see J.E. Smith, 'Race, Emotions, and Socialization', *Race, Gender & Class*, 9 (2002), 94–110, here at p. 102.

38. Smith, 'Race, Emotions', p. 102.

39. B. Eduardo, 'Feeling Race: Theorizing the Racial Economy of Emotions', *American Sociological Review*, 84 (2019), 1–25.

40. Smith, 'Race, Emotions', pp. 102–3.

41. A. Wilkins and J. Pace, 'Class, Race, and Emotions', in J. Stets and J. Turner (eds.), *Handbook of the Sociology of Emotions: Volume II* (Dordrecht: Springer, 2014); Smith, 'Race, Emotions'.

42. S. Broomhall (ed.), *Spaces for Feeling: Emotions and Sociabilities in Britain, 1650–1850* (London: Routledge, 2015); D. Simonton and others, *The Routledge History Handbook of Gender and the Urban Experience* (London: Routledge, 2017); E. Dermineur, V. Langum and Å. Karlsson Sjögren (eds.), *Revisiting Gender in European History, 1400–1800* (London: Routledge, 2018).

43. For such studies of emotions and historical change with a focus on gender dynamics, see A. Brooks, *Genealogies of Emotions, Intimacies and Desire: Theories of Changes in Emotional Regimes from Medieval Society to Late Modernity* (London, 2017) and Bailey and Barclay (eds.), *Emotion, Ritual and Power in Europe*. For gender, emotion and political identity construction, see Kounine, *Imagining the Witch*; M. Seymour, 'Emotional Arenas: From Provincial Circus to National Courtroom in Late Nineteenth-Century Italy', *Rethinking History*, 16 (2012), 177–97 and P. Vasiliev, 'Revolutionary Conscience, Remorse and Resentment: Emotions and Early Soviet Criminal Law, 1917–1922', *Historical Research*, 90 (2017), 117–33.

44. For example, M. Roper, *The Secret Battle: Emotional Survival in the Great War* (Manchester: Manchester University Press, 2009); Stockdale, 'My Death for the Motherland Is Happiness'.

45. J. Butler, *Gender Trouble: Feminism and the Subversion of Gender* (New York: Routledge, 1990).

46. J.W. Scott, 'Gender: Still a Useful Category of Analysis?', *Diogenes*, 57.1 (2010), 7–14 and 'Gender: A Useful Category of Historical Analysis', *The American Historical Review*, 91, 5 (1986), 1053–75.

47. Bourke, 'Fear and Anxiety', pp. 121–2.

48. B.H. Rosenwein, *Emotional Communities in the Early Middle Ages* (Ithaca, NY: Cornell University Press, 2006). See, for example, L. Alston and K. Harvey, 'In Private: The Individual and the Domestic Community', in C. Walker, K. Barclay and D. Lemmings (eds.), *A Cultural History of the Emotions in the Baroque and Enlightenment Age* (London: Bloomsbury, 2019), pp. 137–54.

49. Boddice, 'Cultural Brain as Historical Artefact'.

50. Bourke, 'Fear and Anxiety', p. 125.

51. J.W. Scott, 'The Evidence of Experience', *Critical Inquiry*, 17 (1991), 777.

52. Bourke, 'Fear and Anxiety', p. 123.

53. M. Roper, 'Splitting in Unsent Letters: Writing as a Social Practice and a Psychological Activity', *Social History*, 26 (2001), 319; Ibid., 'Slipping Out of View: Subjectivity and Emotion in Gender History', *History Workshop Journal*, 56 (2005), 57–72.

54. Kounine, *Imagining the Witch.*

55. Barclay, *Men on Trial.*

56. P. Tait, *Performing Emotions: Gender, Bodies, Spaces, in Chekhov's Drama and Stanislavski's Theatre* (London: Routledge, 2002).

57. A.R. Hochschild, 'Emotion Work, Feeling Rules, and Social Structure', *American Journal of Sociology*, 85 (1979), 551–75; E. Goffman, *The Presentation of Self in Everyday Life* (London: Penguin Psychology, 1990).

58. J. Blackwell-Pal, 'The "System" of Service: Emotional Labour and the Theatrical Metaphor', in A. Arnold-Forster and A. Moulds (eds.), *Feelings and Work in Modern History: Emotional Labour and Emotions about Labour* (London: Bloomsbury, 2022), pp. 215–33.

59. Barclay, *Men on Trial*; Kounine, *Imagining the Witch*; Roper, 'Slipping Out of View'.

60. We use the term 'modernity' here tentatively with full awareness of the competing and contradictory uses of the phrase. Here we mean it to encompass the period of focus in the book (1750 to the present day) and the Enlightenment-era philosophies which shaped 'modern' conceptions of colonialism, emotions, gender and the nation state.

61. Rosenwein, *Emotional Communities.*

62. Rosenwein, 'Worrying about Emotions in History', *The American Historical Review*, 106 (2002), 821–45; for emotions as a practice, see M. Scheer, 'Are Emotions a Kind of Practice (and Is That What Makes Them Have a History?): A Bordieuian Approach to Understanding Emotion', *History and Theory*, 51 (2012), 193–220. For 'emotives', see Reddy, *The Navigation of Feeling.*

63. E. Said, *Orientalism* (New York: Vintage Books, 1979).

64. R. Boddice and M. Smith, *Emotion, Sense, Experience* (Cambridge: Cambridge University Press, 2020).

References

Ahmed, S., 'Collective Feelings: Or, the Impressions Left by Others', *Theory, Culture and Society*, 21 (2004), 25–32.

Alston, L., and Harvey, K., 'In Private: The Individual and the Domestic Community', in C. Walker, K. Barclay and D. Lemmings (eds.), *A Cultural History of the Emotions in the Baroque and Enlightenment Age* (London: Bloomsbury, 2019), pp. 137–54.

Anderson, B., *Imagined Communities: Reflections on the Origin and Spread of Nationalism* (London: Verso Books, 2006).

Arnold-Forster, A., and Moulds, A. (eds.), *Feelings and Work in Modern History: Emotional Labour and Emotions about Labour* (London: Bloomsbury, 2022).

Bailey, M.L., and Barclay, K. (eds.), *Emotion, Ritual and Power in Europe, 1200–1920: Family, State and Church* (Basingstoke: Palgrave Macmillan, 2017).

Bailey, V., 'The Fabrication of Deviance: "Dangerous Classes" and "Criminal Classes" in Victorian England', in J. Rule and R. Malcolmson (eds.), *Protest and Survival: The Historical Experience – Essays for E.P. Thompson* (London: Merlin, 1993), pp. 221–56.

Barclay, K., *Men on Trial: Performing Emotion, Embodiment and Identity in Ireland, 1800–45* (Manchester: Manchester University Press, 2018).

Beck, J., 'The Concept Creep of "Emotional Labor"', *The Atlantic*, 26 November 2018, www.theatlantic.com/family/archive/2018/11/arlie -hochschild-housework-isnt-emotional-labor/576637 (accessed 28 June 2022).

Björk, 'Jóga' (music recording), *Homogenic* (One Little Indian, 1997).

Blackwell-Pal, J., 'The "System" of Service: Emotional Labour and the Theatrical Metaphor', in A. Arnold-Forster and A. Moulds (eds.), *Feelings and Work in Modern History: Emotional Labour and Emotions about Labour* (London: Bloomsbury, 2022), pp. 215–33.

Boddice, R., *The History of Emotions* (Manchester: Manchester University Press, 2018).

——, *A History of Feelings* (London: Reaktion, 2019).

——, 'Cultural Brain as Historical Artifact', in L.J. Kirmayer et al. (eds.), *Culture, Mind, and Brain: Emerging Concepts, Models, and Applications* (Cambridge: Cambridge University Press, 2020), pp. 367–74.

Boddice, R., and Smith, M., *Emotion, Sense, Experience* (Cambridge: Cambridge University Press, 2020).

Borges, M.J., Cancian, S. and Reeder, L. (eds.), *Emotional Landscapes: Love, Gender and Migration* (Champaign, IL: University of Illinois Press, 2021).

Bourke, J., 'Fear and Anxiety: Writing about Emotion in Modern History', *History Workshop Journal*, 55 (2003), 111–33.

Brooks, A., *Genealogies of Emotions, Intimacies and Desire: Theories of Changes in Emotional Regimes from Medieval Society to Late Modernity* (London: Routledge, 2017).

Broomhall, S. (ed.), *Spaces for Feeling: Emotions and Sociabilities in Britain, 1650–1850* (London: Routledge, 2015).

Broomhall, S., and Lynch, A. (eds.), *The Routledge History of Emotions in Europe: 1100–1700* (London: Routledge, 2019).

Brubaker, R., and Cooper, F., 'Beyond "Identity"', *Theory and Society*, 29 (2000), 1–47.

Brunotte, U., 'The Beautiful Jewess as Borderline Figure in Europe's Internal Colonialism: Some Remarks on the Intertwining of Antisemitism and Orientalism', *ReOrient*, 5 (2019), 166–80.

Butler, J., *Gender Trouble: Feminism and the Subversion of Gender* (New York: Routledge, 1990).

Charnock, H., '"A Million Little Bonds": Infidelity, Divorce and the Emotional Worlds of Marriage in British Women's Magazines of the 1930s', *Cultural and Social History*, 14 (2017), 363–79.

Churcher, H., 'Understandings of Habitual Criminality in England from 1770 to 1870', unpublished PhD thesis, University of Sheffield (2017).

Delaney, C., 'Father State, Motherland, and the Birth of Modern Turkey', in S. Yanagisako and C. Delaney (eds.), *Naturalizing Power: Essays in Feminist Cultural Analysis* (London: Routledge, 1995), pp. 177–99.

Dermineur, E., Langum, V. and Karlsson Sjögren, A. (eds.), *Revisiting Gender in European History, 1400–1800* (London: Routledge, 2018).

Dixon, T., *From Passions to Emotions: The Creation of a Secular Psychological Category* (Cambridge: Cambridge University Press, 2003).

Durbin, A., 'Ukraine War: Johnson Says If Putin Were a Woman He Would Not Have Invaded', *BBC*, 29 June 2022, www.bbc.co.uk/news/uk-61976526 (accessed 1 July 2022).

Edenborg, E., 'Saving Women and Bordering Europe: Narratives of "Migrants' Sexual Violence" and Geopolitical Imaginaries in Russia and Sweden', *Geopolitics*, 25 (2020), 780–801.

Eduardo, B., 'Feeling Race: Theorizing the Racial Economy of Emotions', *American Sociological Review*, 84 (2019), 1–25.

Eustace, N. et al., 'AHR Conversation: The Historical Study of Emotions', *The American Historical Review*, 117 (2012), 1487–1531.

Fanon, F., *Toward the African Revolution*, trans. H. Chevalier (London: Penguin, 1970).

Federici, S., *Caliban and the Witch: Women, the Body and Primitive Accumulation* (London: Penguin, 2004).

Gammerl, B., 'Emotional Styles: Concepts and Challenges', *Rethinking History*, 16 (2012), 161–75.

Goffman, E., *The Presentation of Self in Everyday Life* (London: Penguin Psychology, 1990).

Greiner, C., and Sakdapolrak, P., 'Translocality: Concepts, Applications and Emerging Research Perspectives', *Geography Compass*, 7, 5 (2013), 373–84.

Häberlen, J.C. and Spinney, R.A., 'Introduction', Special Issue, 'Emotions and Protest Movements in Europe since 1917', *Contemporary European History*, 23 (2014), 489–503.

Halliday, J., 'Boris Johnson Allowing "Wild West" of Misogyny in Parliament, Tracy Brabin Says', *The Guardian*, 29 April 202, www.theguardian.com/politics/2022/apr/29/boris-johnson-misogyny-parliament-tracy-brabin-labour (accessed 1 July 2022).

Heaney, J.G., 'Emotions and Power: Reconciling Conceptual Twins', *Journal of Political Power*, 4 (2011), 259–77.

Hochschild, A.R., 'Emotion Work, Feeling Rules, and Social Structure', *American Journal of Sociology*, 85 (1979), 551–75.

——, *The Managed Heart: The Commercialization of Human Feeling* (Oakland, CA: University of California Press, 2012).

Honarmand Ebrahimi, S., '"Plowing before Sowing": Trust and the Architecture of the Church Missionary Society (CMS) Medical Missions', *Architecture and Culture*, 7 (2019), 197–217.

Hough, C., 'The Metaphorical Landscape', in W. Anderson, E. Bramwell and C. Hough (eds.), *Mapping English Metaphor through Time* (Oxford: Oxford University Press, 2016), pp. 13–31.

Jackson, W., 'Dangers to the Colony: Loose Women and the "Poor White" Problem in Kenya', *Journal of Colonialism and Colonial History*, 14 (2013).

Johnson, G.R., 'In the Name of the Fatherland: An Analysis of Kin Term Usage in Patriotic Speech and Literature', *International Political Science Review*, 8, 2 (1987), 165–74.

Kounine, L., *Imagining the Witch: Emotions, Gender, and Selfhood in Early Modern Germany* (Oxford: Oxford University Press, 2018).

Langhamer, C., *The English in Love: The Intimate Story of an Emotional Revolution* (Oxford: Oxford University Press, 2013).

——, 'Feelings, Women and Work in the Long 1950s', *Women's History Review*, 26 (2017), 77–91.

Langhamer, C. and Vassiliadou, D., 'The Idiom of Love and Sacrifice: Emotional Vocabularies of Motherhood in Nineteenth Century Greece', *Cultural and Social History*, 14 (2017), 283–300.

Mapping Metaphor with the Historical Thesaurus (Glasgow: University of Glasgow, 2020), https://mappingmetaphor.arts.gla.ac.uk (accessed 26 August 2020).

Moreton-Robinson, A., 'Subduing Power: Indigenous Sovereignty Matters', in T. Neale, C. McKinnon and E. Vincent (eds.), *History, Power, Text* (Sydney: UTS ePRESS, 2014), pp. 189–97.

Newman, B., 'The Long History behind the Racist Attacks on Serena Williams', *Washington Post*, 11 September 2018, www.washingtonpost.com/outlook/2018/09/11/long-history-behind-racist-attacks-serena-williams (accessed 1 July 2022).

Nijhar, P., 'Imperial Violence: The "Ethnic" as a Component of the "Criminal" Class in Victorian England', *Liverpool Law Review*, 27 (2006), 337–60.

Noakes, L., Langhamer, C. and Siebrecht, C. (eds.), *Total War: An Emotional History* (Oxford: Oxford University Press, 2020).

O'Connor, S., 'What a Lost Decade of Education Spending Means for the Economy', *Financial Times*, 6 December 2021, www.ft.com/content/3dbbc60e-015d-45ff-8c9f-bf06515af929 (accessed 1 July 2022).

Pernau, M., and Jordheim, H. (eds.), *Civilising Emotions: Concepts in Nineteenth-Century Asia and Europe* (Oxford: Oxford University Press, 2015).

Plamper, J., *The History of Emotions: An Introduction* (Oxford: Oxford University Press, 2015).

Ragins, B.R., and Winkel, D.E., 'Gender, Emotion and Power in Work Relationships', *Human Resource Management Review*, 21 (2011), 377–93.

Reddy, W.M., *The Navigation of Feeling: A Framework for the History of Emotions* (Cambridge: Cambridge University Press, 2001).

Reed, J., 'Emotions in Context: Revolutionary Accelerators, Hope, Moral Outrage, and Other Emotions in the Making of Nicaragua's Revolution', *Theory and Society*, 33 (2004), 653–703.

Romanos, E., 'Emotions, Moral Batteries and High-Risk Activism: Understanding the Emotional Practices of the Spanish Activists under Franco's Dictatorship', *Contemporary European History*, 23 (2014), 545–64.

Roper, M., 'Splitting in Unsent Letters: Writing as a Social Practice and a Psychological Activity', *Social History*, 26 (2001), 318–39.

——, 'Slipping Out of View: Subjectivity and Emotion in Gender History', *History Workshop Journal*, 59 (2005), 57–72.

——, *The Secret Battle: Emotional Survival in the Great War* (Manchester: Manchester University Press, 2009).

Rosenwein, B.H., 'Worrying about Emotions in History', *The American Historical Review*, 107, 3 (2002), 821–45.

——, *Emotional Communities in the Early Middle Ages* (Ithaca, NY: Cornell University Press, 2006).

Said, E., *Orientalism* (New York: Vintage Books, 1979).

Scheer, M., 'Are Emotions a Kind of Practice (and Is That What Makes Them Have a History?): A Bourdieuian Approach to Understanding Emotion', *History and Theory*, 51 (2012), 193–220.

Scott, J.W., 'Gender: A Useful Category of Historical Analysis', *The American Historical Review*, 91, 5 (1986), 1053–75.

——, 'The Evidence of Experience', *Critical Inquiry*, 17 (1991), 773–97.

——, 'Gender: Still a Useful Category of Analysis?', *Diogenes*, 56 (2010), 7–14.

Seymour, M., 'Emotional Arenas: From Provincial Circus to National Courtroom in Late Nineteenth-Century Italy', *Rethinking History*, 16 (2012), 177–97.

Simonton, D. et al., *The Routledge History Handbook of Gender and the Urban Experience* (London: Routledge, 2017).

Smith, J.E., 'Race, Emotions, and Socialization', *Race, Gender & Class*, 9 (2002), 94–110.

Smith, M. et al., 'Introduction: Geography and Emotion – Emerging Constellations', in *Emotion, Place and Culture* (London: Ashgate, 2016), pp. 17–34.

Stockdale, M.K., '"My Death for the Motherland Is Happiness": Women, Patriotism, and Soldiering in Russia's Great War, 1914–1917', *The American Historical Review*, 109 (2004), 78–116.

Tait, P., *Performing Emotions: Genders, Bodies, Spaces in Chekhov's Drama and Stanislavski's Theatre* (London: Routledge, 2002).

Taylor, D., and Chulov, M., 'Home Office Cancels Flight to Deport Kurdish Failed Asylum Seekers to Iraq', *The Guardian*, 31 May 2022, www.theguardian.com/uk-news/2022/may/31/home-office-cancels -flight-to-deport-kurdish-asylum-seekers-to-iraq (accessed 28 June 2022).

'Threat of Sexual Violence Continues for Forced Migrants in Search of Refuge', 29 March 2022, www.birmingham.ac.uk/news/2022/threat-of -sexual-violence-continues-for-forced-migrants-in-search-of-refuge (accessed 28 June 2022)

Vasiliev, P., 'Revolutionary Conscience, Remorse and Resentment: Emotions and Early Soviet Criminal Law, 1917–1922', *Historical Research*, 90 (2017), 117–33.

Vassiliadou, D., 'The Idiom of Love and Sacrifice: Emotional Vocabularies of Motherhood in Nineteenth Century Greece', *Cultural and Social History*, 14 (2017), 283–300.

Virdee, S., *Racism, Class and the Racialised Outsider* (Basingstoke: Bloomsbury, 2014).

Wigger, I., 'Anti-Muslim Racism and the Racialisation of Sexual Violence: "Intersectional Stereotyping" in Mass Media Representations of Male Muslim Migrants in Germany', *Culture and Religion*, 20 (2019), 248–71.

Wilkins, A., and Pace, J., 'Class, Race, and Emotions', in J. Stets and J. Turner (eds.), *Handbook of the Sociology of Emotions: Volume II* (Dordrecht: Springer, 2014), 385–409.

Yeoman, J.M., *Print Culture and the Formation of the Anarchist Movement in Spain, 1890–1915* (Edinburgh: AK Press, 2022).

Part I

GENDER, CLASS AND SEXUALITY IN THE NEGOTIATION OF POLITICAL POWER

Chapter 1

'My old eyes weep but I am proud of my own children'[1]: grief and revolutionary motherhood in the Soviet 1920s

Hannah Parker

A letter from Zherebtsova, a peasant woman from the Komi-Zyryan Autonomous Region, west of the Urals in the newly established Soviet Union, made its way to the editorial board of the peasant women's journal, *Krest'ianka* in 1925.[2] Zherebtsova wrote about the situation of peasant women in her region, asking for attention to be paid to the region's disparate artels and small cooperatives, which were suffering from chronic underfunding. In her preliminary commendation of the Bolshevik Revolution's struggle and success, she prioritized its work among peasant women:

> Previously women lived in the dark and dirt, suffered beatings from [their] husbands, knew the priest and the kulak, and the last bit of butter was taken by the priest and the kulak. The priests and kulaks fattened up, but peasant women and children were hungry and cold. The October Revolution gathered up the chains of lawlessness and oppression, and the Communist Party conducts hard work among the peasants. The peasant woman awakens, learns, and strives to improve her economic situation.[3]

Striking in her letter is the conflation of the fates of women and children, which are cast in stark opposition to the alien elements of the kulak and priest, and historically resigned to suffering in traditional marital relationships. Beyond their shared oppression, the juxtaposition of women and children reflected women's 'essential' responsibility for the upbringing of children. With women subject to domestic abuse, dependent upon religious authority and deprived of resources, children also went hungry until their deliverance by the October Revolution. 'Awakened' by the Revolution, women thus assumed responsibility for their socialist (re)construction.

As implied by Zherebtsova's equivalence of pre-revolutionary life with darkness and dirt, the emancipation of women occurred in tandem with the establishment of what a group of activists from Essentuki termed in a letter to Deputy Minister for Education Nadezhda Krupskaia 'a new system of feelings, new psychology, new emotions and new culture'.[4] The 'bright light of communism' dispelled the dirt and darkness that characterized the tsarist past and opened the path to a bright and joyful communist future.[5] In its mission to transform the mind, body and soul of the pre-revolutionary subject into that of the New Soviet Man and Woman, the Soviet state established particular emotional expectations of its citizens, creating an emotional community whose boundaries were characterized by revolutionary zeal, gratitude and joy.[6] With citizens 'emancipated' from their causes, and the individualism around which daily life had been structured before the Revolution deconstructed, unhappy feelings would be obsolete. The prioritization of the 'public mood' by the Soviet project reflects the 'negotiations of power' involved in the generation of emotional allegiance to governance.[7] For this reason, gratitude was a key landmark on the early Soviet emotional landscape for Soviet citizens, carved out by Lenin in the construction of the vanguard party as the new citizenry's 'benefactor' and fostering what Jeffrey Brooks has called a 'moral economy of the gift'. Civic inclusion increasingly depended upon the expression of public and collective gratitude for the opportunities provided to them to attain the promise of socialist happiness.[8]

Since the newly 'emancipated' Soviet woman had been granted, *in addition to* proletarian liberation, full entitlement to divorce, alimony, suffrage, wage and labour equality, and abortion by 1921, the causes of her unhappiness were, theoretically, abolished.[9] Although the Bolshevik government became the first in history to aim to emancipate women, who were 'doubly oppressed under capitalism' (trebly if subject to 'work amongst women of the East'),[10] the proletarian subject remained resolutely masculine.[11] With class identity continually prioritized over gender, to avoid deterioration into what Lenin rather obliquely referred to as an 'appendage to the sex problem', a crude tension between notions of gender equality and biological difference emerged.[12] Although the association of women with 'the flesh' was widely criticized, the embedding of binary biological sexual difference in Soviet discourse ensured that women's access to 'monumental time' – the eternal cycle of reproduction that straddled past, present and future – placed them at odds with the 'masculine' futurism of the socialist project.[13]

In this chapter, I argue that when motherhood's emotionality was refracted through the prism of revolution, collectivism and socialist construction, the otherwise individual mother–child bond acquired legitimate grievability. Despite the ideological anxieties women embodied, and subsequently a series of fluctuations in what the nuclear family and maternal role should look like, their presumed maternity ensured their indispensability to the Soviet project as 'mothers of the Revolution'. This chapter draws on unpublished letters written by Soviet women to Soviet power in the post-Civil War 1920s to illustrate how 'grief', by connection to socialist construction and social mothering, formed a central tenet of revolutionary motherhood, reinforcing the premise that women were able to establish space in the ideological framework of the Soviet project for their experiences and emotions, even where these appeared to contradict dominant norms.

Throughout the 1920s, thousands of 'public' letters were sent from citizens to Soviet officials. The Soviet government solicited letters from citizens as correspondents to newspapers and journals and sought to assess the 'public mood' through consultation on a range of policies. People also wrote for material assistance, to appeal convictions, to make complaints, to seek advice or simply to confide in a figurehead of Soviet power.[14] In their letters to Soviet authorities, citizens often adopted and reproduced the ideological vernacular of the state, a process described by Stephen Kotkin as 'Speaking Bolshevik'.[15] Tracing the intersection between early Soviet ideology and Soviet selfhood in the language used in these letters, I argue that, while writing oneself into an 'already established master script' may *also* have 'incrementally empowered that text', public letters demonstrate the mutability of early Soviet discourse and constitute an illustration of the 'usable selves' proposed by Sheila Fitzpatrick.[16] By examining the language and content of public letters, the analysis provides a snapshot of the competing emotional expectations within early Soviet society and of Soviet citizens' sense of place among them.

Soviet citizens' engagement of new emotional styles in their letters reflected Sheila Fitzpatrick's suggestion that '[w]hat is most accessible to the historian is the emotional repertoire of a society – which emotions were most frequently performed (expressed) in a specific historical (social, cultural) setting, and what the conventions of performance were'.[17] Attention to the idiosyncrasies in the performance of this emotional repertoire and its staging is crucial to a fuller understanding of the repertoire itself. Public letter-writing in the Soviet Union was ostensibly no *less* authentic than any other genre of letter- or life-writing, since, as Panagiotis Moullas has claimed, the epistolary self is, by definition, 'dual and ambivalent, monological and dialogical, actual and fictitious, private and public'.[18] While, as Miriam Dobson argues, it would be naïve to assume that letters allow us to view the inner life of their authors, the 'transgressions and reworkings of the authoritative text' do provide a sense of their 'understanding of the discursive boundaries of the system in which they operated' and their own priorities and preoccupations.[19] In this sense, public letters facilitated dialogic contact between the individual and the Soviet state, as instigators of policy and ideology, as well as providing some monologic insight into the life and preoccupations of their writers. Practically speaking, the time and energy invested in the writing of a letter by hand would not have been insignificant, and the case can be made that letter-writing constituted a craft used both to construct the social self and to negotiate between the 'emotional communities' of the Soviet collective and the local. Handwritten and invested with social and emotional agency, in the first decades of the Soviet Union's existence material scarcity meant that letter-writing acquired an additional affective property, since the Civil War, war communism and the limited marketization of the New Economic Policy (NEP) caused severe shortages across the Union.[20] Paper was a relative scarcity, and as Jeffrey Brooks has shown, shortages of materials and equipment during war communism and the NEP caused crisis after crisis for press production altogether in the period, with the quantities of paper and cardboard being produced only matching 1913 levels by 1928/9.[21] One correspondent, writing to *Krest'ianka* journal in 1924 to relay the difficulties she faced in fulfilling her duties as a correspondent, made plain her material circumstances with the sentence 'I have no more paper in order to write to you'.[22]

Letter-writing constituted a creative practice in its own right, with the liminal spaces of letters acting, as Dimitra Vassiliadou has argued, as 'key sites for the creation and negotiation of maternal feelings' upon which writers made 'efforts to create presence out of absence'.[23] In this way, they provided a means by which Soviet citizens were able to negotiate and navigate the emotional communities between which they moved. Letters established tangible, if fragile, relationships with the Soviet collective embodied by those at the apex of the institutions of governance, whereby citizens demonstrated their ability to realize their emotions in line with the norms of the Soviet emotional community. For mothers, letters constituted liminal spaces where the emotional contours of motherhood were worked out on the page, in dialogical relationship to the social self and Soviet project. These terms of emotional engagement, as discursive 'paths' trodden, retrodden and diverted, connect Anna Krylova's assertion that Soviet collectivist discourse was not static with the ideological innovations of the post-revolutionary period and with the vacillations of gender ideology after 1917.[24]

Maternal feelings

Recent re-theorizations of Soviet motherhood show that motherhood's place in early Soviet ideology was always ambiguous, with the relationship between motherhood, the individual, the state and socialist labour constantly in flux. The Soviet mother was deeply embedded in the fabric of Soviet society as early as 1921 and her 'resurrection' by the 1930s, along with the resolution of the woman question, signified her legal legitimation rather than a substantive remodelling of gender relations. A source of ideological anxiety to be controlled and supervised, women's bodies simultaneously constituted a chain binding them to the past while fulfilling a vital revolutionary function, and so a consensus on the nature of the maternal relationship was never reached among Bolshevik theorists.[25]

In general terms, motherhood was cast as a social function, concerned with the quality of future generations rather than a private matter. Instructional literature such as the journal *Voprosy materinstva i mladenchestva* (*Questions of Motherhood and Infancy*) placed an emphasis on the conduct of 'future mothers', attempting to scientifically regulate both reproduction and childrearing according to contemporary European, masculine scientific standards.[26] Efforts to dissuade the Soviet population from engagement with folk healers or midwives, or from non-Russian cultural or medical norms, was a near constant characteristic of reproductive health advice throughout the first decades of Soviet power.[27] One poster commissioned by the Department for the Protection of Motherhood and Infancy in 1925, with the headline 'What you must know as a woman', juxtaposed the fates of pregnant women who consulted health professionals through pregnancy and childbirth with those who did not. A cluttered, cautionary panel on the poster featuring an elderly folk healer bore the caption 'Births with a peasant woman-healer (*babka*) end up in the serious illness or even death of the mother and child'.[28]

Figure 1.1: Advice to expectant mothers on healthy practices during pregnancy and at the birth. Colour lithograph after O. Griun, (1925: Izdanie Otdela Okhrany Materinstva i Mladenchestva NKZ, Lit. Goskart Fabr. Narkomfina). Wellcome Collection. In copyright.

By 1930, childcare propaganda still conveyed the benefits of social care over parental care for children, despite the financial limitations upon the state's ability to fulfil its goals.

Thus, motherhood was ideologically constructed simultaneously as a skill to be learnt (from state trained health professionals) and as a natural social function. Yet, as Olga Issoupova has shown, motherhood was not the *only* role for women, nor was the maternal bond her only significant relationship.[29] The new Soviet woman was one who 'rejected femininity and sublimated personal desires, including motherhood, for the sake of building a new socialist society', and although new roles were opened up to her, essentialist notions of maternalism and care persisted.[30] Although external to the nuclear family, the emergence of the *obshchestvennitsa*, or 'wife-activist' movement, whose members 'nurtured, educated, instilled culture and provided comfort', has typically been framed as part of the resurrection of the maternal family in the 1930s, and was described by state departments in typically patriarchal notions of stability and comfort. Although Lauren Kaminsky has argued that the Soviet Union's social policy in the 1930s actually constituted 'the continuation of a radical revolutionary tradition' rather than the earlier traditions of nuclear family life that Engels had cast as the bedrock of capitalism, even within the initial impetus to completely socialize tasks related to domestic labour and childcare, men's participation was conspicuously absent, and assumptions about women's maternal natures went unchallenged.[31] Writing to *Krest'ianka*, an organizer at the 'AVANTGARDE' commune described the day-to-day running of their commune in 1925. Explaining that the bulk of domestic labour on the commune had been socialized, she mentioned in passing that 'each wife washes [laundry] for herself and her husband'.[32] Rebecca Balmas Neary has shown that, despite the fact that some of their activities, such as tracking their children's scholarly progress, did align with traditional notions of motherhood, the *obshchestvennitsy* of the 1930s 'undertook an assortment of activities which could be assumed under the rubric of social mothering', looking beyond the nuclear family.[33]

Despite an emphasis on social over parental care, as Hannah Proctor has argued, 'love remained central to post-revolutionary discourse'.[34] Several writers for *Voprosy materinstva i mladenchestva* openly recognized the problem of 'hospitalism', or the deprivation of emotional interaction from which children raised in overcrowded, underfunded post-revolutionary institutions suffered.[35] Ultimately, though the prioritization of nuclear family ties was controversial, what Proctor has termed 'revolutionary maternal love' retained its importance, establishing an ideological basis upon which legitimate maternal grief might be performed. I argue that 'grief' was a central but unacknowledged means of managing this tension: some women suffered under tsarism to domestic labour and 'the male fist'; others carried the responsibility for future generations; all bore the sorrows of the tsarist past and revolutionary struggle, which could be mobilized behind the Revolution, dialectically resolving women's backwardness and counterrevolutionary potential.

This trajectory is depicted in Pudovkin's 1926 film *Mother* (*Mat'*), based upon Gorky's 1907 novel of the same name.[36] In the film, the unnamed 'mother' is downtrodden by her husband, who is in conflict with their son both at home and in the workplace, an intergenerational conflict culminating in a workers' strike in which the husband is killed and, accidentally betrayed by his mother, the son is arrested and imprisoned. During the son's incarceration, the mother asks for his forgiveness and aids his revolutionary comrades in their plot to free the prisoners during a solidarity march. The uprising is suppressed by tsarist forces, killing son and mother, with her depicted in the final scene stoically holding a red flag in the face of the oncoming tsarist cavalry. Maternal grief could therefore be mobilizing – legitimizing the loss of loved ones by connecting it to the oppression of the proletariat and revolutionary struggle, a journey also depicted by the recurrent motif of grieving maternal figures in other contemporary cinema, such as Eisenstein's 1926 film *Battleship Potemkin*.[37] Women were frequently shown to bear the emotional toll of the old regime and the struggle for the new, it being key to their subjective transformation into builders of socialism.[38] Therefore, though emancipated from tsarist oppression, women remained objects of ambivalence for early Soviet policymakers and theorists who were concerned by the simultaneously revolutionary and counterrevolutionary potential of perpetual cycles of childbearing and childrearing. The task was to 'convert' counterrevolutionary tendencies to an emancipatory form.

Motherhood and grief

As a material means of forging emotional connections with their recipients in the Soviet establishment, letter-writing constituted a way for Soviet citizens to establish common ground between the emotional communities they inhabited and that they established with the new society. Where the feelings they wanted to share with other members, and those who policed it, risked falling beyond its boundaries, women could reaffirm their membership by illustrating their maternal feelings. In requests for material assistance, women frequently described the implications of their need through an emphasis upon the emotional bond between themselves and their children. Writing in 1929 to Mikhail Ivanovich Kalinin, then chairman of the Central Executive Committee, one woman appealed for her children to be able to join her in Central Asia to assist her ailing husband by reflecting upon the emotional toll her absence would have on her boys: 'They're such marvelous little fellows and are so fond of me and if I die – it will be hard for them without a mother.'[39] This bond was often explicitly related to the children's membership of the 'next generation' of Soviet society. A 1924 letter from Petrovskaia in Ekaterinburg in the Urals lamented the subordination of her women's agricultural artel to the needs of the party. She was effectively no longer being paid for her work, which she argued was, above all, highly detrimental both to her children's immediate material needs and to their future: 'I have children and I need to live for them ... they need to learn, their lives are ahead of them, and they need clothes and shoes.'[40] The concurrent constructions of past and future in Petrovskaia's letter underline the centrality of maternal temporality to Soviet womanhood, an 'essence' that enabled women to elucidate their sorrows as mothers.

While the emotions of motherhood were bound with the fate of the child, the inheritance of grief might be alleviated through the rejection of traditions and behaviours associated with life under tsarism. A letter from

Iaknina, a peasant woman from Moscow, in 1924 described the medical implications of Russian folk traditions, which she summed up as the 'senselessness and inattention' of the mother and the influence of 'superstition and prejudice in the life of mother and child'.[41] While reflecting her knowledge of infant mortality rates that were published by the Department for the Protection of Motherhood and Infancy (OMM), the liberation of the mother and child from sorrowing under tsarism was also depicted by Iaknina as a self-evident truth, testament both to the cycles of loss and grief borne by mothers and to the complicity of women themselves in these cycles:

> Everyone knows how many children have died in the first year of life. They know that the reason for this is our darkness, ignorance, and illiteracy ... We, not following the advice of grandmothers [*babok*] and midwives [*povitukh*], the village calls atheists, considering these people inveterate. And here we, the real atheists, must open all the ulcers of Russian life![42]

Elsewhere in her letter, Iaknina revealed the contradictory cultural hierarchies implicit in the construction of the New Soviet Man and Woman, pointing out that '[e]ven the Tatars, dirty dark and ignorant, lose half as many children each year, because under the law of Mohammed the child can only be fed by the mother's breast'.[43] The association between 'poor hygiene' and tradition was thus feminized and conflated with non-Russian and non-Christian minorities, despite an established awareness amongst medical professionals of the obstetric benefits of some aspects of traditional childbearing practices across the former empire.[44]

The implications of this heavy burden of care were not lost on Soviet mothers. Larisa Ia wrote to the deputy minister for education, Nadezhda Krupskaia, in 1930 to request leave from her school following the death of her infant daughter from measles. The school board had already denied her leave to care for her prior to her daughter's death. Larisa's letter describes her social role as a mother and professional role as a teacher as separate yet intrinsically linked identities and commitments: 'I have come to the conclusion that we, who remain strong for the upbringing of the new generation, must not have our own children, the flowers that colour and illuminate our lives.'[45] Larisa may have been referring to the 1926 film *Children – Life's Flowers*, which was shown at an OMM event; the motif also appears in a 1925 Georgian-Russian poster, 'Children are the flowers of the commune', which marked the 'week of the child' and depicts a woman holding her baby up while surrounded by flowers and pomegranates.[46] Despite the metaphor's possible familiarity, Larisa's equivocation between the flowers of life and one's *own* children delivers a poignant insight into her sense of personal grief. She went on to describe the emotional conflict her grief caused her in her work cultivating the flowerbed of the new Soviet generation:

> How could I, tired, and with a sick child in my arms, raise the productivity of the class, what now can I give my pupils? All the cheerfulness, the desire I have to build pupils' freedom, is gone. I function mechanically and am afflicted by this ... but such unfortunate teachers and children's tales are scattered around ... our Union.

Overwhelmed by her grief, Larisa 'functions mechanically' and thus implies the emotionality of the Soviet project – socialist construction *should* be undertaken enthusiastically, although crucially her painful loss prevented this. Continuing, Larisa framed her request in the language of labour regulation, relating her work both as a mother and as a teacher to the new Soviet generation:

> For us there is no regulation ... In the country of the Soviets, there must not be unfortunate children, and unsupervised, neglected children, who spend most of their time under the supervision of semiliterate nannies, with whom childhood passes by grey, and unprepossessing. I'm sorry, a thousand times sorry dear Nadezhda Konstantinovna, that I took from You an hour of precious time, but it is very hard.

Central to Larisa's letter is revolutionary maternal love, its significance for the 'happy childhoods' of the Soviet children and its association with socialist values such as literacy (which had been a key project after the Revolution). Poor supervision and neglect by 'semiliterate nannies' suggest the lingering of roles associated with the old regime, whose oppressed and uneducated domestic workers were emotionally alienated from their labour – the care of children – establishing a stark contrast with the nurture and care provided by Soviet teachers. The letter reflects an understanding of maternal care as fundamental to Larisa's work as a female teacher and to the wellbeing of the new Soviet generation, although motherhood itself is not seen as 'the only' or even the most desirable work available to women.

Grieving suicide

Particularly at the beginning of the decade, the emotional tone of Soviet society was rather mixed, reflecting the perception of ongoing struggle for the fate of the Revolution. A teacher writing from Cherepovets, who signed

'MY OLD EYES WEEP BUT I AM PROUD OF MY OWN CHILDREN' 41

her letter for publication as 'M', suggested the 'difference between 1917 and 1924' was 'not so far apart'.[47] The February Revolution and collapse of the Russian autocracy was well received in Cherepovets, she wrote. 'After the overthrow of [Tsar] Nicholas we breathed a sigh of relief.' The peasants 'waited for what would be', and in October they 'learned of and welcomed' news of the Bolsheviks' success, returning to their homes content and 'full of all sorts of sensations [oshchushchenii] and experiences [perezhivanii]'.[48] Soon after, however, confusion befell the peasants. Confronted for the first time with the question of power, they wondered, 'How will it be without a boss? Are we really going to rule over everything ourselves?' Likewise, a local Zhenotdel delegate, Makaeva, complained to Krest'ianka in 1924 that in Laptevo village in Tula region, where she was based, 'Work among women [was] very bad': there had previously been three Zhenotdel delegates, but now only she remained active.[49] In her letter Makaeva clearly acknowledged the limitations to her achievements – the impact of her efforts diminished as the only Zhenotdel delegate in Laptevo, and the local party congress often forgot to invite her to elections. Significantly, she sought to remedy this and requested acceptance as a correspondent for Krest'ianka: 'Yes, I would like to share my thoughts and impressions with peasant women of other localities, and wish to [know] where and how work is carried out.'[50] Although clearly couched in the language of self-motivated women's emancipation, Makaeva nonetheless had no qualms about sharing her dismay over the dismal state of affairs for women with the editors of a party press.

Key to the effective transmission of dissatisfaction with post-revolutionary conditions was engagement with the transformation wrought by the Revolution, frequently depicted in the nigh-eschatological language of the illumination of darkness. A woman named Viachkova illustrated this when she wrote a note of thanks to the journal, in 1924/5, for their previous issue, which had reached her remote farm:

> Each magazine, like a ray of light cuts through the darkness, connecting us with the world of women, and does not give us the feeling that we are forgotten in our corners ... Reading it we are proud, and follow events around the world. It is difficult and often nearly impossible work, but we see our leaders NK Krupskaia, and Clara Zetkin and other women, wanting to teach us to build our better women's position, as well as to pull our more backwards comrades with us.[51]

The tribulations of life after the Civil War, therefore, constituted a central component of the struggle for revolutionary transformation, a struggle which was implicitly gendered both by women's backwardness and by sexist or apathetic attitudes to women's emancipation across the territories of the Union. The maternal role embodied by leading women in the

Bolshevik Party – potentially reinforced by Krupskaia's marriage to Lenin, the father of the Revolution – and their 'nearly impossible' work for the emancipation of all women perhaps consolidated the significance of mothering for the Revolution's success.

Such was the discursive potential of revolutionary maternal love and sorrow, and its mobilizational potential, that women felt able throughout the 1920s to discuss, quite openly, their children's suicides in the press and in dialogue with high-level officials. Although the emotional tone of the decade was mixed, the preoccupation with the 'public mood' and concerns about counterrevolutionary feeling in the 1920s heightened anxieties about suicide, which was seen as a prioritization of the 'self' over the collective and evidence of counterrevolutionary feeling.[52] In a 1924 biography commemorating her daughter's life in *Krest'ianka* for International Working Women's Day, Maria paid tribute to her daughter. Her account opens: 'On the international day of working women, I, mother of Liza and Volodia, want to share the grief and pride of women.'[53] Reflecting the affective potential of letter-writing to creating presence from absence between writer and recipient, Maria's writing could also be read as a means of creating presence from *loss*. By documenting her daughter's life in a biography intended for publication in a widely circulated print journal, Maria brought Liza back into being on the page.

In the biography, Maria described her daughter's upbringing prior to the Revolution, telling of Liza's generosity of spirit, contributions to her community's work and refusal to live 'as a parasite'. Liza was seventeen when the Revolution, which she joined, took place, and afterwards she undertook political work among women. In 1920, she joined the Red Army in the struggle for the future of the Revolution. Maria explains that Liza 'came home pale, thin, and exhausted'. On 4 June 1921, Liza 'ended her own life'. Liza's brother, Volodia ('also a communist'), was killed 'by bandits' a day earlier, on what Maria describes as 'the eve of Liza's death'. Maria ends the narrative with a eulogy to her children and a pledge to continue their work:

> It is hard for a mother to lose her children, such as [I have lost] mine, and my old eyes weep, but I am proud of my own children Liza and Volodia, who sacrificed their young lives for the struggle against the bourgeoisie. Goodbye my dear children, sleep tight. Change is needed, and it will bring about an end [to the struggle], and your old mother as best [she can] helps Soviet power.[54]

Written two years prior to the film's release, Maria's biography is echoed by Pudovkin's *Mother* in her subjective transformation and subsequent assumption of the revolutionary struggle. Her account underscores her own love – and associated grief – for her own two children as a natural element of motherhood, while emphasizing its centrality to her mobilization for the Revolution. Narrating her daughter's life, Maria took great care to show Liza's good upbringing and selflessness, neutralizing her own apparent distance from the events of the Revolution. Liza's death was eulogized as a sacrifice for the Revolution, legitimizing Maria's grief and managing what Peter Juviler has termed 'the contradiction between revolutionary ideals and the aftereffects of conflict' by framing her political mobilization as an act of mothering.[55]

By the end of the 1920s, while the emotional weather in the Soviet Union had brightened, socialism was still in construction. This ongoing project justified *some* acknowledgement of the emotional work still to be done, but the lingering presence of anti-Soviet elements had become more dangerous. The taboo surrounding suicide intensified correspondingly. Vlasova wrote to Nadezhda Krupskaia five years later in 1929 to demand action on gender relations in schools, introducing herself as a mother of two daughters, one of whom was 'conquered by suicide'. Vlasova's sixteen-year-old daughter, a member of the Soviet youth programme the Pioneers, had been 'humiliated' on her way home from school by three boys. Vlasova's suggestion that her daughter, an active participant in the Soviet project as a Pioneer, 'was conquered' by suicide, rather than having chosen it, posthumously absolved her of responsibility for the presumed rejection of the collective.

Reflecting the negative influence that parents and teachers could have on Soviet children, Vlasova's letter details her protracted struggle with school staff over their approach to gender equality, and responsibility for her daughter's death, remarking: 'I'm even more condemning the teachers here.' Vlasova sought to legitimize her conflict with the workers at the school by evoking her 'natural' maternal feelings, with the entreaty 'I ask you to forgive me, a distressed mother.' Vlasova's motherhood and love not only for her children but for their generation as a whole mitigates the disruption her complaint causes the local Soviet schools. At the end of the letter, Vlasova reiterated the tangible significance of this mission, relating her living daughter to the struggle for gender equality, plainly stating that '[b]etter relations between boys and girls are necessary ... I know you are busy, but I have my daughter to protect'.[56]

Next to Vlasova's file in the archive was a copy of the letter's reply from Krupskaia, itself a relative rarity. In it, Krupskaia corroborated Vlasova's appraisal of gender relations in schools, writing:

Dear comrade,

You are right that there is still a lot left of the old in relations between boys and girls. There is no simple, pure comradeship. I have recently

written on that topic. There is a lot of gossip, gossip, suspicion. We
have much of the old [regime] in children's homes and schools. We
talk all the time about schools' work. By working together, relationships between boys and girls become comradeships. But the poverty
of our country has prevented us from implementing polytechnic
schools, and ordinary school study is not able to fundamentally
change the old [ways]

I am very sorry for the loss of your girl so early.[57]

Krupskaia's letter is surprising in its acknowledgement of the Union's
shortcomings regarding gender relations in schools – though the women's
department, the *Zhenotdel*, was winding down by 1929, and Krupskaia
herself would fall out of favour with Stalin, at this time she was still
deputy minister for education. Acknowledging the Union's financial
shortcomings, her letter implicitly encourages Vlasova's struggle in her
local school system against the persistence of sexist attitudes. The suicide
of Vlasova's daughter, along with Vlasova's grief, were formally, if tacitly,
de-stigmatized.

Conclusions

Public letters were a key site for citizens to negotiate their social identity
and belonging in the decades that followed the October Revolution. As
texts, they demonstrate that women reproduced Bolshevik language carefully and creatively as meaningful historical actors, to accommodate
their own circumstances and feelings firmly within the dominant discourses of Soviet power. Materially, these missives allowed their writers
to forge connections with representatives of Soviet power across great distances. 'Hand-crafted' by their writers, often amid material scarcity,
letters acted as emotional 'agents' on their behalf, seeking to evoke a
desired emotional response from their readers. Whether the intended effect
upon the reader was to provoke material aid, practical advice or simply
confidence and sympathy, as 'efforts to create presence out of absence' letters textually and tangibly emphasized their writer's location in their
social and emotional landscape, and dialogue with the Soviet project.

As demonstrated by their letter-writing, ordinary women were capable
of inhabiting and utilizing the liminal space assigned to them in early
Soviet ideology. Although motherhood was pointedly *not* considered to be
an essential role for women in the Soviet interwar years, its centrality in
women's letters as a justification for the otherwise ideologically ambiguous individualism of personal feelings such as grief and mourning reflects

its significance, not only as an economic and emotional resource but also as a means of shoring up social and ideological cohesion. Although ambivalent in their (counter)revolutionary potential, the grief and sacrifice associated with maternal love could mobilize women behind the Revolution. Women themselves were finely attuned to this discursive nuance, a fact reflected by the careful shift in the tone of their letters throughout the decade. This ideological facet meant that even when lost to suicide, mothers were able to eulogize their children, wielding their emotional power as revolutionary mothers to write their lives back into the Soviet narrative. Despite a clear discursive emphasis upon social mothering, and the ambiguous role of the individual mother–child bond, mothers preserved their individual emotional bonds with their children. Engaging a strong sense of revolutionary commitment to future Soviet generations, and a strong sense of the collective, women deftly navigated the Soviet emotional landscape.

Notes

1. Rossiiskoi Gosudarstvennyi Arkhiv Ekonomiki (RGAE), f. 396, op. 2, d. 30, l. 42.

2. *Krest'ianka* started publication in 1922 and, along with its counterpart for working women, *Rabotnitsa*, continued to circulate for the duration of the Soviet period. K. Romanenko, 'Photomontage for the Masses: The Soviet Periodical Press of the 1930s', *Design Issues*, 26 (2010), 29–39; A. Rowley, 'Spreading the Bolshevik Message? Soviet Regional Periodicals for Women, 1917–1941', *Canadian Slavonic Papers*, 40 (2005), 111–26.

3. RGAE, f. 396, op. 2, d. 33, ll. 461–2.

4. Gosudarstvennyi Arkhiv Rossiiskoi Federatsii (GARF), f. 7279, op. 17, d. 38, l. 1.

5. I. Halfin, *From Darkness to Light: Class Consciousness and Soviet Salvation* (Pittsburgh, PA: University of Pittsburgh Press, 2000), p. 2. Similar metaphors are found frequently in women's descriptions of Soviet life; for example, RGAE, f. 396, op. 2, d. 29, l. 381; RGAE, f. 396, op. 2, d. 33, l. 222; GARF, f. 7279, op. 8, d. 15, l. 24; GARF, f. 7279, op. 6, d. 8, ll. 33–5.

6. B. Rosenwein, 'Worrying about Emotions in History', *The American Historical Review*, 107, 3 (2002), 821–45.

7. N. Eustace et al., 'AHR Conversation: The Historical Study of Emotions', *American Historical Review*, 49 (2012), 1525.

8. J. Brooks, *Thank You, Comrade Stalin! Soviet Public Culture from Revolution to Cold War* (Princeton, NJ: Princeton University Press, 2001), p. 83. See also G. Alexopoulos, 'Soviet Citizenship, More or Less: Rights, Emotions, and States of Civic Belonging', *Kritika*, 7 (2006), 487–528.

9. A detailed overview of the evolution of policies aimed at the liberation of women can be found in W.Z. Goldman, *Women, the State, and Revolution: Soviet Family Policy and Social Life, 1917–1936* (Cambridge: Cambridge University Press, 1993).

10. Yulia Gradskova has published widely on this subject: see, for example, 'Emancipation at the Crossroads between the "Woman Question" and the "National Question"', in M. Ilic (ed.), *The Palgrave Handbook of Women and Gender in Twentieth-Century Russia and the Soviet Union* (Basingstoke: Palgrave Macmillan, 2018), pp. 117–31.

11. V.I. Lenin, 'International Working Women's Day', in *On the Emancipation of Women: Lenin, V.I.* (Moscow: Progress Publishers, 1977), p. 82. The theoretical roots of this argument are found in F. Engels (trans. E. Untermann), *The Origin of the Family, Private Property, and the State* (Chicago, IL: Charles H. Kerr & Co., 1902), available at www.gutenberg.org/files/33111/33111-h/33111-h.htm (accessed 1 June 2018). Although an ambivalence towards the 'woman question' dominated Bolshevik circles in the early twentieth century, innovated and lively discourse on women's liberation was driven by women, such as Aleksandra Kollontai, Inessa Armand and Konkordia Samoilova.

12. K. Zetkin, 'My Recollections of Lenin', in *On the Emancipation of Women* (Moscow: Progress Publishers, 1977), p. 103.

13. J. Kristeva, 'Women's Time', *Signs*, 71 (1981), 13–35. Kristeva's account of the 'monumental time' of women locates the individual woman in a 'cyclical' women's time, characterized by the reproductive cycle; H. Proctor, 'Women on the Edge of Time: Representations of Revolutionary Motherhood in the NEP-Era Soviet Union', *Studies in the Maternal*, 7 (2015), at 14–15.

14. S. Fitzpatrick, 'Supplicants and Citizens: Public Letter-Writing in Soviet Russia in the 1930s', *Slavic Review*, 55 (1996), 78–105.

15. S. Kotkin, *Magnetic Mountain: Stalinism as a Civilization* (Oakland, CA: University of California Press, 1997).

16. E. Naiman, 'On Soviet Subjects and the Scholars Who Make Them', *Russian Review*, 60 (2001), 311. For an explanation of 'usable selves', see S. Fitzpatrick, *Tear Off the Masks! Identity and Imposture in Twentieth Century Russia* (Princeton, NJ: Princeton University Press, 2005). For 'Speaking Bolshevik' as a means of appropriating the bases of social solidarity, see Kotkin, *Magnetic Mountain*; for letters to the press as an 'instrument of power', see M. Lenoe, *Closer to the Masses: Stalinist Culture, Social Revolution and Soviet Newspapers* (Cambridge, MA: Harvard University Press, 2004), especially chapter 3. Anna Krylova argues that there existed a 'Stalinist subject that is neither lost in Stalinist culture, nor securely untouched by its ideals and demands', in 'Identity, Agency and the "First Soviet Generation"', in S. Lovell (ed.), *Generations in Twentieth Century Europe* (Basingstoke: Palgrave Macmillan, 2007), p. 41. See also A. Krylova, 'The Tenacious Liberal Subject in Soviet Studies', *Kritika*, 1 (2000), 119–46.

17. S. Fitzpatrick, 'Happiness and Toska: An Essay in the History of Emotions in Pre-War Soviet Russia', *Australian Journal of Politics and History*, 1 (2004)', p. 357.

18. P. Moullas, *The Discourse of Absence: Essay on Epistolarity, with 40 Unpublished Letters of Fotis Politis (1908–1910)* (Athens: Ikaros, 1992), pp. 151, 158, cited by D. Vassiliadou in 'The Idiom of Love and Sacrifice: Emotional Vocabularies of Motherhood in Nineteenth-Century Greece', *Cultural and Social History*, 14 (2017), 286.

19. M. Dobson, 'Letters', in M. Dobson and B. Ziemann (eds.), *Reading Primary Sources: The Interpretation of Texts from Nineteenth- and Twentieth-Century History* (London: Routledge, 2008), pp. 64–5. Sheila Fitzpatrick also argues that citizen letters reveal a 'remarkably personal flavour' in her study of citizen letters in the 1930s, 'Supplicants and Citizens', p. 82.

20. M. Wassell Smith, '"The Fancy Work What Sailors Make": Material and Emotional Creative Practice in Masculine Seafaring Communities', *Nineteenth-Century Gender Studies Special Issue: Making Masculinity: Craft, Gender and Material Production in the Long Nineteenth Century*, 14 (2018), www.ncgsjournal.com /issue142/smith.html. One anonymous letter, collected by the editorial board of the daily newspaper *Pravda* and forwarded to the Central Committee, lambasted the shortages faced by their community, exhorting: 'Shame on you comrades ... There is no vegetable oil, no cereals, no fat, nothing, and ¾lb bread.' (GARF, f. 3316, op. 16a, d. 426, l. 50.)

21. J. Brooks, 'The Breakdown in Production and Distribution of Printed Material, 1917–1927', in A. Gleason, P. Kenez and R. Stites (eds.), *Bolshevik Culture: Experiment and Order in the Russian Revolution* (Bloomington, IN: Indiana University Press, 1985), especially pp. 153–4.

22. RGAE, f. 396, op. 2, d. 33, l. 83.

23. Vassiliadou, 'The Idiom of Love and Sacrifice', pp. 285, 286.

24. A. Krylova, 'Soviet Modernity: Stephen Kotkin and the Bolshevik Predicament', *Contemporary European History*, 23 (2014), 167–92.

25. Goldman, *Women, the State, and Revolution*, p. 1.

26. O. Issoupova, 'From Duty to Pleasure? Motherhood in Soviet and Post-Soviet Russia', in S. Ashwin (ed.), *Gender, State and Society in Soviet and Post-Soviet Russia* (London: Routledge, 2012), p. 31.

27. For the older, peasant woman as the antithesis of Soviet hygiene and medicine, see R. Glickman, 'The Peasant Woman as Healer', in B.E. Clements, B. Alpert Engel and C. Worobec (eds.), *Russia's Women: Accommodation, Resistance, Transformation* (Oakland, CA: University of California Press, 1991), pp. 148–62.

28. Poster, O. Griun, 1925.

29. T. Starks, 'A Fertile Mother Russia: Pronatalist Propaganda in Revolutionary Russia'. *Journal of Family History*, 28 (2003), 420; Issoupova, 'From Duty to Pleasure?', p. 38; see also A. Rowley, 'Where Are All the Mother Heroines? Images of Maternity in Soviet Films of the 1930s', *Canadian Journal of History*, 44 (2009), 37.

30. T.M. Durfee, '"*Cement* and *How the Steel Was Tempered*": Variations on the New Soviet Woman', in S. Stephan Hoisington (ed.), *A Plot of Her Own: The Female Protagonist in Russian Literature* (Evanston, IL: Northwestern University Press, 1995), p. 96.

31. L. Kaminsky, 'Utopian Visions of Family Life in the Stalin-Era Soviet Union', *Central European History*, 44 (2011), 64.

32. RGAE, f. 396, op. 1, d. 5, ll. 74–6.

33. R. Balmas Neary, 'Mothering Socialist Society: The Wife-Activists' Movement and the Soviet Culture of Daily Life, 1934–1941', *The Russian Review*, 58 (1999), 400.

34. Proctor, 'Women on the Edge of Time', p. 2.

35. Issoupova, 'From Duty to Pleasure?', p. 36.

36. *Mat'* (feature film), dir. Vsevolod Pudovkin. Mezhrabpomfilm, 1926, 89 mins.

37. *Battleship Potemkin* (feature film), dir. Sergei Eisenstein. Mosfilm, 1925, 75 mins.

38. Proctor, 'Women on the Edge of Time', p. 13.

39. Rossiiskoi Gosudarstvennyi Arkhiv Sotsial'no-politicheskoii Istorii (RGASPI), f. 78, op. 1, d. 350, ll. 27–8.

40. RGAE, f. 396, op. 1, d. 5, l. 95.

41. RGAE, f. 396, op. 2, d. 29, ll. 1–3.

42. RGAE, f. 396, op. 2, d. 29, ll. 1–3.

43. Yulia Gradskova has explained the gendered cultural hierarchies related to the 'woman question' in late imperial Russia and the early Soviet Union in more detail, arguing that 'Early Bolshevik policies for the emancipation of non-Russian women were based on a mixture of proletarian slogans and old imperial ideas relating to the need to civilize and educate non-Christian people, who, theretofore, had preserved traditional occupations, hierarchies, and beliefs', in '"The Woman of the Orient Is Not the Voiceless Slave Anymore": The Non-Russian Woman of Volga-Ural Region and "Women's Question"', in M. Neumann and A. Willimott (eds.), *Rethinking the Russian Revolution as Historical Divide* (London: Routledge, 2017), p. 170.

44. Issoupova, 'From Duty to Pleasure?', p. 35.

45. GARF, f. 7279, op. 7, d. 18, l. 42.

46. 'Deti – tsvety kommuny', artist unknown, *Russkii revolutsionnyi plakat* (Moscow, 1925), p. 192, https://commons.wikimedia.org/wiki/File:Неизвестный_художник. _Дети_–_цветы_коммуны.jpg (accessed 14 June 2023).

47. RGAE, f. 396, op. 2, d. 33, l. 442.

48. RGAE, f. 396, op. 2, d. 33, l. 442.

49. RGAE, f. 396, op. 2, d. 33, ll. 271–2.

50. RGAE, f. 396, op. 2, d. 33, ll. 271–2.

51. RGAE, f. 396, op. 2, d. 33, l. 270.

52. K. Pinnow, *Lost to the Collective: Suicide and the Promise of Soviet Socialism, 1921–1929* (Ithaca, NY: Cornell University Press, 2010), p. 250. In the absence of the deceased, the attribution of 'blame' for the practice was assigned to local authorities or the deceased's own family, thereby 'absolv[ing] the socialist environment from any liability'. One letter sent from Yartsevo, Smolensk, which reported cases of worker suicides, was forwarded to the highest rungs of Soviet government and demonstrates the connection of suicide with counterrevolution: 'The mood of the workers is terrible, they are dissatisfied with the existing system, they say that before they lived better, especially the old [workers] ... At Yartsevo factory in connection with the dismissal there were cases of suicide' (GARF, f. 3316, op. 16.a, d. 426, l. 1).

53. RGAE, f. 396, op. 2, d. 30, l. 42.

54. RGAE, f. 396, op. 2, d. 30, l. 42.

55. P.H. Juviler, 'Contradictions of Revolution: Juvenile Crime and Rehabilitation', in A. Gleason, P. Kenez and R. Stites, *Bolshevik Culture: Experiment and Order in the Russian Revolution* (Bloomington, IN: Indiana University Press, 1985), p. 273.

56. GARF, f. 7279, op. 7, d. 18, ll. 15–16.

57. GARF, f. 7279, op. 7, d. 18, l. 14.

References

Unpublished primary sources

Gosudarstvennyi Arkhiv Rossiiskoi Federatsii (GARF)
   f. 3316 Central Executive Committee of the USSR (1922–38)
   f. 7279 Secretariat of the Deputy People's Commissar of
      Education N.K. Krupskaia
Rossiiskoi Gosudarstvennyi Arkhiv Ekonomiki (RGAE)
   f. 396 Editorial board of 'Krest'iankskaia gazeta'
Rossiiskoi Gosudarstvennyi Arkhiv Sotsial'no-politicheskoii Istorii
      (RGASPI)
   f. 78 Kalinin, Mikhail Ivanovich, (1875–1946)
Wellcome Collection
   Advice to expectant mothers on healthy practices during pregnancy
      and at the birth. Colour lithograph after O. Griûn, (1925: Izdanie
      Otdela Okhrany Materinstva i Mladenchestva NKZ, Lit. Goskart
      Fabr. Narkomfina)

Contemporary media and published accounts

Battleship Potemkin (feature film), dir. Sergei Eisenstein. Mosfilm, 1925,
   75 mins.
'Deti – tsvety kommuny', artist unknown, *Russkii revolutsionnyi plakat*
   (Moscow, 1925), p. 192, https://commons.wikimedia.org/wiki
   /File:Неизвестный_художник._Дети_ – _цветы_коммуны.jpg
   (accessed 14 June 2023).
Engels, F., and Untermann, E (trans.), *The Origin of the Family, Private
   Property, and the State* (Chicago, IL, 1902), www.gutenberg.org/files
   /33111/33111-h/33111-h.htm (accessed 22 June 2022).
Mat' (feature film), dir. Vsevolod Pudovkin. Mezhrabpomfilm, 1926,
   89 mins.
On the Emancipation of Women: Lenin, V.I. (Moscow, 1977).

Books and articles

Alexopoulos, G., 'The Ritual Lament: A Narrative of Appeal in the 1920s
   and 1930s', *Russian History*, 24 (1997), 117–29.
——, 'Soviet Citizenship, More or Less: Rights, Emotions, and States of
   Civic Belonging', *Kritika*, 7 (2006), 487–528.

Balmas Neary, R., 'Mothering Socialist Society: The Wife-Activists' Movement and the Soviet Culture of Daily Life, 1934–1941', *The Russian Review*, 58 (1999), 396–412.

Brooks, J., 'The Breakdown in Production and Distribution of Printed Material, 1917–1927', in A. Gleason, P. Kenez and R. Stites (eds.), *Bolshevik Culture: Experiment and Order in the Russian Revolution* (Bloomington, IN: Indiana University Press, 1985), pp. 151–74.

——, *Thank You, Comrade Stalin! Soviet Public Culture from Revolution to Cold War* (Princeton, NJ: Princeton University Press, 1999).

Dobson, M., 'Letters', in M. Dobson and B. Ziemann (eds.), *Reading Primary Sources: The Interpretation of Texts from Nineteenth and Twentieth Century History* (London: Routledge, 1998), pp. 57–73.

Durfee, T.M., '*Cement* and *How the Steel Was Tempered*: Variations on the New Soviet Woman', in S. Stephan Hoisington (ed.), *A Plot of Her Own: The Female Protagonist in Russian Literature* (Evanston, IL: Northwestern University Press, 1995), pp. 89–101.

Eustace, N., Lean, E., Livingston, J., Plamper, J., et al, 'AHR Conversation: The Historical Study of Emotions', *American Historical Review*, 49 (2012), 1487–531.

Fitzpatrick, S., 'Supplicants and Citizens: Public Letter-Writing in Soviet Russia in the 1930s', *Slavic Review*, 55 (1996), 78–105.

——, 'Happiness and Toska: An Essay in the History of Emotions in Pre-War Soviet Russia', *Australian Journal of Politics and History*, l (2004), 357–371.

——, *Tear Off the Masks! Identity and Imposture in Twentieth Century Russia* (Princeton, NJ: Princeton University Press, 2005).

Gammerl, B., 'Emotional Styles: Concepts and Challenges', *Rethinking History*, 16 (2012), 161–75.

R. Glickman, 'The Peasant Woman as Healer', in B.E. Clements, B. Alpert Engel and C. Worobec (eds.), *Russia's Women: Accommodation, Resistance, Transformation* (Oakland, CA: University of California Press, 1991), pp. 148–62.

Goldman, W.Z., *Women, the State, and Revolution: Soviet Family Policy and Social Life, 1917–1936* (Cambridge: Cambridge University Press, 1993).

Gradskova, Y., '"The Woman of the Orient Is Not the Voiceless Slave Anymore": The Non-Russian Woman of Volga-Ural Region and "women's question"', in M. Neumann and A. Willimott (eds.), *Rethinking the Russian Revolution as Historical Divide* (London: Routledge, 2017), pp. 150–70.

———, 'Emancipation at the Crossroads between the "Woman Question" and the "National Question"', in M. Ilic (ed.), *The Palgrave Handbook of Women and Gender in Twentieth-Century Russia and the Soviet Union* (Basingstoke: Palgrave Macmillan, 2018), pp. 117–31.

Halfin, I., *From Darkness to Light: Class, Consciousness, and Soviet Salvation* (Pittsburgh, PA: Pittsburgh University Press, 2000).

Ingold, T., *Making: Anthropology, Archaeology, Art and Architecture* (London: Routledge, 2013).

Issoupova, O., 'From Duty to Pleasure? Motherhood in Soviet and post-Soviet Russia', in S. Ashwin (ed.), *Gender, State and Society in Soviet and Post-Soviet Russia* (London: Routledge, 2012), pp. 30–54.

Juviler, P.H., 'Contradictions of Revolution: Juvenile Crime and Rehabilitation', in A. Gleason, P. Kenez and R. Stites (eds.), *Bolshevik Culture: Experiment and Order in the Russian Revolution* (Bloomington, IN: Indiana University Press, 1985), pp. 261–78.

Kaminsky, L., 'Utopian Visions of Family Life in the Stalin-Era Soviet Union', *Central European History*, 44 (2011), 63–91.

Kotkin, S., *Magnetic Mountain: Stalinism as a Civilization* (Oakland, CA: University of California Press, 1997).

Kristeva, J., 'Women's Time', *Signs*, 71 (1981), 13–35.

Krylova, A., 'The Tenacious Liberal Subject in Soviet Studies', *Kritika*, 1 (2000), 119–46.

———, 'Identity, Agency, and the First Soviet Generation', in S. Lovell (ed.), *Generations in Twentieth Century Europe* (Basingstoke: Palgrave Macmillan, 2007), pp. 101–21.

———, 'Soviet Modernity: Stephen Kotkin and the Bolshevik Predicament', *Contemporary European History*, 23 (2014), 167–92.

Lenoe, M., 'Letter-Writing and the State: Reader Correspondence with Newspapers as a Source for Early Soviet History', *Cahiers Du Monde Russe*, 40 (1999), 139–69.

———, *Closer to the Masses: Stalinist Culture, Social Revolution and Soviet Newspapers* (Cambridge, MA: Harvard University Press, 2004).

Naiman, E., 'On Soviet Subjects and the Scholars Who Make Them', *Russian Review*, 60 (July 2001), 307–15.

Parker, H., 'Voices of the New Soviet Woman: Gender, Emancipation and Agency in Letters to the Soviet State, 1924–1941' (unpublished University of Sheffield PhD doctoral thesis, 2019).

Pinnow, K., *Lost to the Collective: Suicide and the Promise of Soviet Socialism* (Ithaca, NY: Cornell University Press, 2010).

Proctor, H., 'Women on the Edge of Time: Representations of Revolutionary Motherhood in the NEP-Era Soviet Union', *Studies in the Maternal*, 7 (2015), 1–20.

Romanenko, K., 'Photomontage for the Masses: The Soviet Periodical Press of the 1930s', *Design Issues*, 26 (2010), 29–39.

Rosenwein, B., 'Worrying about Emotions in History', *The American Historical Review*, 107 (2002), 821–45.

Rowley, A, 'Spreading the Bolshevik Message? Soviet Regional Periodicals for Women, 1917–1941', *Canadian Slavonic Papers*, 47 (2005), 111–26.

——, 'Where Are All the Mother Heroines? Images of Maternity in Soviet Films of the 1930s', *Canadian Journal of History*, 44 (2009), 25–38.

Spagnolo, R., 'When Private Home Meets Public Workplace: Service, Space, and the Urban Domestic in 1920s Russia', in C. Kaier and E. Naiman (eds.), *Everyday Life in Early Soviet Russia: Taking the Revolution Inside* (Bloomington, IN: Indiana University Press, 2006), pp. 230–55.

Starks, T., 'A Fertile Mother Russia: Pronatalist Propaganda in Revolutionary Russia', *Journal of Family History*, 28 (2003), 411–42.

Vassiliadou, D., 'The Idiom of Love and Sacrifice: Emotional Vocabularies of Motherhood in Nineteenth-Century Greece', *Cultural and Social History*, 14 (2017), 283–300.

Wassell Smith, M. '"The Fancy Work What Sailors Make": Material and Emotional Creative Practice in Masculine Seafaring Communities', *Nineteenth-Century Gender Studies Special Issue: Making Masculinity: Craft, Gender and Material Production in the Long Nineteenth Century*, 14 (2018), www.ncgsjournal.com/issue142/smith.html (accessed 22 June 2022).

Waters, E., 'The Female Form in Soviet Political Iconography, 1917–1932', in B.E. Clement, B. Alpert Engel and C. Worobec (eds.), *Russia's Women: Accommodation, Resistance, Transformation* (Oakland, CA: University of California Press, 1991), pp. 225–42.

——, 'The Modernization of Russian Motherhood, 1917–1937', *Soviet Studies*, 44 (1992), 123–35.

Chapter 2

Emotion as a tool of Russian bisexual and transgender women's online activism: a case study

Olga Andreevskikh

Inherent complexities of gender and sexuality in Russia: emotional communities in women's online activism

The dissolution of the Soviet Union in 1991 led to dramatic social changes in Russia. The decriminalization of homosexuality and the emergence of the first grassroots movements for women's rights, as well as for gay and lesbian rights, led to the rise of feminist and LGBTQ-rights movements in the 2000s and 2010s and discursive shifts in the gender order;[1] that is, societal attitudes to gender roles and societal views and opinions on sexuality.[2] Throughout the 1990s and 2000s, largely because of economic hardships and the 'feminization of poverty', women started to resent the traditional 'double burden' pattern of gendered labour inherited from the Soviet era – the pattern that entailed women being expected to combine the roles of full-time workers and full-time mothers and primary carers.[3] The 'gender contract' of the Soviet era, typified by the 'working mother', was contested by a new post-Soviet gender identity of the self-made career woman, which appealed to many women under the circumstances of growing economic freedom and business opportunities.[4] There was a negative attitude to Soviet-style gender equality, which Francesca Stella and Nadya Nartova argue:

distorted men and women's 'natural' gender roles by 'emasculating' men (by reducing their authority in the private sphere of the family) and 'masculinising' women (by granting them access to 'male' occupations and diverting their energies from their 'natural' calling as mothers and carers).[5]

Similar to the expansion of the range of gender contracts, societal attitudes to sexuality in post-Soviet Russia were also evolving, leading to a higher visibility of non-heteronormative individuals or so-called 'sexual minorities' (*seksual'nye menshinstva*). Laurie Essig pointed out that the discursive implications of the Soviet and post-Soviet Russian term 'sexual minorities' is broader and more complex than the hetero/homo binary opposition: it denotes a similar range of identities, behaviours and images for which the umbrella term of 'queer' is normally used.[6] Since the 1990s, the discursive context of naming and reference of non-heteronormative identities in which contemporary Russian activism for LGBTQ rights is operating has evolved considerably. As I have discussed elsewhere, current public discourses on LGBTQ issues in Russia are characterized by the intermittent use of the terms linked to the Soviet past and discourses of medicalization and criminalization of non-heteronormativity (e.g. homosexualism/*gomoseksualizm*; non-traditional sexual orientation/ *netraditsionnaia seksual'naia orientatsiia*), as well as of the LGBTQ-inclusive terms related to identity politics (e.g. gay/*gei*; homosexual/ *gomoseksual*).[7] LGBTQ-catered initiatives, activist groups and media outlets have been contributing to further diversity of terminology related to non-heteronormativity and non-cisnormativity: thus, among younger LGBTQ Russians the trend of using the term 'queer' as an equivalent of 'gay/lesbian/bisexual/transgender' has become popular in recent years.[8]

The failure of queer grassroots movements to gain momentum after the dissolution of the USSR and the decriminalization of homosexuality in 1993, coupled with an overall neo-conservative political turn towards the state-promoted discourse of institutionalized heteronormativity and 'traditional' values, resulted in a strong societal backlash against feminist and LGBTQ-rights movements. In 2013, this neo-conservative backlash manifested itself in the introduction of article 6.21 of Federal Law 135-FZ (the legislation that aims to protect children from harmful information): similarly to the UK Section 28, the added article banned promotion of non-traditional sexual relationships among minors. In particular, it prohibited the mediation of non-traditional sexuality in a positive, attractive and favourable light.[9] In 2017, restrictive medical procedures for obtaining permission for gender transition were introduced,[10] and in the same year certain forms of domestic violence were decriminalized in Russia.[11]

These legislative attacks on LGBTQ and women's rights significantly complicated the work of feminist and LGBTQ-rights activists. Another piece of legislation restricting such activism (as well as any offline street activism) in contemporary Russia is the notorious article 7 of the Federal Law 54-FZ, requiring any street action which has more than one participant to be authorized and officially permitted by local governments. This effectively means that local governments have the power to stop any oppositional protest, while participation in an unauthorized protest is classified as an administrative offence.

In the patriarchal, heteronormative and sexist culture promoted by the Russian neo-conservative political and media elites since Vladimir Putin's first presidency, the increasing infringement of the rights of both heterosexual and LBT (lesbian, bisexual, transgender) women,[12] as well as the legislation restricting activism, the work of NGOs[13] and digital media, created a complex and difficult environment for feminist and LBT-rights activists to operate in. One of the responses to this conservative pressure was the consolidation of LBT-rights and feminist movements, in particular in the form of online activism on social media platforms. Social networking sites have become a valuable tool of participatory media cultures because of the vast opportunities they offer for 'bridging social capital' by linking various communities, and 'linking social capital' by facilitating communication between different social classes.[14] Lacking such crucial resources as funding, legal support and human resources, feminist and LBT-rights activists have turned to social media platforms as digital activist spaces, where they rely heavily on their individual capital – and in particular on their emotional capital.

The current chapter investigates the ways in which Russian female activists for bisexual and transgender rights can use their 'gendered emotions' to promote their respective agendas, to transgress binary monosexist and cis-normative discourses and to produce mediations and self-mediations of non-binary gender and sexual identities. The choice of bisexual and transgender rights activism is prompted by the fact that these marginalized social groups are minorities within minorities, in the sense that they suffer from double discrimination on the part of LGBTQ communities and of society as a whole.[15] I particularly focus on bisexual and transgender women who, on top of the double stigma on the grounds of their position within LGBTQ communities, as women suffer from further discrimination because of the ubiquity of Russian sexism, as well as from exclusionary rhetoric and policies of some of the factions of the feminist movement.[16]

For the purposes of the current analysis, emotions are interpreted, on the one hand, as a biological and universal aptitude for feeling and the expression of feelings and, on the other, as learned, socially constructed practices, a kind of gendered performance.[17] Social media is known to influence emotions and gender, having a 'distinctive relation to emotion within and across social groups'.[18] The axes of social media and gender are particularly crucial to this research, which aims to identify how women's online activism strategies challenge or support gender-emotion stereotypes existing in contemporary Russia.

Drawing on Bourdieu's concept of capital as accumulated labour[19] which can be exchanged for various benefits (such as services or esteem),[20] I understand 'emotional capital' as a concept composed of 'emotion-based knowledge, management skills, and capacities to feel that links self-processes and resources to group membership and social location'.[21] Building on the idea that activist networks 'act as a link to emotional community while promoting further political activity',[22] I perceive activists' emotional capital as one of the most significant tools in their creation of, and operation within, activist groups as emotional communities.

For the purpose of this analysis, the concept of 'emotional communities' is understood as 'groups in which people adhere to the same norms of emotional expression and value – or devalue – the same or related emotions'.[23] I conceptualize the work of feminist bisexual and transgender activists (performed at the intersection of feminist and LGBTQ-rights movements) as emotional communities themselves. Scholarship on networked activism has highlighted how 'networks of activism ... emerge from the interaction of activists, in shared physical and/or emotional spaces'.[24] I understand contemporary Russian LGBTQ activism as creating and maintaining emotional spaces where marginalized LGBTQ people can feel safe, welcome, and accepted. These emotional spaces are as significant for activists as the physical spaces they create or occupy, and are central to the emergence of emotional communities where freedom of expression is provided and respect for all individual experiences is observed. Digital emotional spaces allow activists, among other things, to share personal confessional narratives which help challenge harmful stereotypes, educate audiences on important issues related to sexuality and gender, deal with sensitive and tabooed topics and, in general, serve as an identity-building tool.[25] Ultimately, such emotional communities provide a basis and support network for further activism.

I am particularly interested in how the intersection of these two emotional communities affects bisexual and transgender women's online activism, what challenges this intersection poses and what opportunities it offers. In order to address this research objective, I apply a tripartite approach to activists' work within emotional communities: I look at the ways in which activists use their own emotional capital in their activist work (e.g. whether they opt for expressing or suppressing certain emotions; whether they choose to invest their emotional resources in others or not). Another aspect I study is how online activism affects activists' own emotional states (i.e. their emotional experience). Finally, I look at how wider communities regulate activists' expression of certain emotions: whether activists testify to any form of censorship and control or whether there is unconditional support of whatever emotions are expressed.

Women's activism as a gendered discourse of 'unruly' emotions

From the 2012 Pussy Riot 'Punk Prayer' in Moscow to the opening of the first women-only coffee shop 'Simona' in Saint Petersburg in 2019, Russian female activists have transgressed and appropriated public spaces as a locus of the fight for gender equality and women's rights. Throughout the 2010s, a similar battle has been taking place in Russian digital spaces, in particular on the global social networking website Facebook (www.facebook.com), its Russian counterpart VKontakte (www.vk.com) and most recently on social media platforms Instagram, YouTube, TikTok and Telegram messenger, the latter being popular among activists because of its extra security and full protection of all shared content from government surveillance.[26] Internet-based activism has become vital for such marginalized and discriminated social groups as bisexual and transgender women, representatives of 'minorities within minorities',[27] and as a result the number of Russian feminist and bisexual and transgender rights activists relying on digital activism has been constantly growing.[28]

The internet as a gendered digital space reflects the gendered discourse of technology as technical objects and machines initially monopolized by men, as part of gendered masculine capital.[29] Computer programming and, in a wider sense, anything related to IT tended to be seen by contemporary societies as predominantly male activities.[30] However, recently, with the gradual closing of a gendered digital divide and with more and more women gaining access to IT, scholars have started conceptualizing the internet and in particular social media platforms as spaces where the transgression and transformation of social institutions are facilitated.[31]

For example, the 2016 campaign #IamNotafraidToTell (*IaNeboiusSkazat'*), a local equivalent of the global #MeToo movement which took place both on the Russophone Facebook and on the Russian social networking site VKontakte, prompted wide debates over whether it is acceptable for women to share such personal, intimate, emotionally charged stories online.[32] Another example of societal debates on how women should express their emotions online is the case of the 2019 'Lushgate' campaign in support of Bella Rapoport, a Russian journalist, gender studies scholar and prominent lesbian feminist activist. In March 2019, in an Instagram story, Rapoport expressed her disappointment in the pro-feminist brand Lush which chose not to support her with a collaboration. This confession made Rapoport a subject of trolling and hate mail from users of Instagram, Twitter and Facebook, and the cyberbullying was further continued by multiple online media and mainstream media.[33] The emotions shared in the Instagram story were interpreted as a transgression of socially acceptable feminine emotional boundaries by an overdemanding and self-absorbed feminist: a 'good' woman does not use her emotions to demand benefits for herself but uses them to benefit others. In the autumn of 2019, a similar case of cyberbullying evolved around Nika Vodvud, one of Russia's most popular and well-known feminist activists and blogger who identifies as a bisexual woman.[34] Vodvud confessed in the media that she had been a victim of cyberbullying for a long time. The media coverage following her confession was far from supportive: the long interview with the activist carried out by Russia's prominent liberally biased media outlet meduza.io[35] portrayed Vodvud as an overly emotional, overreacting woman, whereas Vodvud's detractors, predominantly male, were quoted and represented as rational and sensible individuals.[36]

The examples mentioned above are only a few of the numerous cases where female activists have faced a backlash of complex societal responses to their transgressive emotional expression and gendered behaviour online. Such responses, on the one hand, lead to attempts by female activists to create digital safe spaces for mutual support. On the other hand, they result in the fragmentation of female online activist networks and their respective audiences. Such fragmentation can potentially occur if there are differences in the audiences' attitudes to emotional outbursts online: in other words, if there are dissimilarities in the views on acceptable 'modes of feeling, and ways to express those feelings' and on 'important norms concerning the emotions that they value and deplore and the modes of expressing them'.[37] The two case studies discussed here, of Saint Petersburg-based female activists for bisexual and transgender rights, demonstrate how the complexities and challenges posed by digital activist spaces affect specific online activist practices.

I first met these two female activists in 2015 when I joined one of Russia's largest LGBTQ communities on Facebook – 'LGBT Discussion Board' (*LGBT-diskussionnaia ploshchadka*, www.facebook.com/groups/lgbt.discussion, accessed 14 June 2023; in May 2022 the group counted 9,800 members). It did not take me long to identify that Olga Masina was at that time almost solely responsible for raising awareness of bi-visibility, bi-erasure,

EMOTION AS A TOOL OF RUSSIAN BISEXUAL AND TRANSGENDER WOMEN

bi-phobia and other problems and topics crucial for bisexual communities in Russia and beyond. I also noted a significant contribution made to online discussions by Ekaterina Messorosh, one of the group administrators, who acted as the most prominent advocate for transgender people's rights in the LGBT Discussion Board group.

Between November 2017 and January 2018, I closely monitored the women's own social media pages which they used for their activism,[38] and I approached Olga and Ekaterina with a request to participate in research interviews, to which they eagerly agreed, allowing me to use their real names for the project. In Ekaterina's case, at the time of the project the social media platform she tended to use was her personal Facebook account. In Olga's case, the online activist tools included two public communities she administered: the Facebook community 'Bisexual rights movement "LuBI"' (www.facebook.com/groups/1453792034842926, accessed 14 June 2023; the group had 340 members in May 2022) and the public group 'Bisexuality // Biseksual'nost' on telegram.org (https://t.me/bisexuality_Lubi, accessed 27 June 2023; the community had 509 members in June 2023). The monitoring of these three media pages consisted of daily observations of all media content (own posts, reposted posts, shared links to external websites, memes, photos, videos, comments) published by the activists, which was saved in the form of screengrabs for further analysis.[39]

At the time the research interviews were conducted, Ekaterina Messorosh primarily used her personal Facebook account for online activism. However, when I took brief follow-up interviews with both the respondents in 2019, Ekaterina informed me that she had changed her preferences and was now more active on her personal account on VKontakte, which had subsequently become her primary activist platform. In the respective follow-up interview, Olga informed me of having minimized her involvement in activism for personal and health reasons. Because of these changes in online activism practices that had taken place between the media data collection and the completion of this chapter, I have excluded the media content analysis aspect from the current research as out of date. Thus, the current chapter draws fully on the data obtained during the two research interviews I took from the activists in December 2017 – that is, on first-hand narratives of the activists' experiences of applying their emotional capital while operating in intersecting emotional communities of feminist and LGBTQ-rights movements.

The in-depth semi-structured interviews with Olga and Ekaterina centred on the following topics: what factors influenced the women's decision to take up activism; what forms of offline activism, if any, they used; what online platforms they preferred and why; what kind of activities they considered to be their most important contribution; and how their identities as feminists and representatives of the LGBTQ community intersected. When processing the obtained data for the purpose of the current chapter, I focused on how the activists conceptualized their work in terms of the use of emotions and emotional capital, as well as in terms of emotional responses to their activism on the part of wider activist communities and the general public.

Emotions and acceptance: the challenges of invisibility and bisexual rights activism

At the start of the interview, Olga Masina stated that it was the 2013 Federal Law banning promotion of positive opinions and views about non-traditional sexual relations that brought her to LGBTQ-rights activism: she was 'horrified and outraged' (*uzhasnulas' i vozmutilas'*) when the legislation was passed. Olga said that she joined the already existing bisexual rights initiative 'LuBI' (the name contains a pun: it sounds like the second-person singular form of the verb 'love' in the imperative mood – *liubi*, and it also contains the word 'bi', which in Russian is pronounced as '*bee*'). Olga explained that she was soon left alone to oversee the VKontakte and Facebook pages linked to the initiative. Despite other activists leaving the group because of burnout or relocation, Olga took part in as many activist events devoted to bisexual rights as she could. Olga quoted one particular event as her most memorable and successful because of the overwhelming support of the benevolent, friendly general public and because of the overall feelings of 'solemnity' (*torzhestvennost'*) she experienced when participating in it. A street action called 'The Zoo' was organized by the Alliance of Heterosexuals for LGBT-rights and took place on the bisexual visibility day, 23 September 2017. Olga was handing out leaflets and suggesting the passers-by talk to her female colleague, who was sitting nearby, wearing a costume of a fantasy creature and carrying a placard saying 'Common Bisexual' (*Biseksualka obyknovennaia*). When asked how she felt about being part of the wider LGBTQ community, Olga replied it was a 'striped' (*polosatoe*) feeling: at times she felt included, but sometimes she felt as if she were not exactly unwelcome but rather 'not taken into account, ignored' (*ne vosprinimaiut*). As an illustration of how such ignoring and exclusion on the part of the wider community tends to unfold, Olga narrated her experience of collaboration with Russia's biggest LGBTQ film festival Side-by-Side (*Bok-o-bok*; https://bok-o-bok.com/en, accessed 14 June 2023).

The incident evolved around a brochure on how to write about LGBTQ people correctly, which is published by the Side-by-Side organizers to be distributed amongst media professionals during the annual film festival. Having initially joined Side-by-Side as a volunteer, Olga noted that the first 2013 edition of the brochure contained special sections on inclusive language depicting gays, lesbians and transgender people but had nothing on bisexuals and other non-monosexual people. Since in 2017 a new edition of the brochure was planned, Olga offered to write such a section and the organizers agreed. Although Olga did produce the text and then amended it several times in accordance with all the corrections and suggestions on the part of the editors, her text on bi-inclusive language was not published in the 2017 edition of the brochure. In Olga's own words, she felt 'indignant, resentful' (*vosmushchena*), and it felt as if it were all for naught, as if she were banging her head against a wall (*b'ius' golovoi ob stenu*).

When she approached the editors and organizers for an explanation, Olga was informed that her text was not suitable. At our interview she read aloud from her phone the response from the editors: according to them, the text was too 'oppressive' (*tekst davit*); it did not make it clear to the editors why they 'should bother with and keep in mind yet another group' within the community (*pochemu ia dolzhna zamorachivat'sia i pomnit' o drugoi gruppe*). The suggestions on bi-inclusive language which Olga mentioned as desirable were branded 'aggressive' (*agressivnye zamechaniia*) and 'far-fetched' (*iskustvenno pridumannye*), and the overall tone of the text was said to be marked by 'pretentiousness and weakness of argumentation' (*pretentsioznost' i neubeditel'nost'*). It was recommended that Olga should make the text and the argumentation 'less emotional' (*menee emotsional'nym*).[40]

According to Olga, such an exclusion of bisexual people on the grounds of excess emotionality, lack of argumentation and aggression is not rare in the Russian LGBTQ community. As a social group suffering from double discrimination (stigmatized within the LGBTQ community and by heteronormative society), bisexual people face extreme difficulties in trying to get their message across and in fighting for visibility and inclusion. The exclusion of bisexual people from public discourses, especially media, contributes to the invisibility of this 'minority within minority'.[41] However, bi-activists' insistence on the use of bi-inclusive language in LGBTQ-catered digital and offline spaces and in relevant media texts tends to be perceived by monosexual members of the LGBTQ community as transgressive, threatening or overstepping the boundaries.

The case with the Side-by-Side brochure demonstrated that, as an emotional community, LGBTQ-rights activists can regulate which members of the group are allowed to express emotions and what kind of emotions these should be, and they can also decide whose emotional capital is valid and desirable. An activist whose emotional capital is invalidated, devalued – whose emotional investment in activism is not appreciated – cannot but suffer from such exclusionary policies on the part of the aspired and desired emotional community.

When it comes to feminist communities, bisexual women face certain challenges too. Thus, Olga testified that, although she identifies as a feminist, she cannot always find common grounds with feminist communities: not all sections of the feminist movement in Russia demonstrate acceptance of bisexual people. According to Olga, she encountered the highest level of biphobia when communicating with radical feminists; it was with radical feminists that Olga most often found herself in emotional confrontations while exploring digital spaces. The reasons for the confrontations were primarily related to the gender versus sex debates and misandry, the radical feminist communities tending to discard the concept of gender and demonstrating misandrist rhetoric, which Olga challenged in respective social media threads (*chasche vsego rugaius' v setiakh iz-za etogo*). Queer feminists, on the other hand, as Olga vouched, were generally bi-friendly, largely due to both queer feminists and the Russian bi-community's shared views on fights against binarism and binary approaches to gender and sexuality.

As the interview with Olga Masina demonstrated, the challenges faced by bisexual communities beyond Russia, such as the erasure of bisexual people from and their invisibility in public and media discourses,[42] and the outright or undercurrent biphobia on the part of LGBTQ communities and heteronormative society,[43] are acute problems for Russian bisexual people too. On top of that, the interview also revealed that Russian bisexual female activists identifying as feminist face specific challenges characteristic of the contemporary Russian feminist movement. Apart from consistently strong societal backlashes against the feminist movement in general, these challenges include competition for available resources (especially media and digital spatial resources) amongst various factions, which leads to the problem of hierarchies within the movement.[44] In these circumstances, acceptance by the desired emotional community, and the opportunity that such acceptance establishes to use one's own emotional capital for achieving activist goals and other benefits, becomes crucial for bisexual rights female activists.

Emotions and empowerment: transgender rights activism as a means of activist identity-building

At the beginning of the interview, while discussing the origins of and driving factors behind her activism, Ekaterina Messorosh shared that her transition and the start of her transgender rights activism served as a turning point for her and led to significant changes in her behaviour, emotional expression and communication style. Ekaterina explained that prior to her transition she had considered herself an introvert, but afterwards it turned out she is actually an extrovert: 'I used to think of myself as a misanthrope but it turned out I am very empathetic, I love socializing. ... Now, apart from really odious individuals, I do not feel any enmity for anyone' (*Ia schitala sebia mizantropom; okazalos', chto ia ochen' empatichnaia, mne nravitsia obshchat'sia s liud'mi. ... Seichas u menia net, krome sovsem odioznykh lichnostei, kakoi-to nepriiazni*). As Ekaterina pointed out, her transition resulted not only in the appearance of a keen interest in online activism but also in a consistent necessity for self-advocacy online, which made it easier for her to process the ongoing changes related to her transition.

Soon after starting her transition in 2015, Ekaterina changed her social media accounts accordingly to reflect these changes, which soon led her to realize she was 'an odd duck' (*belaia vorona*) among her friends on social media. Ekaterina explained that for her, stealth (passing as a woman and breaking contact with whoever knew of her previous gendered experience) was never on the cards, and this fact helped her realize that social media gave her an opportunity to promote transgender rights and to raise awareness of transgender issues via the creation, posting and sharing of relevant media content on her personal account pages.

Apart from these educational goals, from the very beginning Ekaterina's online activism was aimed at developing and refining her rhetoric, self-advocacy and argumentation techniques. For example, the activist admitted that she used to intentionally generate debates and confrontations with TERF (trans exclusionary radical feminist) activists. As Ekaterina explained, getting emotionally triggered in those discussions with transphobic opponents helped her to learn how to manage her own emotions and enabled her to develop a habit of relying on logical unemotional argumentation when discussing transgender issues online. As Ekaterina put it, one needs to 'dive headfirst and deep into that swamp' (*zanyrnut' v boloto s golovoi*) and thus to expose oneself to all the possible transphobic stereotypes. Exposure to TERF hatred, and the need to formulate anti-transphobic arguments, eventually enabled her to fully accept her own identity as a transgender woman. As she confessed, at first the hatred used to 'hurt her immensely' (*ochen' sil'no ranilo*): identifying as a feminist and perceiving feminism as a movement for gender equality, it was difficult for her to consider TERFs, whose rhetoric rejects the concept of gender and therefore of transgenderism, as feminist. Soon enough, though, she learned to manage her emotions and to resist transphobic attacks. Quoting Ekaterina, 'sometimes a trigger is necessary – a change is impossible without pain' (*inogda trigger nuzhen, nevozmozhno chto-to meniat' bez boli*).

The experience of confrontations with TERFs helped Ekaterina later on to deal with transphobia in fora and virtual communities for transgender people. According to Ekaterina, 'it is hard to find non-transphobic trans-fora' (*slozhno naiti netransfobnye forumy*) because as soon as transgender transition is mentioned by the forum and virtual community members, the question of 'trueness/genuineness' (*tuiiovost'*) is invariably raised. This issue relates to being a 'true' transgender; that is, someone 'who had it the hardest with the medical evaluation committee' (*u kogo bylo bol'she zhesti na komissii*).

As Ekaterina testified, when challenging biologized and essentialist ideas of gender and sex widespread among Russian transgender people, as well as while fighting to challenge the gender binary in heated debates on binary versus non-binary concepts of gender with other transgender rights activists, she always applied the skills of logical unemotional argumentation and reliance on facts and accurate scientific terminology, which she had developed in confrontations with TERFs. Thus, for example, Ekaterina would point to the fact that since in the Russian language there is no distinction between male/female and man/woman (for each semantic pair the words *muzhchina*/man and *zhenshchina*/woman are used), discussions among transitioning transgender people about becoming 'true men' or 'true women' in the biological meaning of those words made little sense: it would be more appropriate to use the terms applied when talking about male and female species of animals (*samets* and *samka*, respectively). Or, when challenging the use of incorrect expressions like 'he/she changed sex', Ekaterina would confront the opponent by enumerating various aspects comprising the notion of 'sex' (sex hormones; chromosomal, gonadal, morphological, endocrinologic and assigned sex) and would question which of those aspects can actually 'change' during a gender transition and whether it is possible at all to talk about 'sex change' at the current stage of medical advancements.

At the end of the interview, when talking about how her online activism had evolved since 2015, Ekaterina admitted that her activist goals on social media platforms had changed: the primary focus was now on reaching out to wider audiences, whereas before 'the primary goal was to learn to get my arguments across in the right way, avoiding personal attacks, blocking all emotions' (*ran'she osnovnaia tsel' byla nauchit'sia pravil'no argumentirovat', ne perekhodit' na lichnosti, ne ispytyvat' emotsii*). One of the means Ekaterina used to attract new supporters consisted of juxtaposing her unemotional argumentation with the emotional attacks of her opponents. As she confessed, oftentimes she would consciously provoke or manipulate the opponent to make them lose their temper and resort to emotional rhetoric, which conveniently contrasted with Ekaterina's own strong logical argumentation.

The above case study reveals that transgender women's emotional capital can be affected significantly and crucially both by the experience of transitioning and their involvement in activism, with these two factors intersecting. Thus, Ekaterina's transition affected her personality in terms of how she managed emotion-based knowledge, and in her emotion management skills: not only did she develop extroverted features and realize her own potential for empathy, she also acquired valuable skills in controlling and holding her emotions (i.e. withholding, keeping her emotional capital) in order to achieve activist goals. Recognizing that online emotional communities perceive emotional outbursts during heated debates as an undesirable sign of weakness, Ekaterina perfected the skills of both keeping calm under transphobic attacks (as a manifestation of her opinions and views being well grounded) and provoking transphobic opponents for said emotional outbursts (to highlight the weakness of transphobic attitudes and views). The case study of Ekaterina Messorosh's online activism demonstrates how the experience of transgender rights activism performed online in intersecting emotional communities of feminist and LGBTQ activists can serve as a tool for the empowerment and liberation of a transgender woman.

Reflections and suggestions for further study

The two case studies demonstrated the significance of emotions, emotional capital and emotional communities for women's online activism. The adoption of certain practices of using emotional capital (investing emotions in the activist work, as in Olga Masina's case, or holding back emotions while educating social media audiences on transgender issues, as in Ekaterina Messorosh's case) can both offer advantages and pose challenges to Russian female activists for bisexual and transgender rights who operate under the circumstances of double stigmatization, as minorities within minorities. The use of only two case studies makes it difficult to declare with confidence whether the activist strategies and trends presented in this chapter are intrinsic solely to the respondents of the study or whether they are shared by other bisexual and transgender activists across Russia. Nevertheless, the two case studies reveal that transgressive online social activism of this kind is discursively linked to the creation of 'emotional communities' by like-minded bisexual and transgender (feminist) women.

As for the scope of this study, it is important to recognize the inherent limitations of women's and LGBTQ-rights activism in Russia that existed at the time of this project being completed and which still persist at the time of this chapter being written. In contemporary Russia, even more so after the Russian invasion of Ukraine which took place in February 2022 and led to a further crackdown on civil rights and activist groups, activism often becomes a privilege. Participation in street protests can result in being detained and fined, or brought to trial; participation in online activism also presents risks, as social media are being monitored by the Russian police and there have been numerous cases when activists were persecuted for their online publications. There is a practice in Russia that any charges or detainments made by the police can be reported to one's workplace, potentially resulting in a dismissal, and there are cases in which civil rights activists have lost their jobs because of their activism.

Both my respondents at the time of the interviews were in relatively secure jobs, which allowed some freedom or flexibility because of their work. In 2017–18, Olga was working on a PhD in philosophy and carrying out some teaching activities at the university as a postgraduate student, and had a regular salary. She could not be photographed during street protests, but other than that she enjoyed a certain freedom of action and expression. Ekaterina, in her own words, is 'from a university environment': she obtained a university degree in sciences and at the time of the interview was employed in a high-skilled job, where colleagues were accepting of her gender transition. Thus, a secure job and working alongside people with a higher education background can sometimes act as a social support for a female activist, while not having enough social support can potentially prevent women from openly and freely participating in activist groups and initiatives. Another privilege which both my respondents enjoyed is living in Saint Petersburg as a big urban space with a well-developed infrastructure and access to various activist projects and initiatives. LGBTQ-rights and feminist activism are far more problematic for those who live in smaller regional centres or provincial towns. Finally, feminist and LGBTQ-rights activism in contemporary Russia is complicated by Eurocentric and Russocentric discourses promoted by conservative elites and leading activists alike. These discourses permeate the public spheres, impacting societal attitudes to non-Russian, non-white, non-Christian (i.e. Muslim or Jewish) identities,[45] and are also replicated both by Russian and Western media covering feminist and LGBTQ-related events in Russia.[46] This tendency turns Russian LGBTQ-rights and feminist activism into a discursive space of contested 'whiteness'.

In view of the above limitations, further inquiry into the evolvement of and the practices applied by a wider range of Russian emotional communities of bisexual and transgender rights activists in digital spaces would offer opportunities for insightful and innovative findings. An approach which utilizes the concepts of emotional capital and emotional community proves to be an efficient means of investigation into contemporary Russian online activism for women's and LGBTQ rights.

Notes

1. S. Ashwin, 'The Influence of the Soviet Gender Order on Employment Behavior in Contemporary Russia', *Sociological Research*, 41 (2002), 21–37.

2. S. Ashwin (ed.), *Gender, State and Society in Soviet and Post-Soviet Russia* (London: Routledge, 2000).

3. F. Stella, *Lesbian Lives in Soviet and Post-Soviet Russia: Post/Socialism and Gendered Sexualities* (Basingstoke: Springer, 2014).

4. Set of implicit and explicit rules governing gender relations, and which allocate different work, value, responsibilities and obligations to women and men. From *100 Words for Equality: A Glossary of Terms on Equality between Women and Men* (European Commission, 1998).

5. F. Stella, and N. Nartova, 'Sexuality, Nationalism and Biopolitics in Putin's Russia', in F. Stella, Y. Taylor, T. Reynolds and A. Rogers (eds.), *Sexuality, Citizenship and Belonging: Trans/National and Intersectional Perspectives* (London: Routledge, 2015), p. 37.

6. L. Essig, *Queer in Russia: A Story of Sex, Self and the Other* (Durham, NC: Duke University Press, 1999), pp. 56–82.

7. O. Andreevskikh, 'Queering #*MeToo*: Russian Media Discourse on Same-Sex Sexual Harassment in the Context of a Global Anti-Harassment Movement', in G. Miazhevich (ed.), *Queering Russian Media and Culture* (London: Routledge, 2022).

8. O. Andreevskikh, 'Russian Queer (Counter-)Revolution? The Appropriation of Western Queer Discourses by Russian LGBT Communities: A Media Case Study', *Queer Asia Blog Series 'Queer' + Decoloniality in Post-Socialist States* (2021), https://queerasia.com/2021-blog-russian-queer-revolution (accessed 8 July 2022).

9. A. Kondakov (ed.), *Na Pereput'ie. Metodologiia, Teoriia i Praktika LGBT i Kvir-Issledovanii. Sbornik Stat'ei* (Saint Petersburg: Center for Independent Social Research, 2014).

10. Y. Kirey-Sitnikova, 'Who Rejects Depathologization? Attitudes of Russian-Speaking Trans People toward Revision of the International Classification of Diseases', *International Journal of Transgenderism*, 18 (2017), 79–90.

11. E. Couch, 'Engines of Change: The Politicization of the Private Sphere and the Rise of Women's Political Activism in Russia', *Kennan Cable*, 49 (2020).

12. In the Russian language, the word *gei* (gay) tends to be used almost solely in reference to homosexual men, and not women; in this chapter, I therefore use the abbreviation 'LBT' to denote a reference to people who identify as women.

13. Non-governmental organizations; that is, non-profit organizations supporting a socio-political cause.

14. T. Flew (ed.), *New Media* (South Melbourne: Oxford University Press, 2014), pp. 66–78.

15. W.B. Hagen, S.M. Hoover and S.L. Morrow, 'A Grounded Theory of Sexual Minority Women and Transgender Individuals' Social Justice Activism', *Journal of Homosexuality*, 65 (2017), 833–59.

16. J. Serano, *Excluded: Making Feminism and Queer Movements More Inclusive* (Berkeley, CA: Seal Press, 2013).

17. K. Dővling, C. von Scheve and E.A. Konijn (eds.), *The Routledge Handbook of Emotions and Mass Media* (London: Routledge, 2011), p. 62.

18. J.E. Stets and J.H. Turner, *Handbook of Sociology of Emotions* (New York: Springer, 2006).

19. P. Bourdieu, 'The Forms of Capital', in J.E. Richardson (ed.), *Handbook of Theory of Research for the Sociology of Education* (New York: Greenwood Press, 1986), pp. 241–58.

20. M.D. Cottingham, 'Theorizing Emotional Capital', *Theory and Society*, 45 (2016), 451–70.

21. Cottingham, 'Theorizing Emotional Capital'.

22. A. Lacey, 'Networked Communities: Social Centers and Activist Spaces in Contemporary Britain', *Space and Culture*, 8 (2005), 286–301.

23. B.H. Rosenwein, *Emotional Communities in the Early Middle Ages* (Ithaca, NY: Cornell University Press, 2006), p. 2.

24. Lacey, 'Networked Communities', p. 287.

25. O. Andreevskikh, 'Confessional Narratives in Digital Self- and Life-Writing of Bisexual Activists in Russia: A Case Study of Bisexual Identity Building', in *Avtobiografiя: Queer Life-Writing in Russia and Beyond* (forthcoming in 2023).

26. O. Andreevskikh and M. Muravyeva, 'Doing Gender Online: Digital Spaces for Identity Politics', in D. Gritsenko, M. Wijermars and M. Kopotev (eds.), *The Palgrave Handbook of Digital Russian Studies* (Basingstoke: Palgrave Macmillan, 2021), pp. 205–19.

27. Serano, *Excluded*.

28. I. Perheentupa, 'Digital Culture and Feminist Politics in Contemporary Russia: Inside Perspectives', *Studies in Russian, Eurasian and Central European New Media (digitalicons.org)*, 19 (2018), 117–27.

29. P. Bourdieu, *Masculine Domination* (Stanford, CA: Stanford University Press, 2001).

30. E. Green and A. Adam (eds.), *Virtual Gender: Technology, Consumption, and Identity* (London: Routledge, 2001).

31. V. Arvidsson and A. Foka, 'Digital Gender: Perspective, Phenomena, Practice', *First Monday*, 20 (2015).

32. S. Ratilainen, M. Wijemars and J. Wilmes, 'Re-Framing Women and Technology in Global Digital Spaces: An Introduction', *Studies in Russian, Eurasian and Central European New Media (digitalicons.org)*, 19 (2018), 1–10.

33. See, for example, '"I Am a Blogger and I Would Like to Receive Some Cosmetics Set": The Correspondence between Feminist Activist Bella Rapoport and the Cosmetic Brand Lush Gave Birth to a Meme', www.bbc.com/russian/other-news -47640832 (accessed 8 July 2022).

34. In June 2020, Vodvud had over 163,000 followers on Instagram and over 480,000 subscribers on YouTube.

35. 'Nixel Pixel, Russia's Most Famous Feminist, Tells *Meduza* What Prices Nika Vodvud Has to Pay for Her Activism', https://meduza.io/feature/2019/09/10/nixel -pixel-samaya-izvestnaya-feministka-rossii (accessed 8 July 2022).

36. See, for example, 'Public Response: Meduza Released a Profile of Feminist Activist Nika Vodvud (nixelpixel). The Outlet Was Accused in Promotion of Cyberbullying', https://esquire.ru/articles/123352-rezonans-meduza-vypustila -profayl-feministki-niki-vodvud-nixelpixel-izdanie-obvinili-v-pooshchrenii-internet -travli (accessed 8 July 2022).

37. B.H. Rosenwein, *Generations of Feeling: A History of Emotions, 600–1700* (Cambridge: Cambridge University Press, 2016), p. 3.

38. The research was a self-funded three-month project I carried out alongside my primary research on 'Communicating Non-Heteronormative Masculinities in

Contemporary Russian Media: Discourses on "Non-Traditional Sexual Orientation" in the Context of "Traditional Sexuality" Legislation', which I conducted as part of the PhD programme at the University of Leeds, UK between 2015 and 2020.

39. The analysis of the media findings obtained during the three months' monitoring of those social media pages was previously published elsewhere: O. Andreevskikh, 'Social Networking Sites as Platforms for Transgression: Two Case Studies of Russian Women Involved in Bisexual and Transgender Rights Activism', *Digital Icons: Studies in Russian, Eurasian and Central European New Media*, 19 (2018), 11–39, www.digitalicons.org/issue19/social-networking-sites-as-platforms-for-transgression (accessed 8 July 2022).

40. The text on bi-inclusive language in the media was eventually published in the 2018 edition of the Side-by-Side brochure 'How to Write about Gay, Lesbian, Bisexual and Transgender People Correctly' (*Kak korrektno pisat' o geiakh, lesbiankakh, biseksualakh i transgenderakh*), after the joint effort of the bi-community (other bi-activists and I signed an open petition to the editors) and after a fellow LGBTQ-rights activist co-edited with Olga Masina the new version of the document. The text is now used as the primary source of reference of LGBTQ communities and media professionals working with the bisexual rights agenda.

41. K. Yescavage and J. Alexander, 'Bi/Visibility', *Journal of Bisexuality*, 1 (2000), 173–80.

42. I. Capulet, 'With Reps Like These: Bisexuality and Celebrity Status', *Journal of Bisexuality*, 10 (2010), 294–308.

43. K.L. Nutter-Pridgen, 'The Old, the New, and the Redefined: Identifying the Discourses in Contemporary Bisexual Activism', *Journal of Bisexuality*, 15 (2015), 385–413.

44. I. Perheentupa, 'Feminist Politics in Neoconservative Russia', PhD thesis (University of Turku, Finland, 2019).

45. J. Suchland, 'The LGBT Specter in Russia: Refusing Queerness, Claiming "Whiteness"', *Gender, Place & Culture*, 25 (2018), 1073–88.

46. H. Sykes, 'Decolonizing Sporting Homonationalisms', in *The Sexual and Gender Politics of Sport Mega-Events: Roving Colonialism* (London: Routledge, 2016), pp. 157–61.

References

100 Words for Equality: A Glossary of Terms on Equality between Women and Men (European Commission, 1998).

Andreevskikh, O., 'Social Networking Sites as Platforms for Transgression: Two Case Studies of Russian Women Involved in Bisexual and Transgender Rights Activism', *Digital Icons: Studies in Russian, Eurasian and Central European New Media*, 19 (2018), 11–39, www.digitalicons.org/issue19/social-networking-sites-as-platforms-for-transgression (accessed 8 July 2022).

——, 'Russian Queer (Counter-)Revolution? The Appropriation of Western Queer Discourses by Russian LGBT Communities: A Media Case Study', *Queer Asia Blog Series 'Queer' +Decoloniality in Post-Socialist States* (2021), https://queerasia.com/2021-blog-russian-queer-revolution (accessed 8 July 2022).

——, 'Queering #MeToo: Russian Media Discourse on Same-Sex Sexual Harassment in the Context of a Global Anti-Harassment Movement', in G. Miazhevich (ed.), *Queering Russian Media and Culture* (London: Routledge, 2022), pp. 173–90.

——, 'Confessional Narratives in Digital Self- and Life-Writing of Bisexual Activists in Russia: A Case Study of Bisexual Identity Building', *Avtobiografiя: Queer Life-Writing in Russia and Beyond* (forthcoming in 2023).

Andreevskikh, O., and Muravyeva, M., 'Doing Gender Online: Digital Spaces for Identity Politics', in D. Gritsenko, M. Wijermars and M. Kopotev (eds.), *The Palgrave Handbook of Digital Russian Studies* (Basingstoke: Palgrave Macmillan, 2021), pp. 205–19.

Arvidsson, V., and Foka, A., 'Digital Gender: Perspective, Phenomena, Practice', *First Monday*, 20 (2015), https://doi.org/10.5210/fm.v20i4.5930 (accessed 8 July 2022).

Ashwin, S., (ed.), *Gender, State and Society in Soviet and Post-Soviet Russia* (London: Routledge, 2000).

——, 'The Influence of the Soviet Gender Order on Employment Behavior in Contemporary Russia', *Sociological Research*, 41 (2002), 21–37.

Bourdieu, P., 'The Forms of Capital', in J.E. Richardson (ed.), *Handbook of Theory of Research for the Sociology of Education* (New York: Greenwood Press, 1986), pp. 241–58.

——, *Masculine Domination* (Stanford, CA: Stanford University Press, 2001).

Capulet, I., 'With Reps Like These: Bisexuality and Celebrity Status', *Journal of Bisexuality*, 10 (2010), 294–308.

Cottingham, M.D., 'Theorizing Emotional Capital', *Theory and Society*, 45 (2016), 451–70.

Couch, E., 'Engines of Change: The Politicization of the Private Sphere and the Rise of Women's Political Activism in Russia', *Kennan Cable*, 49 (2020), www.wilsoncenter.org/publication/kennan-cable-no-49 -engines-change-politicization-private-sphere-and-rise-womens (accessed 8 July 2022).

Dővling, K., von Scheve, C. and Konijn, E.A., *The Routledge Handbook of Emotions and Mass Media* (London: Routledge, 2011).

Essig, L., *Queer in Russia: A Story of Sex, Self and the Other* (Durham, NC: Duke University Press, 1999).

Flew, T., ed., *New Media* (South Melbourne: Oxford University Press, 2014).

Green, E., and Adam, A. (eds.), *Virtual Gender: Technology, Consumption, and Identity* (London: Routledge, 2001).

Hagen, W.B., Hoover, S.M. and Morrow, S.L., 'A Grounded Theory of Sexual Minority Women and Transgender Individuals' Social Justice Activism', *Journal of Homosexuality*, 65 (2017), 833–59.

Holodynski, M., 'Emotional Commitment and the Development of Collaborative Projects', in A. Blunden (ed.), *Collaborative Projects: An Interdisciplinary Study* (Leiden: Brill, 2014), pp. 351–85.

'How to Write about Gay, Lesbian, Bisexual and Transgender People Correctly' (*Kak korrektno pisat' o geiakh, lesbiankakh, biseksualakh i transgenderakh*, http://bok-o-bok.ru/images/all/files/Korrektny%20 yazyk%200%20LGBT_bi%20additional_2018(1).pdf) (accessed 8 July 2022).

'"I Am a Blogger and I Would Like to Receive Some Cosmetics Set": The Correspondence between Feminist Activist Bella Rapoport and the Cosmetic Brand Lush Gave Birth to a Meme', www.bbc.com/russian /other-news-47640832 (accessed 8 July 2022).

Kirey-Sitnikova, Y., 'Who Rejects Depathologization? Attitudes of Russian-Speaking Trans People toward Revision of the International Classification of Diseases', *International Journal of Transgenderism*, 18 (2017), 79–90.

Kondakov, A. (ed.), *Na Pereput'ie. Metodologiia, Teoriia i Praktika LGBT i Kvir-Issledovanii. Sbornik Stat'ei* (Saint Petersburg: Center for Independent Social Research, 2014).

Lacey, A., 'Networked Communities: Social Centers and Activist Spaces in Contemporary Britain', *Space and Culture*, 8 (2005), 286–301.

'Nixel Pixel, Russia's Most Famous Feminist, Tells *Meduza* What Prices Nika Vodvud Has to Pay for Her Activism', https://meduza.io/feature /2019/09/10/nixel-pixel-samaya-izvestnaya-feministka-rossii (accessed 8 July 2022).

Nutter-Pridgen, K.L., 'The Old, the New, and the Redefined: Identifying the Discourses in Contemporary Bisexual Activism', *Journal of Bisexuality*, 15 (2015), 385–413.

Perheentupa, I., 'Digital Culture and Feminist Politics in Contemporary Russia: Inside Perspectives', *Studies in Russian, Eurasian and Central European New Media (digitalicons.org)*, 19 (2018), 117–27, www.digitalicons.org/issue19/digital-culture-and-feminist-politics-in -contemporary-russia (accessed 1 May 2019).

——, 'Feminist Politics in Neoconservative Russia', PhD thesis (University of Turku, Finland, 2019).

'Public Response: Meduza Released a Profile of Feminist Activist Nika Vodvud (nixelpixel). The Outlet Was Accused in Promotion of Cyberbullying', https://esquire.ru/articles/123352-rezonans-meduza -vypustila-profayl-feministki-niki-vodvud-nixelpixel-izdanie-obvinili -v-pooshchrenii-internet-travli (accessed 8 July 2022).

Ratilainen, S., Wijemars, M. and Wilmes, J., 'Re-Framing Women and Technology in Global Digital Spaces: An Introduction', *Studies in Russian, Eurasian and Central European New Media (digitalicons.org)*, 19 (2018), 1–10, www.digitalicons.org/issue19/re-framing-women-and -technology-in-global-digital-spaces (accessed 1 May 2019).

Rosenwein, B.H., *Emotional Communities in the Early Middle Ages* (Ithaca, NY: Cornell University Press, 2006).

——, *Generations of Feeling: A History of Emotions, 600–1700* (Cambridge: Cambridge University Press, 2016).

Serano, J., *Excluded: Making Feminism and Queer Movements More Inclusive* (Berkeley, CA: Seal Press, 2013).

Stella, F., *Lesbian Lives in Soviet and Post-Soviet Russia: Post/Socialism and Gendered Sexualities* (Basingstoke: Springer, 2014).

Stella, F., and Nartova, N., 'Sexuality, Nationalism and Biopolitics in Putin's Russia', in F. Stella, Y. Taylor, T. Reynolds and A. Rogers (eds.), *Sexuality, Citizenship and Belonging: Trans/National and Intersectional Perspectives* (London: Routledge, 2015), pp. 24–42.

Stets, J.E., and Turner, J.H. (eds.), *Handbook of Sociology of Emotions* (New York: Springer, 2006).

Suchland, J., 'The LGBT Specter in Russia: Refusing Queerness, Claiming "Whiteness"', *Gender, Place & Culture*, 25 (2018), 1073–88.

Sykes, H., 'Decolonizing Sporting Homonationalisms', in *The Sexual and Gender Politics of Sport Mega-Events: Roving Colonialism* (London: Routledge, 2016), pp. 157–61.

Yescavage, K., and Alexander, J., 'Bi/Visibility', *Journal of Bisexuality*, 1 (2000), 173–80.

Chapter 3

Sounding the socialist heroine: gender, revolutionary lyricism and Korean war films

Yucong Hao

In her genealogical inquiry of emotion in modern China, Haiyan Lee observed that during the socialist period (1949–76), as the intimate realm of the heart increasingly came under the scrutiny of the state, the conception of love was deprived of individualistic or romantic implications. Instead, 'class feeling', a class-based, collective amity, became the structuring emotion of the era.[1] The predominant status of class feeling attests to a prevalent understanding of the scarcity of emotion in socialist China: that all personalistic expressions were repressed under the mounting force of the collective. David Wang's study, *The Lyrical in Epic Time*, similarly identified what he considered an irreconcilable tension between the individualistic and the collective, which he termed 'the lyrical and the revolutionary', when the Communists took over China in 1949. The lyrical encompasses both an artistic style and a structure of feeling, which informs the creation of an individualistic, affective subjectivity and ultimately serves as an alternative to collective, political enthusiasm that the Chinese Communist revolution promised.[2]

Wang's conceptualization of the fundamental conflict between the lyrical and the revolutionary is illustrative of a liberal humanist position in which politics is perceived as a repressive force that threatens artistic autonomy and individual subjectivity. Literary scholar Ban Wang, however, reminds us that excessive attention to the incommensurability between the two overlooks a vibrant lyrical impulse undergirding revolutionary aspiration and socialist transformation.[3] Informed by Ban Wang's insight into the symbiosis between lyrical sensibilities and revolutionary passions in Maoist China, I deploy the concept of revolutionary lyricism to characterize the mutual constitution between the lyrical and the revolutionary in Chinese socialist cultural production. In this chapter, I use the case studies of two Korean War films, *Shanggan Ridge* (1956) and *Heroic Sons and Daughters* (1964), which were produced in China's high socialist years, to examine the making of the seemingly incompatible 'revolutionary lyricism'. I explore the representation of gender and the deployment of film music as a means through which personal feelings converged with revolutionary enthusiasm to engender a new socialist structure of emotion beyond the monochromatic 'class feeling'. In this process, Chinese filmmakers mediated a variety of aesthetic resources, both transnational and intermedial, and manufactured the discrete audiovisual attractions of socialist cinema.

Representing the Korean War on screen

The Korean War (1950–53) constitutes a singular moment in the global history of the Cold War as well as the national history of the People's Republic of China. On a global scale, the Korean War, being one of the few 'hot' wars in the era of the Cold War, was one of the most intense forms of confrontation between the two ideologies and two major world powers. To the recently founded People's Republic of China, the decision to enter the Korean War and aid the North Koreans effectively helped the Communist Party to consolidate its political legitimacy. It not only cemented China's internationalist alliance with North Korea in resisting a major Cold War rival – the United States of America – but also firmly asserted the leadership of the ruling Communist Party 'to maintain the inner dynamics of the Chinese Communist revolution'.[4]

After China's entry into the Korean War in October 1950, photographers and filmmakers were sent to the front alongside the Chinese People's Voluntary Force (CPVF) to document China's war efforts. War footage was later edited into several newsreel documentaries that broadcasted sentiments of nationalism and resistance to the domestic audience, most notably Beijing Film Studio's *Resisting the Americans and Assisting the North Koreans* series (1951 and 1952). In addition to documentary film, artists were commissioned to represent the subject of the Korean War across a variety of forms, including literature, performing arts and fiction film. The deployment of mass media for the purpose of political mobilization, as historian Matthew Johnson aptly pointed out, allowed the nascent People's Republic of China 'to communicate new imperatives and to reshape the institutional reach of the state'.[5] Among these state-sanctioned artworks on the Korean War, *Shanggan Ridge* and *Heroic Sons and Daughters* were unparalleled in their long-lasting popularity and strong emotional impacts on the audience. Both films were enthusiastically praised at the time of release by both filmmakers and ordinary audiences as 'spiritually inspiring' and conveying strong 'revolutionary optimism'.[6]

Typifying the Maoist tradition of war films, both *Shanggan Ridge* and *Heroic Sons and Daughters* affirm the central role played by the army in guarding national security and feature stories of war heroes to educate the audience morally and ideologically.[7] The didactic function, however, was hardly the sole consideration for socialist filmmakers, who were then laboriously searching for a cinematic language that could make such moral lessons accessible, memorable and pleasurable. In the cases of *Shanggan Ridge* and *Heroic Sons and Daughters*, the deployment of theme songs and the gendered performance of music helped to synthesize education and entertainment and created cinematic attractions which went beyond ideological indoctrination. In my analysis, I pay particular attention to the intersection between music and gender in the two films and explore how such gendered performance of music contributed to both audiovisual pleasures and a more complex emotive spectrum spanning from lyrical sensibilities to revolutionary enthusiasm. Contextualizing the two films within the genealogy of Chinese sound cinema, I trace the convention of associating female characters with musical expressions back to the media culture of 1930s Shanghai. However, unlike the solo singing of the female vocalists in Shanghai filmic culture, Chinese filmmakers in the Maoist era appropriated this cinematic convention to accompany the female leads' performance with the choral singing of the mass. In this process, the bourgeois songstress is reincarnated into socialist heroines, who acquire a new and more organic relationship with the revolutionary masses, and the aesthetic of decadent sentimentalism is transformed into that of revolutionary lyricism.

Moreover, situating the representation of these socialist heroines within the cultural history of Chinese socialism, I uncover the fast-changing politics of gender from the 1950s to the 1960s: while gender was meaningfully engaged in *Shanggan Ridge*, it became abstract and devoid of substance by the mid-1960s, when Jiang Qing, Madame Mao, who was in charge of cultural work, rose to power and implemented the 'two-line struggle' in the film industry: the struggle between the proletarian and the bourgeois.[8] This shift, I argue, epitomized how the politics of socialist feminism surrendered to that of class struggle on the eve of the Cultural Revolution, when gender, emotion and interiority were removed from the radical politics of 'continuous revolution'.

The making of *Shanggan Ridge*

Shanggan Ridge depicts the military confrontation between the CPVF and the United Nations Command near Shanggan Ridge from October to November 1952.[9] Despite repeated attempts by the United Nations Command to seize the Chinese-controlled military pass, the Chinese army managed to defend their position on Shanggan Ridge, but they also suffered severe losses and casualties in the process. The eponymous film, based on this critical battle that took place in the last stage of the Korean War, was meant to glorify the sacrifice and heroism of the Chinese army in accomplishing such an unusual victory.

The planning of the film began as early as 1954, less than a year after the end of the Korean War. In March 1954, film director Sha Meng embarked on a trip to visit North Korea, where he would meet soldiers who experienced the Battle of Shanggan Ridge and gather materials about heroic stories and military tactics that emerged from the battle.[10] In his North Korean trip, Sha Meng keenly read Konstantine Simonov's *Days and Nights* (1945), a recently translated Russian novel on the Battle of Stalingrad during the Second World War. Simonov's highly engaging characterization of war heroes urged the Chinese director to consider how he could shape his raw materials from the Korean War to make a story comparable to the Soviet fiction.[11]

In his diary, Sha Meng confessed to having encountered some practical challenges when collecting and processing materials for the upcoming film production. For instance, he was quite frustrated at his poor interview skills, which often resulted in unproductive conversations. He also expressed disappointment when talking with the soldiers, who – in his view – were unable to meaningfully narrate their experiences and were often obsessed with insignificant details.[12] For instance, when a soldier recalled how his regiment managed to defend Shanggan Ridge with tactics of tunnel warfare, which later became the central plot of the eponymous film, his recollection was narrated plainly and uneventfully, as if there were nothing heroic of this extraordinary accomplishment.[13] The discrepancy that Sha Meng felt between the requirement of film storytelling and the soldiers' largely fragmented recollections is illustrative of what historian Huw Halstead perceived as a distinction between history as an authoritative narrative and history as an everyday mode of experience, with the latter being 'diffuse, noisy, messy, often confusing, sometimes troubling'.[14]

While Simonov's *Days and Nights* served as a major source of inspiration and exemplified to Sha Meng the importance of constructing a central theme in film narrative, the director also endeavoured to preserve life-like, everyday details that he collected during the interviews. In this process, Sha Meng came to the epiphany that: 'The central theme in an artwork is decisive. Life is meaningful only when it can heighten the expression of the central theme ... [The representation of life] should follow a realist principle.'[15] In other words, as Sha Meng prized the creation of a central theme over the authenticity of life experiences, he also recognized the necessity of exhibiting the richness of life with realist techniques. This realization informed what the director later practised in the making of *Shanggan Ridge*, namely a neo-realist style that combined realism and romanticism to foreground the film's central theme while displaying kaleidoscopic life experiences.[16]

The juxtaposition between realism and romanticism, on the one hand, results in stylistic heterogeneity in the audiovisual language of the film and, on the other, contributes to complex emotive expressions beyond the uncritical celebration of war heroes.[17] The transition between the two styles is most elaborately represented in the culminating scene of the film; that is, when after another round of attacks by the United Nations Command, the Chinese brigade is terribly defeated and cornered in a cave. In this scene, the camera uses a series of close-ups that meticulously visualize the injured bodies and painful looks on the faces of the soldiers. The realist representation forces the audience to directly confront the cruelty of war and to imagine the corporeal experience of bodies in pain. The physical setting of the cave, a cramped, dark and muddy space, further enhances the sense of defeat and despair.

It is at such an overwhelmingly realist moment that the director introduced the singing of 'My Motherland' by Wang Lan, the heroine of the film and a military nurse taking care of the wounded soldiers. Up to this point, the film deploys predominantly realistic sound effects to reenact the soundscape of war. These sonic expressions of war, from the blasts of bomb explosions to the cracking rattle of wounded bodies, not only heighten the sense of military emergency that the Chinese brigade faces but also stir up much psychological anxiety in the mind of the audience. However, when Wang Lan, sitting in the cave with an aura of tranquility, starts to sing, the cacophony of war is suddenly disrupted, and instead the ears of the audience are met with the mellow and soothing voice of the singing heroine.

In this scene, the film seamlessly synthesizes the heroine's singing and the theme song on the soundtrack to create a cinematic illusion of the heroine singing on screen. The careful representation of her performing body – especially when the camera first takes an extreme close-up to her face and later uses a medium close-up to her body – illustrates that the act of singing is a richly embodied experience, of the melodic vibrations of the vocal folds and the rhythmic movement of the female body. As she sings about the vastness of the Chinese landscape and the bravery of the people, the camera crosscuts between the individual faces of the soldiers resting in the cave, who are shown to play musical instruments or join her in singing. An unlikely and yet extraordinarily romanticist scene, the aural intensity of the episode is most emphatically captured through a contrast between sound and sight: a seriously injured soldier, his eyes covered by a bandage, listens attentively to the heroine's voice and hums along the same tune. The loss of vision, therefore, could hardly be considered as a form of deprivation, but is shown to be an enabling process that gives one a new voice, and by extension rejuvenated strength. As the soldiers join the heroine's singing one by one, the solo performance is transformed to group singing, which allegorizes the birth of a collectivized subject. The film's lighting also changes accordingly with the advent of the romanticist soundscape: the dim, narrow and crowded space of the cave is gradually lit up, and the camera transitions from inside the cave to present sequences of panoramic shots of the magnificent landscape and industrial construction of the motherland, the same kind of imageries that the collective singing of 'My Motherland' fondly conjured up.

The film, by self-consciously representing the acts of singing and listening and reflecting on the synchresis between the auditory and the visual, invites the audience to engage with the expanded aural space constructed by film music. Instead of the awe for heroes or hatred for enemies that a conventional historical war film elicits, the romanticist staging of 'My Motherland' creates a much more complex emotive spectrum. Diegetically, it serves as a turning point in the development of the story that boosts the morale of the brigade, and audiovisually it mitigates the sense of depression brought by the realist representation of war and cultivates alternative sentiments of nostalgia, affection and the sheer joy of music. The elaborate depiction of the singing and listening bodies, and the subsequent montage sequence between an acousmatic voice singing about the motherland and shots of China's vast landscape, furthermore contributes to the construction of an organic relationship between the individual and the collective, the personal and the national. In lieu of the ideological indoctrination of patriotism and nationalism, this relationship is forged through the irreducible concreteness of vocal resonance, corporeal experience and affectionate memories about one's compatriots and native soil.

According to Liu Zhi, the songwriter of 'My Motherland', when Sha Meng first approached him for film music, the director presented lyrics about the determination of the Chinese soldiers to guard their motherland. Such plain, straightforward and politically cliched verse, as the musician perceived, could hardly evoke sincere patriotic passions from the film audience.[18] As a result, Liu Zhi recommended Qiao Yu to write the lyrics for this central piece. Qiao's lyrics, without any direct reference to the political event of the Korean War, began with the imagery of a river, a symbol that could immediately arouse a sense of familiarity and nostalgia associated with the local community to which one belonged, and thus the lofty sentiment of nationalism could be translated into a lyrical sensibility of the attachment to specific people and places.[19]

Adapting 'Reunion' to *Heroic Sons and Daughters*

In March 1952, seventeen high-profile artists left Beijing for North Korea, organized by the China Federation of Literary and Art Circles. Their task was to collect first-hand materials of the Korean War to better represent the heroism of China's Voluntary Force. Ba Jin, an accomplished realist writer, was appointed as head of the delegates and led the group to interview Chinese soldiers and North Korean civilians. Nine years after the visit, Ba Jin published 'Reunion', a novella based on his personal experience during the Korean War. Despite the author's fame, the novella received little recognition by state cultural institutions, nor was it consumed widely among popular readership.[20] With a quick glimpse into 'Reunion', one can immediately discern how the novella departs from the convention and expectation of Maoist war culture. Yet when 'Reunion' was adapted into *Heroic Sons and Daughters* in 1964, all such dissonant elements were eliminated to create a model work that celebrated the Chinese army in the Korean War.

The novella is narrated from the first-person perspective of a writer, Li Lin, a character who mirrors Ba Jin's personal experience of the Korean War. Commissioned to report on the heroics of Chinese soldiers, Li Lin arrives in North Korea. There, he comes across a senior commander, Wang Wenqing, and a young girl from the army's art troupe, Wang Fang. It soon turns out that the two are father and daughter who were forced to separate eighteen years ago in Nationalist-ruled Shanghai. The father and the daughter, with the help of the girl's stepfather, eventually reunite with each other.

The story, as well as the metafictional structure of 'Reunion', reveals several layers of dissonance that undermine the intended effort of the novella to propagandize the war. During his visit to the battlefields, the narrator seems to be so preoccupied with the foreign landscape and musical culture in the army that from time to time he confesses to his inability, or even indifference, to portray the heroics of the Chinese soldiers. Such frustration in writing and the indecision in his selection of politically meaningful materials reveals the discrepancy between the political demands of war propaganda and the narrator's (and, to some extent, Ba Jin's) creative mind.

A most profound irony of 'Reunion' lies in the fact that although Li is commissioned to celebrate the bravery and sacrifice of the Chinese army, he ends up presenting a story of family melodrama: a subversive decision of which the writer/narrator was acutely aware. Towards the end of 'Reunion', as Li reflects,

> I initially planned to write reportage on Wang Fubiao (the father of a martyred soldier), but what I actually did with was a story about Commander Wang and Wang Fang (the father and the daughter)... I dare not to show the story to Commander Wang, as I fear that he would tear off my draft.[21]

In *Heroic Sons and Daughters*, the storyline of family reunion is still present, but the central plot of the film is completely altered to revolve around the martyrdom of Wang Cheng, a soldier who is only mentioned in passing in the novella. The shifting focus from the novella to the adapted fiction film, as literary scholar Piao Jie argues, exemplifies the changing cultural ecology of 1960s China, when the subject of war was promoted in state-sanctioned cultural production and the character of soldiers was extensively celebrated.[22] Unlike in the novella, where the narrator repeatedly expresses his frustration over his failure to adequately represent the heroics of the Chinese soldiers, such indecision was completely erased in the film. The act of glorifying war heroics is no longer the solitary, personal quest undertaken by a writer but is turned into a publicly staged event, in which the talented female singer Wang Fang narrates the heroism of Wang Cheng, and by extension the Chinese army, through her very act of singing a praise for them. In this way, heroism is hardly an elusive subject that could not be articulated in language. Instead, it becomes a spectacular performance that is to be witnessed, and participated in, by the collective.

Like *Shanggan Ridge*'s deployment of its theme song, the most emotionally impactful moment in *Heroic Sons and Daughters* similarly takes place at the musical performance of the heroine, Wang Fang. The camera first zooms into Wang Fang's performance of 'Ode to Heroes' as its female lead in front of a group of performers on a makeshift stage. The lyrics of the song open with the lines: 'Amid the raging flames, I sing the hero / Mountains on all sides turn their ears to listen.' The self-reflexive references to the acts of singing and listening from the very beginning reveal the performative, ritualistic nature of the event, and the theatricality of the scene is further reinforced through the film's visual language.

The camera gradually zooms out to present a panoramic view of the audience – both the immediate off-stage spectators and the imagined audience of Chinese soldiers. The visual representation of the collective is matched with the aural performance of choral singing, when Wang Fang's voice is joined by the chorus who jointly acknowledge and glorify the sacrifice and bravery of Wang Cheng. Furthermore, to sublate the collective passion of affection towards the hero and anger over the enemy that the performance of singing elicited to an unambiguously articulated political message, a poignant speech is given at the interlude of the song. In the speech, the heroism of the sacrificed soldier is interpreted through the lens of internationalist struggle, in which Wang Cheng is praised for being a loyal soldier of Mao, who 'harbors profound love for the North Koreans and hatred for the imperialist invaders'. In this way, the revolutionary enthusiasm evoked through the experience of singing and listening is elevated, and yet simultaneously regulated, by a political analysis of Cold War geopolitics as a fundamental conflict between socialist internationalism and capitalist imperialism, thus gesturing towards an ideological leap from spontaneity to consciousness.

The genealogy of the songstress

If we contextualize these representational strategies deployed in Korean War films within the history of Chinese sound cinema, the practice of using music performance to intensify the audiovisual appeals and emotive intensity of cinema could be traced to the tradition of the songstress in 1930s Shanghai film culture. In Jean Ma's study of the filmic tradition of the songstress, she argued that the gendering of lyrical sensibilities and the association of femininity with musical expressions was a signature expression of sound cinema. The expanded urban space of movie theatre, concert hall and dance hall, together with the emerging media technologies of gramophone, music recording and sound cinema, gave rise to a vibrant mediascape in semi-colonial Shanghai of the 1930s. As sound cinema, especially cinema that featured musical performances by singing women, became a prominent form of cultural production in this period, the songstress emerged as one of the most enamoured figures in the media culture of Shanghai. With the ascendance of the songstress on the Shanghai silver screen, the music that they performed became discrete sonic attractions for the moviegoing public and led to a proliferation in the use of theme songs in sound cinema. The popularity of the Shanghai songstress was further boosted through a circuit of intermedial transactions between screen and stage, in which the image and voice of songstress were reproduced and consumed intermedially in film, popular music and print culture.[23]

However, even though songstresses entered the central stage and became heroines in sound cinema, their images were often presented as 'passive objects to be disciplined, sacrificed, rescued, or redeemed'.[24] *Songstress Red Peony* (1931), the earliest sound film that used wax discs to play recorded singing, is a prototype of this narrative convention. The film narrates the misfortune of a Shanghai songstress, Red Peony. Despite the exceptional singing skill of the heroine, her voice, rather than empowering the talented songstress, was shown to cause tragedy in her life and her loss of agency.

As China faced a more urgent need for national salvation after the Manchurian Incident in 1931, theme songs began to convey more complex and urgent messages of political mobilization and mass agitation, and the figure of the songstress also changed. At this time, musicians bricolaged a plethora of musical traditions, from yellow music to Soviet agitprop, to introduce march music and choral singing to the soundtrack of Chinese left-wing cinema.[25] Nie Er, the most accomplished leftist musician in this period, collaborated closely with the burgeoning film industry and Pathé-EMI to produce nearly fifty mass songs.[26] The invention of the politically charged theme song, as Jean Ma argued, signals the gradual disappearance of the songstress, in which 'the female singing voice was joined by male voices and eventually swallowed up in a revolutionary chorus'.[27] In other words, the songstress, a quintessential embodiment of Shanghai's 'decadent' modernity, was sidelined by an emerging political culture that demanded mass mobilization and revolutionary action.

Xiaobing Tang's study of sound cinema in 1930s Shanghai, however, provides a different angle for conceptualizing the changing representation of the figure and music of the songstress. Rather than lamenting the disappearance of the singing heroine, Tang contended that the popularization of left-wing cinema and its theme songs contributed to an emerging voice for working-class women on screen. This updated musical culture, therefore, enabled the exploration of the expressive capacity of human voice to both engender a new sonic expression and foster a new national vocal community.[28] Building on Tang's insight, we may infer that the songstress did not disappear altogether but that she was transformed from a powerless, passive object of vocal attraction to an agitated, awakened modern woman. This awakened modern woman was now capable of articulating an assertive voice for herself and acquiring a new, and perhaps more organic, relationship with the revolutionary masses. In this renewed revolutionary convention of sound cinema, singing was no longer perceived as an 'unfortunate gift', as told in the story of Red Peony, but became an expressive and corporeal instrument for empowerment at both the personal and national level.

Returning to the characterization of singing women in the two Korean War films, we could see how both films were indebted to the representational tradition in 1930s Shanghai sound cinema, both in terms of the sonic pleasure and emotional intensity that the figure of the songstress evoked and the emerging female subjectivity that left-wing cinema envisaged. Such transhistorical borrowing also attests to Paul Clark's historiography of Maoist film culture. Despite the transformation of the cultural ecology of China after the establishment of the People's Republic, the tradition of Shanghai film did not dissolve completely but converged with the Communist tradition of filmmaking in Yan'an to create an accessible and yet politically meaningful mass culture for the public.[29] Singing, first of all, exemplifies the creation of an audiovisual language that reconciles the task of entertainment and that of education in Maoist film culture. Moreover, as singing is depicted as a gendered gift reserved for revolutionary heroines, it is increasingly associated with women's attainment of political subjectivity and revolutionary agency in Chinese socialist cinema. Therefore, in these Korean War films, we can see how different types of heroism are demarcated along the lines of gender: while men fight the battles for the cause of nationalism and internationalism, women sing in an effort to mobilize and agitate the spectators, both on- and off-screen.

The changing politics of gender

Given the similar subject and audiovisual techniques of the two Korean War films, one may conclude that they both belong to the distinctive socialist filmic tradition that utilizes musical spectacles to glorify military struggles and revolutionary heroism. However, if we scrutinize the representation of gender in the two films, we begin to discern how they differ in their characterization of heroines and engagement with gender issues. Such divergence, as exemplified in *Shanggan Ridge* and *Heroic Sons and Daughters* between 1956 and 1964, is indicative of the changing cultural politics of gender in the socialist era, from the early visibility of gender to its eventual erasure on the eve of the Cultural Revolution (1966–76).

The Maoist era witnessed the prominence of female images across almost all mediums of cultural representation. Women were celebrated as exemplary model workers as well as positive fictional characters, embodying a gender egalitarian ideal promised by the socialist state. Despite the favourable status of women, a popular thesis argues that the Maoist era witnessed an 'erasure of female gender'. Mayfair Yang's research on the image of labouring women in *Women of China* in 1960s is representative in this regard, as she argues that 'gender became an unmarked and neutralized category, its role as a vessel of self-identity was greatly diminished, and it lost its significance for gender politics, which was replaced by class politics'.[30] Such a statement, however, overlooks the radical socialist feminist imperative to advocate women's representation in the public and cultural arena, and it further treats the entire history of the socialist period as a monolith dominated by the politics of class struggle.[31]

In *Finding Women in the State*, feminist historian Wang Zheng argues against this prevalent misconception and recognizes heterogeneous articulations of gender in the socialist years. For instance, she traces the critical role played by socialist feminist filmmakers, in particular Chen Bo'er and Xia Yan, who spent their formative years under the May Fourth feminist tradition, in creating revolutionary heroines and transforming gender norms in socialist China. With films such as *Daughters of China* (1949) and *Eternity in Flames* (1965), the feminist filmmakers introduced 'images of brave, selfless revolutionary heroines' as well as powerful critiques of the patriarchal social system to China's mainstream film production.[32] However, before much of their feminist agenda could be actualized, the valorization of revolutionary heroines was soon subsumed by the politics of class struggle on the eve of the Cultural Revolution. Although women continued to be featured in model operas engineered by Jiang Qing, the female protagonists in these artworks 'were not only situated squarely in previous men's turf as leaders but also absolutely detached from familial responsibilities and kinship relations'.[33] In other words, gender was no longer considered as a relevant or meaningful issue with which to engage, and class contention became the focal point of those narratives.

If we come back to the heroines in the Korean War films with the hindsight of the historical trajectory of socialist feminist cultural politics, we can immediately recognize how gender is transformed or erased from *Shanggan Ridge* to *Heroic Sons and Daughters* within the short span of a decade. In *Shanggan Ridge*, the film heroine, Wang Lan, belongs to the genealogy of revolutionary heroines that socialist feminist filmmakers carefully carved. Being a military nurse, she is depicted as affectionate, caring and brave towards the injured soldiers, a character who comes to embody the spirit of revolutionary optimism. Aside from her professional responsibilities, the film also presents the interiority, emotions and gendered experiences of the heroine, and in particular her unexpressed affection towards the commander. Although the private self of the heroine is shown to be occasionally in conflict with and eventually regulated by the public – a narrative convention demanded by socialist cultural production – the acknowledgement of such conflicts nevertheless indicates a process of negotiation and allows for an openness of interpretation.

In the case of *Heroic Sons and Daughters*, we can see clearly how class politics was upheld as a central narrative structure, as well as in structuring feeling in the film, at the cost of the erasure of gender and gendered experiences. The narrative and emotional spectrum of the film is by essence sustained both by the positive bondage between the Chinese and the North Koreans and the negative opposition between the Voluntary Force soldiers and the American aggressors. Although *Heroic Sons and Daughters* still preserves the storyline of the reunion of Wang Wenqing and Wang Fang, in lieu of the reunion of the biological family, the film asserts the construction of an expanded, class-based family of the soldiers and the masses. In this process, the traditional form of family is rendered an empty signifier in which biological ties are displaced, and the trope of the family becomes a miniature of class fraternity that substantiates the new political order of class struggle. Moreover, the film features extensive cross-cultural exchanges between the Chinese and the North Koreans to explore the making of an international(ist) family. The heroine Wang Fang is oftentimes shown as interacting with the North Koreans, dressing herself in Korean attires and diligently learning about Korean folk culture. While the presence of North Korean elements embellishes a foreign attraction in this film, more importantly it helps to situate the heroine within a transcultural contact zone and allegorize the formation of an international family between North Koreans and the Chinese that was founded on a shared national experience of imperialist aggressions. As Ban Wang observed, the establishment of this transnational family structure illustrates 'a particular feature of Chinese nationalism that projects an internationalist dimension'.[34] In this process, the mourning for her deceased stepbrother that Wang Fang performs through her singing of 'Ode to Heroes' is no longer personal or familial, but is transformed into a more abstract glorification that aims to inspire young revolutionaries to resist enemies, be they imperialist or class. In this light, it is hardly surprising that *Heroic Sons and Daughters* was among the very few fiction films that were still allowed to be screened openly during the Cultural Revolution, a period in which the principle of class struggle became the orthodoxy in cultural production.

Coda

In *One Second* (dir. Zhang Yimou, 2020), a contemporary Chinese film about a group of 'cinephiles' during the Cultural Revolution, a central conflict takes place at the screening site of *Heroic Sons and Daughters* in a poorly equipped movie theatre in Northwest China. Even though the audience have watched the film many times, they still eagerly line up and cram into the movie theatre to see it. As *One Second* later reveals, people come to see *Heroic Sons and Daughters* for a variety of reasons: to see the newsreel attached to the film, to join in the communal ritual of moviegoing and to enjoy the power of exhibiting a film, but crucially none of them are for the ideological lesson or revolutionary enthusiasm orchestrated by the Korean War film.

This revisionist citation of *Heroic Sons and Daughters* illustrates, perhaps, as much the complex emotive terrain of ordinary Chinese people in the socialist era as the changing mediascape of contemporary China.[35] When political passions about class, nation and revolution become exhausted or obsolete, what else could account for the continued emotive appeal of these Korean War films to socialist and post-socialist audiences? While the present chapter focuses predominantly on the mechanisms of cultural production, Zhang's cinematic remediation illuminates a different angle of approaching gender and emotion in Chinese revolutionary war films: to recognize the highly individualized cinematic experiences and understand the plural ways of making sense (and sensibility) of socialist cinema.

Notes

1. H. Lee, *Revolution of the Heart: A Genealogy of Love in China, 1900–1950* (Stanford, CA: Stanford University Press, 2007), p. 286.

2. D.D. Wang, *The Lyrical in Epic Time: Modern Chinese Intellectuals and Artists through the 1949 Crisis* (New York: Columbia University Press, 2015), p. x.

3. B. Wang, 'Review of *The Lyrical in Epic Time: Modern Chinese Intellectuals and Artists Through the 1949 Crisis*', *Chinese Literature: Essays, Articles, Reviews (CLEAR)*, 37 (2015), 218–20, at p. 220.

4. J. Chen, *China's Road to the Korean War: The Making of the Sino-American Confrontation* (New York: Columbia University Press, 1997), p. 215.

5. M. Johnson, 'International and Wartime Origins of the Propaganda State: The Motion Picture in China, 1897–1955', PhD dissertation (University of California San Diego, 2008), p. 452.

6. See Liu Zuyi, 'A Brief Discussion of the Portrayal of Film Characters in *Shanggan Ridge*', *China Film*, 3 (1957), 54–5 at p. 54 and Zhao Lantian, 'On Heroic Sons and Daughters', *Film Art*, 1 (1965), 16–17. Even in the post-socialist era, they are fondly remembered as 'red classics' and widely cited and remediated in the contemporary Chinese mediascape; for instance, a recent blockbuster on the Korean War, *Sacrifice* (2020), paid homage to *Heroic Sons and Daughters* by employing the same theme song as the 1964 film.

7. B. Wang, 'Art, Politics, and Internationalism', in C. Rojas (ed.), *The Oxford Handbook of Chinese Cinemas* (Oxford: Oxford University Press, 2013), p. 252.

8. The 'two-line struggle' refers to the struggle between the proletarian and the bourgeois. While the theory was first formulated by Mao, Jiang Qing adopted it to the realm of culture and prescribed that the depiction of class struggle was the sole legitimate subject in socialist cultural production, and henceforth the Manichean class feeling became the dominant structure of emotion in the subsequent decade of the Cultural Revolution. See Z. Wang, *Finding Women in the State: A Socialist Feminist Revolution in the People's Republic of China, 1949–1964* (Oakland, CA: University of California Press, 2017), p. 218.

9. Shanggan Ridge is commonly known as Triangle Hill in English.

10. M. Sha, 'Diary When Conducting Interviews for *Shanggan Ridge*', in L. Kailuo (ed.), *Approaching Sha Meng* (Beijing: Beijing dianying chubanshe, 2002), p. 66.

11. M. Sha, 'Diary When Conducting Interviews for *Shanggan Ridge*', pp. 67–75.

12. M. Sha, 'Diary When Conducting Interviews for *Shanggan Ridge*', p. 66.

13. M. Sha, 'Diary When Conducting Interviews for *Shanggan Ridge*', p. 76.

14. H. Halstead, 'Everyday Public History', *Journal of the Historical Association*, 107 (2022), 235–48 at p. 236.

15. M. Sha, 'Diary When Conducting Interviews for *Shanggan Ridge*', p. 75.

16. L. Meng, 'Neo-Realism and the Heroic Epic', in L. Kailuo (ed.), *Approaching Sha Meng* (Beijing: Beijing dianying chubanshe, 2002), p. 121.

17. Because of the intensely realist depiction of the war, the film was heavily criticized during the Cultural Revolution as such realism risked undermining the positive image of the Chinese army. See L. Meng, 'Neo-Realism and the Heroic Epic', p. 124.

18. Z. Liu, 'The Experience of Composing for *Shanggan Ridge, Heroic Sons and Daughters*, and *Ode to the Motherland*', *Zongheng*, 22 (1997), 41–2.

19. The composition of 'My Motherland' borrows both from folk music and resistance music produced during the Second Sino-Japanese War (1937–45). The pre-Communist origin of the music and the ordinary folk imageries deployed in the lyrics, however, make 'My Motherland' a patriotic song but without direct reference to socialism. Therefore, it is hardly surprising that the song could evoke so many different layers of emotions that may not align entirely with official ideology. This echoes what Anna Toropova observed in *Feeling Revolution* about the porousness and polysemy of emotion that defies, escapes or exceeds official values. See A. Toropova, *Feeling Revolution: Cinema, Genre, and the Politics of Affect under Stalin* (Oxford: Oxford University Press, 2020), pp. 10–12.

20. N. Chen, 'Not Just the Travel of a Story: A Study of the Adaptation of "Reunion" and *Heroic Sons and Daughters*', *Literature and Art Forum*, 10 (2014), 179–83 at p. 180.

21. Ba Jin, 'Reunion', *Shanghai Literature*, 8 (1961), 15–29 at p. 29.

22. J. Piao, 'Reading *Heroic Sons and Daughters*: The Internal Logic of the Production of the Image of Hero in the People's Republic of China', *Literature and Art Studies*, 11 (2020), 100–11 at p. 103.

23. J. Ma, *Sounding the Modern Woman*, p. 5; Z. Zhang, *An Amorous History of the Silver Screen: Shanghai Cinema, 1896–1937* (Chicago, IL: University of Chicago Press, 2005), p. 315.

24. Ma, *Sounding the Modern Woman*, p. 17.

25. A. Jones, *Yellow Music: Media Culture and Colonial Modernity in the Chinese Jazz Age* (Durham, NC: Duke University Press, 2001), p. 69.

26. J. Howard, '"Music for a National Defense": Making Martial Music during the Anti-Japanese War', *Cross-Currents: East Asian History and Culture Review*, 4 (2015), 1–50 at p. 10.

27. Ma, *Sounding the Modern Woman*, p. 12.

28. X. Tang, 'Radio, Sound Cinema, and Community Singing: The Making of a New Sonic Culture in Modern China', *Twentieth-Century China*, 45 (2020), 3–24, p. 10.

29. P. Clark, *Chinese Cinema: Culture and Politics since 1949* (Cambridge: Cambridge University Press, 1987), p. 25.

30. M. Yang, 'From Gender Erasure to Gender Difference: State Feminism, Consumer Sexuality, and Women's Public Sphere in China', in M.M. Young (ed.), *Spaces of Their Own* (Minneapolis, MN: University of Minnesota Press, 1999), p. 41.

31. Z. Wang, 'Creating a Socialist Feminist Cultural Front: "Women of China" (1949–1966)', *The China Quarterly*, 204 (2010), 844.

32. Z. Wang, *Finding Women in the State*, p. 198.

33. Z. Wang, *Finding Women in the State*, p. 216.

34. B. Wang, 'Art, Politics, and Internationalism', p. 264.

35. Z. Ma, 'War Remembered, Revolution Forgotten: Recasting the Sino-North Korean Alliance in China's Post-Socialist Media State', *Cross-Currents: East Asian History and Culture Review*, 22 (2017), 54–82 at p. 74.

References

Ba Jin, 'Reunion', *Shanghai Literature*, 8 (1961), 15–29.

Chen, J., *China's Road to the Korean War: The Making of the Sino-American Confrontation* (New York: Columbia University Press, 1997).

Chen, N., 'Not Just the Travel of a Story: A Study of the Adaptation of "Reunion" and *Heroic Sons and Daughters*', *Literature and Art Forum*, 10 (2014), 179–83.

Clark, P., *Chinese Cinema: Culture and Politics since 1949* (Cambridge: Cambridge University Press, 1987).

Halstead, H., 'Everyday Public History', *Journal of the Historical Association*, 107 (2022), 235–48.

Howard, J., '"Music for a National Defense": Making Martial Music during the Anti-Japanese War', *Cross-Currents: East Asian History and Culture Review*, 4 (2015), 1–50.

Johnson, M., 'International and Wartime Origins of the Propaganda State: The Motion Picture in China, 1897–1955', PhD dissertation (University of California San Diego, 2008).

Jones, A., *Yellow Music: Media Culture and Colonial Modernity in the Chinese Jazz Age* (Durham, NC: Duke University Press, 2001).

Lee, H., *Revolution of the Heart: A Genealogy of Love in China, 1900–1950* (Stanford, CA: Stanford University Press, 2007).

Liu, Z., 'A Brief Discussion of the Portrayal of Film Characters in *Shanggan Ridge*', *China Film*, 3 (1957), 54–5.

——, 'The Experience of Composing for *Shanggan Ridge*, *Heroic Sons and Daughters*, and *Ode to the Motherland*', *Zongheng*, 12 (1997), 41–2.

Ma, J., *Sounding the Modern Woman: The Songstress in Chinese Cinema* (Durham, NC: Duke University Press, 2015).

Ma, Z., 'War Remembered, Revolution Forgotten: Recasting the Sino-North Korean Alliance in China's Post-Socialist Media State', *Cross-Currents: East Asian History and Culture Review*, 22 (2017), 54–82.

Meng, L., 'Neo-Realism and the Heroic Epic', in L. Kailuo (ed.), *Approaching Sha Meng* (Beijing: Beijing dianying chubanshe, 2002), pp. 115–37.

Piao, J., 'Reading *Heroic Sons and Daughters*: The Internal Logic of the Production of the Image of Hero in the People's Republic of China', *Literature and Art Studies*, 11 (2020), 100–11.

Sha, M., 'Diary When Conducting Interviews for *Shanggan Ridge*', in L. Kailuo (ed.), *Approaching Sha Meng* (Beijing: Beijing dianying chubanshe, 2002), pp. 65–89.

Tang, X., 'Radio, Sound Cinema, and Community Singing: The Making of a New Sonic Culture in Modern China', *Twentieth-Century China*, 45 (2020), 3–24.

Toropova, A., *Feeling Revolution: Cinema, Genre, and the Politics of Affect under Stalin* (Oxford: Oxford University Press, 2020).

Wang, B., 'Art, Politics, and Internationalism', in C. Rojas (ed.), *The Oxford Handbook of Chinese Cinemas* (Oxford: Oxford University Press, 2013), pp. 251–67.

——, 'Review of *The Lyrical in Epic Time: Modern Chinese Intellectuals and Artists Through the 1949 Crisis*', *Chinese Literature: Essays, Articles, Reviews (CLEAR)*, 37 (2015), 218–20.

Wang, D.D., *The Lyrical in Epic Time: Modern Chinese Intellectuals and Artists through the 1949 Crisis* (New York: Columbia University Press, 2015).

Wang, Z., 'Creating a Socialist Feminist Cultural Front: "Women of China" (1949–1966)', *The China Quarterly*, 204 (2010), 844.

——, *Finding Women in the State: A Socialist Feminist Revolution in the People's Republic of China, 1949–1964* (Oakland, CA: University of California Press, 2017).

Yang, M., 'From Gender Erasure to Gender Difference: State Feminism, Consumer Sexuality, and Women's Public Sphere in China', in M.M. Young (ed.), *Spaces of Their Own* (Minneapolis, MN: University of Minnesota Press 1999), pp. 35–67.

Zhang, Z., *An Amorous History of the Silver Screen: Shanghai Cinema, 1896–1937* (Chicago, IL: University of Chicago Press, 2005).

Zhao, L., 'On Heroic Sons and Daughters', *Film Art*, 1 (1965), 16–17.

Chapter 4

Emotions at work: solidarity in the Liverpool dock dispute, 1995–8

Emma Copestake

In 2017, twenty-two years after he had been sacked for refusing to cross a picket line, Kevin remembered the 'camaraderie', 'love' and 'affection' that had defined his time as a dock worker in Liverpool since the late 1960s. Kevin explained that the relationships he formed on the waterfront were 'something unique'.[1] These bonds of solidarity bridged two industrial and political eras in Britain. As Britain's twentieth-century economy moved away from primary and secondary industries to become largely service based, over a million jobs were lost in engineering and metal manufacturing alone between 1951 and 1991.[2] The rise of neoliberalism from the 1970s also weakened the power of trade unions and increased the political currency of individualism. Nevertheless, sacked dock workers and their families fought on the edge of this transformation between September 1995 and January 1998 as they attempted to force the Mersey Docks and Harbour Company (MDHC) and Torside Ltd to reinstate approximately 500 men. While Alice Mah and Brian Marren have demonstrated elsewhere that solidarity persisted in this dock dispute, I argue here that emotions, such as Kevin's, are crucial to understanding how and why.[3]

In this chapter, I examine the emotional malleability of solidarity, as opposed to its more visible manifestations, in relation to class and gender in Liverpool.[4] David Featherstone has defined solidarity as a 'relation forged through political struggle which seeks to challenge forms of oppression'.[5] Sociologists have been at the forefront of understanding the role of emotions within this relationship. Erika Summers-Effler, for example, has proposed that solidarity encompasses experiencing the 'needs and feelings of others as our own' and James Jasper has demonstrated how this experience is underpinned by 'reciprocal emotions' directed towards one another and 'shared emotions' directed at those outside of the group.[6] Emotions construct, define and sustain relations of power by operating as 'social signals' expressed by individuals in relation to their cultural values.[7] On the docks in Liverpool, this process was defined by the struggle for job security that began under the system of casual employment in place until 1967 and continued as a result of containerization. The National Dock Labour Scheme (NDLS) had provided some form of protection for registered dock workers from 1947 until it was abolished in 1989.[8] As these significant changes took place in the Port of Liverpool, relationships evolved and new challenges emerged. Informed by Diarmaid Kelliher's assessment of the new forms of solidarity that emerged between striking miners and the Lesbians and Gays Support the Miners group in the 1984–5 strike, I examine how reassessments of solidarity shaped the industrial action taken by Liverpool's dock community during the 1990s.[9] I am concerned primarily with the emotional resonance of solidarity in an era which had devalued collectivism, the impact this shift had upon the relationships between male and female members of the dock community and how the emotional negotiations that took place impacted understandings of solidarity itself.

I use Barbara Rosenwein's concept of 'emotional communities' in this chapter because it refers directly to the shared values and expectations of behaviour that experiences of solidarity depended upon.[10] To understand what Rosenwein has termed the 'systems of feeling' that defined Liverpool's dock community, I draw upon a range of sources.[11] Primarily, I focus on two interviews I shared with people involved in the 1995–8 dock dispute in 2017 and ten accounts shared with Bill Hunter at the time. Oral history shares commonalities with the history of emotions through its emphasis on subjectivity, therefore interviews are a valuable source for understanding how 'individual life stories converge with, overlap and are shaped by collective narratives and experiences'.[12] Further context for my analysis is provided by the website created and updated by men and women during the dispute, *The Flickering Flame* documentary made by Ken Loach in 1996, newspaper articles, official trade union correspondence and Jimmy McGovern's film *Dockers* which was written by those involved.

I begin the chapter by examining the core values of men and women who depended upon dock work for their livelihoods to outline the historical composition of the working-class solidarity that existed between them. I then assess how these bonds evolved through the expression of gendered emotions as existing values were assessed in the new context of the 1990s. To reveal the emotional processes that sustained a sense of solidarity within the dock community, I consider the role of pride and fear in regulating masculine boundaries and the negotiations of anger, embarrassment and dignity that enabled the creation of Women of the Waterfront (WOW). Finally, I examine the dock community's relationship with external actors involved in the dispute more specifically to outline how these relationships helped to redefine the parameters of solidarity and the action taken based upon it. My approach demonstrates how solidarity has been continually 'fashioned and constructed' while encompassing a broad range of shared emotional experiences.[13]

Solidarity, gender and Liverpool's dock community

The shared emotions of solidarity within the 1995–8 dock dispute were rooted in generations of history in the Port of Liverpool, particularly in relation to experiences of casualism which operated in the port until 1967. Dock work was traditionally the preserve of Irish-Catholic immigrants in the city, and both men and women shared memories of dock workers being 'treated like animals' in the hiring pens. Men would scramble over one another to catch the eye of the foreman to secure low-paid work in poor conditions.[14] Kevin Bilsborrow summarized the harm caused by this system to Hunter when he stated that 'there's only one type of employer and that's a bad employer, because he's after you and if you're not strong he'll get you'.[15] Although a gendered division of labour ensured male breadwinners dominated the industrial sphere, both men and women remembered the importance of their fathers getting 'lucky' in the pen.[16] Carol, whose husband and father had worked on the docks, explained to me in 2017 that anything that happened in her husband's job had a 'knock-on' effect in family life: 'it affects everybody'.[17] Sons often followed their fathers on to the docks and, until the housing programmes of the 1950s and 1960s were introduced, families lived in tight-knit communities close to the port. As families were surrounded by others experiencing the hardships of casualism, these shared negative experiences nurtured a strong support system.[18] Gang work also helped to embed the value of co-operation, as opposed to competition, on the docks, as men had a high degree of autonomy over their work and received their pay based upon productivity.[19] In other words, working together produced the most favourable outcome for everyone. As a result, the collective goals of men and women in the dock community centred on ensuring dock work was a secure job with fair pay for all, including future generations.

Historically, heteronormative understandings of men and women led to gendered roles in securing these goals.[20] Since the formation of the

National Union of Dock Labourers in 1889, a date referenced by shop stewards during the 1995 to 1998 dispute over 100 years later, the method of achieving these goals had been male, collective action.[21] Each victory gained through the trade union movement fostered a reciprocal sense of pride among men that reinforced the bonds between them by confirming their sense of morality.[22] This established method of acting upon solidarity explains why dock workers themselves used the term mostly in relation to the union but contextualized it through male relationships at work.[23] Ted Woods described the nature of these relationships to Hunter as a 'macho comradeship' expressed as though men were 'going to murder each other'.[24] Dangerous and physically exhausting work on the docks led to the development of a tough attitude that relied upon the use of humour to avoid the expression of negative emotions. This toughness helped men to keep one another going and served to demonstrate to employers that they could overcome the environment they had to work in.[25] The strength of male relationships at work was evident in 2017 when Kevin used 'we' instead of 'I' consistently while discussing the fight for better conditions throughout his working life. Kevin also explained to me explicitly that the 'love' he had for his colleagues depended upon whether a man would 'put themselves out big time for the union or the other men'.[26] Evidently, masculinity centred not just upon a man's responsibility as the breadwinner but also his willingness to ensure this role could be fulfilled under fair conditions.

Women were not subject to the same work environment and were therefore expected to act upon solidarity differently to men. Carol referred to her own experience of the docks in the late twentieth century to explain that women were expected to leave work to bring up children and then get 'pin-money' jobs once their children had grown up.[27] Femininity centred upon alleviating the perils of the casual system at home which ensured that male power over the family economy did not always translate into an abuse of this power. The nature of bonds between husbands and wives was often characterized by mutual respect and appreciation. Kevin expressed this respect when he said that 'men can talk the talk, but women can walk the walk when it comes to ... coping mechanisms, dealing with the kids, dealing with the bills, dealing with the household chores, dealing with the school'.[28] Madeline Kerr's sociological study of families living on Ship Street, a name given to a collection of inner-city streets in Liverpool, in the 1950s demonstrated that women knew the value of their role within the family as they demanded their fair share of their partner's wages. This study also highlighted that bonds between women centred upon female relatives living nearby rather than friendships forming specifically between the wives and partners of dock workers.[29] These strong bonds continued as many families moved outside of the city centre in the 1950s and

1960s.[30] Therefore, feminine experiences of solidarity within the dock community had an imagined component outside the family unit or local friendship group as they rested upon the assumption that other women connected to dock work would share similar experiences.[31] While solidarity itself was rooted in the shared condemnation of employer power, the emotional experiences of it were shaped by the relationships between men and women.

Never cross a picket line

Traditions of masculine pride, particularly in relation to the principle of refusing to cross a picket line, are crucial to understanding why solidarity and solidarity action persisted into the 1990s. On 25 September 1995, twenty-two men employed by Torside were ordered to carry out overtime on short notice without the usual rates of pay. Torside had been voted on to the docks by ex-registered MDHC dock workers in 1991 and its employees worked on lower rates of pay with the expectation these rates could be improved later.[32] The five men who left the ship to discuss the situation with their shop stewards were dismissed alongside the remaining men who refused to work on these terms. The sacked men then mounted a picket line at Nelson and Seaforth to persuade the MDHC employees to support their case for reinstatement. The result was that in just four days, approximately 500 men were sacked from companies on the docks.[33] In Hunter's interviews, 'pride and admiration' dominated the accounts of these events, particularly in relation to the redundancy payments and pensions that the MDHC men were willing to give up when they breached their contracts to take secondary action.[34] By not crossing the picket line, they were supporting Torside men who were employed by a different company, though the two worked closely together. This action had been made illegal by the Employment Act of 1982.[35] Financial risk had always been a fundamental feature of going on strike but this had been the loss of wages that were offset by the potential success of achieving a long-term benefit.

In this dispute, the context was different. Dock workers no longer had the protection of the NDLS which was administered by employers and representatives from the Transport and General Workers' Union (TGWU).[36] Following the Devlin Report's two-phased modernization programme for the scheme, a stamp system had ensured regular work and most port employers recognized the powerful shop stewards committee in Liverpool.[37] Alongside decasualization, modernization also included a reduction of the workforce as the number of labour hours needed to move 11,000 tonnes of cargo fell from 10,584 to just 546 in 1970 thanks to the introduction of containers.[38] The situation in Liverpool was worsened by its geographical position as shipping firms closed because of increased British trade with European ports.[39] Nevertheless, the values of collectivism held political currency in Britain at this time, which meant that dock workers were in a strong position to achieve their goals. The nationwide strike in 1972 that freed the five London-based dock workers who had been imprisoned in Pentonville for illegally picketing container depots was just one example of this strength.[40] The subsequent Aldington-Jones agreement ensured that there were no compulsory redundancies for dock workers registered under the NDLS and established voluntary severance schemes as the method for reducing the number of workers.[41] From 1979, the Conservative government restructured the relationship between the state, economy and trade unions which meant that the National Association of Port Employers was successful in their attempts to remove the NDLS in 1989 by arguing that worker control had become detrimental to profit.[42] Dock workers were choosing to fight in the industrial climate of the 1990s in which employers had the upper hand.

Long traditions of pride in fighting injustice on the docks meant men expressed any uncertainty carefully. Terry Southers, a shop steward, acknowledged to Hunter that by 1995 some men had become 'despondent'. If men had expressed this emotion towards the prospect of the dispute directly, they would have undermined the value placed upon supporting one another against the actions of employers and, in the process, contravened expectations of tough behaviour. To avoid negating their entitlement to the pride that solidarity depended upon, men questioned whether the Torside employees were worth fighting for. The notion that Torside had only been working on the docks for 'five minutes' tapped into the significance of pride as the suggestion was that these men had not earned the respect of others by demonstrating their commitment to fighting for them.[43] Before the dispute had ended, Bob Ritchie, a shop steward at the time, described to Hunter that he had watched the sacked Torside employees grow up to become men as they gained a 'hatred for the establishment and for what's happened'.[44] Kevin, who had also been a shop steward, articulated this process in 2017 in the way he explained that 'they', the 'young Torside kids', had 'savvy' ideas such as the 'DoCKers' T-shirt that incorporated the popular Calvin Klein logo before stating that 'it come from us'.[45] Men drew upon longstanding notions of pride to express concern, yet ultimately this sense of pride reaffirmed the solidarity amongst those willing to fight.

The close relationship between masculine pride and negative emotions demonstrated how the two were dependent upon one another. Throughout the dispute, fear, as a judgement of something bad occurring, was referred to by men as predominantly located elsewhere in others.[46] Nevertheless,

The Flickering Flame documentary explained that 'everyone has a fear of going back to the bad old days' before 1967 when there were no regular hours or income.[47] Between 1989 and 1992, approximately 80 per cent of dock workers left the industry nationwide, opting for redundancy pay over working under tougher managerial control.[48] Kevin Robinson explained to Hunter that men had felt as though 'their heart had been somewhat ripped out of them temporarily' when it ended.[49] Similarly, Ted Woods identified 1989 as a 'time of fear' and told Hunter that the men who had left the industry then had been 'scared of the future'.[50] Liverpool's dock workers maintained the recognition of their shop stewards system, but this did not prevent the forced introduction of new contracts in 1994 for ex-registered men. These contracts introduced a three-week hourly work schedule which meant that daily hours could vary on short notice depending on management requirements.[51] The prevalence of fear in accounts of the dispute insinuated that it was a driving force behind action, especially as the accompanying pride taken in fighting relied upon preventing many fears from being realized. This point is particularly relevant to reflections of the origins of Torside. In our interview, Carol remembered warning her husband that allowing a new company on to the docks to employ workers on lower rates of pay would undermine his job and that, when he voted for the company's creation, he explained to her that he had allowed his 'heart' to rule his 'head'. The distinction between hearts, as the desire to continue the tradition of sons following their fathers on to the docks, and heads, as preventing the port from returning insecure working conditions, reiterated that separating the internal values of the dock community from the ongoing power struggle with the port employers was detrimental to achieving long-term security.[52]

The initial concession made by MDHC employees with the creation of Torside defined the dispute emotionally for men. Kevin, for example, stated in our interview that the dispute had been about 'bringing people [in] on decent wages' and that his job was not his to sell.[53] This motivation was why men rejected offers made by the MDHC in October 1995, January 1996, November 1996 and then again in October 1997. The latter offer was rejected in an imposed ballot on a reformulated offer from June earlier that year which had included a potential labour supply company.[54] The reinstatement of Torside employees was a main point of contention as the MDHC claimed they were unable to do anything regarding this issue, despite the overlapping remit between the two companies. Frank Lannigan, who had been a shop steward since 1981, told Hunter that men had believed they would be able to help fight for better conditions for Torside employees at a later date. Yet this did not happen because, in Lannigan's words, 'the employers started taking us on at the same time'. Therefore, the fight over

Torside did not 'worry' Frank because the men had no other option for negotiations after being 'fettered' by the managing directors of the MDHC.[55] The negative shared emotions surrounding the prospect of making further concessions towards returning to pre-1967 conditions worked to reinforce the reciprocal pride men took in trying to prevent this from happening.[56]

Ultimately, the mobilizing effect of pride and fear in September 1995 determined who was included and excluded within solidarity. The film *Dockers* was written by the dock community with the support of Jimmy McGovern, and its accompanying documentary, *Writing the Wrongs*, shows how the script was created. In this documentary, men and women described the mindset of crossing a picket line as 'alien' and they were reluctant to give this action any coverage in the film. McGovern then insisted on probing the emotions surrounding this issue further, which resulted in a sacked dock worker writing the most fruitful scene between the protagonist, Tommy, and his best friend who returned to work, Macca.[57] In this scene, the script referred to the 180 new contracts that the MDHC issued immediately after the sackings. Macca had taken one of these contracts and explained to Tommy that 'it's fucking easy to be brave when you're wanted'.[58] The two men were divided by their definitions of bravery. Tommy's reason for not taking the contract he was issued was because others, like Macca, had not received one, whereas Macca had allowed his belief that the dispute was 'doomed' because of the lack of men involved, lack of union support and the political climate it took place in to override his commitment to others. Tommy was scripted to challenge Macca's claims that crossing the picket line took 'bottle' by arguing that sneaking into work did not show 'courage' and that the right way to handle fear was to stand up to those causing it.[59] The script for *Dockers* then focused on the pride Macca had lost by showing that he no longer held the esteem of his male friends, which caused arguments between him and his family when they were ostracized. These sentiments were echoed in Hunter's interviews during the dispute when Andy Dwyer stated that 'scabs' had 'got no history on the dock' because they were 'today people'.[60] The immediate disassociation of 'history' from those who crossed the picket line showed that they prioritized immediate personal gains and removed them from the historical pride solidarity depended upon.

Women of the Waterfront

While industrial action on the docks had traditionally been carried out by men, women shared the conception of pride associated with collective action as it protected working conditions and therefore families. As women evaluated this action in the context of the 1990s, their anger carved out space for the gender roles underpinning solidarity to evolve and shift. During an interview in 2017, Carol remembered being 'furious' that the MDHC would call her husband constantly to come to work or to alter his hours.[61] Increased employer control had collapsed the separation between work and home, which brought female members of the dock community directly into the arena of struggle. Just as masculine pride depended upon an expression of indignation, Carol's expression of anger demonstrated her sense of wrongdoing and served to defend the dignity of being able to provide and care for a family.[62] During the dispute, Sue Mitchell, whose husband was a sacked dock worker, discussed the effect that long consecutive shifts were having on family life and said, 'I was absolutely choking, thinking this can't go on.' She explained that the 1995 to 1998 dispute was different to those that had preceded it because women could 'see what the management had done'.[63] Both Carol and Sue remembered women calling into local radio stations to express their anger at the situation and women reaching out to others they had not known previously. Carol recalled feeling a 'perverse relief' when her husband was sacked because she had wanted a reason to fight the dock company after the 'misery' they had caused. This understanding was formulated not only by the intrusion of employers into homes but also by the knowledge that the fight was 'bigger than just the men' and that it entailed a broader struggle to maintain established ways of life. She understood 1995 as the final stand following the fight of the miners and Women Against Pit Closures in the 1980s and explained that it changed how the working class had to fight.[64] Women's desire for action culminated in the creation of an official support group for the dock workers, with support from the shop stewards, within a few weeks of the original sackings. WOW picketed the houses of the managing directors of the MDHC, raised funds and promoted the case of the sacked men on delegations.[65]

WOW's integration into the industrial dispute centred on an emotional 'give and take' between men and women that was rooted in concepts of respect and dignity.[66] *The Dockers Charter*, published in December 1995 by those involved in the dispute, included an article about WOW. Cathy Dwyer's interview for this article was also published on the dockers' website. She stated that she had been 'embarrassed' when she first attended a picket line. Cathy had not wanted the men to think she was there because her husband did not 'totally respect' her.[67] Cathy is also quoted as saying that men felt 'embarrassed' to admit needing help because they were 'dignified', 'tough men'. Cathy's emotions demonstrated how WOW constituted a departure from traditional masculine and feminine roles by suggesting that men could no longer protect and provide for families on their own. Nevertheless, Cathy focused upon explaining that she 'admired' her husband for not crossing the picket line because he was protecting the industry, and their grandchildren, from the return of casualism. By explaining that respect had to be earned and could not be 'bought', Cathy located and reinforced male dignity in fighting injustice as opposed to simply earning money.[68] This reinforcement helped women to earn respect for their new role. During our interview in 2017, Kevin explained that he had been involved in the creation of WOW because he recognized that the dispute would not be as successful if men were under pressure to earn money. The 'dignity' that he used to describe WOW's actions stemmed from them demonstrating that they knew the men were right and their fathers had been right before them. Any concerns that men had about protecting women were alleviated by separate meetings for WOW and, particularly in the early days of the dispute, male-escorted delegations for its members.[69] WOW were able to fully embrace their new responsibilities after gaining the support of men like Kevin.

The readjustment of gender roles rested upon the reinforcement of existing notions of pride and respect. Therefore, the emotions that men and women expressed about the pressures of the dispute remained gendered.[70] Kevin explained his appreciation for WOW by outlining how women would be more likely to let him, or other shop stewards, know when more support was needed to ensure a family could continue to fight. He also appreciated WOW's ability to communicate the dispute emotionally by focusing on the hardship of families at rallies or on delegations at a time when public discourse emphasized the anachronism of industrial action. Kevin recalled instances when members of WOW had cried during their speeches. He would stand up afterwards to say, 'and you wonder why we get angry'.[71] In this memory, crying presented a simultaneous gendered portrayal of strength and weakness. The strength of masculinity depended upon avoiding expressions of the negative emotions that crying was associated with, but there remained an appreciation of the powerful reasons for these feminine tears.[72] In footage of WOW's discussions in *The Flickering Flame*, Sue is shown fighting off tears while she explained the 'social injustice' of families losing their homes and savings. She talked about how visible the 'strain' and 'stress' of everyone involved was to her and then contextualized this in the trends towards flexible, casual jobs with little security and low pay.[73] Even twenty years later, Carol remembered the 'stress, stress, stress' that women encountered as they juggled daily life, including paid work, with supporting the men.[74] Men were more likely to express the injustices they were experiencing by focusing on the inner workings of the dispute rather than the household. For example, Micky Tighe described the treatment of men who had dedicated forty years of

EMOTIONS AT WORK   105

their life to the MDHC as 'criminal' in *The Dockers Charter*. The sacked dock workers referenced an inability to understand how a company that boosted their profits from almost £8.5 million in 1989 to just over £33.5 million in 1994 could sack its entire workforce in favour of casualism.[75] This return to casualism was proven by the Merseyside Port Shop Stewards Committee (MPSSC) when they presented a case successfully to the Education and Employment Committee at the House of Commons in 1996.[76] Collectively, these negative emotions continued to cement the value of looking after one another.

Empathetic boundaries

The inclusion of women in the industrial sphere was only one way in which the emotional specificities of the 1995–8 dispute shaped the nature of solidarity action. The dock community's traditional support network had been transformed by the closure of industries across Britain and the restrictions placed upon trade unions during the 1980s. Dock workers and WOW had expected the union to share the same values as them and in March 1996, Bill Morris, then general secretary of the TGWU, gave a speech which recognized the 'pride' dock workers could take in fighting the MDHC.[77] However, the TGWU never made the dispute official and instead facilitated negotiations while providing financial support. In 2017, Carol spoke highly of John Pilger whose article in *The Guardian* in November 1996 had stated that the TGWU had contained the 'anger' of its members to serve 'the aims of the British establishment'.[78] Morris's 'One Union' approach had centralized power within the union and favoured social partnership methods that avoided direct confrontation with employers. In part, this approach was intended to reduce a deficit of approximately £12 million at the time that had resulted from falling membership in the previous decade.[79] Consequently, Morris's response to Pilger's article in *The Guardian* and *T&G Record* argued that dock workers had inhibited the union's ability to act by taking secondary action and the union had a duty to protect its 900,000 members from possible financial sanctions.[80]

Accounts of the dispute consistently focused upon how the TGWU acted. The reply from the MPSSC to Morris's letter, for example, outlined the union's rejection of four ballot requests for industrial action between 1989 and 1995, the failure to organize a ballot after the dismissal of the Torside men and that the financial aid provided equated to £15 a week per family.[81] Men and women interviewed during the dispute highlighted the moral code the union had violated by referring to their 'bloody disgusting' behaviour and stating that they should have been 'ashamed'.[82]

When reflecting on the TGWU's position more recently, both Carol and Kevin referred repeatedly to the union refusing to make the dispute official. Kevin stated that the union had been 'frightened' of sequestration when they should have been challenging the law and he believed that 'the whole country would have stopped' if the union had supported the dispute fully.[83] The lack of support could have translated simply into a lack of action, but past successes provided a reference point for what could have happened and these notions of shame helped to drive the dispute forward through new methods of fighting.

Hope was also necessary to continue the fight because, as Manuel Castells has argued, it is 'fundamental' to goal-seeking action because it projects positive outcomes into the future.[84] The dock community found 'hope' in their appeals for international support that were made possible by new technologies such as fax machines and the internet.[85] Picket lines, stoppages and demonstrations that took place in ports across the world aimed to disrupt the shipping companies that operated in Liverpool. Action taken on the east coast of the United States, for example, caused a 20 per cent drop in the MDHC's share prices when Atlantic Container Line withdrew from the Port of Liverpool in June 1996.[86] Support across the globe culminated in two international days of action on 20 January 1997 and 9 September 1997.[87] An MPSSC press release in September 1997 underlined that international support in the dispute was a 'symbol for all dockers' determined to resist the threats of casual labour and the deregulation of the industry.[88] Earlier that year, the Dockers' Section Steering Committee of the International Transport Workers' Federation had outlined that docks in Taiwan, Colombia and Honduras had been threatened with privatization, and attacks on trade unionists' rights had been made in Australia and New Zealand.[89] In the interviews I conducted, international support was discussed at length. Kevin said that this support was the 'most pleasing' aspect of the fight because it supplemented the support they had lost in Britain.[90] Furthermore, Carol explained to me that the events of the dispute had pushed empathy beyond the docks industry to encompass 'human suffering'. The international delegations that Carol attended shaped her understanding that what was happening on the docks was part of a broader fight against the effects of an intensified phase of global capitalism. This understanding explained why WOW and the sacked dock workers gave their support to the women of Srebrenica as well as Turkish citizens fighting for democracy, and how the radical ecologist and anti-corporate group Reclaim the Streets came to support the dock community's cause.[91] Through new forms of action and the hope it provided, 'imagined' solidarity was strengthened with others in struggle beyond industrial workers in Britain.[92]

Following the dispute, this broadened understanding of solidarity continued to operate and define the emotions of the dock community. The MPSSC wrote a letter with 'great sadness' to their supporters in January 1998 explaining that the hardship of families and lack of sustained action on the international front meant a settlement had to be made.[93] The final settlement included a register of former dock workers who wished to be considered for future vacancies, a labour supply organization which created between twenty-five and twenty-eight jobs initially, joint MDHC and TGWU pensions, a twelve-week fixed term contract with a payment of £3,000, and redundancy payments of £25,000 for those who had worked for fifteen years or more.[94] Nevertheless, the dock community did not view 1998 as the end of their fight. They founded The Initiative Factory, a charitable trust, shortly after the dispute ended, which aimed to build international communities and retrain those who had 'suffered as a result of the changing economic circumstances of the past two decades'.[95] *Dockers* was written through this organization and the revenue received from it was used to create The Casa, or the Community Advice Service Association, that has since provided employment, welfare and legal advice to many people across Merseyside.[96] Despite the tension between the TGWU and Liverpool's dock community, many dock workers and their wives remained active in trade unions because of their important role in defending workers' rights with some even returning to Seaforth to help re-unionize the workforce in 2012.[97] The emotional malleability of solidarity during the dispute shifted value from a specific form of collective bargaining alone to a multi-pronged approach that focused on all those harmed by the capitalist system. This malleability extended to the interviews that I conducted in The Casa in 2017 as Kevin asserted that he was 'handing the baton' to me because 'you can't win every fight, but you can't lose every fight either'.[98] The interviews provided an opportunity to share the values of the dock community, present a fight against exploitation and continue to build a shared solidarity.

Conclusion

In this chapter, I have focused on the gendered emotional experiences of solidarity for men and women who fought for the reinstatement of sacked dock workers in Liverpool between 1995 and 1998. The emotional community on the docks developed from a specific period of British industrial history that had changed dramatically by the 1990s. Nevertheless, the values that underpinned this community led to new forms of pride, fear, anger, shame and hope as they were evaluated in the context of the 1990s.

These shared emotions defined solidarity and by focusing on them I have demonstrated how men and women navigated changing structures of power to drive the dispute forward. While their longstanding aim to secure fair pay and conditions at work to support families and future generations remained largely unchanged, the boundaries of solidarity and the typical action associated with it evolved. Without an emotional analysis, the nuances of this evolution, and the relationships it was based upon, cannot be appreciated fully.

As solidarity had been channelled through male industrial action on the docks throughout the twentieth century, pride dominated men's narratives of the dispute. The expression of pride related to overcoming shared negative emotions such as fear, yet solidarity itself only extended to those who expressed these emotions in line with expectations of behaviour. A politicized sense of pride regulated the boundaries of masculinity by defining who was worth fighting for. The examples I explored in this chapter showed that acknowledging fear was acceptable only when used as a reason to keep fighting. The severity of the situation in the 1990s meant that adhering to this expectation was not straightforward and explained why some MDHC men had questioned whether Torside employees were included within established notions of pride. Women had understood the value of fighting the employer but their role in this fight, and within understandings of solidarity, had centred on caring for a family. The dispute forced these gender roles to be reassessed. The encroachment of the MDHC's managerial practices into the family home led women to express anger that created space for them to form new connections with other women. These connections led to the formation of WOW. The transgression that WOW represented had to be reconciled by emphasizing certain aspects of masculinity and femininity while de-emphasizing others. For men, dignity was located primarily in taking a stand and fighting for future generations as opposed to earning money. For women, their dignity was located in supporting this cause and being able to communicate it to others in order to gain support. Therefore, emotions remained gendered when expressing the impact of the dispute despite the ways that expectations of behaviour had evolved.

Employers had always been expected to act in ways that were antithetical to the dock community's values, thus their increased power was insufficient to alter perceptions of solidarity and solidarity action. In the final section of this chapter, I examined how the TGWU's actions impacted how men and women chose to fight the MDHC. The ability of the TGWU to support the sacked dock workers had been restricted by the labour laws of the 1980s and financial strain meant the union was not willing to make the dispute official. A divide developed between the TGWU and the dock community that centred on its close association with conceptions of solidarity. The union prioritized protecting itself financially so it could continue to support its membership. However, men and women of the dock community understood the restrictions on trade unions as part of the dispute and therefore something to be challenged. Without their usual allies, dock workers and members of WOW sought hope in new international connections that they formed outside the framework of the union. The delegations that men and women attended overseas strengthened the solidarity between them and workers beyond industrial Britain. Combined with the outcome of the final settlement, internationalism helped to formulate a stronger sense of imagined solidarity with those suffering from the effects of economic restructuring across the globe. The focus on a wider sense of solidarity led to a new emphasis on different methods of action. Broader explorations of the emotional communities of port employers, official union structures and the government were beyond the remit of this chapter. However, the close attention paid to dock workers and their families in Liverpool has demonstrated that solidarity was not a static feature of working-class communities tied to a specific form of industrial action. Instead, the emotional fluidity of solidarity was, and still is, embedded in the ebb and flow of power that defined who could act and how.

Notes

1. Kevin, interview with the author, The Casa, Liverpool, 12 July 2017.

2. A. McIvor, *Working Lives: Work in Britain Since 1945* (London: Bloomsbury, 2013), pp. 11–13.

3. A. Mah, *Port Cities and Global Legacies: Urban Identity, Waterfront Work and Radicalism* (Basingstoke: Springer, 2014), pp. 113–35 and B. Marren, *We Shall Not Be Moved: How Liverpool's Working Class Fought Redundancies, Closures and Cuts in the Age of Thatcher* (Manchester: Manchester University Press, 2016), pp. 201–33.

4. See, for example, P. Turnbull and V. Wass, 'The Greatest Game No More: Redundant Dockers and the Demise of Dock Work', *Work, Employment & Society*, 8 (1994), 487–506 and J. Phillips, 'Class and Industrial Relations in Britain: The "Long" Mid-Century and the Case of Port Transport, c. 1920–70', *Twentieth Century British History*, 16, 1 (2005), 52–73.

5. D. Featherstone, *Solidarity: Hidden Histories and Geographies of Internationalism* (London: Bloomsbury, 2012), p. 5.

6. E. Summers-Effler, 'The Emotional Significance of Solidarity for Social Movement Communities: Sustaining Catholic Worker Community and Service', in H. Flam and D. King (eds.), *Emotions and Social Movements* (New York: Routledge, 2005), p. 138 and J.M. Jasper, 'Constructing Indignation: Anger Dynamics in Protest Movements', *Emotion Review*, 6 (2014), 208–13 at p. 209.

7. B.H. Rosenwein, 'Problems and Methods in the History of Emotions', *Passions in Context*, 1 (2010), 1–32 at p. 21.

8. Phillips, 'Class and Industrial Relations in Britain', pp. 52–73.

9. D. Kelliher, 'Solidarity and Sexuality: Lesbians and Gays Support the Miners 1984–5', *History Workshop Journal*, 77 (2014), 240–62 at pp. 248–52.

10. B.H. Rosenwein, 'Worrying about Emotions in History', *American Historical Review*, 107 (2002), 821–45 (pp. 842–5) and Rosenwein, 'Problems and Methods', 1–32.

11. Rosenwein, 'Worrying about Emotions in History', p. 842.

12. R. Clifford, 'Emotions and Gender in Oral History: Narrating Italy's 1968', *Modern Italy*, 17 (2012), 209–21 at p. 211.

13. Featherstone, *Solidarity*, p. 246.

14. Kevin, interview with the author, The Casa, Liverpool, 12 July 2017 and J. Belchem, *Irish, Catholic and Scouse: The History of the Liverpool-Irish, 1800–1940* (Liverpool: Liverpool University Press, 2007), pp. 27–55.

15. Kevin Bilsborrow, interview with Bill Hunter, 1995–8, www.billhunterweb.org.uk/interviews/History_as_Told.htm (accessed 3 June 2019).

16. *The Flickering Flame*, dir. Ken Loach (Parallax Pictures, AMIP, BBC, La Sept Arte, 1996).

17. Carol (pseudonym), interview with the author, The Casa, Liverpool, 21 July 2017.

18. P. Ayers, 'Work, Culture and Gender: The Making of Masculinities in Post-War Liverpool', *Labour History Review*, 69 (2004), 153–67 at pp. 161–2.

19. Turnbull and Wass, 'The Greatest Game No More', pp. 489–94.

20. E.K. Kelan, 'Gender Logic and (Un)doing Gender at Work', *Gender Work and Organization*, 17 (2010), 174–94.

21. Warwick, Modern Records Centre (MRC), MSS.126/BM/3/1/4/2, 'Liverpool: The Dockers Fight Back!', Papers of Bill Morris, Lord Morris of Handsworth, OJ (b.1938),

trade union leader and B. Hunter, *They Knew Why They Fought: Unofficial Struggles and Leadership on the Docks 1945–1989* (London: Index Books, 1994).

22. T.J. Scheff, *Bloody Revenge: Emotions, Nationalism and War* (Boulder, CO: Westview Press, 1994), p. 3.

23. Micky Tighe, interview with Bill Hunter, 1995–8, www.billhunterweb.org.uk /interviews/History_as_Told.htm (accessed 3 June 2019).

24. Ted Woods, interview with Bill Hunter, 1995–8, www.billhunterweb.org.uk /interviews/History_as_Told.htm (accessed 3 June 2019).

25. McIvor, *Working Lives*, pp. 91–2 and 163–5.

26. Kevin, interview with the author, The Casa, Liverpool, 12 July 2017.

27. Carol (pseudonym), interview with the author, The Casa, Liverpool, 21 July 2017.

28. Kevin, interview with the author, The Casa, Liverpool, 12 July 2017.

29. M. Kerr, *The People of Ship Street* (London: Routledge, 1958), pp. 40–51.

30. Ayers, 'Work, Culture and Gender', pp. 161–2, Kevin, interview with the author, The Casa, Liverpool, 12 July 2017 and Carol (pseudonym), interview with the author, The Casa, Liverpool, 21 July 2017.

31. B. Anderson, *Imagined Communities: Reflections on the Origin and Spread of Nationalism*, rev. ed. (London: Verso Books, 2006), p. 6.

32. M. Lavalette and J. Kennedy, *Solidarity on the Waterfront: The Liverpool Lock Out of 1995/96* (Birkenhead: Liver Press, 1996) pp. 1–2, 39–41.

33. Lavalette and Kennedy, *Solidarity on the Waterfront*, pp. 1–2.

34. Bob Ritchie, interview with Bill Hunter, 1995–8, www.billhunterweb.org.uk /interviews/History_as_Told.htm (accessed 3 June 2019).

35. Lavalette and Kennedy, *Solidarity on the Waterfront*, p. 28 and P. Dorey, 'Weakening the Trade Unions, One Step at a Time: The Thatcher Governments' Strategy for the Reform of Trade-Union Law, 1979–1984', *Historical Studies in Industrial Relations*, 37 (2016), 169–200 (pp. 177 and 184).

36. B. Towers, *Waterfront Blues: The Rise and Fall of Liverpool's Dockland* (Lancaster: Carnegie Publishing, 2011), pp. 253–4, 286–9.

37. Lavalette and Kennedy, *Solidarity on the Waterfront*, pp. 20–23.

38. T. Lane, *Liverpool: City of the Sea* (Liverpool: Liverpool University Press, 1997), p. 25.

39. G. Taylor, 'The Dynamics of Labour Relations at the Port of Liverpool, 1967–1989', unpublished PhD thesis (Manchester Metropolitan University, 2012), pp. 158–241.

40. Kevin, interview with the author, The Casa, Liverpool, 12 July 2017.

41. Taylor, 'The Dynamics of Labour Relations at the Port of Liverpool, 1967–1989', pp. 141–2.

42. Towers, *Waterfront Blues*, pp. 284–9.

43. Terry Southers, interview with Bill Hunter, 1995–8, www.billhunterweb.org.uk /interviews/History_as_Told.htm (accessed 3 June 2019).

44. Bob Ritchie, interview with Bill Hunter, 1995–8, www.billhunterweb.org.uk /interviews/History_as_Told.htm (accessed 3 June 2019).

45. Kevin, interview with the author, The Casa, Liverpool, 12 July 2017.

46. M. Weiss, 'Introduction: Fear and Its Opposites in the History of Emotions', in M. Laffan and M. Weiss (eds.), *Facing Fear: The History of Emotion in Global Perspective* (Princeton, NJ: Princeton University Press, 2012), pp. 1–9.

47. *The Flickering Flame*, dir. Ken Loach.

48. Marren, *We Shall Not Be Moved*, p. 213.

49. Kevin Robinson, interview with Bill Hunter, 1995–8, www.billhunterweb.org.uk /interviews/History_as_Told.htm (accessed 3 June 2019).

50. Ted Woods, interview with Bill Hunter, 1995–8, www.billhunterweb.org.uk /interviews/History_as_Told.htm (accessed 3 June 2019) and Frank Lannigan, interview with Bill Hunter, 1995–8, www.billhunterweb.org.uk/interviews/History _as_Told.htm (accessed 3 June 2019).

51. Lavalette and Kennedy, *Solidarity on the Waterfront*, pp. 39–43.

52. Carol (pseudonym), interview with the author, The Casa, Liverpool, 21 July 2017.

53. Kevin, interview with the author, 12 July 2017.

54. M. Clua-Losada, 'Solidarity, Global Restructuring and Deregulation: The Liverpool Dockers' Dispute 1995–98', unpublished doctoral thesis (University of York, 2010), pp. 150, 156–61, 168–70, 174–7.

55. Frank Lannigan, interview with Bill Hunter, 1995–8, www.billhunterweb.org.uk /interviews/History_as_Told.htm (accessed 3 June 2019).

56. Jasper, 'Constructing Indignation', p. 209.

57. *Writing the Wrongs*, dir. Solon Papadopoulos (Planet Wild, 1999).

58. Lavalette and Kennedy, *Solidarity on the Waterfront*, p. 77.

59. *Dockers*, dir. Bill Anderson (Parallax Pictures, 1999).

60. Andy Dwyer, interview with Bill Hunter, 1995–8, www.billhunterweb.org.uk /interviews/History_as_Told.htm (accessed 3 June 2019).

61. Carol (pseudonym), interview with the author, The Casa, Liverpool, 21 July 2017.

62. Jasper, 'Constructing Indignation', pp. 208–13.

63. Sue Mitchell and Doreen McNally, interview with Bill Hunter, 1995–8, www.billhunterweb.org.uk/interviews/History_as_Told.htm (accessed 3 June 2019).

64. Carol (pseudonym), interview with the author, 21 July 2017 and C. Stephenson and J. Spence, 'Pies and Essays: Women Writing through the British 1984–1985 Coal Miners' Strike', *Gender, Place and Culture*, 20 (2013), 218–35.

65. Lavalette and Kennedy, *Solidarity on the Waterfront*, p. 47.

66. Rosenwein, 'Problems and Methods', p. 20.

67. '"Me on a Picket Line!" (Cathy Dwyer, 21 Nov 1995)', Labournet, www.labournet .net/docks2/9511/cathy.htm (accessed 3 June 2019).

68. MRC, 601/R/20/2/3, 'Dockers Charter, no. 2, Dec 1995', p. 3, The Socialist Party (formerly the Revolutionary Socialist League, Militant Tendency and Militant Labour).

69. Kevin, interview with the author, The Casa, Liverpool, 12 July 2017.

70. D. Cantor and E. Ramsden, 'Introduction', in D. Cantor and E. Ramsden (eds.), *Stress, Shock, and Adaptation in the Twentieth Century* (Rochester: Boydell & Brewer, 2014), pp. 1–18.

71. Kevin, interview with the author, The Casa, Liverpool, 12 July 2017.

72. T. Dixon, *Weeping Britannia: A Portrait of a Nation in Tears* (Oxford: Oxford University Press, 2015), p. 7.

73. *The Flickering Flame*, dir. Ken Loach.

74. Carol (pseudonym), interview with the author, The Casa, Liverpool, 21 July 2017.

75. MRC, 601/R/20/2/3, 'Dockers Charter, no. 2, Dec 1995', p. 3, The Socialist Party (formerly the Revolutionary Socialist League, Militant Tendency and Militant Labour).

76. 'Casualisation. Dockers Prove Charges', Labournet, www.labournet.net/docks2/9605/CASUAL.HTM (accessed 3 June 2019).

77. 'Speech by Bill Morris, Gen. Secretary of T&GWU, to Liverpool Dockers, 14 March 1996', Labournet, www.labournet.net/docks2/9608/MORRIS.HTM (accessed 3 June 2019).

78. Carol (pseudonym), interview with the author, The Casa, Liverpool, 21 July 2017 and MRC, MSS.126/BM/3/1/4/10, John Pilger, 'They Never Walk Alone', Papers of Bill Morris, Lord Morris of Handsworth, OJ (b. 1938), trade union leader.

79. M. Clua-Losada, 'Solidarity, Global Restructuring and Deregulation', p. 107 and A. Murray, *The T&G Story: A History of the Transport and General Workers' Union 1922–2007* (London: Lawrence and Wishart, 2008), pp. 174–9, 184.

80. Bill Morris, 'Union Dues', *The Guardian*, 7 December 1996, p. 94 and MRC, MSS.126/BM/3/1/4/15, 'Setting the Record Straight', T&G Record February/March 1997, p. 4, Papers of Bill Morris, Lord Morris of Handsworth, OJ. (b. 1938), trade union leader.

81. MRC, MSS.126/BM/3/1/4/15, Merseyside Port Shop Stewards Response to 'Setting the Record Straight', 9 April 1997, Papers of Bill Morris, Lord Morris of Handsworth, OJ. (b. 1938), trade union leader.

82. Jean Fox, 'The Rats, the Weasels, the Snakes! ... How Can They Do It to Us?', Labournet, www.labournet.net/docks2/9710/FOX.HTM (accessed 3 June 2019) and Bob Ritchie, interview with Bill Hunter, 1995–8, www.billhunterweb.org.uk/interviews/History_as_Told.htm (accessed 3 June 2019).

83. Kevin, interview with the author, 12 July 2017 and Carol (pseudonym), interview with the author, 21 July 2017.

84. M. Castells, *Networks of Outrage and Hope: Social Movements in the Internet Age* (Malden, MA: Polity Press, 2012), p. 15.

85. 'Internationalism Is about Our Only Hope (Richie Gerrard at Seaforth, 20 November 1995)', Labournet, www.labournet.net/docks2/9511/gerrard.htm (accessed 3 June 2019) and C. Carter et al., 'The Polyphonic Spree: The Case of the Liverpool Dockers', *Industrial Relations Journal*, 34 (2003), 290–304.

86. N. Castree, 'Geographic Scale and Grass-Roots Internationalism: The Liverpool Dock Dispute, 1995–1998', *Economic Geography*, 76 (2000), 272–92 (p. 283).

87. B. Marren, *We Shall Not Be Moved*, pp. 219–22.

88. 'Merseyside Port Shop Stewards Press Release', Labournet, www.labournet.net/docks2/9709/PREREL.HTM (accessed 3 June 2019).

89. MRC, MSS.159/4/557/2, ITF Dockers' Section Steering Committee, 27 February 1997, International Transport Workers' Federation, Dockers and Portworkers, 1996–8.

90. Kevin, interview with the author, The Casa, Liverpool, 12 July 2017.

91. Carol (pseudonym), interview with the author, The Casa, Liverpool, 21 July 2017 and P. Bradley and C. Knight (eds.), *Another World Is Possible: How the Liverpool Dockers Launched a Global Movement* (London: Radical Anthropology Group, 2004), http://radicalanthropologygroup.org/reading/all (accessed 3 June 2019).

92. B. Anderson, *Imagined Communities*, p. 6.

93. MRC, 601/D/2/4/5, Letter from Merseyside Port Shop Stewards, 'Liverpool Dockworkers Final Settlement', The Socialist Party (formerly the Revolutionary Socialist League, Militant Tendency and Militant Labour).

94. MRC, MSS.126/BM/3/1/4/21, Copy of the final settlement, February 1998, Papers of Bill Morris, Lord Morris of Handsworth, OJ (b. 1938), trade union leader.

95. MRC 601/D/2/4/5, The Liverpool Dockers and Stevedores Co-Operative, 'The Initiative Factory', The Socialist Party (formerly the Revolutionary Socialist League, Militant Tendency and Militant Labour), p. 14.

96. P. Shennan, 'Save The Casa', *Liverpool Echo*, 19 January 2015, www.liverpoolecho .co.uk/news/liverpool-news/save-casa-ex-echo-writer-8475662 (accessed 3 June 2019).

97. A. Mah, *Port Cities*, pp. 127–33.

98. Kevin, interview with the author, The Casa, Liverpool, 12 July 2017.

References

Primary sources

Andy Dwyer, interview with Bill Hunter, 1995–8, www.billhunterweb
.org.uk/interviews/History_as_Told.htm (accessed 3 June 2019).

Bill Morris, 'Union Dues', *The Guardian*, 7 December 1996.

Bob Ritchie, interview with Bill Hunter, 1995–8, www.billhunterweb.org
.uk/interviews/History_as_Told.htm (accessed 3 June 2019).

Carol (pseudonym), interview with the author, The Casa, Liverpool, 21
July 2017.

'Casualisation. Dockers Prove Charges', Labournet, www.labournet.net
/docks2/9605/CASUAL.HTM (accessed 3 June 2019).

Dockers, dir. Bill Anderson (Parallax Pictures, 1999).

Frank Lannigan, interview with Bill Hunter, 1995–8, www.billhunterweb
.org.uk/interviews/History_as_Told.htm (accessed 3 June 2019).

'Internationalism Is about Our Only Hope' (Richie Gerrard at Seaforth, 20
November 1995)', Labournet, www.labournet.net/docks2/9511/gerrard
.htm (accessed 3 June 2019).

Jean Fox, 'The Rats, the Weasels, the Snakes! … How Can They Do It to
Us?', Labournet, www.labournet.net/docks2/9710/FOX.HTM
(accessed 3 June 2019).

Kevin, interview with the author, The Casa, Liverpool, 12 July 2017.

Kevin Bilsborrow, interview with Bill Hunter, 1995–8, www.billhunter-
web.org.uk/interviews/History_as_Told.htm (accessed 3 June 2019).

Kevin Robinson, interview with Bill Hunter, 1995–8, www.billhunterweb
.org.uk/interviews/History_as_Told.htm (accessed 3 June 2019).

'"Me on a Picket Line!" (Cathy Dwyer, 21 Nov 1995)', Labournet,
www.labournet.net/docks2/9511/cathy.htm (accessed 3 June 2019).

'Merseyside Port Shop Stewards Press Release', Labournet,
www.labournet.net/docks2/9709/PREREL.HTM (accessed 3
June 2019).

Micky Tighe, interview with Bill Hunter, 1995–8, www.billhunterweb
.org.uk/interviews/History_as_Told.htm (accessed 3 June 2019).

P. Bradley and C. Knight (eds.), *Another World Is Possible: How the
Liverpool Dockers Launched a Global Movement* (London: Radical
Anthropology Group, 2004), http://radicalanthropologygroup.org
/reading/all (accessed 3 June 2019)

'Speech by Bill Morris, Gen. Secretary of T&GWU, to Liverpool Dockers,
14 March 1996', Labournet, www.labournet.net/docks2/9608/MORRIS
.HTM (accessed 3 June 2019).

Sue Mitchell and Doreen McNally, interview with Bill Hunter, 1995–8, www.billhunterweb.org.uk/interviews/History_as_Told.htm (accessed 3 June 2019).

Ted Woods, interview with Bill Hunter, 1995–8, www.billhunterweb.org .uk/interviews/History_as_Told.htm (accessed 3 June 2019).

Terry Southers, interview with Bill Hunter, 1995–8, www.billhunterweb .org.uk/interviews/History_as_Told.htm (accessed 3 June 2019).

The Flickering Flame, dir. Ken Loach (Parallax Pictures, AMIP, BBC, La Sept Arte, 1996).

Warwick, Modern Records Centre, MSS.126/BM/3/1/4/2, 'Liverpool: The Dockers Fight Back!', Papers of Bill Morris, Lord Morris of Handsworth, OJ (b. 1938), trade union leader.

—— 601/R/20/2/3, 'Dockers Charter, no. 2, Dec 1995', The Socialist Party (formerly the Revolutionary Socialist League, Militant Tendency and Militant Labour).

—— MSS.126/BM/3/1/4/10, John Pilger, 'They Never Walk Alone', Papers of Bill Morris, Lord Morris of Handsworth, OJ (b. 1938), trade union leader.

—— MSS.126/BM/3/1/4/15, 'Setting the Record Straight', T&G Record February/March 1997, p. 4, Papers of Bill Morris, Lord Morris of Handsworth, OJ. (b. 1938), trade union leader.

—— MSS.126/BM/3/1/4/15, Merseyside Port Shop Stewards Response to 'Setting the Record Straight', 9 April 1997, Papers of Bill Morris, Lord Morris of Handsworth, OJ. (b. 1938), trade union leader.

—— MSS.159/4/557/2, ITF Dockers' Section Steering Committee, 27 February 1997, International Transport Workers' Federation, Dockers and Portworkers, 1996–8.

—— 601/D/2/4/5, Letter from Merseyside Port Shop Stewards, 'Liverpool Dockworkers Final Settlement', The Socialist Party (formerly the Revolutionary Socialist League, Militant Tendency and Militant Labour).

—— MSS.126/BM/3/1/4/21, Copy of the final settlement, February 1998, Papers of Bill Morris, Lord Morris of Handsworth, OJ (b. 1938), trade union leader.

—— 601/D/2/4/5, The Liverpool Dockers and Stevedores Co-Operative, 'The Initiative Factory', The Socialist Party (formerly the Revolutionary Socialist League, Militant Tendency and Militant Labour).

Writing the Wrongs, dir. Solon Papadopoulos (Planet Wild, 1999).

Secondary sources

Anderson, B., *Imagined Communities: Reflections on the Origin and Spread of Nationalism*, rev. ed. (London: Verso Books, 2006).

Ayers, P., 'Work, Culture and Gender: The Making of Masculinities in Post-War Liverpool', *Labour History Review*, 69 (2004), 153–67.

Belchem, J., *Irish, Catholic and Scouse: The History of the Liverpool-Irish, 1800–1940* (Liverpool: Liverpool University Press, 2007).

Cantor, D., and Ramsden, E., 'Introduction', in D. Cantor and E. Ramsden (eds.), *Stress, Shock, and Adaptation in the Twentieth Century* (Rochester, NY: Boydell & Brewer, 2014), pp. 1–18.

Carter, C., Cless, S., Hogan, J. and Kornberger, M., 'The Polyphonic Spree: The Case of the Liverpool Dockers', *Industrial Relations Journal*, 34 (2003), 290–304.

Castells, M., *Networks of Outrage and Hope: Social Movements in the Internet Age* (Malden, MA: Polity Press, 2012).

Castree, N., 'Geographic Scale and Grass-Roots Internationalism: The Liverpool Dock Dispute, 1995–1998', *Economic Geography*, 76 (2000), 272–92.

Clifford, R., 'Emotions and Gender in Oral History: Narrating Italy's 1968', *Modern Italy*, 17 (2012), 209–21.

Clua-Losada, M., 'Solidarity, Global Restructuring and Deregulation: The Liverpool Dockers' Dispute 1995–98', unpublished doctoral thesis (University of York, 2010).

Dixon, T., *Weeping Britannia: A Portrait of a Nation in Tears* (Oxford: Oxford University Press, 2015).

Dorey, P., 'Weakening the Trade Unions, One Step at a Time: The Thatcher Governments' Strategy for the Reform of Trade-Union Law, 1979–1984', *Historical Studies in Industrial Relations*, 37 (2016), 169–200.

Featherstone, D., *Solidarity: Hidden Histories and Geographies of Internationalism* (London: Bloomsbury, 2012).

Hunter, B., *They Knew Why They Fought: Unofficial Struggles and Leadership on the Docks 1945–1989* (London: Index Books, 1994).

Jasper, J.M., 'Constructing Indignation: Anger Dynamics in Protest Movements', *Emotion Review*, 6 (2014), 208–13.

Kelan, E.K., 'Gender Logic and (Un)doing Gender at Work', *Gender Work and Organization*, 17 (2010), 174–94.

Kelliher, D., 'Solidarity and Sexuality: Lesbians and Gays Support the Miners 1984–5', *History Workshop Journal*, 77 (2014), 240–62.

Kerr, M., *The People of Ship Street* (London: Routledge, 1958).

Lane, T., *Liverpool: City of the Sea* (Liverpool: Liverpool University Press, 1997).

Lavalette, M., and Kennedy, J., *Solidarity on the Waterfront: The Liverpool Lock Out of 1995/96* (Birkenhead: Liver Press, 1996).

Mah, A., *Port Cities and Global Legacies: Urban Identity, Waterfront Work and Radicalism* (Basingstoke: Springer, 2014).

Marren, B., *We Shall Not Be Moved: How Liverpool's Working Class Fought Redundancies, Closures and Cuts in the Age of Thatcher* (Manchester: Manchester University Press, 2016).

McIvor, A., *Working Lives: Work in Britain since 1945* (London: Bloomsbury, 2013).

Murray, Andrew, *The T&G Story: A History of the Transport and General Workers' Union 1922–2007* (London: Lawrence and Wishart, 2008).

Phillips, J., 'Class and Industrial Relations in Britain: The "Long" Mid-Century and the Case of Port Transport, c. 1920–70', *Twentieth Century British History* 16, 1 (2005), 52–73.

Rosenwein, B.H., 'Worrying about Emotions in History', *American Historical Review* 107 (2002), 821–45.

——, 'Problems and Methods in the History of Emotions', *Passions in Context*, 1 (2010), 1–32.

Scheff, T.J., *Bloody Revenge: Emotions, Nationalism and War* (Boulder, CO: Routledge, 1994).

Shennan, P., 'Save The Casa', *Liverpool Echo*, 19 January 2015, www.liverpoolecho.co.uk/news/liverpool-news/save-casa-ex-echo -writer-8475662 (accessed 3 June 2019).

Stephenson, C., and Spence, J., 'Pies and Essays: Women Writing through the British 1984–1985 Coal Miners' Strike', *Gender, Place and Culture*, 20 (2013), 218–35.

Summers-Effler, E., 'The Emotional Significance of Solidarity for Social Movement Communities: Sustaining Catholic Worker Community and Service', in H. Flam and D. King (eds.), *Emotions and Social Movements* (New York: Routledge, 2005), pp. 135–49.

Taylor, G., 'The Dynamics of Labour Relations at the Port of Liverpool, 1967–1989', unpublished doctoral thesis (Manchester Metropolitan University, 2012).

Towers, B., *Waterfront Blues: The Rise and Fall of Liverpool's Dockland* (Lancaster: Carnegie Publishing, 2011).

Turnbull, P., and Wass, V., 'The Greatest Game No More: Redundant Dockers and the Demise of Dock Work', *Work, Employment & Society*, 8 (1994), 487–506.

Virdee, S., *Racism, Class and the Racialized Outsider* (Basingstoke: Palgrave Macmillan, 2014).

Weiss, M., 'Introduction: Fear and Its Opposites in the History of Emotions', in M. Laffan and M. Weiss (eds.), *Facing Fear: The History of Emotion in Global Perspective* (Princeton, NJ: Princeton University Press, 2012).

Part II

POWER AND PLACE-MAKING: CLASS, HYGIENE AND RACE IN THE BRITISH EMPIRE

Chapter 5

White pride, male anger and the shame of poverty: gendered emotions and the construction of white working-class identity in interwar Southern Rhodesia

Nicola Ginsburgh

Colonialism relies upon the power to deploy essentializing categories which reduce diverse and complex societies into relatively homogeneous and oppositional racial groups. Yet across the British Empire, imperial and settler ideologues proselytized their conviction in the absoluteness of racial difference while gripped by an acute doubt regarding the ability to maintain and perform such difference. As Harald Fischer-Tine and Christine Whyte have argued, despite prevalent images of omniscient and all-powerful colonial states, the British Empire was largely structured by anxiety, fear and embarrassment.[1] Historians have explored colonial and settler anxieties of indigenous rebellion and defiance, disease and contagion, mental and physical breakdown and of the failure to maintain racial boundaries essential to colonial rule, as well as the affective strategies employed to allay such fears and reinforce colonial categories. Dane Kennedy has explored these phenomena with regards to Southern Rhodesia and Kenya, arguing that prestige functioned as an emotional amulet which whites used to perform their difference from Africans.[2] In considering the power of Native Commissioners to punish Africans, Alison Shutt has argued that manners, etiquette and emotions were embedded in expressions and contests of social and political power. Native Commissioners portrayed themselves as sober, rational and detached while Africans were depicted as ill-mannered and emotional.[3]

Turning our attention to white worker communities offers a unique lens through which to explore the classed, racial and gendered components of colonial anxieties, and the role of emotions in projecting difference as well as the impact of economic insecurity and poverty on experienced and expressed emotions. In Southern Rhodesia, as well as receiving better job opportunities, wages, housing, education and healthcare than the African population, white workers manufactured a pride in their white skin to proclaim racial difference so that even the poorest, most unskilled and uneducated whites could feel distinguished. Certainly, in order to maintain the racial boundaries fundamental to settler rule, white workers had to *feel* superior to Africans.[4] Yet, as Deborah Posel has indicated in relation to Apartheid South Africa, rather than white skin being an uncomplicated source of pride and content, racial ideologies often provoked psychological distress for white workers, who struggled to reconcile their supposed racial superiority with their class status and how they were negatively perceived in broader settler society.[5] In the first decades of white settlement, lower-class whites were both feared and repulsed by elite white settler society, variously seen as self-important and a rowdy mob capable of infecting Africans with ideas of trade unionism and collective action against employers. They were also regarded as more susceptible to racial degeneration and likely to encourage the blurring of racial boundaries. The tensions between self-identification as inherently superior and the reality of low-paid work and relative poverty could be a source of profound dislocation. White skin could offer a sense of pride and status but also profound anxiety over racial status.

This chapter explores how colonial anxieties shaped white racial identities in a period of white worker weakness and increased precariousness in Southern Rhodesia. White workers employed numerous emotional strategies to create a sense of shared community, police white worker behaviours and overcome the shame induced by poverty. The Rhodesian Railway Workers Union's trade union journal, the *Rhodesian Railway Review*, and parliamentary debates of the Rhodesia Labour Party provide insight into aspects of white working-class identity during this period. However, they tend to exclude female perspectives. By contrasting these male-dominated trade union sources with white female-authored memoirs, this chapter demonstrates how pride, shame, anger and contentment were differentially expressed and wielded by white men and women. It contends that class, race and gender influenced emotional expression and that, in turn, emotions were used to create loyalty within social groups and mark others as outsiders. White workers' fraught relationship to the settler colonial state and their idiosyncratic positionality within the settler colonial structure shaped their emotional expression as well as their power to control the emotional expression of others. The chapter ends with a consideration of how particular emotions were projected onto Africans and white women to reassert established hierarchies.

Background to Southern Rhodesian white labour

From the turn of the twentieth century, the steady growth of mining and railway industries across Southern Rhodesia brought a steady stream of white migrants from Britain and South Africa. Yet the bulk of the territory's unskilled labour needs were met by coerced African labour. In many fledgling industries, profitability rested on the super-exploitation of Africans who toiled in oppressive, violent conditions.[6] White workers fiercely struggled to protect their monopoly over skilled work and feared undercutting from low-paid African labour. Despite this relative privilege, in the first decades of settlement white workers laboured under harsh conditions and struggles to establish trade union organizations were met with fierce resistance from management.[7]

The position of white workers was strengthened with the outbreak of the First World War. As shortages of skilled white labour deepened, a lightning strike of firemen at Bulawayo in 1916 saw the men gain an extra shilling a day, and the Rhodesian Railway Workers' Union (RRWU) was established in the same year. Two successful strikes in 1919 and 1920 saw railway workers secure a 25 per cent raise and eight-hour day and white trade unions gradually proliferated across the colony.[8] Although the RRWU had sought to unite European men from all grades, a rival craft union, the Amalgamated Engineers Union, was successfully established in 1916 and proved more attractive to most of the skilled workers on the railways and mines.[9] Yet by the 1920s white trade unions were weakened as the post-war slump intensified and unemployment steadily rose.[10] For Rhodesian rail workers, 1922 saw reductions in pay and in the cost of living allowance, an increase in working hours and the removal of the eight-hour working day. These events form the context for the first half of this chapter. The second half focuses on the Great Depression as conditions for white workers worsened and fears of unemployment and economic degradation flared.

Pride in wage labour

Emotions, Barbara Rosenwein contends, result from judgements made about whether something will be pleasurable, painful or impact upon us negatively or positively but are also the product of cultural practices, morals and language. As such, particular social groups – including trade unions – have their own 'systems of feeling' and rules for the expression of emotions.[11] This chapter shows how white workers' emotional expression was shaped by bourgeois imperial notions of masculinity and femininity and was rooted in white workers' antagonistic relationship both to their white employers and the African majority. It shows how white trade unions attempted to proscribe and encourage particular forms of emotional expression, and that they wielded emotions to discipline those who were deemed to be failing to meet 'white' standards.

Expressed emotions were central to the ways in which white workers imagined themselves as a distinct community. Despite the fundamental heterogeneity of Southern Rhodesia's white labouring class – divided by skill, gender, occupation and nationality – emotions of pride, shame, anger and empathy created a sense of shared identity and experience based on perceived collective injustices which offered a route to subsume these divisions. In RRWU's journal the *Review*, different classes and racial groups were imagined as mediums for different emotions, which reflected perceived and actual threats to white worker status. Emotional states marked class and racial boundaries as well as trade union identity. Thus, while the phrase 'happiness and contentment' was repeatedly attached to active participation in the RRWU and Rhodesia Labour Party, Africans and upper-class whites were presented as sources of distress – parasitical figures that drew upon the strength and productive capacity of the white worker.[12]

White labouring men invested in a hypermasculine identity which relied heavily on their occupations and pride in work. This was contrasted with African manual labouring, which was seen as unskilled, repetitive work in which Africans took no care or pride. For white male workers, respectability was accrued by a relative education and skill, a claim to pioneering spirit, sobriety and provision for dependants. But it was the feelings of pride in 'white work' which underpinned a shareable, amorphous white worker identity. Certainly, as Jon Lunn has demonstrated, where white men undertook unskilled or semi-skilled work, they redefined the work as 'skilled' in their own minds in order to feel this sense of pride and thus differentiate themselves from Africans.[13] For white male workers, manual work was not something to be ashamed of, or something that only non-whites did, but something in which to take pride, even if the middle classes and white-collar workers perceived such blue-collar work as defiling. As one poem printed in the *Review* asserted:

to wish is the play of an office boy:
To do is the job of a man.[14]

These white workers both borrowed from dominant constructions of masculinity and challenged and reformulated their own sense of manliness through work. This labouring ideal was positioned as the authentic expression of maleness.

Those who remained un-unionized were castigated as 'nons' and ridiculed as lazy and effeminate workshy cowards. One article began with the assertion that:

> If you haven't got manhood enough to be concerned with the comfort and welfare of your own family, then do not read this article. If you haven't got the backbone enough to be a free man in a free country, then stop reading right here, for this article is intended for the real he-men, who do not shiver in their boots when the Roadmaster passes; men who are men enough to fight their own fights; men who are not too cowardly to demand a wage sufficient to properly care for their families whether the railroad officials like it or not.[15]

Manliness was claimed through union activity and taking a stand against management; union successes were explained through the actions of 'men – white men who were not prepared to knuckle down to it'.[16] One letter to the *Review* explained that intimidation and the blacklist had lowered attendance at branch meetings but went on to encourage men to overcome these fears, to 'brace up ... make a firm stand and come out boldly as one solid body of workers ... In conclusion brothers, "be white."'[17] For these workers, being white was about experiencing and fighting against injustices; it was about courage and mastering and overcoming the fear of failure and of employer reprisals. 'Nons' and those who failed to support the trade union were presented in contrast to this bravery and portrayed as slaves to fear.

Maintaining racial difference took on a pressing significance for workers who worked alongside Africans. The gold miner H.J. Lucas's reflections upon his early experiences show how emotional and psychological distance from African workers was maintained despite physical closeness:

> many smallworkers did not employ an assistant and in the remote parts might not see a white man for a month or more at a stretch ... it was a lonely life for the white man. He could not sit and gossip with the Africans but often of an evening he would watch the boys laughing and gossiping around their fires and wish he could join in.[18]

On the railways there was particular concern over gangers – railway workers who looked after a particular stretch of line and were often stationed many miles away from established areas of white settlement. The *Review* bemoaned the position of the ganger as 'practically an outcast, who knows no joy of human society'.[19] Antony Croxton, an ex-railwayman, described the ganger's outposts in the 'heavy rain in the lonely forest, with lions, leopards, elephants and other wildlife as neighbours and only a momentary glimpse of the infrequent train [which] induced nerves and depression'.[20] The Africans who worked under the ganger are erased in this picture. Loneliness and self-imposed ostracism seemed preferable to fraternization that could endanger the respectability of white workers and throw the racialized performance of labour into disarray.

Shame was also particularly important in the policing of racial boundaries. Those who appeared to be offering support for certain non-white organizations were publicly castigated. In 1927 a European railwayman signed a petition in support of an Indian-led campaign to remove a European Market Master from his post after he had called Indians 'Coolies'. The *Review* joked that 'our comrade must have come off a long and tiresome shift and signed the petition without realising what he signed'.[21] Solidarity beyond the boundaries of whiteness was unthinkable, and the European railwayman who crossed this line was publicly ridiculed in the pages of the union journal for providing support. In this sense, not only did the platform serve the function of policing white workers' behaviour, it also acted as a warning to others: loyalty must only be given to other white workers.

Pride and domesticity

White male workers rallied against the employment of Africans in semiskilled and skilled work, but they also tried to prevent white women from entering the ranks of formal wage labour. White male workers generally opposed the employment of white women not only on the basis that women represented a form of cheap labour which threatened to undercut their own wages but also because they represented a psychological threat. White women's wage labour undermined the ability of men to prove their manliness by being the sole breadwinner. The RRWU and Rhodesia Labour Party (RLP) consistently argued that women should stick to their 'natural roles' in the home as mothers and wives. As one trade unionist put it, female wage labour endangered 'a most sacred law of nature that a father must provide food and all necessities of life for his family'.[22]

More generally, white women's presence in the colonies was envisioned as a calming force and natural corrective to the male excesses and general rowdiness which were seen to characterize early settler societies.[23] Cullen Gouldsbury, a keen observer of white Rhodesian society who wrote verse for the glory of Empire, surmised that white women were important 'to lessen drink, to tame the bachelor colonial', but stressed that their role was one which was essentially subordinate and passive, indeed 'hardly more than ornamental':

> to swish the skirt: to smile: to flirt,
> to captivate the detrimental! –
> To spend our cash, to cook our hash;
> To sew for us the sportive button,
>
> ...
>
> Yet still, we fear, the day draws near
> When women will no longer heed us,
> When beings in skirts will scorn our shirts,
> And bid the heathen savage feed us[24]

White women were encouraged to feel and express emotions in ways which supported existing gendered and racial hierarchies. Outside of the home and out of the control of their husbands, white women became a source of anxiety.

As homemakers, white women were required to maintain white standards in the domestic sphere and to provide a barrier between their children and corrupting racial influences.[25] They were encouraged to take pride in creating homes, producing children and investing in community activities, such as organizing dances or craft competitions.[26] White women were generally absent from white trade union journals. Articles directed at women usually reaffirmed social norms, addressing cooking skills or giving domestic tips. One poem in the *Review*, written by a white woman, described the position of railway wives in the 1920s:

> We knew it when we married him
> Some twenty years ago –
> That he would be away a lot,
> In fact he told us so,
> But the real truth we didn't guess,
> Not all... or even half –
>
> ...
>
> They have no hours, these railroad men,
> Their work is never done,
> They just remember that it's night
> When everyone goes home.
> We wives and mothers learn to smile,
> The young as well as old –

And keep the meat from burning up,
The beans from getting cold.

We go to church and club, alone,
To pictures, lectures too,
We rear the children, cook the meals
And pay the bills when due.
The youngsters get the whooping cough,
And measles, mumps and grippe –
We carry on both day and night,
And don't give up the ship.[27]

Women could feel pride in the labour of the home and motherhood by keeping a 'tight ship' and by struggling through loneliness and using ingenuity to stretch wages to cover household costs. To 'smile' and to 'flirt'; women were expected to manufacture an air of contentment to reassure the working man. Moreover, the process of investing status into these tasks of domesticity acted as a form of cognitive dissonance, manufacturing a sense of fulfilment to suppress dissatisfaction. Here, women's feelings of distress were accepted as a part of their daily experience, yet it was the endurance of these feelings of isolation and the suppression of emotions which was also valorized as a source of pride. Like the white male workers who laboured beside Africans, they were expected to promote emotional disengagement from the Africans they or their children were most likely to form bonds with – their domestic staff. Again, loneliness was lauded as a sign of differentiation; racial propriety meant one would rather endure and publicize the pain of being alone than engage friendliness or intimacy which could damage racial boundaries.

Mobilizations of shame

Lower-class whites never achieved the image of respectability, status and skill that they manufactured. In reality, a substantial disjuncture existed between idealized representations of white workers and the daily experiences of a heterogeneous social group who failed to maintain 'white standards'. Many workers in fact proved to be acute sources of embarrassment for the trade union bureaucracy. There were numerous complaints that rank-and-file members had failed to educate themselves, as well as concerns over sobriety, porous racial boundaries and the dubious racial status of some who identified as white. The desired respectable and masculine characteristics that labour organizations were attempting to project were not automatically possessed by all white male workers. The *Review* argued that white labour was 'entitled' to a 'standard of respect' but that a cross-section of workers from different social and industrial grades were endangering the reputation of the majority:

> The term 'common railway man' hurts the feelings of the great majority of railway workers, who are as respectable and noble-minded as any class in the land. If those members of our craft, who act in such a manner as to lower the status of railway men, would pause and think of the intense injury they are inflicting on themselves and all other railway workers.[28]

The consequences of this inability to educate oneself and attain respectability were not confined to the individual violating expected standards of whiteness but were recognized as a source of embarrassment and hurt for the white labouring class in its entirety. White workers were again encouraged to take pride and joy in their work: to see it as something that required fierce protection and to educate themselves in order to protect white workers' prestige.[29]

As many men increasingly failed to think and feel in 'white' ways, the RRWU encouraged women to use familial and gender ideologies to police male workers' behaviours. Women were encouraged to wield shame to discipline men into correct behaviours; they were directed to humiliate men who were unable to provide, who remained un-unionized or who did not pay union fees. In one such piece, a railwayman detailed how he had resisted joining RRWU until his wife had shamed him into doing so: 'she reproached me for letting other men fight her battles and the children's. We were not quarrelsome about it, but she clinched the argument when she said, hotly, one night: "do you want me to think my husband a cad, Jim?"'[30] The RRWU also suggested women should manage their husbands' finances, making sure they did not spend too much on drink.[31] The role of the railwayman's wife, according to the *Review*, was one of support, reproduction and regulation, all of which should enforce gendered norms.

Depression

These attempts to maintain a respectable white working-class identity based upon the skilled working man who provided for dependants were put under increasing strain as the Great Depression reverberated across the global economic system.[32] The settler administration effectively used the African population as a shock absorber to protect Europeans from economic strife, but white workers were not completely protected. While the numbers of whites registered as unemployed in the early 1920s had never reached 350, by September 1931 Bulawayo district alone noted 417 unemployed men and 600 dependants.[33] Decreasing traffic on the railways saw at least 1,600 railwaymen retrenched from 1930 to 1932 as the white workforce on the railways was reduced by around 25 per cent. Although retrenchment on the railways primarily targeted African workers, with the number of black workers falling from 18,492 in April 1930 to 7,898 just three years later in June 1933, unemployment was nonetheless conceptualized as a white, and specifically male, affliction.[34]

Southern Rhodesian approaches to poverty and unemployment were largely influenced by international debates surrounding 'poor whiteism'. Poor whiteism was fundamentally an ideological construction; a set of beliefs embedded in the association of poverty with miscegenation, racial decline and the inability of whites to live and rule in Africa.[35] Poor whiteism meant much more than material impoverishment. It signified a range of behavioural and racial defects. The Southern Rhodesian *Report on Unemployment* defined poor whites as 'men accustomed to and content with a very low standard of living' who lacked any sense of ambition or responsibility, and who preferred to live with continual assistance from the state. They continued that the poor white should be treated differently to the 'impoverished European' as it was 'by the standard of living, and the psychological traits, more than actual financial position, that the class is defined'.[36]

While accepting many dominant ideas about eugenics and poor whiteism, white worker organizations tried to recast discussions around unemployment and white poverty in order to reject stereotypes of sloth and protect the character of white workers. The RRWU and RLP argued that the numbers provided by unemployment registries could not be trusted, as the individual pride of white workers prevented many from openly admitting that they were unemployed and seeking government help.[37] Men and women who sought government relief were required to undergo a rigorous application process, which included providing statements to the unemployment officers and the Criminal Investigation Department followed by an interview, and the taking of fingerprints. Leading trade unionists argued that this 'criminalization' of the poor and the 'indignity' of the process of applying for relief was so demeaning that many Europeans would rather starve than go through it.[38] Negotiating wider assertions about poor whiteism, shame was used to dispute official unemployment statistics and was also held up as proof of lower-class respectability; that they would 'rather starve' than compromise their dignity was heralded as a testament to white workers' moral strength.

Yet this shame was expressed differently by men and women, and anxieties over poor whiteism had clearly gendered dimensions. For white labouring men, poverty was imagined as a process of emasculation. Not only did it remove the ability of men to provide for dependants, it also endangered the ways in which their racial and gendered identities were expressed through work. The *Review* noted with alarm how unemployment would lead Rhodesian whites to endure social debasement, writing that the unemployed men of South Africa 'must consort in slums with negroes and half castes to whose jeers and insolence he and his womenfolk especially are then subject'. This, they argued, led to white men selling liquor to Africans and white women forced into prostitution.[39] As a temporary measure, white male workers argued that unskilled work which was previously performed solely by Africans should be allocated to white men; these unskilled roles were subsequently reformulated as character building and sources of pride. White female employment was also reconfigured as a necessary *temporary* measure to prevent the shame of poverty and prevent Africans taking 'white' jobs.[40]

Despite trade union attempts to reconfigure emotional response to economic crisis, black peril anxieties flared as white women entered wage labour.[41] In 1928 one leading white trade unionist claimed that

> near the large towns there is scarcely a week goes by without hearing of a sexual offence being committed by natives and the white women of the towns are becoming more and more afraid of venturing outside the precincts of their own dwellings; indeed, it is hardly too much to say that even within their own houses they do not feel safe.[42]

The RLP and RRWU increasingly stressed the vulnerability of white women and children as they strove to mobilize sympathy for figures of white wretchedness. The *Review* remarked upon white children who walked around in the street barefooted.[43] RRWU described 'horrible dens ... insanitary conditions, families of ten wandering about the sanitary buckets, picking up crusts on account of inability to get sufficient rations from the Department'.[44] Images of white women and children, distressed and endangered, encouraged shared feelings of empathy and community, but also acted to emphasize white women's weakness as traditional gender roles came under threat.

Poverty and gendered shame

White women predominantly expressed anxieties over poverty through the idiom of the home, conspicuous consumption and 'fitting in' to white social life. Novelist Doris Lessing, who had moved to Southern Rhodesia with her family in 1925, recalled that her childhood friend, Cynthia, an impoverished white who lived by the railway line, confided in her one day her intense shame of having to buy fabrics from the Indian store. Cynthia lamented, 'it's so horrible to be poor. It's horrible to have people despising you'.[45] Daphne Anderson, a self-described 'poor-white', expressed acute anxiety over her clothing which she recognized visibly marked her as an outsider. At school she wore ill-fitting cast-offs: 'a blouse or a gym frock borrowed here and there from another's cupboard ... as a result of all this my inferiority complex threatened to overwhelm me and I no longer worked hard, feeling it would make no difference to my life and that no one really cared'.[46] Even as an adult this shame inhibited her participation in community functions: 'the real reason I refused invitations was that I did not possess a bathing suit or the most elementary clothes for outings ... [I] was determined not to make a fool of myself again'.[47]

Hylda Richards, a British middle-class migrant from Kent, detailed her experiences of the Depression in her autobiography *Next Year Will Be Better*. Hylda and her husband Tom had settled in Southern Rhodesia in the early 1920s to pursue a new life in tobacco farming. Yet their hopes of quickly establishing themselves as wealthy producers were dashed as the reality of the arduous and unpredictable nature of white agriculture set in. Attempting to 'wipe out a little of the awful sense of failure that rankled' her, Hylda turned her hand to master the domestic sphere where she produced an inedible cake and failed to complete basic laundry tasks. She recalled how she found her 'woollen socks covered with blackjacks and grass seeds like hedgehogs'. What disturbed her most, however, was the realization that 'I had been the washer [as] I would never trust woollen socks with the boys'. In response her 'temper raged' and she lamented, 'I was inefficient, foolish, criminally careless. I was no good. *I wish I were dead.*'[48] Such an acute sense of anger and self-loathing emerged from a complex of interrelated anxieties regarding the failure to reproduce British bourgeois culture and rapidly establish economic and domestic success in the colonies. It also reflected Hylda's deep discomfort with her dependency on African staff, whom she both despised and feared. Significantly, what these memoirs reveal is that both middle- and lower-class white women repeatedly expressed broader anxieties around poverty and economic failure through the language of domesticity.

Economic insecurity uprooted idealized gender roles but also deeply affected the nuclear family and interpersonal relationships. Emma Griffin's work on the emotional bonds of love – or their absence – in British working-class mother–child relationships explores how poverty and economic precariousness seeped into the core of Victorian family life. Working-class autobiographies demonstrate that bonds of familial love were neither universal nor static and that emotions of affection were deeply shaped by the material reality of poverty.[49] With regards to Southern Rhodesia, an edition of the *Review* from 1922 suggests that bonds of affection within the white family unit were often expressed through affirmations of idealized gender roles. When asked as a competition for the 'Children's Corner' of the *Review* 'which member of your family do you like best and why?', the responses of the children who wrote in were strikingly similar:

> *Ripe Fig*: 'I love my father because he teaches me boxing and my mother looks after my clothes'
>
> ...
>
> *Pleasant One*: 'I love my father best as he is the one who is working to provide us with food and clothing and he has such a gentle heart and forgiving spirit'
>
> ...
>
> *Buster*: 'I like my mother and father because she mends my clothes and my father buys me books'
>
> ...
>
> *'Jolly Joan'* ... likes her mother best: 'All my dainty dresses she *strached* and ironed for me. My meals I always find in good time and all other luxuries of comfort in general. Also correcting my manners so that I can be polite and ladylike. She very seldom has to correct me in my manners.'[50]

The emotions of familial love were expressed in highly gendered ways. This affection valorized male provision and female domesticity and rewarded kindness and forgiveness, but also recognized the role of white mothers in reproducing racial and gendered sensibilities.

In contrast to the bonds of affection recorded in the Children's Corner of the *Review*, Daphne Anderson's memoir, *The Toe-Rags*, provides a vivid depiction of strained and abusive parent–child relationships in a context of white poverty. Anderson's childhood memories of the Depression are characterized by emotional and material neglect inflicted by both her immediate and extended family. Notably, because of her parents' poverty, Anderson's servant, Jim, took what was deemed an inappropriate role in her upbringing: her relationship with her servant was so close Anderson's first language was not English, but Shona. In this context, familial material and emotional neglect encouraged the formation of meaningful affective bonds which crossed over the racial divide. Certainly, poverty was widely acknowledged as compromising white women's abilities to reproduce racial boundaries in the home.

As a young child Anderson was unaware of the perceived incongruous nature of her contact with her servant, but as she aged, she struggled with this emotional attachment. Anderson wrote that the affection she felt for Jim became tainted by fears that he could turn into a 'savage' and murder them, which in turn plunged her into an intense guilt for allowing such thoughts into her mind.[51] When Daphne's mother eventually abandoned her and her siblings, their father and aunt were forced to intervene to separate them from the servant, reintegrate them into white respectability and instruct them in the appropriate relationships and performances regarding Africans. Anderson, in other words, had to be instructed in shame, how to perform it and when to feel it. Moreover, these familial interventions appear to be motivated by a collective shame of having poor whites in the family, rather than any deep-rooted affection of the aunt or father for Daphne and her siblings. Nevertheless, Anderson's rehabilitation into white respectability and white modes of feeling was partially successful. As Anderson entered adulthood, she increasingly recognized the impropriety of the affection she held for her past servants, which consequently incited feelings of shame and fear that it could compromise her social standing. Conversing with a wealthier friend, Anderson wrote, 'what would she say if I told her that I had been brought up by native servants and had been treated as one?'[52]

Anger

As the Depression deepened, white male workers increasingly turned to anger to reassert their own sense of pride and attempt to demean and frighten those social groups they saw as a threat. Anger had always been a part of white masculine expression amongst workers; by no means an exclusively 'male emotion', it was nonetheless cultivated more explicitly amongst men as part of their white gendered identities. Within the adversarial culture which pitted bosses against workers and white workers against Africans, anger – when channelled through appropriate mediums such as the trade union – became a mark of righteousness and was tolerated and encouraged in various forms. Anger was seen as a natural reaction when the liberty or dignity of the white man was encroached upon. Expressing righteous anger was an important demonstration of principles, characterized as a natural reaction to exploitation and to those who were disloyal to the trade union and industrial action.

WHITE PRIDE, MALE ANGER AND THE SHAME OF POVERTY   135

Violence and anger directed at Africans had always served an important role for white workers in maintaining racial hierarchies. Lawrence Vambe, a prominent African journalist, noted that the Depression had intensified the level of bile and hatred directed from white workers to Africans:

> Especially deep was their humiliation arising from the fact that they were seen doing pick-and-shovel tasks by the Africans, who walked or rode their bicycles past them. As it was, the Africans did not have to starve or go on the dole. If they lost their jobs, they simply returned to their villages, where they grew their own food. Probably for the first time, the European workers understood that black people had a freedom which they themselves did not possess. The indigenous people seemed unaffected by the white man's financial system that had gone so crazily wrong and brought poverty, insecurity and bitterness to men who had always behaved like demi-gods … Their bitterness showed itself openly in the streets and on outlying roads. Those of them who knew our language swore at innocent black passers-by, using the most obscene terms in Chisezuru.[53]

In this scene white men work with a pick and shovel, using their hands in the mud and dirt, while Africans appear carefree, riding bicycles, the image of urban, recreational modern life. Whites had continually preached the virtues of European culture and systems of governance, but this system had created unemployment and threatened the ability of white workers to lay claim to their presumed racial superiority. Whites, whose self-identification as the productive driving force in the country, creating wealth and prosperity on what would otherwise be unprofitable, disused land, were now confronted with figures of Africans whose links to rural villages were able to provide for them during the Depression.[54] Moreover, Africans seeing whites working menial jobs and living in relative poverty brought the assumption of white racial superiority crashing down. Liberal MP Jacob Smit outlined why whites walking the streets – their unemployed and destitute status laid bare for all to see – were a particular problem, as 'it might have to some extent a very bad effect on the minds of the natives when they see these white people doing the work which in the past was only done by natives'.[55] For Smit, the debased white gave the black man confidence, and this confidence was despised and feared. The confidence to challenge white authority, to refuse to follow instructions or display submissive behaviours, was the same confidence that led to revolt and rebellion against white rule.[56]

As white workers suffered and felt their racial prestige under attack, they turned to violent intimidation and hostility to reassert their presumed superiority. Letters to the *Review* proliferated, complaining of Africans laughing, talking or walking in the street.[57] In part, the transgression lay in the incursion of African bodies into those urban and residential spaces imagined as white, but it was also the visible reminder of African contentment and individual agency. White workers desired Africans to perform their own humiliation; for them to accept that they were a lower race and to behave accordingly, observing the emotional norms prescribed by whites. When automatic deference was not forthcoming, frustration and bitterness resulted.[58] Increasing levels of anger were directed at the government and its refusal to prevent Africans fulfilling skilled jobs. Africans seen to be performing 'white work' were routinely harassed. White workers also complained to management, attempted to shame those firms that hired African staff in skilled positions and threatened industrial action in a bid to maintain their racialized monopoly over certain jobs.[59] Here anger was characterized as a natural reaction of white men to this transgression, intimately tied to performances of white masculinity. Anger offered a route through which white men could restore their masculinity just as their confidence in their manhood was undermined by poverty.

Conclusion

In white lower-class communities, what was regarded as legitimate, or rational, emotional expression was constituted within existing racial, gendered and class power relations. White workers' emotional expression was conditioned by fears of racial degeneration, African agency and threats to traditional notions of masculinity and femininity, as well as the threat and lived experience of material impoverishment. Trade union journals were inflected with passion, outrage and anger, but white men and women were encouraged to experience and wield emotions in highly gendered ways which reaffirmed existing social norms. For white men, anger was a legitimate expression of righteousness against employers or Africans who were deemed to be a threat to their position in the racial hierarchy. Pride in specific types of wage labour offered a route of differentiation to white workers, both from white elites, and white women and Africans. Particular emotions were projected onto racialized and gendered others: emphasizing the fear and distress of women and children in descriptions of poverty protected masculine pride and allowed for damning assessments of those deemed responsible, and positioned women as weak and frail to counteract their increasing autonomy outside of the home. For white women, on the other hand, emotional expression was conditioned by their experience in the domestic realm and the failure to perform an idealized white femininity.

Expressions of loneliness were conspicuous testaments to white workers' vigilance in maintaining emotional and physical distance from Africans. Yet, the regularity with which lower-class whites publicized their loneliness spoke to underlying anxieties; fears that some whites – particularly the poor, isolated workers or low-class housewives – were engaged in transgressive interracial interactions. To help quell these anxieties, settlers compelled Africans to express themselves in specific ways which supported racial hierarchies; for Africans, simply appearing to be happy in the presence of anxiety-ridden whites could make them the target of white violence. Yet white skin was never an uncritical source of consolation or pride. Shame was instrumentalized and used by lower-class whites to lay claim to white racial propriety. Fundamentally, this shame was also deeply felt by individuals, as tensions between the idealized white worker and their experiences of material insecurity disrupted self-imaginings of an inherently superior race.

Notes

1. H. Fischer-Tine and C. Whyte (eds.), *Anxieties, Fear and Panic in Colonial Settings: Empires on the Verge of a Nervous Breakdown* (Basingstoke: Springer, 2016).

2. D. Kennedy, *Islands of White: Settler Society and Culture in Kenya and Southern Rhodesia, 1890–1939* (Durham, NC: Duke University Press, 1987).

3. A. Shutt, '"The Natives Are Getting Out of Hand": Legislating Manners, Insolence and Contemptuous Behaviour in Southern Rhodesia, c.1910–1963', *Journal of Southern African Studies*, 33 (2007), 653–72.

4. W. Jackson, 'Bad Blood: Poverty, Psychopathy and the Politics of Transgression in Kenya Colony, 1939–59', *Journal of Imperial and Commonwealth History*, 39 (2011), 73–94; A. Stoler, *Race and the Education of Desire: Foucault's History of Sexuality and the Colonial Order of Things* (Durham, NC: Duke University Press, 1995).

5. D. Posel, 'Whiteness and Power in the South African Civil Service: Paradoxes of the Apartheid State', *Journal of Southern African Studies*, 25 (1999), 99–119.

6. See I. Phimister, *An Economic and Social History of Zimbabwe, 1890–1948: Capital Accumulation and Class Struggle* (London: Longman, 1988); C. van Onselen, *Chibaro: African Mine Labour in Southern Rhodesia, 1900–1933* (London: Pluto Press, 1976).

7. M.E. Lee, 'Politics and Pressure Groups in Southern Rhodesia, 1898–1923' (unpublished doctoral thesis, University of London, 1974), p. 166.

8. Phimister, *Economic and Social*, p. 189.

9. Lee, 'Politics and Pressure', p. 170; L.H. Gann and M. Gelfand, *Huggins of Rhodesia* (London: Allen & Unwin, 1964), p. 61.

10. Phimister, *Economic and Social*, p. 93.

11. B. Rosenwein, 'Worrying about Emotions in History', *The American Historical Review*, 107 (2002), 821–45.

12. J. Keller, 'Who Pays?', *RRR* (March 1923), p. 19.

13. J. Lunn, *Capital and Labour on the Rhodesian Railway System, 1888–1947* (Basingstoke: Springer, 1997), p. 83.

14. R. Lord, 'The Tally', *RRR* (August 1922), p. 7.

15. J. Keller, 'Solid Reasoning: Are You Helping to Starve Your Own Family?', *RRR* (April 1928), pp. 19–20.

16. *RRR* (December 1930), p. 37.

17. 'Correspondence', *RRR* (December 1922), p. 10.

18. H.J. Lucas, 'Early Days on a Small Working', *Rhodesiana*, 20 (1969), 14–15.

19. J. Keller, 'The Truth about the Rhodesian Railwayman', *RRR* (November 1921), pp. 2–9.

20. A. Croxton, *Railways of Zimbabwe: The Story of the Beira, Mashonaland and Rhodesia Railways* (Newton Abbot: David & Charles, 1982), p. 107.

21. 'Umtali Branch Notes', *RRR* (June 1927), p. 36.

22. H. Killeen, 'Female Unemployment', *RRR* (November 1921), p. 35.

23. P. Levine, 'Introduction: Why Gender and Empire?', in *Gender and Empire* (Oxford: Oxford University Press), p. 8. See also D. Jeater, 'No Place for a Woman: Gwelo Town, Southern Rhodesia, 1894–1920', *Journal of Southern African Studies*, 26 (2000), 29–42.

24. C. Gouldsbury, 'For Women Only. Land Settlement in Rhodesia, Rider Haggard's Report Condemned', *Rhodesian Rhymes* (Salisbury, 1969). Every reasonable effort

has been made to locate the copyright holder and we will aim to rectify any omissions in future reprints or editions should further information be brought to our attention.

25. A. Stoler, *Carnal Knowledge and Imperial Power: Race and the Intimate in Colonial Rule* (Berkeley, CA: University of California Press, 2010).

26. For a deeper discussion of white femininity, domesticity and work in Southern Rhodesia, see U. Kufakurinani, *Elasticity in Domesticity: White Women in Rhodesian Zimbabwe, 1890 to 1980* (Leiden: Brill, 2019).

27. J.M. Scott, 'What Every Railroad Woman Knows', *RRR* (December 1928), p. 64. Every reasonable effort has been made to locate the copyright holder and we will aim to rectify any omissions in future reprints or editions should further information be brought to our attention.

28. Givelo, 'Musings without Method', *RRR* (April 1922), p. 18.

29. Abraham Lincoln, 'The Native Industrial Position and Problems in the Congo Belge', *RRR* (November 1922), p. 9.

30. 'Am I to Think You a Cad Jim?', *RRR* (December 1928), p. 111.

31. 'Branch Notes Salisbury: What the Women Can Do', *RRR* (August 1929), p. 41.

32. See chapter 4 in Phimister, *An Economic and Social History*.

33. *Southern Rhodesia Report upon the Census taken on 3rd May 1921*, p. 17. National Archives of Zimbabwe, S480/95 C.H. Berger's Records of Unemployment. 'Editorial', *RRR* (December 1931), p. 15.

34. Lunn, *Capital and Labour*, p. 125.

35. R. Morrell (ed.), *White but Poor: Essays on the History of Poor Whites in Southern Africa, 1880–1940* (Pretoria: Unisa Press, 1992); S. Dubow, 'Race, Civilisation and Culture: The Elaboration of Segregationist Discourse in the Inter-War Years', in S. Marks and S. Trapido (eds.), *The Politics of Race, Class and Nationalism in Twentieth Century South Africa* (New York: Taylor & Francis, 1987), pp. 71–94; Stoler, *Carnal Knowledge*.

36. G.E. Wells, *Report on Unemployment and the Relief of Destitution in Southern Rhodesia* (Salisbury, 1934), pp. 24–5.

37. *Debates of the Legislative Assembly* (Southern Rhodesia, 1932), p. 412.

38. 'Plight of the Workless', *RRR* (December 1931), p. 19.

39. 'The Story of a Crime', *RRR* (January 1925), p. 19. See also *Debates of the Legislative Assembly* (1932), p. 421.

40. 'Women Workers of the Past', *RRR* (December 1930), p. 55.

41. See also T. Keegan, 'Gender, Degeneration and Sexual Danger: Imagining Race and Class in South Africa, ca.1912', *Journal of Southern African Studies*, 27 (2001), 461.

42. 'The General Election', *RRR* (September 1928), p. 16.

43. P. Levine, 'States of Undress: Nakedness and the Colonial Imagination', *Victorian Studies*, 50, 2 (2008), 189–219.

44. 'The Unemployment Problem', *RRR* (June 1934), pp. 7–18.

45. D. Lessing, *Going Home* (London: Panther, 1957).

46. D. Anderson, *The Toe-Rags: The Story of a Strange Up-Bringing in Southern Rhodesia* (London: Andre Deutsch Limited, 1989), p. 154.

47. Anderson, *Toe-Rags*, p. 235.

48. H. Richards, *Next Year Will Be Better* (Bulawayo: Books of Rhodesia, 1975), pp. 78–9.

49. E. Griffin, 'The Emotions of Motherhood: Love, Culture, and Poverty in Victorian Britain', *The American Historical Review*, 123 (2018), 60–85.

50. 'Our Little Children's Little Corner', *RRR* (September 1922), pp. 32–3.

51. Anderson, *Toe-Rags*, pp. 45–6.

52. Anderson, *Toe-Rags*, p. 197.

53. L. Vambe, *From Rhodesia to Zimbabwe* (London: Heinemann, 1976), pp. 58–9.

54. W. Dopcke, '"Magomo's Maize": State and Peasants During the Depression in Colonial Zimbabwe', in I. Brown (ed.), *The Economies of Africa and Asia in the Inter-War Depression* (London: Taylor & Francis, 1989), pp. 29–58.

55. *Debates of the Legislative Assembly* (1932), p. 419.

56. B. Shadle, *The Souls of White Folk: White Settlers in Kenya, 1900s–1920s* (Manchester: Manchester University Press, 2015).

57. 'A SUFFERER', 'Letters to the Editor: A Complaint against the Native', *RRR* (July 1933), p. 21.

58. On prestige, see Kennedy, *Islands of White*; Shadle, *Souls of White Folk*.

59. Vambe, *From Rhodesia to Zimbabwe*, p. 165.

References

Primary sources

Anderson, D., *The Toe-Rags: The Story of a Strange Up-Bringing in Southern Rhodesia* (London: Andre Deutsch Limited, 1989).

Croxton, A., *Railways of Zimbabwe: The Story of the Beira, Mashonaland and Rhodesia Railways* (Newton Abbot: David & Charles, 1982).

Debates of the Southern Rhodesian Legislative Assembly.

Lessing, D., *Going Home* (London: Panther, 1957).

National Archives of Zimbabwe, S480/95 C.H. Berger's Records of Unemployment.

Rhodesiana.

Rhodesian Railway Review. [cited as *RRR*]

Richards, H., *Next Year Will Be Better* (Bulawayo: Books of Rhodesia, 1975).

Vambe, L., *From Rhodesia to Zimbabwe* (London: Heinemann, 1976).

Wells, G.E., *Report on Unemployment and the Relief of Destitution in Southern Rhodesia* (Salisbury 1934), pp. 24–5.

Secondary sources

Davie, G., *Poverty Knowledge in South Africa: A Social History of Human Science, 1855–2005* (Cambridge: Cambridge University Press, 2015).

Dopcke, W., '"Magomo's Maize": State and Peasants During the Depression in Colonial Zimbabwe', in I. Brown (ed.), *The Economies of Africa and Asia in the Inter-War Depression* (London: Taylor & Francis, 1989), pp. 29–58.

Dubow, S., 'Race, Civilisation and Culture: The Elaboration of Segregationist Discourse in the Inter-War Years', in S. Marks and S. Trapido (eds.), *The Politics of Race, Class and Nationalism in Twentieth Century South Africa* (New York: Taylor & Francis, 1987), pp. 71–94.

——, *Scientific Racism in Modern South Africa* (Cambridge: Cambridge University Press, 1995).

Fischer-Tine, H., and Whyte, C. (eds.), *Anxieties, Fear and Panic in Colonial Settings: Empires on the Verge of a Nervous Breakdown* (Basingstoke: Springer, 2016).

Gann, L.H. and Gelfand, M., *Huggins of Rhodesia* (London: Allen & Unwin, 1964).

Griffin, E., 'The Emotions of Motherhood: Love, Culture, and Poverty in Victorian Britain', *The American Historical Review*, 123 (2018), 60–85.

Jackson, W., 'Bad Blood: Poverty, Psychopathy and the Politics of Transgression in Kenya Colony, 1939–59', *Journal of Imperial and Commonwealth History*, 39 (2011), 73–94.

Jeater, D., 'No Place for a Woman: Gwelo Town, Southern Rhodesia, 1894–1920', *Journal of Southern African Studies*, 26 (2000), 29–42.

Keegan, T., 'Gender, Degeneration and Sexual Danger: Imagining Race and Class in South Africa, ca.1912', *Journal of Southern African Studies*, 17 (2001), 459–77.

Kennedy, D., *Islands of White: Settler Society and Culture in Kenya and Southern Rhodesia, 1890–1939* (Durham, NC: Duke University Press, 1987).

Kufakurinani, U., *Elasticity in Domesticity: White Women in Rhodesian Zimbabwe, 1890 to 1980* (Leiden: Brill, 2019).

Lee, M.E., 'Politics and Pressure Groups in Southern Rhodesia, 1898–1923', unpublished doctoral thesis (University of London, 1974).

Levine, P. (ed.), 'Introduction: Why Gender and Empire?', in *Gender and Empire* (Oxford: Oxford University Press, 2007), pp. 1–13.

Levine, P., 'States of Undress: Nakedness and the Colonial Imagination', *Victorian Studies*, 50, 2 (2008), 189–219.

Lonsdale, J., 'Kenya: Home County and African Frontier', in R. Bickers (ed.), *Settlers and Expatriates: Britons over the Seas* (Oxford: Oxford University Press, 2010), pp. 74–111.

Lunn, J., *Capital and Labour on the Rhodesian Railway System, 1888–1947* (Basingstoke: Springer, 1997).

Morrell, R. (ed.), *White but Poor: Essays on the History of Poor Whites in Southern Africa, 1880–1940* (Pretoria: Unisa Press, 1992).

Phimister, I., *An Economic and Social History of Zimbabwe, 1890–1948: Capital Accumulation and Class Struggle* (London: Longman, 1988).

Posel, D., 'Whiteness and Power in the South African Civil Service: Paradoxes of the Apartheid State', *Journal of Southern African Studies*, 25 (1999), 99–119.

Rosenwein, B., 'Worrying about Emotions in History', *The American Historical Review*, 107 (2002), 821–45.

Shadle, B., *The Souls of White Folk: White Settlers in Kenya, 1900s–1920s* (Manchester: Manchester University Press, 2015).

Shutt, A., '"The Natives Are Getting Out of Hand": Legislating Manners, Insolence and Contemptuous Behaviour in Southern Rhodesia, c.1910–1963', *Journal of Southern African Studies*, 33 (2007), 653–72.

Stoler, A., *Race and the Education of Desire: Foucault's History of Sexuality and the Colonial Order of Things* (Durham, NC: Duke University Press, 1995).

——, *Carnal Knowledge and Imperial Power: Race and the Intimate in Colonial Rule* (Oakland, CA: University of California Press, 2010).

van Onselen, C., *Chibaro: African Mine Labour in Southern Rhodesia, 1900–1933* (London: Pluto Press, 1976).

Chapter 6

'Africans smell different': disgust, fear and the gendering of interracial intimacy in Kenya and Zambia

Josh Doble

In February 2017 Terry Marks* sat in his house just outside Lusaka, and pondered his own racism and its impact upon the intimate relationships in his life.

> The visceral prejudice ... it's very difficult to get rid of that. With the [African] girls there [in the UK], it wasn't an intimate thing. I wouldn't have had an affair with them. I think because of my upbringing ... that ingrained racism. When I was a kid poverty was widespread, Africans tended to be much poorer than we were. The ramification was that they didn't wash, or couldn't wash, so they were a bit whiffy. That would separate us ...[1]

Terry stated explicitly the deeply embedded colonial notions of racial bodily difference which separated white and black Zambians romantically, despite an increasingly mixed social scene after independence in 1964. Even when in the foreign context of the UK, he did not feel comfortable to engage in romantic relationships with the black Africans he befriended. Notably, he rooted this separation in his childhood memories, specifically the memory of African smell, which signified not only racial difference but also poverty and class difference.

Encapsulated by the smell that Terry recalled were all of the assumptions of the racial hierarchy of colonialism, which sought to distinguish, differentiate and regulate. This recalcitrant colonial mentality elicited a distinct emotional response: that of disgust with African smell. Through this disgust the actions of Terry were restrained. Smell aroused disgust, which in turn invoked racial memories and psychologically secured colonial hierarchies, reinforcing the boundaries of whiteness – as a structural privilege and skin colour – which were increasingly unstable in the post-colonial period. These tenuous boundaries were imperilled by rising black African prosperity and the influx of 'expatriate' whites, whose willingness to act on desire for, and emotional connection with, Africans weakened white claims to aloofness and superiority. This chapter argues that the post-colonial retrenchment of white emotional norms relied upon the delineation of 'visceral' emotions, such as disgust, as somehow distinct from intellectual or other mental responses. The conceptualization of 'visceral' emotions as instinctive, and thus inevitable, was a way of rationalizing and legitimizing informal behaviours of racial segregation.

Attempts to differentiate white communities, and subsequently forge a more coherent sense of post-colonial white identity, have relied upon emotional strategies akin to Barbara Rosenwein's theory of 'emotional communities', also evident in Nicola Ginsburgh's example of the policing of white working-class identities in Rhodesia in this volume.[2] The construction and regulation of coded systems of emotional expression and intimate interracial behaviour have been central to white attempts to maintain homogeneity in the face of existential concerns about the fracturing of whiteness. The theory of emotional communities focuses upon the fact that certain expressions, gestures and bodily symptoms are privileged within certain groups.[3] In this instance, I focus on how fear and disgust have structured intimate white interactions with black Africans. This corresponds closely to Adi Kuntsman's and Jonathan Dollimore's conceptions of disgust in the formation of sexual and class boundaries. Building upon their work, this chapter considers the embodied, sensorially derived feeling of disgust required to retrench both racialized and gendered sexual boundaries in post-colonial African nations with a history of white settlement.[4] The social conditioning and self-regulation of this emotional community point towards the deeply engrained and often unconscious emotional work that disgust and fear did to deny Africans as full sexual or social beings, and therefore as viable romantic partners.[5]

Furthermore, this chapter argues that these emotional responses were explicitly gendered as a means of regulating white women's sexuality, while allowing for a degree of white male sexual freedom. The development of a communal emotional language amongst white settler groups regulated and shaped behaviour and mentalities.[6] In this sense, the emotional discourse of the colonial period can be seen to have lingered and morphed into the post-colonial, as while the political and social changes of decolonization forced whites in both Kenya and Zambia to reposition themselves as legitimate members of African society, they also struggled to escape the colonial mentalities which sustained the tenuous boundaries of whiteness.[7] However, this chapter moves beyond the purely discursive by developing the notion of sensory knowledge, the idea that knowledge of people and places is expressed through the senses. For example, 'knowing' a smell of a person or environment, especially one in which evocative memories are entangled, entails a close knowledge of what that smell *should* smell like. Thus, smell has to be considered within a framework of intimacy and power. The knowledge of someone's smell is a demonstration not only of familiarity but also of power. In this context, Africans conform to white ideas of what they should smell like. This is a point of particular urgency for whites in contexts where their previous claims to power have been invalidated or openly challenged. Sensory knowledge as an idea weaves together the embodied aspects of sensory history and the cultural facets of the history of emotions. This approach develops existing cultural histories of fear and disgust to consider how sensory reactions, emotional responses and social regulation are co-existent and mutually supportive.[8] Through so doing, the chapter acknowledges how the cultural and linguistic dynamics of fear and disgust are inseparable from the visceral and embodied.

Oral history and participant observation became central to investigating sensory knowledge as research participants' troubled relationships with the past were explored and described through their sensory memories, often while in the spaces that evoked them.[9] The senses matter in this history, as both a means of defining white identity and as a means of stressing white knowledge of the continent through emotional connections deeply rooted to childhood. The intimate day-to-day nature of this research meant that I naturally became close to participants with whom I spent a lot of time, partially experiencing the lives of my research subjects. This study into the emotions of proximity required my own navigation of emotional interactions with research subjects. This often provided a seemingly more candid experience, albeit tempered by an awareness that while participants seemed more open with me than I had expected; like all sources there were concealments, self-censorship and self-deceits. This proximity had the methodological benefit of not only providing examples of individual context and experiences but also illuminating the wider trends within white groups through social situations. This allowed for an interrogation of an individual's subjectivity and their engagement with the emotional norms of their community.[10]

The period of study in this chapter ranges from the late-colonial period of the mid-1950s to the present day. Compared to the nearby settler territories of Rhodesia and South Africa, the decades between the 1960s and

1990s were relatively peaceful. While civil war raged in Rhodesia, Mozambique, Namibia and Angola between European settlers and African guerrillas, Kenya and Zambia's settlers maintained a precarious yet persistent peace with the post-colonial African state, largely protecting their power and privilege.[11] While they remained physically safe and propertied, the mental discomfort unleashed by African independence prompted a new search for white belonging and legitimacy in Africa amidst the long-term uncertainty of the white position. The strategies developed after independence to emphasize the 'naturalness' and permanence of whites in Africa, while also reinforcing their separation and difference, are central tenets of the chapter, which frame the analysis of how post-colonial intimacy has been gendered through the emotive language of the senses.

The emotions of smell

Smells excite particular emotions. The smell of African places – the rains, wood smoke – could render longing, while the smell of African people could render disgust; disgust because the smell of African people reminded whites that the place is not 'theirs', hence their longing for *it*, the mythical place in which Africans could be absented.[12] Smell is central to intimate knowledge and ideas of proximity and distance. Power was at the heart of the colonial discourse of smell; it was used to foster both physical and psychological distance between whites and Africans. The paradox herein is the proximate nature of smell: it required an intimate familiarity with those marked as 'other', even as such stereotypes worked to erase this knowledge, relying on assumptions about social gulfs.[13] The tension is not only between the necessary proximity to be able to smell and the fact that it is on the basis of smell that otherness is described, but also the fact that the smell of difference gave rise to a particular emotional response – that of disgust. While proximity was central to the ability to be able to 'know' a smell, the supposed visceral white reaction of disgust to the 'smell' of Africans strikes a note of interest: if that particular smell was always noticeable, it has not been entirely normalized; it evidently retains a sense of novelty despite everyday contact between black Africans and whites. Displaying an act of memory work outside everyday experience, whites re-remembered the associations of blackness with distinct smells, having to provoke an emotional response to what was a routine occurrence.

The smell of Africa is sweat, body odour and smoke.[14]

June Rasch, an elderly white Zambian living outside Lusaka, made this comment in late 2016, demonstrating how the colonial discourse which linked race and smell has had striking resilience beyond independence. It also indicates the homogenization of smell that whites have associated with Africa.[15] The notion that Africa has a smell is, in reality, absurd. A continent of over 1.2 billion people and 30.37 million km^2 cannot be distilled into a series of aromas. However, this false homogenization is instructive nonetheless. The homogenization of Africa into a small group of aromas by whites speaks more to a lingering settler understanding of the supposed 'simplicity' of the continent and their knowledge of it than the continent or its indigenous inhabitants. The small number of aromas which are used to invoke this are part of a shared 'smellscape' which helped provide an emotionally reassuring sense of shared white experience and homogeneity in the face of the reality of disparate knowledge and identities.[16]

The colonial racialization of smell

During the colonial period, smell began to be used within a wider discourse of racial difference in European colonies as visceral 'evidence' of the difference between the clean and the unclean; the civilized and the uncivilized. In early twentieth-century colonial Dutch Java, Javanese servants were told to hold their European wards away from their bodies so that they 'wouldn't smell of their sweat'.[17] In settler colonial Africa, 'body racism', as Timothy Burke termed it, and the politics of smell were further amplified, with the black African body becoming the site of a disciplinary hygiene discourse, in which cleanliness became synonymous with whiteness and dirtiness with blackness.[18] Closely tied to the discourse of hygiene and race was the importance of smell. The supposed ability of Africans to 'pick up dirt by instinct' led to complaints about 'the omnipresent odour which streams from these people'.[19] At the heart of these concerns was a settler fixation upon African sweat.[20] In this case, sweat, and connectedly alleged body odour, became both racialized and classed to depict the black worker.[21]

The apparent innateness of different races' aromas, and the supposed links between diseases, race and smell, became part of a rationale of difference and separation between races.[22] In the settler territories of Africa, as in the south of the United States, olfactory-based assumptions of racial difference were used to build and legitimize systems of segregation which policed the arrangement of such 'different' bodies in public spaces.[23] Peter Barak, a white anti-colonial activist in his nineties, remembered Northern Rhodesia in the 1950s: 'Body odour [BO] was a big issue and that applied socially. You couldn't work in an office with an African next to you. It [BO] became symbolic, a rationale for non-social contact (between races).'[24]

The notion of Africans smelling different to Europeans became pointedly politicized during the heated atmosphere of the early 1960s with the desegregation of hotels, bars and restaurants. Europeans opposed to desegregation used the apparent 'smell' of Africans as a point of justification in keeping the races separated.[25] Mr Veliades, the owner of the Rhodes Café in Kitwe who had been accused of racial discrimination in 1962, defended his right to refuse Africans entry to his premises unless they were 'reasonably dressed' and this meant 'clean, tidy and not smelly'.[26]

The long history of blackness, dirt and sweat being both commodified and naturalized became part of post-colonial whites' sensory knowledge. It was normalized that black Africans 'smell', a fact reinforced by the divergent material conditions of whites in Africa and the domestic staff and agricultural employees whom they most frequently interacted with. Thus, the idea of an innate African aroma has lingered into the post-colonial white imagination but has become more intimately linked to discomfort with the idea of sexual and emotional integration through mixed marriages. The 'voluntary segregation' myth of the colonial period morphed into post-colonial thought through the discourse of smell.[27] The supposed difference in smell between the races is no longer used to segregate shopping, toilets or swimming pools but instead has been reformulated as a physical manifestation of the unnaturalness of mixed marriages.

Decolonization and fear of African sexuality

While the colonial discourse of unclean African bodies and body odour has remained resilient amongst whites since independence, there has been a growing African middle class conforming to 'white standards' of middle-class bourgeois norms, and challenging the older colonial notion of 'unclean, primitive Africans'.[28] Mel Teevan, an Anglo-Irish Zambian resident in her eighties, encapsulated this distinction when asked what the biggest change since independence was: she promptly replied that 'African women certainly don't smell in church anymore'.[29] The social challenge decolonization posed to whites' supposed 'knowledge' of African smells required the re-entrenchment of such claims but they became even more pointedly gendered, as the real possibility of formal interracial sexual relationships arose through the closer proximities between white and black material existence.

'Innate' African smell was supposedly a marker of biological difference and therefore a preclusion to emotional and intimate engagement with

Africans. However, for white men, the discourse of disgust evidently did not always prevent sexual interaction, behaviours which undermined any essentialized 'truth' in these patterns of emotional regulation. Instead, attempts were made to limit formal romantic arrangements through the structure of marriage. While sexual relationships with Africans had been taking place since the first colonial encounter, they were always at the edge of white society – an inadmissible fact which few wanted to openly broach.[30] Fear of relationships developing 'beyond the physical' and fostering genuine emotional attachment brought the greatest risks to the European male partner in the colonial period, as romantic affection would blur the supposed boundaries of whiteness.[31] This reflects Dane Kennedy's assertion that the function of fears of interracial intimacy, whether legitimate or not, was to enforce racial unity, 'of compelling white settlers to delineate material and symbolic boundaries between themselves and those people upon whom their livelihoods so heavily depended'.[32]

In settler society it was the prospect of white women having any romantic or sexual contact with African men which was the source of greatest white fear, reflecting dominant scholarly reflections upon social reproduction and the role of the white woman as the future of the settler project. The latent threat posed by white women's intimacy – sexually or otherwise – with African men is of a future of white demographic obliteration. Historically this was articulated through the phenomenon of black peril – white, notably male, fear of black male sexuality. The prospect of physical and sexual contact between white women and black men had long been held up as the harbinger of the end of white rule, and was the reason for the vociferous policing of 'black peril' through punitive miscegenation and interracial rape legislation.[33] It was the failure to secure white hegemony in Kenya and Northern Rhodesia which fixed 'Africa' as unconquerable, dangerous and untamed; it remained a black space despite settler attempts to make it white, a fact only further reinforced by independence in the early 1960s. Following the desegregation of schools in both territories in the years before independence, white fears developed over the 'physically developed and sexually more sophisticated' African students mixing with European girls 'at tender ages'.[34] Similarly, Charles Braithwaite, an elderly rancher in Laikipia, recalled of independence that 'people [white settlers] with young daughters had nightmares about their daughters being a tiny minority in a black community. It was slightly different for sons'.[35] The fear of black male sexuality was evident in his comment, as was the gendered difference in the potential of sexual partners. Charles's statement that 'it was slightly different for sons' indicated that, unlike their female counterparts, who required protection through close regulation of the boundaries of intimacy, men need not fear the sexual advances of African women.[36]

The lingering British tropes of white women's sexuality and desire being shaped by love and reproduction, as opposed to male innate sexual 'needs', were made sharper and more pointedly racialized in these emotional communities by the widespread preconception, both real and imagined, of the sexual availability of black women for white men.[37] This availability was most commonly presumed to occur either through formal sex work, or informal sexual patronage/transactional sex in the racialized socio-economic power dynamics of both countries.[38] Contrastingly, the prospect of a liberated black African male sexuality raised specific fears of annihilation in the white male imagination. It was the emotive and sensory strategies of separation, created in the colonial period, which would be reinvigorated in the post-colony as a means of securing the racial and sexual boundaries of white emotional communities and therefore protect some form of a white future in Africa.

'What a waste of a white skin': marriage, reproduction and the white family unit

The fear of social censure and ostracization of interracial relationships has remained remarkably strong since independence. In 142 interviews with white Kenyans and Zambians, only two were in open mixed marriages or relationships. Deidre Walton, an elderly female settler in Nanyuki, typified the response to such issues:

> My grandson is married now and lives in Dubai [Is he married to an African lady?] Oh no no! [laughs] I say it like that but he's not, it sounds awful doesn't it? I don't think I'd like that. I've always thought birds of a feather, frankly ... I can't really think of any [whites] that are [in mixed marriages].[39]

There was remarkable consensus amongst almost all participants that mixed marriages were a bad idea for both the couple and any children born of the relationship. Charles Braithwaite described his discomfort with mixed marriages.

> There's always a hidden ... [pause] I don't mean it maliciously, but we've got several half-caste young friends who are doing very well in Kenya, but they're quite unusual people already. Because I'm a bloody old colonial I'd be very unhappy [if his grandchildren married an African]. There's not edge to that, but my instinct goes against it.[40]

It was Charles's 'instinct' which indicated the deeply innate and emotive contours to the regulation of interracial intimacy, despite his attempt to laugh off his visceral reaction as being the preserve of an 'old colonial'. By stressing the supposedly unnatural nature of mixed-race children, racial categories were reified, and miscegenation vilified, a process which was particularly gendered by the strength of feeling attached to the preoccupation with daughters' partners, and correspondingly to African men's sexuality. The prospect of this particular dynamic was one of the few liberalizations of race relations which was repeatedly and vociferously refuted by whites. Mike and Clare Webster, white farmers living outside Kabwe, provided one such striking example. While taking part in a candid and wide-ranging discussion, Mike became sharply defensive as conversation turned to their daughter, Catherine. Catherine was living with a black Zambian man, something which was attributed to her education in a mixed-race school. However, the couple were quick to justify their objections to the arrangement by emphasizing that Clare used to employ her daughter's housemate, drawing hierarchical class distinctions upon the relationship. When this prompted a question about whether Catherine had a black boyfriend, Clare, her mother, pondered, 'we'd really struggle with that'. Mike had a more visceral reaction, as he firmly stated, 'you're really testing the depths, aren't you?'[41] This strength of feeling was part of a communal fear and disgust at the idea of white women – often imagined as a white daughter – being sexually or romantically intimate with a black African. This shared emotional norm drew one of the clearest boundaries of a post-colonial white emotional community.

While this chapter has thus far focused upon the significance of olfactory reactions, both discursive and embodied, in shaping the emotional boundaries of white communities in Kenya and Zambia, I would be remiss not to reflect upon the presence of interracial couples in both countries. Independence and the growth of the African middle class have been key to the emergence of formal and public interracial relationships. Leyton Moran was a white farmer in southern Zambia. In many respects he had the upbringing and life of any other colonial white child, yet he decided to marry Gloria, a local woman 'from the village' with whom he had fallen in love.[42]

> For me it was hard. My dad was dying of cancer, so I didn't want to bring it up [his relationship]. The local people loved my dad. But to broach the subject, that I'd found a beautiful young black lady that I wanted to marry, I just couldn't bring myself to do that. I secretly got married in the village ... my family took it quite badly initially. 'Why didn't you just got a marry some white woman somewhere?' It was a hiccup to the family for a bit. Sometimes my kids find it hard, because they aren't treated the same as the other cousins.[43]

Leyton reiterated how interracial marriage was 'the final frontier' in whites' emotional and psychological decolonization. Despite his white family's 'good relations' with the local African community, the prospect of marriage would have been out of the question. The severity of the family's discomfort meant that his father died not knowing his son had married a black Zambian, which caused an angry rupture in the family, which was still 'not sitting 100 per cent right'.[44] Leyton recalled the vitriol and disgust he faced in the wider white community when the marriage became public: 'you must get out of here, you must leave ... what a waste of a white skin', as a neighbouring farmer put it.[45] Leyton's traumatic experience demonstrated the ways in which disgust and anger were mobilized by the white emotional community in reaction to his romantic choices. While his actions were not censured, the liminal position he now occupied within that community demonstrated how embarking on a marriage, and the establishment of a family, with a black Zambian were policed. Edward Fisher, a self-declared 'white African' living in Nairobi who had no connection to Leyton, put this logic in stark terms: 'If you want to go and shag one [an African] that's fine but don't marry one. You want to associate with people who are the same as you and smell the same. Africans smell different.'[46]

The biological determinism of his statement is striking. In his mind it was the smell of people which binds them: the innate aroma of different individuals was demonstrative of their innate difference.

White women and the 'black worker': racializing class through smell

Edward's statement acknowledged how in the post-colonial period, as in the colonial period, white men have had far greater freedom to pursue sexual relationships with Africans compared to white women as long as they avoided a publicly loving, familial relationship as Leyton had done. This underlines how, despite the strength of the communal emotional language of fear and disgust, desire, lust or love could override the fear of transgression within certain gendered contexts. However, a clear distinction was drawn between casual sexual relationships and relationships thought of as familial, reproductive or affective. It was the latter relationships which brought forth the prospect of white demographic fragility, emotional and social equality with black Africans and therefore remained key sites of social censure. Moreover, the direct challenge white women taking African partners posed to white men's idea of their cultural and racial superiority, as well as the demographic 'fading out' of the white community, added deeply emotive elements to control over white women's sexuality. These concerns have been made all the sharper by the growth in white expatriate populations, and a gradual increase in social interaction between white and black. White imaginations and emotive responses have been incensed by the apparent presence of 'half-castes everywhere', reinforcing a determination amongst whites that such transgressions would not befall 'my grandchildren'.[47] This has underpinned attempts to reinforce African difference, thereby safeguarding against the prospect of sex or intermarriage with middle-class Africans. The form that these attempts took drew upon the existing history of olfactory discourse around sweat and body odour, and the emotions of fear and disgust they were supposed to invoke.

The legitimization of this boundary delineation has required the continual intertwining of smell and blackness into the post-colonial period, and has become intimately connected to domestic social hierarchies, a point made clear by the white farmer Deborah Strathern on her farm in Zambia's southern province:

> You associate [blackness] with workers [here] and maybe there is [sic] educated nice [black] people in the UK, but the moment you say that, [mixed marriage] I think of the garden boy, who I like very much but ... I suppose it's not very Christian of me to say ... but someone who doesn't smell.[48]

Deborah foregrounded manual work and sweat – just as colonial settlers and missionaries had done – in a conditioned revulsion to the idea of romantic and sexual intimacy with black Africans. Through this conditioning she indicated the emotional work whites did to deny Africans as full sexual or social beings. This was made easier through the association made between race and class, by redefining sweat as labour, and smell as 'Africanness'. This worked to homogenize 'Africans' into a pastiche of stereotypes attached by whites to their domestic servants, typified by their apparent 'smell', a process only made possible by the lack of social interaction between whites and Africans upon an equal social footing, Africans instead being relegated within existing hierarchical constructions to domestic servitude. Thus, when Deborah thought of interracial marriages, she automatically envisaged her daughter marrying the 'garden boy', which constituted not only a racial transgression but a class one. Strikingly, Deborah's discomfort with this imagination was firmly rooted in the 'smell' of the 'garden boy', a sensorial articulation of her underlying psychological discomfort with the idea of the relationship. In this instance his apparent smell – and the visceral response of disgust – encapsulates all of the reasons why Africans and whites should not marry.

The racialization of class, and the gendered dynamics of interracial relationships, were explained further when Deborah continued:

> I would battle, I seriously would battle [against interracial marriage]. Maybe more with my girls than with Andy. I don't know why that is. Just the thought of a mixed marriage with my daughters ... I just think it's the sexual connotation really. I don't know why I say that ... I don't know why I can justify this bold statement. It's just oohhh no no no no. You see some of these [black Zambians] really nicely spoken ... speaks better than most of us you know, but just no. We are associating ourselves with a lower-class person. Same as in England.[49]

Deborah openly admitted that it was the thought of sex between 'her girls' and Africans which raised such hostility. She attempted to rationalize her emotions in terms of the dynamics of class by appealing to a shared knowledge of the class structure of England. However, the viscerality and jarring racial dynamics contained in her response betrayed the disgust that the imagined scenario invoked. Although Deborah recognized that many Africans are now better educated than whites, there was still a visceral rejection of the idea of mixed-race relationships. Race was asserted *despite* the language competence of many black Zambians, and class was made to stand in for race in this instance. The well-spoken Africans she described were, in her view, simply masking the underlying inherent difference between the races. She invoked the scepticism of the 'civilized native' which had been common colonial discourse since the 1920s, and which Ginsburgh clearly delineates in her chapter in this volume. Her disapproval and outright refusal to contemplate both a black Zambian equal to her or her kin and the prospect of interracial romance failed to recognize the reality of twenty-first-century Zambia, and instead relied on much older discourses of the subterfuge of the 'well-spoken', fluent and 'nicely dressed' African.[50]

The dissonance between white reliance upon African staff and the continual denial of black African legitimacy as potential romantic partners rested on a continual conceptualization of the imagined 'African' as a worker. This was reiterated by Reg Turner and Mel Turnbull, a white Zambian couple living and working in Lusaka. They emphasized that, 'we have Christmas lunch with our staff. We have no problem with mixing'. Reg went on, 'but I wouldn't marry a black girl'.[51] In Kenya, Mark Benson, a retired white hunter living on the shores of Lake Naivasha, was even more explicit in his emphasis upon the class contours to this regulated behaviour.

I'm more educated than 99.9 per cent of the people here, I've trav-
elled all over the world, and I've employed people here. Now am I
racist? Yes, because I would not be happy having my son-in-law be
a Sabgi [sic] Singh from Delhi or from here. I would like her to marry
an Englishman.[52]

Mark went on to explain his sense of superiority over the 'lower-class'
Kenyans he employed: 'do I feel superior to the man on the street here?
Yes, I do quite frankly. He grew up in a mud hut, sitting around a fire eating
with his fingers'.[53] Mark's focus upon the manner of eating contained a
clear sensory element: Africans' and South Asians' culture of eating with
their hands marked them out as sensorially unrefined and indulging in a
baser culinary experience associated with manual tactility. It was this
apparent sensory difference between whites and Africans which marked
out their different levels of sophistication, and which, ultimately, defined
who Mark could envisage as a future son-in-law. Closely allied to these
classed depictions of Africans was the nebulous category of 'culture', itself
often a byword for race.[54]

Deidre Walton, an elderly retired white farmer living on the outskirts
of Nanyuki in Central Kenya, explained:

I wouldn't be best pleased if one of my grandchildren married an
African. Because I think culturally, is that the right word? We're all
different really. But you know I suppose there used to be a lot [of
interracial sex], it used to be called the Khaki Highlands (here)! We
used to have all these little 'chocolate drops', I think they were called,
running around.[55]

Deidre repeatedly returned to the idea of mixed marriages during a wide-
ranging interview, evidently preoccupied by the thought of it. Deidre
herself was unsure about the term 'culture', betraying her awareness of
its usage to delineate race, which she justified with the suggestion that her
black Kenyan staff would feel the same about 'cultural mixing'. Although
she recalled the colonial period as being a time of acknowledged, if illicit,
interracial sex, she clearly considered present-day desires to be more
closely regulated. It would seem that, for Deidre at least, post-colonial
whites' urges to racially transgress had been restrained through careful
observation of emotional norms. While schools have become racially
mixed and middle-class Africans take part in the businesses and social
activities of whites, informal social segregation in people's homes and private social clubs has remained strong. At the heart of this continued
separation has been the consistent and widespread emotional response

of disgust with African bodies and sexuality, an emotional norm regulating white, particularly women's, behaviour and continuing to reinforce the untenable discourse of African's biological difference. It remains one of the last colonial mentalities to which whites visibly and vociferously adhere, as interracial marriage, and thus legitimate offspring, most visibly represent the prospect of the physical 'fading out' of the last of the white population.

Conclusion

Colonial sensory discourse has died hard in Kenya and Zambia. The white search for legitimacy and racial coherence has led to reinvigorated sensorially justified notions of racial difference. Decolonization, and whites' associated loss of political power, has prompted a retrenchment of racial difference through the senses as means of consolidating and legitimizing the increasingly unsustainable aloofness of the white population. The senses, in turn, helped to define the boundaries of whites' emotional communities. The tangible social and physical entities of white communities have often been disparate and fleeting, as decolonization, transnational mobility and ill-health have chipped away at white populations in both countries. In the face of physically transient white communities, emotional norms from the colonial period have retained currency through the formation of post-colonial emotional communities, preoccupied with interracial relationships.[56] The emotional boundaries of white communities determined the principles regulating interracial intimacy, as well as establishing post-colonial emotional norms, which also stressed deep bonds of belonging and longing to and for African environments.

The way olfactory language, and the emotional norms it conveys, has been used by whites as a means of dividing themselves from Africans while attempting to legitimize their presence in Africa illuminates the contradiction at the heart of post-colonial whiteness. The position of the post-colonial white in Africa is never secure because of their colonial heritage of power, privilege and wealth, of which their conspicuous whiteness marks them out as colonial remnants. Smell, and the emotional norms it was supposed to invoke, legitimized white senses of self through the vilification of Africans and an emphasis upon an 'inherent connection' to Africa. The construction of post-colonial emotional communities has been a means for whites to try and mitigate the decline in their own standing over the past sixty years. However, such communities have illuminated the contradictory space which whites continue to occupy between an affective claim to 'belonging' to Africa and meaningful integration with African society.

*All of the participants in this research have been anonymized, with their names changed and discerning features of employment and/or location changed.

Notes

1. Interview with Terry Marks, ZI039. For similar arguments, see interviews with Deborah Strathern, Edward Fisher and Sharon Mintram.

2. B. Rosenwein, *Emotional Communities in the Early Middle Ages* (Ithaca, NY: Cornell University Press, 2006).

3. B. Rosenwein, 'Worrying about Emotions in History', *The American Historical Review*, 107 (2002), 821–45, at p. 16; Rosenwein, *Emotional Communities*.

4. A. Kuntsman, '"With a Shade of Disgust": Affective Politics of Sexuality and Class in Memoirs of the Stalinist Gulag', *Slavic Review*, 68, 2 (2009), 308–28, at p. 308; J. Dollimore, 'Sexual Disgust', in T. Dean and C. Lane (eds.), *Homosexuality and Psychoanalysis* (Chicago, IL: University of Chicago Press, 2001), p. 368.

5. The use of 'emotional work' builds upon Hochschild's conception of 'emotion-work'; see A. Hochschild, 'Emotion Work, Feeling Rules, and Social Structure', *American Journal of Sociology*, 85 (1979), 551–75.

6. This takes instruction from Reddy's theory of emotives and emotions being brought to life through language; see W. Reddy, *The Navigation of Feeling: A Framework for the History of Emotions* (Cambridge: Cambridge University Press, 2001), pp. 105–7.

7. For work on the colonial boundaries of whiteness, see A. Stoler, 'Rethinking Colonial Categories: European Communities and the Boundaries of Rule', *Comparative Studies in Society and History*, 31 (1989), 134–61; B. Shadle, *The Souls of White Folk: White Settlers in Kenya, 1900s–20s* (Manchester: Manchester University Press, 2015).

8. C. Classen, *The Deepest Sense: A Cultural History of Touch* (Champaign, IL: University of Illinois Press, 2012); M. Smith, 'Producing Sense, Consuming Sense, Making Sense: Perils and Prospects for Sensory History', *Journal of Social History*, 40 (2007), 841–58; J. Bourke, *Fear: A Cultural History* (London: Virago, 2006); H.J. Rindisbacher, 'A Cultural History of Disgust', *KulturPoetik*, 5 (2005), 119–27; C.E. Forth, 'Fat, Desire and Disgust in the Colonial Imagination', *History Workshop Journal*, 73 (2012), 211–39.

9. This methodology was informed by the 'walking interviews' which geographers and anthropologists have used. See P. Jones et al., 'Exploring Space and Place with Walking Interviews', *Journal of Research Practice*, 4 (2008), 2; J. Evans and P. Jones, 'The Walking Interview: Methodology, Mobility and Place', *Applied Geography*, 31 (2011), 849–58.

10. P. Summerfield, *Histories of the Self: Personal Narratives and Historical Practice* (London: Routledge, 2018); L. Roper, 'Beyond Discourse Theory', *Women's History Review*, 19 (2010), 307–19.

11. S.C. Lubkemann, 'Unsettling the Metropole: Race and Settler Reincorporation in Postcolonial Portugal', in C. Elkins and S. Pedersen (eds.), *Settler Colonialism in the Twentieth Century* (London: Routledge, 2005), pp. 257–70; F. Chung, *Re-Living the Second Chimurenga: Memories from the Liberation Struggle in Zimbabwe* (Harare: Weaver Press, 2006).

12. For the notion of 'absenting' the native, see P. Wolfe, 'Settler Colonialism and the Elimination of the Native', *Journal of Genocide Research*, 8 (2006), 387–409. For apparent white attempts to absent Africans from natural environments, see D. Hughes, *Whiteness in Zimbabwe: Race, Landscape, and the Problem of Belonging* (New York: Routledge, 2010).

13. H. Dugan and L. Farina, 'Intimate Senses/Sensing Intimacy', *Postmedieval: A Journal of Medieval Cultural Studies*, 3 (2012), 373–9, at p. 375.

14. Interview with June Rasch, ZI033.

15. For homogenization, see J.D. Porteous, 'Smellscape', *Progress in Geography*, 9 (1985), 356–78, at pp. 362–3.

16. For 'smellscape', see Porteous.

17. A.L. Stoler, 'Tense and Tender Ties: The Politics of Comparison in North American History and (Post) Colonial Studies', *The Journal of American History*, 88, 3 (2001), 829–65, at p. 832.

18. T. Burke, 'Nyamarira That I Loved: Commoditisation, Consumption and the Social History of Soap in Zimbabwe', in *Collected Seminar Papers* (London: Institute of Commonwealth Studies, 1992), pp. 195–216; T. Burke, *Lifebuoy Men, Lux Women: Commodification, Consumption, and Cleanliness in Modern Zimbabwe* (Durham, NC: Duke University Press, 1996).

19. Burke, 'Nyamarira That I Loved', pp. 201–2; D. Kidd, *The Essential Kafir* (London: Black, 1904). Some ethnic groups were also recognized by early twentieth-century European travellers due to their wearing of imperfectly cured skins and the use of smoked ghee as a skin moisturizer.

20. It is worth noting that smell is subjective and connectedly notions of body odour are too. Similarly, Africans' use of soap did increase over the colonial period (in Uganda it was one of the primary products people bought by the 1950s). Deodorant may not have been so effective in the colonial era, or universally used by whites. However, the reality of smell and body odour did not especially matter as social segregation was an irrational matter.

21. G. Waitt, 'Bodies That Sweat: The Affective Responses of Young Women in Wollongong, New South Wales, Australia', *Gender, Place & Culture*, 21 (2014), 666–82; G. Waitt and E. Stanes, 'Sweating Bodies: Men, Masculinities, Affect, Emotion', *Geoforum*, 58 (2015), 30–38; A. McClintock, *Imperial Leather: Race, Gender, and Sexuality in the Colonial Contest* (London: Routledge, 2013); E. Shove, 'Converging Conventions of Comfort, Cleanliness and Convenience', *Journal of Consumer Policy*, 26 (2003), 395–418.

22. For discussions of race, smell and disease, see M. Smith, 'Transcending, Othering, Detecting: Smell, Premodernity, Modernity', *Postmedieval: A Journal of Medieval Cultural Studies*, 3 (2012), 380–90, at p. 386.

23. Smith, 'Transcending, Othering, Detecting', p. 387.

24. Interview with Peter Barak, ZI028.

25. ZNA, Cabinet Office, Co-ordination and supervision of Government CO3/01, 6841 008, 'Race Relations and Discrimination General 1960–63', Letter from EA Last, Manager of Kachalola Rest House to Mr Goodfellow, PC, Fort Jameson 11/6/1961.

26. Mr Veliades, the owner of the Rhodes Café in Kitwe who had been accused of racial discrimination in 1962, Zambia National Archives, Local Government and Housing, Native Affairs, LGH 7/9 3777 32 – Racial discrimination 1957–8, Kitwe 1962 Report.

27. Interviews with Brendon Lang, ZI042; in Kenya, see interviews with Charles Braithwaite, KI069 and Deidre Walton, KI062. For voluntary apartheid, see correspondence with Dom Walker, KI057.

28. M.O. West, *The Rise of an African Middle Class: Colonial Zimbabwe, 1898–1965* (Bloomington, IN: Indiana University Press, 2002); N. Cheeseman, '"No Bourgeoisie, No Democracy"? The Political Attitudes of the Kenyan Middle Class', *Journal of International Development*, 27 (2015), 647–64.

29. Interview with Mel Teevan, ZI020.

30. D. Kennedy, *Islands of White: Settler Society and Culture in Kenya and Southern Rhodesia, 1890–1939* (Durham, NC: Duke University Press, 1987); Shadle, *The Souls of White Folk*. See interview with Deidre Walton, KI062.

31. Kennedy, *Islands of White*, p. 176.

32. Kennedy, *Islands of White*, p. 188.

33. D. Anderson, 'Sexual Threat and Settler Society: "Black Perils" in Kenya, c. 1907–30', *The Journal of Imperial and Commonwealth History*, 38, 1 (2010), 47–74; J. McCulloch, *Black Peril, White Virtue: Sexual Crime in Southern Rhodesia, 1902–1935* (Bloomington, IN: Indiana University Press, 2000); O.C. Phillips, 'The "Perils" of Sex and the Panics of Race: The Dangers of Inter-Racial Sex in Colonial Southern Rhodesia', in S. Tamale (ed.), *African Sexualities: A Reader* (London: Fahamu/Pambazuka, 2011); Kennedy, *Islands of White*, pp. 177–9.

34. ZNA, Ministry of Education, ED 1/4/812/225, 'Separation of the Sexes', in *Northern News*, 8/8/1963.

35. Interview with Charles Braithwaite, KI069.

36. The ideas of intimate boundaries in this chapter draw upon A. Stoler, *Race and the Education of Desire: Foucault's History of Sexuality and the Colonial Order of Things* (Durham, NC: Duke University Press, 1995).

37. A. Harris and T. Jones, *Love and Romance in Britain, 1918–1970* (New York: Springer, 2014); C. Langhamer, *The English in Love: The Intimate Story of an Emotional Revolution* (Oxford: Oxford University Press, 2013); S. Szreter and K. Fisher, *Sex before the Sexual Revolution: Intimate Life in England 1918–1963* (Cambridge: Cambridge University Press, 2010), p. xvi.

38. R.K. Omondi and C. Ryan, 'Sex Tourism: Romantic Safaris, Prayers and Witchcraft at the Kenyan Coast', *Tourism Management*, 58 (2017), 217–27; R.K. Omondi, 'Gender and the Political Economy of Sex Tourism in Kenyas Coastal Resorts', a paper first presented at the International Symposium/Doctorial Course on Feminist Perspective on Global Economic and Political Systems and Women's Struggle for Global Justice at Sommoroya Hotel, Tromso, Norway, 24–26 September 2003, www.arsrc.org/downloads/features/omondi.pdf (accessed 15 June 2023).

39. Interview with Deidre Walton, KI062.

40. Interview with Charles Braithwaite, KI069.

41. Interview with the Websters, ZI008.

42. Interview with Leyton Moran, ZI005.

43. Interview with Leyton Moran, ZI005.

44. Interview with Leyton Moran, ZI005.

45. Interview with Leyton Moran, ZI005.

46. Interview with Edward Fisher, KI037.

47. Interviews with Sharon Mintram, KI002 and Charles Braithwaite, KI069.

48. Interview with Deborah Strathern, ZI041.

49. Interview with Deborah Strathern, ZI041. For other examples of racialized class, see interview with Tony Williams, ZI023; Sharon Mintram, KI002; Deidre Walton, KI062; Charles Braithwaite, KI069; and Trevor Donaldson, KI078.

50. Burke, *Lifebuoy Men, Lux Women*, pp. 99–104; Shadle, *The Souls of White Folk*, p. 32.

51. Interview with Reg Turner and Mel Turnbull, ZI027.

52. Interview with Mark Benson, KI043. This was reiterated by Charles Braithwaite, KI069.

53. Interview with Mark Benson, KI043.

54. R.J.C. Young, *Colonial Desire: Hybridity in Theory, Culture and Race* (London: Psychology Press, 2005).

55. Interview with Deidre Walton, KI062.

56. For arguments about the importance of emotional norms to maintaining the boundaries of settler colonial society in Kenya, see Shadle, *The Souls of White Folk*.

References

Primary sources

Oral history

All oral history dialogues and participant observations were collected by the author in 2016/17 and have been classmarked based upon a pseudonym, followed by Kenyan interviews (KI) or Zambian interviews (ZI) and an identifying number; for example, Deidre Walton, KI062.

Archives

Zambia National Archives (ZNA), Local Government and Housing, Native Affairs, LGH 7/9 777 32.
ZNA, Cabinet Office, Co-ordination and supervision of Government CO3/01, 6841 008.
ZNA, Ministry of Education, ED 1/4/812/225.

Secondary sources

Anderson, D., 'Sexual Threat and Settler Society: "Black Perils" in Kenya, c. 1907–30', *The Journal of Imperial and Commonwealth History*, 38, 1 (2010), 47–74.
Bourke, J., *Fear: A Cultural History* (London: Virago, 2006).
Burke, T., 'Nyamarira That I Loved: Commoditisation, Consumption and the Social History of Soap in Zimbabwe', in *Collected Seminar Papers Institute of Commonwealth Studies* (London, 1992), vol. 42, pp. 195–216.
——, *Lifebuoy Men, Lux Women: Commodification, Consumption, and Cleanliness in Modern Zimbabwe* (Durham, NC: Duke University Press, 1996).
Cheeseman, N., '"No Bourgeoisie, No Democracy"? The Political Attitudes of the Kenyan Middle Class', *Journal of International Development*, 27 (2015), 647–64.
Chung, F., *Re-Living the Second Chimurenga: Memories from the Liberation Struggle in Zimbabwe* (Harare: Weaver Press, 2006).
Classen, C., *The Deepest Sense: A Cultural History of Touch* (Champaign, IL: University of Illinois Press, 2012).
Dollimore, J., 'Sexual Disgust', in T. Dean and C. Lane (eds.), *Homosexuality and Psychoanalysis* (Chicago, IL: University of Chicago Press, 2001), pp. 367–87.

Dugan, H., and Farina, L., 'Intimate Senses/Sensing Intimacy', *Postmedieval: A Journal of Medieval Cultural Studies*, 3 (2012), 373–9.

Evans, J., and Jones, P., 'The Walking Interview: Methodology, Mobility and Place', *Applied Geography*, 31 (2011), 849–58.

Forth, C.E., 'Fat, Desire and Disgust in the Colonial Imagination', *History Workshop Journal*, 73 (2012), 211–39.

Harris, A., and Jones, T., *Love and Romance in Britain, 1918–1970* (New York: Springer, 2014).

Hochschild, A.R., 'Emotion Work, Feeling Rules, and Social Structure', *American Journal of Sociology*, 85 (1979), 551–75.

Hughes, D., *Whiteness in Zimbabwe: Race, Landscape, and the Problem of Belonging* (New York: Springer, 2010).

Ignatieff, N., *How the Irish Became White* (New York: Routledge, 1995).

Jones, P., Bunce, G., Evans, J., Gibbs, H. and Hein, J.R., 'Exploring Space and Place with Walking Interviews', *Journal of Research Practice*, 4 (2008), Article D2.

Kashita, J., *This Was My Africa: Living with Changes* (Charleston, SC: CreateSpace Independent Publishing Platform, 2018).

Kennedy, D., *Islands of White: Settler Society and Culture in Kenya and Southern Rhodesia, 1890–1939* (Durham, NC: Duke University Press, 1987).

Kidd, D., *The Essential Kafir* (London: Black, 1904).

Kuntsman, A., '"With a Shade of Disgust": Affective Politics of Sexuality and Class in Memoirs of the Stalinist Gulag', *Slavic Review*, 68, 2 (2009), 308–28.

Langhamer, C., *The English in Love: The Intimate Story of an Emotional Revolution* (Oxford: Oxford University Press, 2013).

Lubkemann, S.C., 'Unsettling the Metropole: Race and Settler Reincorporation in Postcolonial Portugal', in C. Elkins and S. Pedersen (eds.), *Settler Colonialism in the Twentieth Century* (London: Routledge, 2005), pp. 257–70.

McClintock, A., *Imperial Leather: Race, Gender, and Sexuality in the Colonial Contest* (London: Routledge, 2013).

McCulloch, J., *Black Peril, White Virtue: Sexual Crime in Southern Rhodesia, 1902–1935* (Bloomington, IN: Indiana University Press, 2000).

Omondi, R.K., 'Gender and the Political Economy of Sex Tourism in Kenyas Coastal Resorts', 2003. A paper first presented at the International Symposium/Doctorial Course on Feminist Perspective on Global Economic and Political Systems and Women's Struggle for Global Justice at Sommoroya Hotel, Tromso, Norway, 24–26

September 2003, www.arsrc.org/downloads/features/omondi.pdf (accessed 15 June 2023).

Omondi, R.K., and Ryan, C., 'Sex Tourism: Romantic Safaris, Prayers and Witchcraft at the Kenyan Coast', *Tourism Management*, 58 (2017), 217–27.

Phillips, O.C., 'The "Perils" of Sex and the Panics of Race: The Dangers of Inter-Racial Sex in Colonial Southern Rhodesia', in S. Tamale (ed.), *African Sexualities: A Reader* (London: Fahamu/Pambazuka, 2011).

Porteous, J.D, 'Smellscape', *Progress in Geography*, 9 (1985), 356–78.

Reddy, W.M., *The Navigation of Feeling: A Framework for the History of Emotions* (Cambridge: Cambridge University Press, 2001).

Rindisbacher, H.J., 'A Cultural History of Disgust', *KulturPoetik*, 5 (2005), 119–27.

Roper, L., 'Beyond Discourse Theory', *Women's History Review*, 18 (2010), 307–19.

Rosenwein, B.H., 'Worrying about Emotions in History', *The American Historical Review*, 107 (2002), 821–45.

——, *Emotional Communities in the Early Middle Ages* (Ithaca, NY: Cornell University Press, 2006).

Shadle, B.L., *The Souls of White Folk: White Settlers in Kenya, 1900s–20s* (Manchester: Manchester University Press, 2015).

Shove, E., 'Converging Conventions of Comfort, Cleanliness and Convenience', *Journal of Consumer Policy*, 26 (2003), 395–418.

Smith, M.M., 'Producing Sense, Consuming Sense, Making Sense: Perils and Prospects for Sensory History', *Journal of Social History*, 40 (2007), 841–58.

——, 'Transcending, Othering, Detecting: Smell, Premodernity, Modernity', *Postmedieval: A Journal of Medieval Cultural Studies*, 3 (2012), 380–90.

Stoler, A., 'Rethinking Colonial Categories: European Communities and the Boundaries of Rule', *Comparative Studies in Society and History*, 31 (1989), 134–61.

——, *Race and the Education of Desire: Foucault's History of Sexuality and the Colonial Order of Things* (Durham, NC: Duke University Press, 1995).

——, 'Tense and Tender Ties: The Politics of Comparison in North American History and (Post) Colonial Studies', *The Journal of American History*, 88, 3 (2001), 829–65.

Summerfield, P., *Histories of the Self: Personal Narratives and Historical Practice* (London: Routledge, 2018).

Szreter, S., and Fisher, K., *Sex before the Sexual Revolution: Intimate Life in England 1918–1963* (Cambridge: Cambridge University Press, 2010).

Waitt, G., 'Bodies That Sweat: The Affective Responses of Young Women in Wollongong, New South Wales, Australia', *Gender, Place & Culture*, 21 (2014), 666–82.

Waitt, G., and Stanes, E., 'Sweating Bodies: Men, Masculinities, Affect, Emotion', *Geoforum*, 58 (2015), 30–38.

West, M.O., *The Rise of an African Middle Class: Colonial Zimbabwe, 1898–1965* (Bloomington, IN: Indiana University Press, 2002).

Wolfe, P., 'Settler Colonialism and the Elimination of the Native', *Journal of Genocide Research*, 8 (2006), 387–409.

Wray, M., *Not Quite White* (Durham, NC: Duke University Press, 2006).

Young, R.J.C., *Colonial Desire: Hybridity in Theory, Culture and Race* (London: Psychology Press, 2005).

Chapter 7

Gender, mission, emotion: building hospitals for women in northwestern British India[1]

Sara Honarmand Ebrahimi

In 1864, Reverend Robert Clark, a missionary of the Church Missionary Society (CMS) in Punjab, and his wife, Elizabeth Mary Browne, visited Kashmir to find an 'opening' for evangelistic work. They were greeted with 'opposition' by the officials of the Maharajah and by 'the masses' who showed 'Mr. and Mrs. Clark that neither they nor their religion was welcome in Kashmir'. Despite these obstacles, Mrs Clark opened a dispensary that 'was largely attended' and this was taken as a sign of the need for a medical mission. Subsequently, the CMS Committee passed a resolution, and Dr William Jackson Elmslie, a medical graduate of the University of Edinburgh, was appointed to Kashmir to start a medical mission.[2] On 9 May 1865, Elmslie wrote, 'to-day is memorable in the history of the Kashmir Medical Mission from the fact that I opened my dispensary this morning'. The dispensary was in a small veranda in Elmslie's bungalow which had been 'rudely fitted up'. He then altered another veranda for inpatients and wrote that he had opened his 'small hospital'.[3] Obligated to leave Kashmir for the winter upon the order of the Maharajah, Elmslie returned the following spring to find that the landlord of his old quarters 'had been forbidden to let the house to the Padre Doctor Sahib, on the excuse that it was too near the city'. After some negotiations, a dispensary was built for him near the city. Again, 'in spite of sepoys placed at the different avenues leading to his house to prevent people coming to him', Elmslie wrote that a 'few days ago I had as many as a hundred and eighty patients in a morning, and at this moment a fine-looking elderly Mussulman of rank, from

169

the east end of the valley, has called to ask my advice'. While the opposition of authorities persisted, Elmslie not only reported an increase in the number of patients but also stated that 'the people are much less bigoted than formerly ... and a very large number of the inhabitants of the valley now look upon us as their friends, and in their difficulties and sorrows come to us for advice and sympathy'.[4] Elmslie died in 1872 and was succeeded by Dr Theodore Maxwell and his wife, Elizabeth Eyre, who arrived in Kashmir in autumn 1873. They managed to gain permission from the *wazir* (governor) to build a hospital. The number of patients grew in subsequent years. The hospital was enlarged by Maxwell's successors, Dr Arthur Neve and Dr Ernest Neve, and became one of the biggest medical missions of the CMS.[5]

This narrative summary, extracted from a series of articles published in the first volume of *Mercy and Truth*, a CMS medical magazine, is testimony to how the publications of different Protestant missionary organizations represented medical missions as instrumental in opening the door to evangelistic work. With few exceptions, published letters and reports uniformly discuss how, after experiencing a series of ups and downs, medical missionaries overcame the distrust of the local people, who would otherwise be unreceptive of the missionaries and gained access to their homes. It is important not to draw a false equivalence between present configurations of trust and friendship and the stated feelings of historical missionaries situated in different places. One should also avoid too readily interpreting these terms to imply 'pacifying' or 'solidifying' and assuming that the missionaries understood them in a way similar to other colonial actors across time and space.[6] To understand the meaning of these terms in the context of medical mission work, we should consider what changed with the introduction of medical work. Missionaries, who were not allowed to preach (and were greeted with stoning according to some accounts[7]) or failed to reach diverse people through Bible sales and distributions and schools, could, through medicine, get closer to a larger and more varied group of local people and visit them in their homes. Therefore, these terms imply a change in the sensory relationship between missionaries and local people. They emerged out of a century of mission work marked by frustration and failure to reach a large audience.

There were differences in how building trust was understood and practised, depending on the national affiliation of individual missionary organizations and where they worked. Complicating this picture further was how building trust concerned female missionaries in a different way and quality to male missionaries.[8] While coming into close contact with indigenous people was relevant to both male and female missionaries, it took on an extra shape for female missionaries in the form of 'familial connections' or 'sisterhood' with (potential) converts.[9] Thus, mission hospitals for women played a crucial role in changing the sensory relationships between missionaries and the local people.

The missionaries spent a great deal of time contemplating their own and prospective converts' emotions. The medical missionaries' practice of attempting to gain people's trust is an integral part of this history, which has recently gained new impetus because of the growing attention to the role of emotions in history making. Studies have gone beyond seeing emotions as limited to the private sphere of missionary family interactions and intimacy[10] and have shown that we need to investigate emotions if we are to understand colonial missions and colonialism fully.[11] But these have mainly focused on linguistic utterances and, to some extent, on habits, rituals, prayers and less on architecture or physical expressions. This chapter draws on Monique Scheer's concept of emotional practices and Rob Boddice's emphasis on biocultural historicism to examine how missionaries sought to change their sensory relationship with local people through the architecture of women's hospitals.[12] Scheer's emphasis on emotions as 'doing' allows examining architecture as emotional prescription that facilitated certain bodily practices (habits and routines) and thus 'doing emotions', while Boddice's biocultural, or body-mind-world dynamic, model helps acknowledge patients' diverse experiences and variations in the relationship between the management of space and the management of emotions.[13] The chapter shows how missionaries' concern with gaining trust resulted in a new architectural solution known as the '*purdah* hospital'. The emotional practices that this type of planning facilitated – such as cooking in the hospital and interacting with family and friends – did not take place against 'stable backgrounds' of experiential feelings that existed 'out there'; patients would appropriate – arrange, rearrange and categorize – these practices and construct experiences.[14]

Before turning to architecture, the chapter briefly highlights some of the different ways female missionaries were active players in British India. It demonstrates, by reading between the lines of missionary records, that there was more to female missionary work than most scholarship has recognized. More specifically, it argues that women's work in mission should include their involvement in the construction of the hospitals (and mission buildings more generally). Female missionaries were not only educators, doctors, nurses, traveller writers and collectors but were also amateur architects.[15] This recognition in turn means that scholarship on women and architecture in the late nineteenth and early twentieth centuries should include women who set sail for different countries across the British Empire. Their inclusion deepens our understanding of the relationship between women and the material and spatial environment. According to Lynne

Walker, houses and churches were two building types that were 'thought appropriate for women to design' in the nineteenth century because of beliefs in women's supposedly caring qualities and their superior moral and spiritual nature.[16] In contrast, many female missionaries designed not only houses and churches but also hospitals.[17] They contributed to the built environment by drawing plans, supervising building construction and renovating existing buildings solely and jointly with their male colleagues.

By introducing and examining the *purdah* hospital, the chapter also contributes to the historiography of hospital architecture in the nineteenth and early twentieth centuries, which is predominantly about the pavilion plan hospital. The advocates of pavilion design aimed to limit the spread of hospital infection by allowing air – and natural light – to permeate every part of the hospital. Pavilion plan hospitals often consisted of long rectangular wards that were housed in a separate pavilion. Each ward had windows facing each other along its length to ensure cross-ventilation as well as its own sanitary facilities – baths, sinks and water closets – that were usually placed at the end of the ward. According to Cor Wagenaar, the pavilion plan was 'the first revolution' in the history of hospital architecture: 'a victory of science, philosophy and technology'.[18] Scholars such as Jeremy Taylor and Jeanne Kisacky further argue that this type of hospital planning became an *international* standard by the late nineteenth century.[19] These arguments are based on the examination of a few military and state hospitals, with no due consideration to mission hospitals and hospitals built in China, Africa and South America, those constructed by non-British empires and those by North Americans in the colonized world.[20] An examination of all these hospitals is required to address the extent to which the pavilion plan became an international standard. Protestant mission hospitals are a particularly important lens through which a history of hospital architecture in the global context can be written. This is because they had emerged as one of the main providers of 'Western biomedical services' in colonial territories, if not the only one in some regions, by the early twentieth century.[21] Although the secular and mission medicine in colonies shared characteristics in terms of disease conceptions and healing perceptions, it was the latter that engaged in major spending on medical facilities at the local level.[22] A focus on mission hospitals challenges the assumption that the pavilion plan became an international standard.[23]

Female missionaries as amateur architects

While women (including single women) were increasingly accepted as missionaries in their own rights from the second half of the nineteenth century, as stated by Rhonda Anne Sample, their labour 'remained undervalued in terms of both remuneration and administrative advancement, until well into the twentieth century'.[24] Mrs Clark is an exemplary instance of female exclusion from official mission histories. Mrs Clark was a hospital worker (a sister of St John at King's College Hospital) before marrying Robert Clark in 1858. Moreover, her father was a medical doctor, Dr Robert Browne, who had worked in Calcutta for forty-five years.[25] She was also instrumental in the foundation of the hospital of the Church of England Zenana Missionary Society in Amritsar, which was known as the St Catherine Hospital.[26] Yet the CMS publications deny her any active role. In 1939, the CMS medical magazine, *The Mission Hospital*, published an article entitled, 'CMS Medical Missions: Our Yesterdays'. After stating that the medical work of the CMS is focused in 'seventy-seven hospitals, 200 welfare centres, and thirty-three leper colonies', the article asked, 'How did it all begin?' Although it acknowledged the vision and achievement of 'giant men and women', it only referred to male missionaries when explaining 'the first days'.[27] It is telling to note that guidelines for the recruitment and training of women candidates were only formally presented at the Edinburgh Missionary Conference in 1910.[28] Moreover, the CMS accepted women to its General Committee for the first time in 1917.[29] The contribution of female (medical) missionaries to building construction was another excluded area.

Dr Minnie Gomery is among the female medical missionaries who contributed to building construction. She established the John Bishop Memorial Hospital in Islamabad (Anantnag) in 1902, where she worked until her retirement in 1935. The hospital was named after the Scottish doctor, John Bishop, whose wife, Isabella Bird, a well-known explorer, established a hospital in his name in Kashmir in the 1880s. A severe flood damaged this hospital in 1891 and the John Bishop Memorial Hospital in Islamabad took its place.[30]

In her obituary, E.H. Bensley, the head of the Faculty of Medicine at McGill University, explained about Gomery's time in Islamabad and her life after retirement but left out her involvement in the construction process of the John Bishop Memorial Hospital.[31] This omission mirrors missionary publications which played down the role of female missionaries in building construction, referring to their involvement, at the very best, only in passing. According to Annmarie Adams, women's role as 'regulators' of the household system 'fitted well with Victorian theories of sexual difference, which claimed that because of the smallness of their brains, women were better at arranging or finishing work started by men rather than initiating the work themselves'.[32] Moreover, as Lynne Walker writes, designing chapels or churches 'reinforced the idea of women's supposedly superior moral and spiritual nature'.[33] These beliefs underwent a change with the acceptance of women as professional architects by the late nineteenth century. But female missionaries, many of whom were not from middle-class backgrounds, were involved in planning, repairing and supervising buildings long before this period. Their range of activities fell outside the contemporary accepted definition of women's capacity. As early as the middle decades of the nineteenth century, Bessie Price, the daughter of the London Missionary Society missionary to South Africa, Robert Moffat, lent a hand in repairing buildings when needed.[34] By the late nineteenth century, female missionaries were sharing the design of the buildings with their male colleagues. Gomery did not initiate building construction – this task was left to the Neve brothers of the Kashmir medical mission – but she designed the buildings with their help. She and Miss Newnham, a nurse, also 'marked out on the site the proposed position of the buildings, according to plans'.[35] Additionally, she looked after the 'plastering, floor-ing, &c' upon the completion of building construction.[36] Moreover, in a 1902 report, Gomery stated that 'I carefully planned a window for one of our bedrooms'.[37]

The female missionaries of the CMS in Persia also left their mark on the architectural landscape, as did those of the Society for the Promotion of Gospel in Foreign Lands (SPG) in China, British India and Africa. A few examples include Dr Winifred Westlake of the CMS and Jenny C. Muller, Emily Lawrence and Ethel Margaret Phillips of the SPG. When the decision was made to build a separate hospital for women in Kerman, G. Everard Dodson and Westlake drew the plan of the hospital together: 'Enclosing preliminary plan of new women's hospital drawn by himself and Dr Westlake', wrote Dodson in a letter on 7 June 1904.[38] Muller 'care-fully and skilfully planned' St Stephen's Hospital in Delhi and the hospital in Karnal.[39] The 1934 report of SPG called her 'the creator of St. Stephen's Hospital'.[40] Phillips drew the plans of St Agatha's Hospital for Women in Shandong, China and superintended the construction of the buildings, and Lawrence oversaw the construction of the first medi-cal mission on Madagascar's eastern coast.[41] Their involvement in building design and construction demonstrates what Elizabeth Prevost describes as the 'highly independent nature of single missionary activ-ity'.[42] Female missionaries were able to escape metropolitan pressures and gain professional experience while stretching the 'boundaries of socially sanctioned notions of femininity', thus experiencing 'opportunities nor-mally reserved for men'.[43]

In her examination of the design of Australian Inland Mission's cottage hospitals, Cathy Keys argues that nursing sisters' 'knowledge of social and climatic conditions' influenced their design. They not only offered advice on building materials, the number of doors and windows and the size of verandas but also sought to 'combine nursing, medical and social work in a single plan under one roof'.[44] In other words, they acted as reformers while innovating new architectural designs.

Purdah hospital

The John Bishop Memorial Hospital was one of the active ninety-three mission hospitals for women in British India in 1927. Under colonial health policies, the provision of medical relief to Indian women was most conspicuously inadequate. As Rosemary Fitzgerald states, 'Western responses to Indian women's health needs came largely from philanthropic organizations, and, most notably, the missionary societies'.[45] The ninety-three mission hospitals for women that were recorded in *A Survey of the Status and Conditions of Women in India* represented over half of all women's hospitals in India.[46] This statistic highlights what was stated at the start of this chapter; that is, mission hospitals are an essential lens through which we can explore hospital architecture in the British Empire.

The design of mission hospitals was often left to the care of the medical missionaries. Although archival materials offer little help in understanding how they designed the hospitals, they show that they had access to new and approved design criteria including models of pavilion plan hospitals. But many mission hospitals did not live up to the principles of the pavilion plan. If there was one place where they should have built a pavilion hospital, or at least a 'miniature pavilion hospital',[47] it was in Islamabad, because the Neve brothers had designed a pavilion plan hospital in Kashmir built between 1886 and 1895.[48] The first John Bishop Memorial Hospital was also a pavilion plan hospital. It consisted of 'an out-patient department, a waiting-room, consulting-room, operating room, dispensary; two pavilions, fifty feet long, to hold thirty-two patients'.[49] Yet the missionaries (the Neve brothers and Gomery) opted instead for two bungalows, one containing four small wards for twelve inpatients and the other comprising the operating room, the consulting and dressing rooms and a dispensary for outpatients.[50] Although not in layout and appearance, in being a bungalow, the hospital was a variation on the Dera Ismail Khan or the Bannu hospitals, both of which were not very different from the bungalows of the Public World Department of British India.[51] In other words, they can be examined side by side if the topic is the global production of the bungalow. But if the topic is hospital architecture, then the Islamabad Hospital is aligned with cottage or small local hospitals. In Britain, the cottage hospital originated in the mid-nineteenth century and, in time, became the ideal type for meeting the medical and surgical needs of rural districts, small towns or specific communities.[52] Gomery and the Neve brothers might have drawn on such pattern books as *A Handy Book of Cottage Hospitals* (1870) and Henry Burdett's *Cottage Hospitals: General, Fever and Convalescent.*[53]

Because of financial and practical factors, and in order to accumulate interest, missionaries often established medical missions in a step-by-step manner. First, they opened outpatient dispensaries, after which they started inpatient departments, followed by the construction of a purpose-built hospital. Thus, Gomery went against the grain of medical missionaries' standard practice by building a hospital straight away after her arrival. She wanted to build a hospital as quickly as possible and opted for a cottage hospital because of financial constraints. Gomery and the Neve brothers might also have been motivated by the fact that a cottage hospital was small in scale and could be constructed using 'domestic-scale' details, and hence could fit into its surroundings, thus making it less likely to stand as a threat.[54] They sourced stone from the surrounding mountains, and Neve described the hospital as 'unpretentious' in his 1904 report.[55] The importance the missionaries assigned to hospital buildings as emotional setups in accumulating interest is clear here. While building a hospital straight after their arrival was not advisable, architecture could intervene and cancel out potential alarming feelings. The missionaries' hope was that the patients would be confronted with familiar, if not necessarily local, buildings, and thus be more willing to go to the hospital.

Although the missionaries hoped the three free-standing buildings (including the missionary house), built out of rough stone with their tiled roof and chimneys, fit into their surroundings, they might still have appeared different to people. This might have even been desirable to some missionaries. Gomery noted in her report in 1902 that 'as these are the first buildings in other than native style in Islamabad, the people are naturally much interested and often amused at all they see, and their remarks are very interesting'.[56] The hospital's location away from the town of Islamabad might also point to the role of missionaries as guardians of social and cultural change in the imperial enterprise. They viewed the 'native city' as a source of illness and disease, and the spatial separation was supposed to bring change.[57] Yet Islamabad, according to Neve, was 'a populous district, and on all sides, we see flourishing villages and scattered homesteads. Within a twenty-mile radius must be a quarter of a million people, for whom Islamabad is a commercial centre'.[58] If buildings like those of the John Bishop Hospital were new in Islamabad, they were not in many other parts of the country. They could neither have 'amused' nor could they have a 'civilizing' influence on everyone.

Moreover, the hospital was not merely a cottage hospital. Arthur Neve's 1904 report indicated that the hospital had, in fact, a distinct design, where it described the hospital as a *purdah* hospital: 'It is a *Purdah* hospital, kept strictly for women, but the waiting-room is by the roadside, and is occasionally used for men.'[59] *Purdah* (literally 'a curtain') is the term that is commonly used for referring to the system of secluding women through clothing and architecture in the Middle East and South Asia. It is practised among both Muslims and Hindus, although each has a different understanding of the practice, meaning that they observe or keep *purdah* differently and to varying degrees.[60] By *purdah*, Neve might have merely meant that the hospital was strictly for women. Yet, the location of the inpatient block on the steep slope part of the compound behind the outpatient block ensured that it was, to some extent, invisible from the road. Indeed, the design of the hospital facilitated the implementation of the *purdah* system. Being part of many patients' daily life, the *purdah* arrangement could allow certain experiences and thus confront the patients with feelings of trust and affection. Practices such as observing seclusion were meant to facilitate the experience of these feelings.

The idea of a *purdah* hospital was executed on a different, more tangible level in the design of the Multan Hospital, which was described as having an 'extreme purdah arrangement'.[61] Eger established the Multan Hospital in 1885 under the auspices of the Society for Promoting Female Education in China, India and the East (FES).[62] When the CMS took over the FES's work and workers in 1899, the Multan Hospital was transferred to the CMS.[63] The hospital was divided between Muslims and Hindus, with each group having their own compound that consisted of wards and a courtyard. The hospital also had an inner, walled area and an outer section. The interior space was composed of an entrance block and an inpatient block and the outpatient department, with 'operating-room and special surgical and private wards, besides a large hall where the out-patients assemble for Bible teaching'.[64] The outer section consisted of rooms, or a *caravanserai*, for male relatives of the female patients. In other words, like houses in some parts of Persia and India, the hospital had an *andarūni* (inner section) and a *birūni* (outer section). The only difference was that the hospital's *andarūni* was not a family quarter and was reserved for women.[65]

Eliza F. Kent states that missionaries in India generally did not aim to force women to disregard *purdah*. Their goal was instead to transform women's identification with home so that they could be 'preservers of the home' based on the ideals of Christian faith.[66] The CMS missionaries might have been thinking along similar lines when designing the Multan Hospital. Eger's statement in 1901 is telling:

> One very purdah Mohammedan woman whom, with great difficulty, I got into the hospital, explained on arrival, 'Oh, keep me here; I have come from their own tiny dark rooms!' ... After her recovery her husband told me he was looking for a house built after the hospital pattern, as his wife had been so happy there![67]

Medical missionaries sought to teach new ideas about health and hygiene through a pre-existing architecture that was meaningful to the women. The *purdah* arrangement of the hospital was meant to be reminiscent of patients' homes and thus attract them to the hospital. In this way, the patients were confronted with an emotional setup that could cause them to 'do' an emotion, such as feeling attracted to the hospital. Once they were in the hospital, they followed certain rules and regulations, learning in turn new ideas about health and hygiene. Nevertheless, Sister A.R. Simmonds made a statement in 1937 that contradicts Eger's perspective: '[t]his may sound strange to those who only know English hospitals, but in the East our patients like to be out on the veranda or open compound until the sun gets hot; then every one [sic] goes into the ward, and the fierce heat is shut out'.[68] Simmonds does not present wards as airy and bright and the hospital as similar to an English hospital. The buildings were dark and were not cross-ventilated. Simmonds's focus was instead on patients' movement in the hospital; she spoke of the shifting balance between outside and inside spaces in mission hospitals and thus the extent to which they displayed surveillance and order.[69] The missionaries provided a familiar environment but they did so by disregarding some of their own ideals in favour of patients' needs. In this way, they hoped to facilitate certain practices, thus attracting patients to the hospital while encouraging them to stay. There would have been more chance of converting the patients if they stayed, so the missionaries thought.

Analysing the Multan Hospital as simply a hybrid structure overlooks how male and female missionaries experienced spaces and places differently, which could influence their architectural decisions. Female missionaries had access to women and their sex-segregated private and domestic realm. They offered a 'corrective vision' of the veil through the *purdah* hospital, hoping to strengthen their identification with women.[70] The *purdah* arrangement could facilitate certain practices: an outer section for male relatives welcomed many women who 'would not [have been] able to stay with us [missionaries] unless provision was made for their men', stated Eger in 1901.[71] This illustrates that designing a *purdah* hospital was linked to the missionaries' desire to attract as many people as possible. It could also assure the male relatives that their wives or daughters were protected and separated from the eyes of male strangers. Moreover, patients were able to move in and out of the wards whenever desired, thus they could interact with one another and exchange news as they would in their homes or in public spaces such as *hammam*. The *purdah* system was an architectural solution to the practical problem of attracting female patients, viewed as essential to their experiences. Take, for example, Eger's statement regarding 'unappreciative Hindus' in 1906:

> Picture No. 1 shows the interior of the large wards – it was built in three rooms connected by large arches in the hope that Hindu patients would occupy a part of it, and also to make it easy to hold a service for a number of patients together. But we cannot get Hindus to see with us in this matter. They do not like our large, tiled room, but prefer small mud rooms on the outside of the purdah wall, where they can squeeze in various members of their family, and which they can on taking possession cleanse to their own satisfaction from all ceremonial defilement of the last inhabitant.[72]

While Eger's language is racially charged not least because of her use of the term 'unappreciative', it highlights how the material arrangement of the hospital allowed the Hindu patients to make a special provision for themselves. They were permitted to bring their utensils and cook their food in the hospital. A picture of 'friends of Hindu patients cooking in hospital' accompanied Simmonds's report, showing patients and their female family members surrounded by pots and pans. The decision of the Hindu patients was not a form of transgression; the design of the hospital encouraged this activity. The Hindu patients' move was in conformity with the expectations inherent in a *purdah* arrangement and their culturally and historically specific preconceptions of the *purdah* system. In other words, this form of spatial arrangement facilitated the practices of staying with family and friends, brining utensils and cooking in the hospital. If these practices did not arouse patients' interest in medical missionaries and their work, they at least attracted them to the hospital and encouraged them to remain.

Returning to Sister Simmonds's report, she also described part of the 'inner working of' the Multan Hospital: 'the whole hospital is quiet, the porter is asked to prevent men at the gate calling to their wives inside ... for it is so disturbing when this happens, and the wife calls back *"Andi pai"* [I am coming] and goes!'[73] This statement demonstrates that female missionaries' evaluations of the *purdah* system collided with that of indigenous women.[74] Meanwhile, public areas such as *hammam*, where women could gather, were also subject to strict rules, social conventions and religious laws.[75] Missionaries' efforts in controlling female patients' interaction with their male relatives did not necessarily alter the emotional significance of the practice of observing *purdah*. Rather, some female patients might have understood missionaries' prescriptions according to their previous experiences and thus still found the hospital familiar and habitable.

Nevertheless, *purdah* was not a meaningful practice among all members of a community.[76] Some women did not favour the *purdah* system and manipulated the meanings and representations associated with this system. Others, who observed *purdah*, also acted as religious leaders, storytellers and healers and even promoted women's welfare and education.[77] As Ann Grodzins Gold states, '[w]omen may think of purdah ... as a cover behind which they gain the freedom to follow their own lights, rather than as a form of bondage or subordination'.[78] How women observed *purdah* also varied between rural and urban areas and between elite and non-elite families. In other words, there were internal differences in the emotional charges of *purdah* based on religion, profession and class. Receiving treatment in a *purdah* hospital may have conformed only to some patients' expectations and preconceptions. Missionaries' plans to attract the patients by facilitating the practice of *purdah* could sometimes fail, leading to a form of 'feeling differently'; that is, 'failing to feel correctly'.[79]

The women's hospital opened in Bannu was also described as a *purdah* hospital; it was separated from the men's block by a small by-road.[80] Moreover, in 1923 a new building was added to the Peshawar Hospital consisting of 'three private wards' where 'a purdah family could be housed and remain separate from the rest of the patients'.[81] Notably, the *purdah* hospital was a new type of hospital architecture, unknown in Britain. Hospital wards in Britain were separated based on gender, but did not have a separate walled section for women.

The missionaries did not disseminate the design of the Multan Hospital widely and did not build a *purdah* hospital in other mission fields. Yet, providing privacy for women was as much of a concern in Persia and Palestine as in northwestern British India. As Philippe Bourmand states regarding the Nablus Hospital, besides being 'finance-related' and 'hygiene-concerned', discussions regarding the design of the hospital were 'part of a moral agenda: where were the women's wards and their toilets, or the entrances of the hospital and to the consultation room, so as to create as much gender separation as possible, and prevent an occasion for scandal?'[82] The women hospitals built in these regions might be described as *purdah*-like. For example, while access to the men's hospital in the Isfahan Hospital in Persia was direct, access to the women's hospital was indirect; it was planned at a distance from the inpatient section and was connected to it by an L-shaped passageway. This arrangement was similar to courtyard houses where the entrance was set at a distance from the central yard to prevent a direct view of the interior, thereby providing privacy.[83]

Apart from the private environment of the inpatient sections of the Kerman and Isfahan hospitals for women, entering them through an L-shaped passageway was a practice that could affect many patients as they would be able to practically appreciate it. It was meant to be reminiscent of local women's daily lives and thus attract them to the hospital. Female missionaries were familiar with such architectural features because of their access to the female quarters of the houses. Thus, they most likely pushed for them or even handled their execution.

Conclusion

This chapter focused on female missionaries, their involvement in the construction process of mission hospitals and their importance in gaining trust and friendship. There were multiple layers of exclusion and inclusion in official histories and reports of mission societies. In particular, these publications failed to acknowledge the contribution of female medical missions to the built environment. One of the female medical missionaries involved in building construction was Dr Minnie Gomery, the founder of the John Bishop Memorial Hospital in Islamabad. Gomery shared the design of the hospital with the Neve brothers. Although she did not supervise building construction, there were female medical missionaries who were involved in planning, repairing and superintending the construction of the buildings as early as the middle decades of the nineteenth century, and it is possible to speculate about their role by analysing the hospitals' layout.

In appearance, the women's hospitals were either like models in Britain, such as the Islamabad Hospital, which was modelled after cottage hospitals or mimicked men's hospitals. However, a closer examination reveals that they were designed to provide women with a private and segregated space. The missionaries in northwestern British India employed the term 'purdah hospital' to highlight this distinctive feature of women's hospitals, and the Multan Hospital had a *purdah* arrangement. Consisting of an outer section for male relatives and an inner section, the plan of the Multan Hospital was not dissimilar to traditional courtyard houses. The *purdah* arrangement of the hospitals was essential to patients' experience of women's hospitals. While the *purdah* system was not a meaningful practice for every woman, it could, at the very least, prevent 'occasions of scandal'.

Notes

1. This chapter is extracted from chapter 5 of S. Honarmand Ebrahimi, *Emotion, Mission, Architecture: Building Hospitals in Persia and British India, 1865–1914* (Edinburgh: Edinburgh University Press, 2023). Reproduced in a revised format with permission of Edinburgh University Press through PLSclear.

2. A.W.F.H., 'The Opening of the Door in Kashmir, Part I', *Mercy and Truth*, 1, 8 (1897), 173–7 at p. 174.

3. A.W.F.H., 'The Opening of the Door in Kashmir, Part I', p. 175.

4. A.W.F.H., 'The Opening of the Door in Kashmir, Part I', pp. 176–7.

5. T. Maxwell, 'The Opening of the Door in Kashmir, 1873–1876', *Mercy and Truth*, 1, 9 (1897), 199–203.

6. S. Honarmand Ebrahimi, 'Medical Missionaries and the Invention of the "Serai Hospital" in North-Western British India', *European Journal for the History of Medicine and Health*, 79 (2022), 67–93, https://doi.org/10.1163/26667711-bja10013. To read about the importance of avoiding using emotion words as if their meanings are readily understandable, see R. Boddice, *A History of Feelings* (London: Reaktion Books, 2019), p. 19.

7. For example, see D.W. Carr, 'Progress in Persia', *Mercy and Truth*, 11, 128 (1907), 236–41 at p. 238.

8. To read about how emotions are gendered, see U. Frevert, *Emotions in History: Lost and Found* (Budapest: Central European University Press, 2013), pp. 87–247.

9. R.A. Sample, *Missionary Women: Gender, Professionalism and the Victorian Idea of Christian Mission* (Woodbridge: Boydell Press, 2003), p. 3; H. Murre-van den Berg, 'Dear Mother of My Soul: Fidelia Fiske and the Role of Women Missionaries in Mid-Nineteenth Century Iran', *Exchange*, 30 (2001), 33–48. For sisterhood, see D.L. Robert, *American Women in Mission: A Social History of Their Thought and Practice* (Macon: Mercer University Press, 1997), p. 133.

10. E.J. Manktelow, *Missionary Families: Race, Gender and Generation on the Spiritual Frontier* (Manchester: Manchester University Press, 2013), p. 6.

11. C. McLisky, D. Midena and K. Vallgårda (eds.), *Emotions and Christian Missions: Historical Perspectives* (Basingstoke: Springer, 2015); R. Swartz, 'Educating Emotions in Natal and Western Australia, 1854–65', *Journal of Colonialism and Colonial History*, 18 (2017), doi: 10.1353/cch.2017.0022; T. Ballantyne, 'Moving Texts and "Humane Sentiment": Materiality, Mobility and the Emotions of Imperial Humanitarianism', *Journal of Colonialism and Colonial History*, 17 (2016), doi: 10.1353/cch.2016.0000; K.A.A. Vallgårda, 'Tying Children to God with Love: Danish Mission, Childhood, and Emotions in Colonial South India', *Journal of Religious History*, 39 (2015), 595–613, doi: 10.1111/1467-9809.12265. Also see chapters 5 and 6 of J. Lydon, *Imperial Emotions: The Politics of Empathy across the British Empire* (Cambridge: Cambridge University Press, 2020), pp. 123–63; J. Van Gent, 'Global Protestant Missions and the Role of Emotions', in U. Rublack (ed.), *Protestant Empires: Globalizing the Reformations* (Cambridge: Cambridge University Press, 2020), pp. 275–95; S. Cummins and J. Lee, 'Missionaries: False Reverence, Irreverence and the Rethinking of Christian Mission in China and India', in B. Gammerl, P. Nielsen and M. Pernau (eds.), *Encounters with Emotions: Negotiating Cultural Differences since Early Modernity* (New York: Routledge, 2019), pp. 37–60.

12. R. Boddice and M. Smith, *Emotion, Sense, Experience* (Cambridge: Cambridge University Press, 2021); also see R. Boddice, *Human Professions: The Defence of Experimental Medicine, 1876–1914* (Cambridge: Cambridge University Press, 2021), pp. 1–19; R. Boddice, 'The Cultural Brain as Historical Artifact', in L.J. Kirmayer et al.

(eds.), *Culture, Mind, and Brain: Emerging Concepts, Models, and Applications* (Cambridge: Cambridge University Press, 2020), pp. 367–74.

13. It also helps to distinguish between the approach of missionaries and present-day architects with access to a large body of guidebooks suggesting users' enhancement. Also see S. Honarmand Ebrahimi, 'Introduction: Exploring Architecture and Emotions through Space and Place', *Emotions: History, Culture, Society*, 6 (2022), 65–77, doi: https://doi.org/10.1163/2208522X-02010146.

14. As Boddice states, 'There is no experimental feeling inherent in events, in objects, in relations. They all have to be made.' R. Boddice, *The History of Emotions* (Manchester: Manchester University Press, 2018), p. 162. Also see M. Pernau, 'Space and Emotion: Building to Feel', *History Compass*, 12 (2014), 541–9, doi: https://doi.org/10.1111/hic3.12170; A. Reckwitz, 'Affective Spaces: A Praxeological Outlook', *Rethinking History*, 16 (2012), 241–58, doi: 10.1080/13642529.2012.681193.

15. I. Livne, 'The Many Purposes of Missionary Work: Annie Royle Taylor as Missionary, Travel Writers, Collector and Empire Builder', in H. Nielssen, I.M. Okkenhaug and K. Hestad Skeie (eds.), *Protestant Missions and Local Encounters in the Nineteenth and Twentieth Centuries: Unto the Ends of the World* (Leiden: Brill, 2011), pp. 43–70.

16. L. Walker, 'Women and Architecture', in J. Attfield and P. Kirkham (eds.), *A View from the Interior: Feminism, Women and Design* (London: The Women's Press, 1989), p. 94.

17. For the contribution of female missionaries to church architecture, see D.K. Martin, 'The Churches of Bishop Robert Gray & Mrs Sophia Gray', unpublished PhD thesis (University of Cape Town, 2002).

18. C. Wagenaar, 'Five Revolutions: A Short History of Hospital Architecture', in C. Wagenaar (ed.), *The Architecture of Hospitals* (Rotterdam: NAi Publishers, 2006), p. 26.

19. J. Taylor, *Hospital and Asylum Architecture in England 1840–1914: Building for Health Care* (London: Mansell, 1991); J. Kisacky, *Rise of the Modern Hospital: An Architectural History of Health and Healing, 1870–1940* (Pittsburgh, PA: University of Pittsburgh Press, 2017), pp. 23–4.

20. For three exceptions, see S. De Nys-Ketels, 'A Hospital Typology Translated: Transnational Flows of Architectural Expertise in the Clinique Reine Elisabeth of Coquilhatville, in the Belgian Congo', *ABE Journal*, 19 (2021), doi: https://doi.org/10.4000/abe.12715; C. Bastos, 'The Hut-Hospital as Project and as Practice: Mimeses, Alterities, and Colonial Hierarchies', *Social Analysis: The International Journal of Anthropology*, 62 (2018), 76–97, doi: https://doi.org/10.3167/sa.2018.620204; M. Campbell Renshaw, *Accommodating the Chinese: The American Hospital in China, 1880–1920* (London: Routledge, 2016).

21. See M. Jennings, 'Healing of Bodies, Salvation of Souls: Missionary Medicine in Colonial Tanganyika, 1870s–1939', *Journal of Religion in Africa*, 38 (2008), 27–56 at p. 28; D. Hardiman, 'The Mission Hospital, 1880–1960', in M. Harrison, M. Jones and H. Sweet (eds.), *From Western Medicine to Global Medicine: The Hospital Beyond the West* (Hyderabad: Orient BlackSwan, 2009), p. 198.

22. D. Hardiman, 'Introduction', in D. Hardiman (ed.), *Healing Bodies, Saving Souls: Medical Missions in Asia and Africa* (Amsterdam: Brill, 2006), pp. 5–6. Also see R. Fitzgerald, 'Rescue and Redemption: The Rise of Female Medical Missions in Colonial India during the Late Nineteenth and Early Twentieth Centuries', in A.M. Rafferty, J. Robinson and R. Elkan (eds.), *Nursing History and the Politics of Welfare* (London: Routledge, 1997), p. 67; M. Vaughan, *Curing Their Ills: Colonial Power and African Illness* (Palo Alto, CA: Stanford University Press, 1991), p. 56.

23. Honarmand Ebrahimi, 'Medical Missionaries and the Invention of the "Serai Hospital"'.

24. Sample, *Missionary Women: Gender, Professionalism.*

25. H.M. Clark, *Robert Clark of the Punjab: Pioneer and Missionary Statesman* (London: A. Melrose, 1907), pp. 139–40.

26. 'Women's Medical Missions in India', *The Church Missionary Gleaner*, 19, 223 (1892), 100–101 at p. 100.

27. 'CMS Medical Missions: Our Yesterdays', *The Mission Hospital*, 43, 492 (1939), 12–16 at p. 15; G. Kings, 'Abdul Masih: Icon of Indian Indigeneity', *International Bulletin of Missionary Research*, 23 (1999), 66–9 at p. 69.

28. Sample, *Missionary Women: Gender, Professionalism*, p. 2.

29. K.J. Trace Farrimond, 'The Policy of the Church Missionary Society Concerning the Development of Self-Governing Indigenous Churches, 1900–1942', unpublished PhD thesis (University of Leeds, 2003), p. 45.

30. 'The Mission-Field'. *Church Missionary Intelligencer*, 16, new series (1891), 766–72 at p. 769.

31. P170 Minnie Gomery Fonds, Folder 2, Osler Library Archive, McGill University.

32. A. Adams, *Architecture in the Family Way: Doctors, Houses, and Women, 1870–1900* (Montreal: McGill-Queen's University Press, 1996), p. 152.

33. Walker, 'Women and Architecture', p. 94.

34. D. Gaitskell, 'Rethinking Gender Roles: The Field Experience of Women Missionaries in South Africa', in A. Porter (ed.), *The Imperial Horizons of British Protestant Missions 1880–1914* (Grand Rapids, MI: William B. Eerdmans Publishing Company, 2003), pp. 134–5.

35. From Dr M. Gomery, *Extracts from the Annual Letters of the Missionaries for the Year 1901* (London, 1902), p. 553.

36. 'Items: Home and Foreign', *Mercy and Truth*, 6, 61 (1902), 4–8 at p. 6.

37. M. Gomery, 'Work in the New Hospital at Islamabad', *Mercy and Truth*, 6, 72 (1902), 362–3 at p. 362.

38. G.E. Dodson, 7 June 1904, CMS/M/C 2/1 4, no. 56, Cadbury Research Library, Special Collection, University of Birmingham (CRL).

39. Edited by her mother, *Letters of Marie Elizabeth Hayes, M. B. Missionary Doctor, Delhi, 1905–8* (London: Marshall Brothers, 1909), pp. 218–19.

40. *The Eternal Purpose: Being the Report of the Year 1934 of the Society for the Propagation of the Gospel in Foreign Parts* (London, 1934), p. 96.

41. C.H. Phillips, *The Lady Named Thunder: A Biography of Dr. Ethel Margaret Phillips (1876–1951)* (Alberta: University of Alberta Press, 2003), pp. 131–44; E. Prevost, 'Married to the Mission Field: Gender, Christianity, and Professionalization in Britian and Colonial Africa, 1865–1914', *Journal of British Studies*, 47 (2008), 796–826 at p. 814, doi: 10.1086/590171.

42. Prevost, 'Married to the Mission Field'.

43. J. Lee, 'Between Subordination and She-Tiger: Social Constructions of White Femininity in the Lives of Single, Protestant Missionaries in China, 1905–1930', *Women's Studies International Forum*, 19 (1996), 621–32 at p. 624, https://doi.org/10.1016/S0277-5395(96)00073-8.

44. C. Keys, 'Designing Hospitals for Australian Conditions: The Australian Inland Mission's Cottage Hospital, Adelaide House, 1926', *The Journal of Architecture*, 21 (2016), 68–89 at pp. 82–3, doi: 10.1080/13602365.2016.1141790.

45. Fitzgerald, 'Rescue and Redemption', p. 63.

46. M. Balfour and R. Young, *The Work of Medical Women in India* (London: H. Milford, 1930), pp. 45–79, referred to in Fitzgerald, 'Rescue and Redemption', p. 64.

47. J. Taylor, *Hospital and Asylum Architecture in England*, p. 73.

48. For detailed discussion, see Honarmand Ebrahimi, 'Medical Missionaries and the Invention of the "Serai Hospital"', pp. 10–12.

49. A.M. Stoddart, *The Life of Isabella Bird (Mrs. Bishop)* (London: J. Murray, 1906), p. 206.

50. M. Gomery, 'The New John Bishop Memorial, Islamabad', *Mercy and Truth*, 6, 65 (1902), 146–7 at p. 146.

51. A.D. King, *The Bungalow: The Production of a Global Culture* (New York: Routledge & Kegan Paul, 1995).

52. Taylor, *Hospital and Asylum Architecture in England*, p. 73. Also see R.M.S. McConaghey, 'The Evolution of the Cottage Hospital', *Medical History*, 11 (1967), 128–40, doi: https://doi.org/10.1017/S0025727300011984.

53. H. Swete, *Handy Book of Cottage Hospitals, Issue 133* (London: Hamilton, Adams and Co., 1870); H.C. Burdett, *Cottage Hospitals: General, Fever, Convalescent: Their Progress, Management, and Work in Great Britain and Ireland and the United States of America*, 3rd ed. (London: Scientific Press, 1896).

54. Taylor, *Hospital and Asylum Architecture in England*, p. 73.

55. A. Neve, 'John Bishop Memorial Hospital, Islamabad', *Mercy and Truth*, 8, 91 (1904), 199–201 at p. 199.

56. Gomery, 'The New John Bishop Memorial, Islamabad', p. 147.

57. King, *The Bungalow*, p. 35.

58. Neve, 'John Bishop Memorial Hospital, Islamabad', p. 199.

59. Neve, 'John Bishop Memorial Hospital, Islamabad', p. 200.

60. H. Papanek, 'Purdah: Separate Worlds and Symbolic Shelter', *Comparative Studies in Society and History*, 15 (1973), 289–325 at p. 289. *Purdah* also constitutes behaviours including veiling, silence and bodily gestures such as seeking a place of lower elevation.

61. A.W. Eger, 'The Mission Hospital at Multan', *Mercy and Truth*, 5, 56 (1901), 180–83 at p. 180.

62. 'CMS Medical Missions: A Comparative Survey', *Mercy and Truth*, 18, 214 (1914), 347–50 at p. 347.

63. 'Things to Be Noted', *Mercy and Truth*, 3, 32 (1899), 181–4 at p. 182.

64. Eger, 'The Mission Hospital at Multan', p. 180.

65. G. Memarian and F. Brown, 'The Shared Characteristics of Iranian and Arab Courtyard Houses', in B. Edwards, M. Sibley, M. Hakmi and P. Land (eds.), *Courtyard Housing: Past, Present, and Future* (London: Taylor & Francis, 2006), pp. 21–30.

66. E.F. Kent, *Converting Women: Gender and Protestant Christianity in Colonial South India* (Oxford: Oxford University Press, 2004), p. 128.

67. Eger, 'The Mission Hospital at Multan', p. 180.

68. Sister A.R. Simmonds, 'Pressing Forward in Multan', *The Mission Hospital*, 41, 469 (1937), 27–30 at p. 28.

69. The same was the case in the Isfahan Hospital. See S. Honarmand Ebrahimi, '"Ploughing before Sowing": Trust and the Architecture of the Church Missionary

Society (CMS) Medical Missions', *Architecture and Culture*, 7 (2019), 197–217 at p. 205, doi: 10.1080/20507828.2019.1608051.

70. I am inspired here by Ambereen Dadabhoy's examination of Lady Mary Wortley Montagu's *Turkish Embassy Letters*. Montagu is known for her poems, her contribution to the fight against smallpox and, last but not least, her life in Turkey where her husband worked as the British ambassador. See A. Dadabhoy, '"Going Native": Geography, Gender, and Identity in Lady Mary Wortley Montagu's *Turkish Embassy Letters*', in M. Narain and K. Gevirtz (eds.), *Gender and Space in British Literature, 1660–1820* (London: Routledge, 2016), p. 52.

71. Eger, 'The Mission Hospital at Multan', p. 180.

72. W. Eger, 'Some of Our Multan Patients', *Mercy and Truth*, 10, 118 (1906), 300–304 at p. 301.

73. Simmonds, 'Pressing Forward in Multan', p. 28.

74. S. Mills, 'Gender and Colonial Space', *Gender, Place and Culture: A Journal of Feminist Geography*, 3 (1996), 125–48 at p. 142, doi: 10.1080/09663699650021855.

75. Dadabhoy, '"Going Native": Geography, Gender, and Identity', p. 54.

76. To read about the highly differentiated voices and viewpoints of Muslim woman on any social and political issue, see G. Falah and C. Nagel (eds.), *Geographies of Muslim Women: Gender, Religion, and Space* (New York: Guilford Press, 2005).

77. Begum Wali-ud-Dowla was the president of the Hyderabadi Women's Association. S. Chakraborty, 'European Nurses and Governesses in Indian Princely Households: "Uplifting That Impenetrable Veil"?', *Journal of Colonialism and Colonial History*, 19 (2018), doi: 10.1353/cch.2018.0001.

78. A. Grodzins Gold, 'Purdah Is as Purdah's Kept: A Storyteller's Story', in G. Goodwin and A. Grodzins Gold (eds.), *Listen to the Heron's Words: Reimagining Gender and Kinship in North India* (Berkeley, CA: University of California Press, 1994), p. 164. Also see J. Burkhalter Flueckiger, *In Amma's Healing Room: Gender and Vernacular Islam in South India* (Bloomington, IN: Indiana University Press, 2006).

79. B. Gammerl, J.S. Hutta and M. Scheer, 'Feeling Differently: Approaches and Their Politics', *Emotion, Space and Society*, 25 (2017), 87–94, https://doi.org/10.1016/j.emospa.2017.07.007.

80. Miss E. Giles, 'First Impressions of Bannu', *The Mission Hospital*, 35, 396 (1931), 8–12 at p. 9.

81. J.H. Cox, 'Peshawar Hospital: Extension', *The Mission Hospital*, 28, 312 (1924), 3–4 at p. 3.

82. P. Bourmaud, 'Public Space and Private Spheres: The Foundation of St Luke's Hospital of Nablus by the CMS (1891–1901)', in H. Murre-van den Berg (ed.), *New Faith in Ancient Lands: Western Missions in the Middle East in the Nineteenth and Early Twentieth Centuries* (Leiden: Brill, 2006), p. 140.

83. Memarian and Brown, 'The Shared Characteristics of Iranian and Arab Courtyard Houses', p. 26.

References

Primary sources

A.W.F.H., 'The Opening of the Door in Kashmir, Part I', *Mercy and Truth*, 1, 8 (1897), 173–7.

Balfour, M., and Young, R., *The Work of Medical Women in India* (London: H. Milford, 1930).

Burdett, H.C., *Cottage Hospitals: General, Fever, Convalescent – Their Progress, Management, and Work in Great Britain and Ireland and the United States of America*, 3rd ed. (London: Scientific Press, 1896).

Carr, D.W., 'Progress in Persia', *Mercy and Truth*, 11, 128 (1907), 236–41.

Clark, H.M., *Robert Clark of the Punjab: Pioneer and Missionary Statesman* (London: A. Melrose, 1907).

'CMS Medical Missions: A Comparative Survey', *Mercy and Truth*, 18, 214 (1914), 347–50.

'CMS Medical Missions: Our Yesterdays', *The Mission Hospital*, 43, 492 (1939), 12–16.

Cox, J. H., 'Peshawar Hospital: Extension', *The Mission Hospital*, 28, 312 (1924), 3–4.

Dodson, G.E., 7 June 1904, CMS/M/C 2/1 4, 56, Cadbury Research Library, Special Collection, University of Birmingham.

Eger, A.W., 'The Mission Hospital at Multan', *Mercy and Truth*, 5, 56 (1901), 180–83.

Eger, W., 'Some of Our Multan Patients', *Mercy and Truth*, 10, 118 (1906), 300–304.

Giles, Miss E., 'First Impressions of Bannu', *The Mission Hospital*, 35, 396 (1931), 8–12.

Gomery, M., *Extracts from the Annual Letters of the Missionaries for the Year 1901* (London, 1902).

——, 'The New John Bishop Memorial, Islamabad', *Mercy and Truth*, 6, 65 (1902), 146–7.

——, 'Work in the New Hospital at Islamabad', *Mercy and Truth*, 6, 72 (1902), 362–3.

Hayes, M.E. *Letters of Marie Elizabeth Hayes, M. B. Missionary Doctor, Delhi, 1905–8* (edited by her mother) (London: Marshall Brothers, 1909), pp. 218–19.

'Items: Home and Foreign', *Mercy and Truth*, 6, 61 (1902), 4–8.

Maxwell, T., 'The Opening of the Door in Kashmir, 1873–1876', *Mercy and Truth*, 1, 9 (1897), 199–203.

Neve, A., 'John Bishop Memorial Hospital, Islamabad', *Mercy and Truth*, 8, 91 (1904), 199–201.

P170 Minnie Gomery Fonds, Folder 2, Osler Library Archive, McGill University.

Simmonds, Sister A.R., 'Pressing Forward in Multan', *The Mission Hospital*, 41, 469 (1937), 27–30.

Stoddart, A.M., *The Life of Isabella Bird (Mrs. Bishop)* (London: J. Murray, 1906).

Swete, H., *Handy Book of Cottage Hospitals, Issue 133* (London: Hamilton, Adams & Co., 1870).

The Eternal Purpose: Being the Report of the Year 1934 of the Society for the Propagation of the Gospel in Foreign Parts (London, 1934).

'The Mission-Field', *Church Missionary Intelligencer*, 16, new series (1891), 766–72.

'Things to Be Noted', *Mercy and Truth*, 3, 32 (1899), 181–4.

'Women's Medical Missions in India', *The Church Missionary Gleaner*, 19, 223 (1892), 100–101.

Secondary sources

Adams, A., *Architecture in the Family Way: Doctors, Houses, and Women, 1870–1900* (Montreal: McGill-Queen's University Press, 1996).

Ballantyne, T., 'Moving Texts and "Humane Sentiment": Materiality, Mobility and the Emotions of Imperial Humanitarianism', *Journal of Colonialism and Colonial History*, 17 (2016), doi: 10.1353/cch.2016.0000.

Bastos, C., 'The Hut-Hospital as Project and as Practice: Mimeses, Alterities, and Colonial Hierarchies', *Social Analysis: The International Journal of Anthropology*, 62 (2018), 76–97, doi: https://doi .org/10.3167/sa.2018.620204.

Boddice, R., *The History of Emotions* (Manchester: Manchester University Press, 2018).

——, *A History of Feelings* (London: Reaktion Books, 2019).

——, 'The Cultural Brain as Historical Artifact', in L.J. Kirmayer et al. (eds.), *Culture, Mind, and Brain: Emerging Concepts, Models, and Applications* (Cambridge: Cambridge University Press, 2020), pp. 367–74.

——, *Human Professions: The Defence of Experimental Medicine, 1876–1914* (Cambridge: Cambridge University Press, 2021).

Boddice, R., and Smith, M., *Emotion, Sense, Experience* (Cambridge: Cambridge University Press, 2021).

Bourmaud, P., 'Public Space and Private Spheres: The Foundation of St Luke's Hospital of Nablus by the CMS (1891–1901)', in H. Murre-van den Berg (ed.), *New Faith in Ancient Lands: Western Missions in the*

Middle East in the Nineteenth and Early Twentieth Centuries (Leiden: Brill, 2006), pp. 133–50.

Burkhalter Flueckiger, J., *In Amma's Healing Room: Gender and Vernacular Islam in South India* (Bloomington, IN: Indiana University Press, 2006).

Campbell Renshaw, M., *Accommodating the Chinese: The American Hospital in China, 1880–1920* (London: Routledge, 2016).

Chakraborty, S., 'European Nurses and Governesses in Indian Princely Households: "Uplifting That Impenetrable Veil"?', *Journal of Colonialism and Colonial History*, 19 (2018), doi: 10.1353/cch.2018.0001.

Cummins, S., and Lee, J., 'Missionaries: False Reverence, Irreverence and the Rethinking of Christian Mission in China and India', in B. Gammerl, P. Nielsen and M. Pernau (eds.), *Encounters with Emotions: Negotiating Cultural Differences since Early Modernity* (New York: Routledge, 2019), pp. 37–60.

Dadabhoy, A., '"Going Native": Geography, Gender, and Identity in Lady Mary Wortley Montagu's *Turkish Embassy Letters*', in M. Narain and K. Gevirtz (eds.), *Gender and Space in British Literature, 1660–1820* (London: Routledge, 2016), pp. 49–66.

Falah, G., and Nagel, C. (eds.), *Geographies of Muslim Women: Gender, Religion, and Space* (New York: Guilford Press, 2005).

Fitzgerald, R., 'Rescue and Redemption: The Rise of Female Medical Missions in Colonial India During the Late Nineteenth and Early Twentieth Centuries', in A.M. Rafferty, J. Robinson and R. Elkan (eds.), *Nursing History and the Politics of Welfare* (London: Routledge, 1997), pp. 64–79.

Frevert, U., *Emotions in History: Lost and Found* (Budapest: Central European University Press, 2013).

Gaitskell, D., 'Rethinking Gender Roles: The Field Experience of Women Missionaries in South Africa', in A. Porter (ed.), *The Imperial Horizons of British Protestant Missions 1880–1914* (Grand Rapids, MI: William B. Eerdmans Publishing Company, 2003), pp. 131–57.

Gammerl, B., Hutta, J.S. and Scheer, M., 'Feeling Differently: Approaches and Their Politics', *Emotion, Space and Society*, 25 (2017), 87–94, https://doi.org/10.1016/j.emospa.2017.07.007.

Grodzins Gold, A., 'Purdah Is as Purdah's Kept: A Storyteller's Story', in G. Goodwin and A. Grodzins Gold (eds.), *Listen to the Heron's Words: Reimagining Gender and Kinship in North India* (Berkeley, CA: University of California Press, 1994), pp. 164–81.

Hardiman, D., 'Introduction', in D. Hardiman (ed.), *Healing Bodies, Saving Souls: Medical Missions in Asia and Africa* (Amsterdam: Brill, 2006), pp. 5–58.

———, 'The Mission Hospital, 1880–1960', in M. Harrison, M. Jones and H. Sweet (eds.), *From Western Medicine to Global Medicine: The Hospital beyond the West* (Hyderabad: Orient BlackSwan, 2009), pp. 198–220.

Honarmand Ebrahimi, S., '"Ploughing before Sowing": Trust and the Architecture of the Church Missionary Society (CMS) Medical Missions', *Architecture and Culture*, 7 (2019), 197–217, doi: 10.1080/20507828.2019.1608051.

———, 'Introduction: Exploring Architecture and Emotions through Space and Place', *Emotions: History, Culture, Society*, 6 (2022), 65–77, doi: https://doi.org/10.1163/2208522X-02010146.

———, 'Medical Missionaries and the Invention of the "Serai Hospital" in North-Western British India', *European Journal for the History of Medicine and Health*, 79 (2022), 67–93, https://doi.org/10.1163/26667711 -bja10013.

Jennings, M., 'Healing of Bodies, Salvation of Souls: Missionary Medicine in Colonial Tanganyika, 1870s–1939', *Journal of Religion in Africa*, 38 (2008), 27–56.

Kent, E.F., *Converting Women: Gender and Protestant Christianity in Colonial South India* (Oxford: Oxford University Press, 2004).

Keys, C., 'Designing Hospitals for Australian Conditions: The Australian Inland Mission's Cottage Hospital, Adelaide House, 1926', *The Journal of Architecture*, 21 (2016), 68–89, doi: 10.1080/13602365.2016.1141790.

King, A.D., *The Bungalow: The Production of a Global Culture* (New York: Routledge & Kegan Paul, 1995).

Kings, G., 'Abdul Masih: Icon of Indian Indigeneity', *International Bulletin of Missionary Research*, 23 (1999), 66–9.

Kisacky, J., *Rise of the Modern Hospital: An Architectural History of Health and Healing, 1870–1940* (Pittsburgh, PA: University of Pittsburgh Press, 2017).

Lee, J., 'Between Subordination and She-Tiger: Social Constructions of White Femininity in the Lives of Single, Protestant Missionaries in China, 1905–1930', *Women's Studies International Forum*, 19 (1996), 621–32, https://doi.org/10.1016/S0277-5395(96)00073-8.

Livne, I., 'The Many Purposes of Missionary Work: Annie Royle Taylor as Missionary, Travel Writer, Collector and Empire Builder', in H. Nielssen, I.M. Okkenhaug and K. Hestad Skeie (eds.), *Protestant Missions and Local Encounters in the Nineteenth and Twentieth Centuries: Unto the Ends of the World* (Leiden: Brill, 2011), pp. 43–70.

Lydon, J., *Imperial Emotions: The Politics of Empathy across the British Empire* (Cambridge: Cambridge University Press, 2020).

Manktelow, E.J., *Missionary Families: Race, Gender and Generation on the Spiritual Frontier* (Manchester: Manchester University Press, 2013).

Martin, D.K., 'The Churches of Bishop Robert Gray & Mrs Sophia Gray', unpublished PhD thesis (University of Cape Town, 2002).

McConaghey, R.M.S., 'The Evolution of the Cottage Hospital', *Medical History*, 11 (1967), 128–40, doi: https://doi.org/10.1017 /S0025727300011984.

McLisky, C., Midena, D. and Vallgårda, K. (eds.), *Emotions and Christian Missions: Historical Perspectives* (Basingstoke: Springer, 2015).

Memarian, G., and Brown, F., 'The Shared Characteristics of Iranian and Arab Courtyard Houses', in B. Edwards, M. Sibley, M. Hakmi and P. Land (eds.), *Courtyard Housing: Past, Present, and Future* (London: Taylor & Francis, 2006), pp. 21–30.

Mills, S., 'Gender and Colonial Space', *Gender, Place and Culture: A Journal of Feminist Geography*, 3 (1996), 125–48, doi: 10.1080/09663699650021855.

Murre van den Berg, H., 'Dear Mother of My Soul: Fidelia Fiske and the Role of Women Missionaries in Mid-Nineteenth Century Iran', *Exchange*, 30 (2001), 33–48.

Nys-Ketels, S. De, 'A Hospital Typology Translated: Transnational Flows of Architectural Expertise in the Clinique Reine Elisabeth of Coquilhatville, in the Belgian Congo', *ABE Journal*, 19 (2021), doi: https://doi.org/10.4000/abe.12715.

Papanek, H., 'Purdah: Separate Worlds and Symbolic Shelter', *Comparative Studies in Society and History*, 15 (1973), 289–325.

Pernau, M., 'Space and Emotion: Building to Feel', *History Compass*, 12 (2014), 541–9, doi: https://doi.org/10.1111/hic3.12170.

Phillips, C.H., *The Lady Named Thunder: A Biography of Dr. Ethel Margaret Phillips (1876–1951)* (Alberta: University of Alberta Press, 2003).

Prevost, E., 'Married to the Mission Field: Gender, Christianity, and Professionalization in Britain and Colonial Africa, 1865–1914', *Journal of British Studies*, 47 (2008), 796–826, doi: 10.1086/590171.

Reckwitz, A., 'Affective Spaces: A Praxeological Outlook', *Rethinking History*, 16 (2012), 241–58, doi: 10.1080/13642529.2012.681193.

Robert, D.L., *American Women in Mission: A Social History of Their Thought and Practice* (Macon: Mercer University Press, 1997).

Sample, R.A., *Missionary Women: Gender, Professionalism and the Victorian Idea of Christian Mission* (Woodbridge: Boydell Press, 2003).

Swartz, R., 'Educating Emotions in Natal and Western Australia, 1854–65', *Journal of Colonialism and Colonial History*, 18 (2017), doi: 10.1353/cch.2017.0022.

Taylor, J., *Hospital and Asylum Architecture in England 1840–1914: Building for Health Care* (London: Mansell, 1991).

Trace Farrimond, K.J., 'The Policy of the Church Missionary Society Concerning the Development of Self-Governing Indigenous Churches, 1900–1942', unpublished PhD thesis (University of Leeds, 2003).

Vallgårda, K.A.A., 'Tying Children to God with Love: Danish Mission, Childhood, and Emotions in Colonial South India', *Journal of ReHistory*, 39 (2015), 595–613, doi: 10.1111/1467-9809.12265.

Van Gent, J., 'Global Protestant Missions and the Role of Emotions', in U. Rublack (ed.), *Protestant Empires: Globalizing the Reformations* (Cambridge: Cambridge University Press, 2020), pp. 275–95.

Vaughan, M., *Curing Their Ills: Colonial Power and African Illness* (Palo Alto, CA: Stanford University Press, 1991).

Wagenaar, C., 'Five Revolutions: A Short History of Hospital Architecture', in C. Wagenaar (ed.), *The Architecture of Hospitals* (Rotterdam: NAi Publishers, 2006), pp. 26–42.

Walker, L., 'Women and Architecture', in J. Attfield and P. Kirkham (eds.), *A View from the Interior: Feminism, Women and Design* (London: The Women's Press, 1989), pp. 90–105.

Part III

MODERN EUROPE'S PUBLIC SPHERE AND THE POLICING OF THE GENDERED BODY

Chapter 8

'The sap that runs in it is the same': how the ideal of romantic love challenged the myth of 'primitive' polygamy in Paolo Mantegazza's sexual science

Francesca Campani

In the second half of the eighteenth century, the spread of the ideal of romantic love set off an epochal change in European societies. In opposition to previous marriage customs that were mainly based on the practice of arranged marriages, the new emotional paradigm – namely, a new common understanding about sentimental relationships – spread in the West, an ideal for which the only valid reason for marriage had to be a strong love bond between a man and a woman. Although slow and uneven, the diffusion of this ideal in many ways represented a real revolution, as it triggered deep changes not only in the way emotional relationships between individuals were understood but also with respect to how family ties, child-rearing and, not least, sexuality were experienced. Nevertheless, few historians to date have considered this phenomenon in relation to the emergence of a discipline, sexual science, that contributed greatly to the development of the modern Western conception of sexuality.[1]

One of the reasons for this is certainly that Michel Foucault, in his seminal work *The Will to Knowledge* (1976), does not consider romantic love among the factors influencing the emergence of sexual science. Despite the fact that the philosopher acknowledges that, starting in the eighteenth century, the family became 'an obligatory place of affection, of feelings, of love', his analysis does not go much further, concentrating on the development of the medical-scientific discourses on sexuality and the mechanisms of power connected to it without considering the influence of the new affective paradigm.[2]

Among the first to point out this lacuna in Foucault's texts is Anthony Giddens. Building on the work of historian Lawrence Stone, in *The Transformation of Intimacy* (1992) Giddens stresses the importance of considering the spread of the ideal of romantic love as a key element in the development of the modern understanding of sexuality.[3] Developing Giddens's work, historian Henry Oosterhuis also emphasized the need to take into consideration the influence of the social and cultural context in which scientific theories on sexuality developed and how they were received, accepted or retracted by individuals. In doing so, Oosterhuis turns his attention to romantic love as a cultural and emotional element that contributed decisively to the conceptualization of sexuality as the quintessence of an individual's identity. In other words, he writes: 'in the wake of romantic love, sexuality was individualised, and it grew into a separate, largely internalised, sphere of human life'.[4] Although Oosterhuis emphasizes the importance of taking a broad view that also considers long-term cultural phenomena, he focuses his research primarily on psychiatry as the context within which these changes took shape. As will be shown in this chapter, however, the ideal of romantic love had a much wider influence and also influenced anthropological research and its analysis of the marriage bonds of colonized peoples within European empires.

A second aspect overlooked by Foucault in his analysis of the development of Western sexual science is precisely how the image of the non-Western 'Others' influenced the European understanding of sexuality and love, namely how it contributed to the idea that the monogamous heterosexual couple was the 'civilized' normative model to be followed. As Andrew and Harriet Lyons argue, Foucault did not consider 'the "differently sexed savage", nor did he examine the places of the anthropologist in the structure of knowledge and power he ... elaborated'.[5] Yet, a substantial amount of historiography has been produced on how the Western sexualized (male) gaze was not a secondary issue in the construction of colonial discourse and how, at the same time, Western ways of understanding sexuality were shaped by the racial conceptions of the time.[6] From this point of view, however, in the Italian context more attention has been paid to the dynamics inherent to the fascist era, leaving the nineteenth-century context largely unexplored.[7] Within this framework, the construction of scientific knowledge about sexuality was also influenced by contact with the Other. This has only been highlighted in recent years, leading historiography to explore how constructions of the 'primitive' mirrored and provided a counterpart to the construction of Western sexuality within the emergence of sexual science.[8]

This chapter aims to combine these two perspectives and to contribute to the analysis of the complex intersections and interweavings that involve categories such as sexuality, race and gender in scientific discourses during the second half of the nineteenth century. I will demonstrate how the emotional paradigm of romantic love influenced anthropological research on the sexual habits of both Western and colonized peoples, and in particular on adopted marriage structures. To do so, I will focus on an analysis of the intellectual production of Paolo Mantegazza (1831–1910), one of the leading anthropologists and sexual scientists of post-unification Italy. First, I will illustrate how romantic love became the emotional paradigm championed by the Italian elites who undertook the task of laying the societal foundations of the new-born nation. Mantegazza, part of the Italian positivist bourgeoisie, advocated love's relevance to his readers, targeting women in particular. Second, I will show how romantic love not only influenced Mantegazza's scientific thinking but was also in some ways at the root of nineteenth-century investigations into human sexuality because of its influence on Charles Darwin's (1809–82) theories. Third, I will compare Mantegazza's work with that of Henry Westermarck (1862–1939), considered, so far, among the first to question the perspectives of nineteenth-century evolutionary anthropology. This discussion substantiates my hypothesis that Mantegazza's challenge of the myth of 'primitive' polygamy was a consequence of the influence that romantic love had on his sexual science and anthropology. This will lead me to question the existence of a clear shift from evolutionary anthropology to the culturalist approach, and to claim that discourses tending to relativize the behaviour of a people according to their culture – or generalizing features of human beings regardless of their 'race' – were already present within evolutionary hierarchical discourses, as in Mantegazza's case.

The ideal of romantic love in post-unification Italy

In nineteenth-century Italy, the diffusion of the ideal of romantic love appears to have been closely intertwined with the rise of the national patriotic movement.[9] Strongly influenced in their ideals by Romanticism, the Risorgimento elites were committed not only to shaping the political, economic and social contours of the new-born Italian state but also to spreading a new emotional and sexual morality. In the aftermath of unification, the institution of marriage was beset by a series of tensions, such as the debate around the civil rite introduced in 1865 by the first Italian civil code, the so-called 'Pisanelli code', the proposed divorce law and the socialist propaganda of free love.[10]

Conceiving of the family as the link in a wider chain of parental ties, the post-unification bourgeoisie felt the need to secure the stability of Italian society and reaffirm the centrality of marriage as an institution, rejecting divorce and the search for paternity and extending marital authorization to the entire peninsula.[11] Among the motivations behind this stance was adherence to the ideals of romantic love. National patriotic rhetoric had in fact insisted on the idea that at the basis of every good marriage there should be a strong love bond. In contrast to the habits of the aristocracies of the *ancien régime* whereby marriages tended to be arranged, the Italian bourgeoisie was convinced that only a marriage for love would guarantee a future of happiness for individuals and, consequently, a future of prosperity and peace for the entire nation. Paolo Mantegazza can undoubtedly be counted among the ranks of those who committed themselves, in the aftermath of unification, to drawing the contours of the new society or, in other words, to 'making Italians'. Elected first as a deputy (1865) and later as a senator of the kingdom (1875), during his career Mantegazza devoted his scientific investigation to improving the living conditions of the citizens of the newly formed Italian state, showing a particular interest in issues related to their sexuality and affectivity. Trained as a physician, he began his career by engaging in the study of hygiene, writing works that variously fell into the genre of so-called guides to 'matrimonial hygiene'. Together with *Igiene dell'amore* (*Hygiene of Love*) (1877), a compendium and deepening of his other earlier works such as *Fisiologia del piacere* (*Physiology of Pleasure*) (1854) and *Elementi di igiene* (*Elements of Hygiene*) (1865), Mantegazza wrote the famous *Fisiologia dell'amore* (*Physiology of Love*) (1873).

In this work, he undertakes a detailed analysis of love as a 'feeling' from a philosophical and psychological point of view. Focusing mainly on European civilization, Mantegazza describes a feeling that largely mirrored the characteristics underlying the ideal of romantic love. A deep and all-embracing bond between a man and a woman, the presence of a space in which it was possible to have (within certain limits) a free experience of sexuality and pleasure, and recognition of the need – for both men and women – to choose their partner in complete freedom were the elements that characterized the bond that should underlie matrimonial relationships for him. Moreover, Mantegazza deemed love to be the 'prince of affections'.[12] In his view, it was a profound feeling that, in its highest form, involved an individual in all aspects. Therefore, in line with the scientific trends of the central decades of the nineteenth century, Mantegazza divided psychic phenomena into the three classes of 'senses', 'feelings' and 'thoughts', considered as the main components of human beings.[13] Thus, while it was true that there were types of love that intersected, the apex of human affectivity – or what Mantegazza called 'perfect love' – could only be achieved through the perfect harmony of all three elements.

In the book, Mantegazza goes on to advocate the adoption of the new emotional paradigm by the couples of the new-born Italian state. In doing so, he addressed himself primarily to the female audience or, as he called them at the opening of the work, 'the daughters of Eve'.[14] His readers expressed great enthusiasm for the work, addressing letters to Mantegazza through which they described their adherence to the new emotional paradigm in its various aspects, including those more related to the body and eroticism. His targeting of female readers was in line with the conviction of the time that women were naturally closer to the sphere of feelings and affections. Whereas men were generally associated with the public sphere, with matters related to politics, economics and civil society, women were to be seen as the queens of the affections, those who had to take care of the domestic sphere related to the family and raising children.

Women, therefore, were for Mantegazza a kind of specialist in the field of feelings. Unlike men, who were more inclined to stop superficially at the aesthetics of forms, in love relationships women were more often capable of achieving what we have seen described as 'perfect love'. The woman, in fact,

> can hardly ever love without esteem ... This difference alone is enough to show that in the psychic evolution of the two sexes woman advances us in the aesthetics of feeling than we advance her in intellectual development. Woman has already reached perfect love, which is the fusion of all human elements, which is the election of elections; we also see in the lover and the bride the concubine ... In love we are more often disciples than masters in the field of feelings.[15]

Without any doubt, even if women were deemed to be specialists in feelings, it was still Mantegazza – a white bourgeois man – who drew the guidelines of amorous affection. At the same time, however, female readers' responses show that it was becoming a widely shared emotional ideal – by both men and women – to such an extent that one could suggest the emergence in the nineteenth century of an 'emotional community' sharing the same understanding of love.[16]

Mantegazza therefore conducted a real campaign in support of romantic love and marriage by free choice. As will be seen later, in the scientific investigations conducted throughout his career, the ideal of romantic love constituted one of the cornerstones of his sexual science, continuing to represent the interpretative framework within which he developed his interests in human sexuality, even when he orientated them towards non-Western populations. Before looking at this, it is perhaps worth considering how, from the mid-nineteenth century onwards, the ideal of romantic love was adhered to in scientific discourse by a number of scholars, including Mantegazza.

The influence of romantic love at the roots of sexual science

In the nineteenth century, sexual science emerged alongside anthropology. The parallel development of these two disciplines favoured the creation of close interconnections between issues such as race and sexuality, an aspect of both fields of study that has only recently begun to be explored.[17] From this perspective, Mantegazza represents an interesting example of this interconnection. Known as the father of Italian anthropology and a scientist of sexuality, he stands at the crossroads of this process of disciplinary and epistemological development. Mantegazza in fact grounded his sexual science in his anthropological method. Although he intended the anatomical and biological component of humans as the starting point of his investigation, he was convinced that at the same time it was also necessary to investigate its psychological, social and cultural aspects. Therefore, even in his analysis of human sexuality, he adopted an all-encompassing perspective, which included not only the physiological mechanics of reproduction but also the investigation of human sexual behavioural habits set in their social and cultural context.

From this perspective, human psychology, and within it the sphere of feelings, represented one of the most important aspects of the human which needed to be investigated through the analysis of its manifestations. Certainly, Mantegazza did not deny the physiological origin of psychic phenomena, convinced that they were no different from other physical forces 'except for the forms in which they manifest themselves and the special organs that produce them'.[18] However, he believed that science at the time was not yet sufficiently advanced in the histological analysis of the human brain, so he considered it inevitable that the psyche would be studied through 'external and apparent acts, actions and works', pursuing a comparative study of human behaviours.[19]

In the psychological study of the emotions, Mantegazza was strongly influenced by the scientific trends of the time, not only by the studies of Herbert Spencer (1820–1903) who wrote the *Principles of Psychology* (1855)[20] but above all by the research carried out by Charles Darwin who, in 1872, published *The Expression of the Emotions in Man and Animals*, one year before Mantegazza's *Fisiologia dell'amore*.[21] Although throughout 1871

Mantegazza repeatedly noted in his diary the need to focus on writing his book, it was not until September 1872 that it took shape. In particular, in December of the same year, Mantegazza noted that he had 'read Darwin's last work' and immediately afterwards that he wrote '68 pages of the Physiology of Love' followed by the note 'I revise them all and send them to the printer',[22] suggesting that Darwin's work did indeed have some influence on the drafting of his book. Like the English scientist, Mantegazza was convinced that complex emotions such as love were the result of a long evolutionary process. Thus, not only were elementary expressions of the emotions to be found in animals but European civilization, considered to be the most advanced, carried forward – or rather had to tend towards – its most advanced forms. In essence, both Mantegazza and Darwin regarded romantic love as the apex of the emotionality of living beings, for which the study of the feeling in its earlier stages of evolution would be useful. For this reason, they were convinced that to study the earlier stages of the development of this emotion was necessary in order to fully understand its deeper meanings in contemporary times. The anthropologist wrote in this regard:

> if the anatomist and the physiologist, in the study of generation in the various animals, find valuable materials for marking the highest laws of the morphology of living beings, the psychologist finds in the loves of the brutes sketched almost all the elements which man clutches under his robust wings.[23]

Darwin, however, was also influential from another important point of view. By electing the sexual instinct as the main human drive, his theories also gave a great boost to scientific research on human sexuality. In fact, unlike in *The Origin of Species* (1859), in which he assigned only relative importance to it, in *The Descent of Man* (1871) Darwin gives crucial importance to sexual selection, an aspect also shared by Mantegazza who, after reading the work, coined the motto 'to live means to generate'.[24] One of the fundamental characteristics of sexual selection as applied to the human species is its fundamental reliance on the ability of each individual to choose their partner – the partner they consider the best. It is precisely this element of 'human agency', which Mantegazza interestingly translates as 'sexual choice', that allows the species to evolve not only in terms of health but also in terms of morality. Supporting Darwin's theory, Mantegazza defines love as one of the fundamental elements of human progress. On the one hand, it enabled the health of a species to be improved by choosing strong healthy individuals and discarding sick ones, but on the other, it also allowed the moral improvement of an entire society. Indeed, according to Mantegazza, 'if tomorrow woman would only grant

FRANCESCA CAMPANI

her love to the honest and hard-working man, if it were possible for man to love only the modest woman, we would see the human family regenerated in the course of a generation'.[25]

Although Mantegazza differed from Darwin on the modalities of sexual selection,[26] he agreed with him on the fact that nature advocated the need to put individuals in the foreground, who are invested with the responsibility for the advancement of the species or the improvement of humanity. Following Darwin's theories, Mantegazza was in fact going to give a scientific explanation to the citizens of post-unification Italy of the key element underlying the spread of romantic love, namely the free choice of a partner. However, the importance that the emotional paradigm of romantic love acquired in nineteenth-century society not only influenced the investigation of the mechanisms underlying human sexuality but also played an important role in directing the interest of anthropological research towards the various declinations assumed by marriage at a global level.

The sexuality of the so-called 'primitives'

If, at first, Mantegazza's interest seems to be focused on the way in which the feeling of love was understood within Western society, he soon orientated his interest towards the study of sexuality according to a broader perspective that also involved the so-called 'savage' populations, namely non-Western populations. Indeed, when Mantegazza published the *Fisiologia dell'amore*, he had recently moved to Florence where he obtained what is officially considered the first chair of anthropology in Italy. From that moment on, Mantegazza began to develop his anthropology and sexual science in parallel.

The interest in the sexuality of people deemed 'primitive' was not exclusive to the nineteenth century, but was a fundamental part of Europe's colonial expansion and already established by the eighteenth century. Accounts of Other societies conveyed by white European travellers, missionaries, explorers, merchants and naturalists developed into stereotypical images concerning the sexual habits of non-European peoples which began to be more widely spread in Western culture. There are two main types of images concerning the sexuality of non-European peoples that became widespread.

Some of these representations emphasized the greater freedom and closeness to nature that supposedly characterized the sexual behaviour of so-called 'primitive peoples'. The progenitor of this discursive strand is in many ways Denis Diderot's (1713–84) book *Addendum to the Journey of*

Bougainville (1772) in which he describes how the inhabitants of Tahiti – men and women – experienced their sexuality 'without shame and without fear',[27] thus fuelling the Western erotic imagination of the myth of a new Kythera – as Bougainville himself called it – an earthly Eden where the inhabitants lived 'innocent and happy' following 'the pure instinct of nature'.[28]

Other representations, on the other hand, showed the imagined 'savage' as an individual dominated by an animal sensuality that led them to commit the worst nefarious deeds and engage in the lowest sexual perversions. The discourse was primarily linked to the reflections of naturalists and anthropologists concerning the size of the genitals of non-Western populations, particularly Africans. Still influenced by legacies of ancient medicine, these scientists, largely educated as physicians, believed that if African men had, on average, larger penises than Western men, this must inevitably entail a greater erotic charge that would consequently condition their sexuality.[29] Albeit with different declinations, these images both emphasized that 'primitive peoples' possessed a greater degree of eroticism than Western populations and as such needed to be colonized and civilized to temper their 'base' feelings. During the nineteenth century, indeed, these stereotyped images crystallized within the scientific discourse of the time, contributing to the affirmation of the supposed biological inferiority of so-called 'primitive peoples' and thereby justifying colonialism and slavery. Both images occurred at length over the past centuries within Western culture and continue to constitute deeply rooted, and not yet completely eradicated, racist discourses on non-Western populations.[30]

As is well known, exotic sexuality had a key role in shaping Western culture's self-image as it was employed as a foil in constructing ideas about European sexual behaviours. During the nineteenth century, 'primitive' sexualities were mainly used in a comparative function to show the superiority of Western morality.[31] Historians, including Doble and Ginsburgh in this volume, have demonstrated how in the colonial context the sexuality of the Other, especially that of Africans, was depicted as a threat to 'white purity'.[32] Africans were imagined as sexually excessive, lustful 'savages',[33] with the potential to subvert the colonial order through miscegenation and the blurring of racial boundaries.[34]

When Mantegazza obtained the first chair in anthropology in Italy, he also 'expanded' his studies on human beings by exploring the so-called 'savage races'. At the time, however, the emerging Italian anthropological discourse was not yet closely linked to colonial ambitions, which developed mainly during the 1880s. In the decades following Italian unification (1860s and 1870s), Mantegazza's interest in the Other was still largely influenced by a romantic-liberal attitude that, based on a monogenism more dictated by his moral than scientific convictions, led the anthropologist to affirm the existence of a 'universal human brotherhood'.[35] His concern was therefore to study 'l'uomo e gli uomini' ('man and men'): not only the variations in human manifestations but also the features they have in common. Of course, this also concerned the emotional expressions associated with human sexuality and the emotional bonds derived from them. In his anthropology, in fact, Mantegazza also wanted to focus

> on the mores, the feelings, the thoughts of all those men, yellow or black, who in regions so far from us and with almost nothing in common with our history, have nevertheless thought and struggled, enjoyed and mourned in the forest or desert, which nature has assigned them.[36]

Although in the course of his career, Mantegazza undertook a few journeys himself – to South America between 1854 and 1858, to Lapland in 1879 and to India between 1881 and 1882 – his can mainly be described as an 'armchair anthropology', or a science that was not based on fieldwork as in the case of twentieth-century anthropology. Like many anthropologists at the time, in fact, to gather evidence of human sexual behaviour he mainly drew on the accounts of other anthropologists and scientists, travellers, explorers, traders and priests and on novels and works by classical authors. With regard to sexuality, the work in which he concentrates his research from an ethnological point of view is *Gli amori degli uomini* (*Loves of Mankind*) (1885–6). This work is thus a sort of large catalogue in which, interestingly, the attitudes of peoples considered 'savage', as well as those of past civilizations (particularly the classics), are described and compared with Western sexual behaviours.

The publication of the book came at an important moment in the history of Italian colonialism. Indeed, in the same year (1885) the so-called 'overseas campaign' received a considerable boost due to occupation of territories in the Horn of Africa that eventually went on to constitute the colony of Eritrea, the Italian *colonia primogenita*, officially recognized in 1889 with the Treaty of Wuchale. The last among European nations to participate in the so-called 'scramble for Africa', the fledgling Italian kingdom was driven primarily by economic purposes and the desire to join the circle of European powers. Nevertheless, the idea of 'Oltremare' ('Overseas') represented one of the great myths of liberal Italy, not only politically and economically but also culturally.[37] In the 1880s, indeed, Italian publications saw a flourishing of articles and accounts by scholars and travellers whose central theme was Africa.

Mantegazza, for his part, also sought to ride the wave of that exotic *vogue* and to help support the Italian colonization campaign. In fact, from the 1880s onwards, Mantegazza's attitudes changed, becoming more and more supportive of Italian expansionist aims, as demonstrated by his participation as Italian representative at the Conference of Berlin in 1884, though he nevertheless played a rather marginal role.[38] Notwithstanding, the focus on the sexual habits of non-Western populations does not seem to be directed towards a moralizing purpose on the part of the West: unlike much of the impassioned racism of nineteenth-century evolutionary anthropology, Mantegazza's attitude towards so-called 'savage peoples' remained rather ambivalent. On the one hand, in fact, Mantegazza spoke towards 'primitive peoples' as populations that generally possessed an overflowing sensuality, as they were less subject to the 'religious and moral extinguishments'[39] that act instead on individuals within 'civilized' society. On the other hand, however, Mantegazza very often used examples taken from the sexual habits of 'primitives' to question the absolutism of Western customs, showing that sometimes non-Western populations demonstrated similar, if not imitable, behaviours. As will be seen shortly, this was also the case of customs related to emotional relationships and marriage bonds.

Questioning the polygamy of non-Western peoples

In contrast to the belief held by much of nineteenth-century evolutionary anthropology,[40] Mantegazza's investigation of non-European and past sexual habits did not have as its primary aim the creation of reductive views that served to secure the supposedly moral superiority of the West. Nevertheless, Mantegazza's perspectives fit into the colonial and racist visions of the time. Certainly, like most of his contemporaries, Mantegazza was convinced that human 'races' were organized along a hierarchical scale, in his case a tree. In the highest branches were the Western peoples, while descending to the bottom were the 'Semites', 'Asians', 'Americans', 'Finns', 'Laplanders', 'Hottentots' and 'Negroes', down to the lowest branch occupied by 'Australians'.[41] At the same time, however, in Mantegazza's anthropology, this discourse does not apply univocally to the manifestations of the sexuality and emotions of racialized people. Like other scholars at the time, Mantegazza was undoubtedly convinced that romantic love was the highest form of sentimental relationship and that it should serve as the legitimizing basis for the marital relations of the 'high races' such as those in Europe. This does not mean that Mantegazza understood marriage as the best form of union between a man and a woman; rather, it was in his opinion 'the least worst'[42] of the possible types that could be adopted in the Italian society of the time.

Mantegazza was also aware that it was a human-made contract and that consequently every era and race had different marriage customs. Nevertheless, the love bond remained the element that, in his opinion, had to be the basis of marital unions. Indeed, his anticlericalism led him to advocate the need for a divorce law reform 'to be made now' to preserve the institution of marriage as the seal of true love.[43] With regard to 'primitive races', on the other hand, Mantegazza was undoubtedly convinced that 'a polygamy limited to a few females is the most common form of human society of the lower races', but at the same time he believed that amorous sentiment and monogamy were also widespread among them. He wrote in the *Fisiologia dell'amore*:

> even the most libertine and wildest man feels needs other than that to fecundate the female; he feels the need to love a woman. And to love does not mean to bind the limbs of two bodies in a single knot, but to possess and desire and defend and protect each other for a long time ... it means taking responsibility ... for the future of the one we have created and brought into the world.[44]

More than ten years later, in *Gli amori degli uomini*, he reiterates: 'Love by free choice is to be found at the very bottom and at the very top of the human ladder.'[45] Not only the Celts 'among whom girls freely choose their husbands'[46] but also among the 'Loango negroes', in the Western part of the present-day Republic of the Congo, if 'the young couple are in love with each other, they can always manage to get along without either marital consent or a dowry'.[47] The reason for this belief is explained a few pages later. Expressing his opposition to the 'strange theory' held by a number of ethnologists that 'the most ancient form of love was communal marriage', Mantegazza states 'however distant and however low-reaching may be the boughs of that great tree [of humankind] to which we all belong, the sap that runs in it is the same'.[48] Convinced of the existence of races but also of the common nature of all human beings, Mantegazza had no doubt that the capacity to love, and thus to bond to a single individual, was intrinsic to human nature. These contradictions were partly embedded in nineteenth-century Italian science. As historian Sandra Puccini argues, at the time,

> racist prejudice was still intertwined with the consideration of *primitives* as our ancestors, inferior nowadays but also capable, in a distant future, of ascending to *civilisation* thanks to the identity of the human mind and the progressive force of evolutionary law.[49]

However, it is also possible to identify some peculiarities of Mantegazza's scientific perspective. His anthropological methodology – aimed at studying both the variations of human beings and their common features – added to his anticlericalism – which led him to emphasize the negative influence of the Church on sexuality – probably caused him to overlap different and apparently contradictory discourses: the inferiority of non-Western races and the ubiquity of certain human behaviours. However, regarding the claim of the human tendency towards monogamy, adherence to the ideals of romantic love also played an important role.

In this respect, Mantegazza seems to anticipate the work of another important anthropologist, Edward Westermarck (1862–1939). With his important studies on homosexuality and marriage in Morocco, Westermarck is generally regarded as one of the forerunners of the twentieth-century tendency to question the hegemony of Western sexual mores and the supposed inferiority of the sexual morality of 'savage' peoples. In particular, thanks to his work *The History of Human Marriage* (1893), he is regarded as one of the first anthropologists to begin deconstructing the myth of the original promiscuity of non-European peoples, arguing on the contrary that humans were fundamentally monogamous.[50] Westermarck, in fact, wrote that:

> love has slowly become the refined feeling it is in the mind of culti-vated persons in modern times, although conjugal affection is far from being unknown, even among very rude savages.[51]

A Darwin supporter as much as Mantegazza, Westermarck also believed in sexual selection and, at the same time, in the ideal of romantic love as the foundation of marriages in the West. There is no explicit evidence to suggest that Westermarck derived his thoughts directly from Mantegazza's works, which were published several years before his own. Westermarck was undoubtedly familiar with Mantegazza's intellectual production, quot-ing him extensively in his book. He also sent the Italian anthropologist a copy of his *The History of Human Marriage* with a direct dedication.[52] Mantegazza, for his part, recognized the importance of Westermarck's work, writing in the review published in his journal *Archivio per l'antropologia e l'etnologia*, the same year that the work was published:

> We are especially pleased to note how the A. strenuously fights the theory of the promiscuity of the sexes in the earliest epoch of human history, an idea that we have long fought in our work on the psychol-ogy and ethnography of love.[53]

While Westermarck is regarded as a transitional figure from evolution-ary anthropology to cultural relativism, Mantegazza on the other hand is generally considered a traditional evolutionary anthropologist. However, Mantegazza, as we have seen, already held this belief in the 1870s. Overlaying the ideal of romantic love with their endorsement of Darwinist theories, Mantegazza, before Westermarck, believed that the tendency to create a couple by selecting a partner according to their preferences was innate to human beings. However, at the same time, it seems difficult to deny that the election of the romantic ideal as the emotional paradigm of the time did not contribute to establishing among scientists a propensity to search for the roots of such an emotional paradigm in supposedly 'primitive' people – not only Mantegazza and Westermarck but also Darwin himself, who from a young age was a great lover of romantic literature.[54]

Conclusions

The ideal of romantic love was a profound influence upon the evolutionary anthropologist Paolo Mantegazza's research on human sexuality, helping to cast doubt on the hypothesis of polygamy originating with 'primitive' peoples. In fact, Mantegazza, by emphasizing that humans naturally tended towards monogamy, wanted to scientifically legitimize the need to adopt romantic love as the emotional paradigm underpinning the society of the new-born Italian kingdom, the aim of this being the stability of the new society under construction. Mantegazza addresses the Italian bourgeoisie in his works, especially women, who were considered specialists in the field of emotions, portraying romantic love as a guarantee of a happy future not only for the nation but also for individuals.

If, as was often the case in the nineteenth century, the gaze on the 'primitive Other' represents a projection of the anxieties and aspirations of Western society,[55] also in this case the image of the Other disseminated by Mantegazza is conditioned by the perspectives of the post-unification Italian bourgeoisie and the prominent place that romantic love occupied in their psycho-emotional horizons. However, the sexuality of the 'Other' was not used here in a negative sense but rather as a virtuous mirror to demonstrate that love and monogamy were intrinsic to humankind. This brings further evidence to overcome an overly simplistic view of the nineteenth-century investigation of human sexuality. Indeed, scholars have stated the existence of an 'unsolved epistemological tension' between, on the one hand, an 'older largely ethnocentric and deductive tradition of cross-cultural evolutionary anthropology' and, on the other, a 'new inductive science that recognised sexual and cultural variability as natural'.[56] The occurrence, not only in Westermarck but also, years before, in Mantegazza's sexual anthropology, of different and sometimes contradictory elements shows the need to think of a more nuanced view of the development from evolutionism to culturalism in anthropological thought. In fact, placed side by side, Westermarck's and Mantegazza's cases show that already within the evolutionary paradigm there were discourses that aimed to describe the complexity and multiplicity of non-European sexualities.

Notes

1. For an accurate account of historiographical developments related to sexual science, see C. Waters, 'Sexology', in M. Houlbrook and H. Cocks (eds.), *Palgrave Advances in the Modern History of Sexuality* (Basingstoke: Palgrave Macmillan, 2006), pp. 41–63.

2. M. Foucault, *La volontà di sapere. Storia della sessualità 1* (Milan: Feltrinelli, 2006), p. 97. (Translation from Italian texts are my own.)

3. A. Giddens, *La Trasformazione dell'intimità. Sessualità, amore ed erotismo nelle società moderne* (Bologna: Il Mulino, 1992), pp. 27–37.

4. H. Oosterhuis, *Stepchildren of Nature: Krafft-Ebing, Psychiatry, and the Making of Sexual Identity* (Chicago, IL: University of Chicago Press, 2000), pp. 233–5.

5. A.P. Lyons and H. Lyons, *Irregular Connections: A History of Anthropology and Sexuality* (Lincoln, NE: University of Nebraska Press, 2004), p. 101. On Foucault's discourses on sexuality and race, see also A.L. Stoler, *Race and the Education of Desire: Foucault's History of Sexuality and the Colonial Order of Things* (Durham, NC: Duke University Press, 1995).

6. For an overview on the subject, see C. Schields and D. Herzog (eds.), *The Routledge Companion to Sexuality and Colonialism* (New York: Routledge, 2021).

7. On the connections between race and sexuality in the fascist era, see S. Ponzanesi, 'The Color of Love: Madamismo and Interracial Relationships in the Italian Colonies', *Research in African Literatures*, 43 (2012), 155–72; D. Garvin, 'Imperial Wet-Nursing in Italian East Africa', in C. Schields and D. Herzog (eds.), *The Routledge Companion to Sexuality and Colonialism* (New York: Routledge, 2021). For an initial attempt to investigate the connections between Italian colonialism from the perspective of non-conforming sexualities, see N. Camilleri and V. Fusari, 'Queering Italian Colonialism: Mapping a Blind Spot', *Contemporanea*, 25 (2022), pp. 477–87.

8. H.H. Chiang, 'Double Alterity and the Global Historiography of Sexuality: China, Europe, and the Emergence of Sexuality as a Global Possibility', *E-Pisteme*, 2 (2009); J. Funke, 'Navigating the Past: Sexuality, Race, and the Uses of the Primitive in Magnus Hirschfeld's *The World Journey of a Sexologist*', in K. Fisher and R. Langlands (eds.), *Sex, Knowledge, and Receptions of the Past* (Oxford: Oxford University Press, 2015), pp. 111–34; P. Schrader, 'Fears and Fantasies: German Sexual Science and Its Research on African Sexualities, 1890–1930', *Sexualities*, 23 (2020), pp. 127–45.

9. P.A. Ginsborg and A.M. Banti, 'Romanticismo e Risorgimento: L'io, l'amore e la nazione', in *Storia d'Italia. Annali 22. Il Risorgimento* (Turin: Einaudi, 2007).

10. L. Tasca, 'Il "senatore erotico". Sesso e matrimonio nell'antropologia di Paolo Mantegazza', in Bruno P.F. Wanrooij (ed.), *La mediazione matrimoniale in Italia e in Europa tra Otto e Novecento. Il terzo (in)comodo* (Rome: Storia e Letteratura, 2004), p. 300.

11. L. Schettini, *Il gioco delle parti: travestimenti e paure sociali tra Otto e Novecento* (Florence: Le Monnier, 2011), p. 152.

12. P. Mantegazza, *Fisiologia dell'amore* (Milan: G. Bernardoni, 1873), p. viii.

13. T. Dixon, *From Passions to Emotions: The Creation of a Secular Psychological Category* (Cambridge: Cambridge University Press, 2003), p. 139.

14. Mantegazza, *Fisiologia dell'amore*, p. v.

15. Mantegazza, *Fisiologia dell'amore*, p. 204.

16. On this concept, see B.H. Rosenwein, *Emotional Communities in the Early Middle Ages* (Ithaca, NY: Cornell University Press, 2006).

17. Funke, 'Navigating the Past', pp. 111–34.

18. P. Mantegazza, 'Saggio sulla trasformazione delle forze psichiche', *Archivio per l'Antropologia e l'Etnologia*, 27 (1897), p. 290.

19. 'Rendiconto della Società di Antropologia', *Archivio per l'Antropologia e l'Etnologia*, 3 (1873), p. 317.

20. On Spencer and psychology, see J.W. Burrow, *La crisi della ragione. Il pensiero europeo 1848–1914* (Bologna: Il Mulino, 2002), pp. 73–6.

21. On the relationship between Darwin and Mantegazza with regard to expressions of emotion, see, D. Martín Moruno, 'Pain as Practice in Paolo Mantegazza's Science of Emotions', *Osiris*, 31 (2016), pp. 137–62.

22. Mantegazza, *Giornale della mia vita* (Rendiconto, December 1872).

23. Mantegazza, *Fisiologia dell'amore*, p. 24.

24. Mantegazza, *Fisiologia dell'amore*, p. 1.

25. Mantegazza, *Fisiologia dell'amore*, p. 193.

26. G. Landucci, *Darwinismo a Firenze: tra scienza e ideologia: 1860–1900* (Florence: L.S. Olschki, 1977), pp. 131–3.

27. D. Diderot, *Supplemento al viaggio di Bougainville e altri scritti sulla morale e sul costume*, Renato Pastore (ed.) (Rome: Salerno Editrice, 1977), p. 34.

28. Diderot, *Supplemento al Viaggio di Bougainville e altri scritti sulla morale e sul costume*, p. 31.

29. Lyons and Lyons, *Irregular Connections*, pp. 28–9.

30. On the racial and gender stereotypes still surviving in Italian society, see S. Ponzanesi, 'Edges of Empire: Italy's Postcolonial Entanglements and the Gender Legacy', *Cultural Studies ↔ Critical Methodologies*, 16 (2016), pp. 373–86.

31. K. Fisher and J. Funke, '"Let Us Leave the Hospital; Let Us Go on a Journey around the World": British and German Sexual Science and the Global Research for Sexual Variation', in V. Fuechtner, D.E. Haynes and R.M. Jones (eds.), *A Global History of Sexual Science (1880–1960)* (Oakland, CA: University of California Press, 2017), p. 55; Lyons and Lyons, *Irregular Connections*.

32. J. McCulloch, *Black Peril, White Virtue: Sexual Crime in Southern Rhodesia, 1902–1935* (Bloomington, IN: Indiana University Press, 2000); D. Anderson, 'Sexual Threat and Settler Society: "Black Perils" in Kenya, c. 1907–30', *The Journal of Imperial and Commonwealth History*, 38 (2010), pp. 47–74.

33. C. Forth, 'Fat, Desire and Disgust in the Colonial Imagination', *History Workshop Journal*, 73 (2012), pp. 211–39.

34. A. McClintock, *Imperial Leather: Race, Gender, and Sexuality in the Colonial Contest* (New York: Routledge, 1995).

35. P. Mantegazza, 'L'uomo e gli Uomini. Lettera Etnologica del Prof. Paolo Mantegazza al Prof. Enrico Giglioli', in *Viaggio Intorno al Globo della R. Pirocorvetta Italiana Magenta* (Milan: V. Maisner & Compagnia, 1876), p. xx. On the evolution of Mantegazza's racism, see N. Labanca, '"Un nero non può esser bianco". Il Museo Nazionale di Antropologia di Paolo Mantegazza e la Colonia Eritrea', in *L'Africa in Vetrina. Storia di musei e di esposizioni coloniali in Italia* (Paese Treviso: Pagus, 1992), pp. 79–83.

36. P. Mantegazza, 'Fra i Micmac', *L'Illustrazione Italiana*, 21, 31 (1894), p. 91.

37. N. Labanca, *Oltremare. Storia dell'espansione coloniale italiana* (Bologna: Società editrice il Mulino, 2002), pp. 15–56.

38. Labanca, '"Un nero non può esser bianco". Il Museo Nazionale Di Antropologia Di Paolo Mantegazza e La Colonia Eritrea', pp. 86–94.

39. P. Mantegazza, *Gli amori degli uomini* (Rome: l'Osservatore, 1967), p. 51.

40. Funke, 'Navigating the Past', p. 121; E.W. Said, *Orientalismo: l'immagine europea dell'Oriente* (Milan: Feltrinelli, 2015).

41. Mantegazza, 'L'uomo e gli uomini. Lettera etnologica del Prof. Paolo Mantegazza al Prof. Enrico Giglioli' (fig. I).

42. P. Mantegazza, *L'arte di prender moglie, l'arte di prender marito*, Lucia Rodler (ed.) (Rome: Carocci, 2008), pp. 49–50.

43. Mantegazza, *Fisiologia dell'amore*, p. 336.

44. Mantegazza, *Fisiologia dell'amore*, p. 322.

45. P. Mantegazza, *The Sexual Relations of Mankind*, trans. Samuel Putnam (New York: Eugenics Publishing Company, 1935), p. 161.

46. Mantegazza, *The Sexual Relations of Mankind*, p. 162.

47. Mantegazza, *The Sexual Relations of Mankind*, p. 161.

48. Mantegazza, *The Sexual Relations of Mankind*, p. 190.

49. S. Puccini, 'I Viaggi di Paolo Mantegazza. Tra divulgazione, letteratura e antropologia', in C. Chiarelli and W. Pasini (eds.), *Paolo Mantegazza e l'evoluzionismo in Italia* (Florence: Florence University Press, 2010), p. 61.

50. Funke, 'Navigating the Past'; R. Leck, 'Westermarck's Morocco: Sexology and the Epistemic Politics of Cultural Anthropology and Sexual Science', in V. Fuechtner, D.E. Haynes and R.M. Jones (eds.), *A Global History of Sexual Science (1880–1960)* (Oakland, CA: University of California Press, 2017), pp. 70–96.

51. E. Westermarck, *The History of Human Marriage* (London: Macmillan, 1891), p. 546.

52. M.E. Frati (ed.), *Le carte e la biblioteca di Paolo Mantegazza. Inventario e catalogo* (Milan: Giunta regionale Toscana & Editrice Bibliografica, 1991), p. 316.

53. P. Mantegazza, 'Edward Westermarck "The History of Human Marriage"', *Archivio per l'Antropologia e l'Etnologia*, 23 (1893), p. 470.

54. G. Beer, 'Darwin and Romanticism', *The Wordsworth Circle*, 41 (2010), 3–9.

55. Lyons and Lyons, *Irregular Connections*, p. 8.

56. Leck, 'Westermarck's Morocco', p. 87.

References

Anderson, D., 'Sexual Threat and Settler Society: "Black Perils" in Kenya, c. 1907–30', *The Journal of Imperial and Commonwealth History*, 38 (2010), 47–74.

Beer, G., 'Darwin and Romanticism', *The Wordsworth Circle*, 41 (2010), 3–9.

Burrow, J.W., *La crisi ella ragione. Il pensiero europeo 1848–1914* (Bologna: Il Mulino, 2002).

Camilleri, N., and Fusari, V., 'Queering Italian Colonialism: Mapping a Blind Spot', *Contemporanea*, 25 (2022), 477–87.

Chiang, H.H., 'Double Alterity and the Global Historiography of Sexuality: China, Europe, and the Emergence of Sexuality as a Global Possibility', *E-Pisteme*, 2 (2009).

Diderot, D., *Supplemento al Viaggio di Bougainville e altri scritti sulla morale e sul costume*, Renato Pastore (ed.) (Rome: Salerno Editrice, 1977).

Dixon, T., *From Passions to Emotions: The Creation of a Secular Psychological Category* (Cambridge: Cambridge University Press, 2003).

Fisher, K., and Funke, J., '"Let Us Leave the Hospital; Let Us Go on a Journey around the World": British and German Sexual Science and the Global Research for Sexual Variation', in V. Fuechtner, D.E. Haynes and R.M. Jones (eds.), *A Global History of Sexual Science (1880–1960)* (Oakland, CA: University of California Press, 2017), pp. 51–69.

Forth, C., 'Fat, Desire and Disgust in the Colonial Imagination', *History Workshop Journal*, 73 (2012), 211–39.

Foucault, M., *La volontà di sapere. Storia della sessualità 1* (Milan: Feltrinelli Editore, 2006).

Frati, M.E. (ed.), *Le carte e la biblioteca di Paolo Mantegazza. Inventario e catalogo* (Milan: Giunta Regionale Toscana & Editrice: Bibliografica, 1991).

Funke, J., 'Navigating the Past: Sexuality, Race, and the Uses of the Primitive in Magnus Hirschfeld's *The World Journey of a Sexologist*', in K. Fisher and R. Langlands (eds.), *Sex, Knowledge, and Receptions of the Past* (Oxford: Oxford University Press, 2015), pp. 111–34.

Garvin, D., 'Imperial Wet-Nursing in Italian East Africa', in C. Schields and D. Herzog (eds.), *The Routledge Companion to Sexuality and Colonialism* (New York: Routledge, 2021).

Giddens, A., *La Trasformazione dell'intimità. Sessualità, amore ed erotismo nelle società moderne* (Bologna: Il Mulino, 1992).

Ginsborg, P.A., and Banti, A.M., 'Romanticismo e Risorgimento: L'io, l'amore e la nazione', in *Storia d'Italia. Annali 22. Il Risorgimento* (Turin: Einaudi, 2007).

Labanca, N., '"Un nero non può esser bianco". Il Museo Nazionale di Antropologia di Paolo Mantegazza e la Colonia Eritrea', in *L'Africa in Vetrina. Storia di musei e di esposizioni coloniali in Italia* (Paese Treviso: Pagus, 1992), pp. 69–106.

——, *Oltremare. Storia dell'espansione coloniale italiana* (Bologna: Il Mulino, 2002).

Landucci, G., *Darwinismo a Florence: tra scienza e ideologia: 1860–1900* (Florence: L.S. Olschki, 1977).

Leck, R., 'Westermarck's Morocco: Sexology and the Epistemic Politics of Cultural Anthropology and Sexual Science', in V. Fuechtner, D.E. Haynes and R.M. Jones (eds.), *A Global History of Sexual Science (1880–1960)* (Oakland, CA: University of California Press, 2017), pp. 70–96.

Lyons, A.P., and Lyons, H., *Irregular Connections: A History of Anthropology and Sexuality* (Lincoln, NE: University of Nebraska Press, 2004).

Mantegazza, P. *Giornale della mia vita* (unpublished personal diary) (Rendiconto, December 1872).

——, *Fisiologia dell'amore* (Milan: G. Bernardoni, 1873).

——, 'L'uomo e gli Uomini. Lettera etnologica del Prof. Paolo Mantegazza al Prof. Enrico Giglioli', in *Viaggio Intorno al Globo della R. Pirocorvetta Italiana Magenta*, pp. 16–26 (Milan: V. Maisner & Compagnia, 1876).

——, 'Edward Westermarck "The History of Human Marriage"', *Archivio per l'Antropologia e l'Etnologia*, 23 (1893), p. 470.

——, 'Fra i Micmac', *L'Illustrazione italiana*, 21, 31 (1894), 91.

——, 'Saggio sulla trasformazione delle forze fisiche', *Archivio per l'Antropologia e l'Etnologia*, 27 (1897), pp. 285–306.

——, *The Sexual Relations of Mankind*, trans. S. Putnam (New York: Eugenics Publishing Company, 1935).

——, *Gli amori degli uomini* (Rome: l'Osservatore, 1967).

——, *L'arte di prender moglie, l'arte di prender marito*, L. Rodler (ed.) (Rome: Carocci, 2008).

Martín Moruno, D., 'Pain as Practice in Paolo Mantegazza's Science of Emotions', *Osiris*, 31 (2016), pp. 137–62.

McClintock, A., *Imperial Leather: Race, Gender, and Sexuality in the Colonial Contest* (New York: Routledge, 1995).

McCulloch, J., *Black Peril, White Virtue: Sexual Crime in Southern Rhodesia, 1902–1935* (Bloomington, IN: Indiana University Press, 2000).

Oosterhuis, H., *Stepchildren of Nature: Krafft-Ebing, Psychiatry, and the Making of Sexual Identity* (Chicago, IL: University of Chicago Press, 2000).

Ponzanesi, S., 'The Color of Love: Madamismo and Interracial Relationships in the Italian Colonies', *Research in African Literatures*, 43 (2012), pp. 155–72.

——, 'Edges of Empire: Italy's Postcolonial Entanglements and the Gender Legacy', *Cultural Studies ↔ Critical Methodologies*, 16 (2016), pp. 373–86.

Puccini, S., 'I viaggi di Paolo Mantegazza. Tra divulgazione, letteratura e antropologia', in C. Chiarelli and W. Pasini (eds.), *Paolo Mantegazza e l'evoluzionismo in Italia* (Florence: Florence University Press, 2010), pp. 53–78.

'Rendiconto della Società di Antropologia', *Archivio per l'Antropologia e l'Etnologia*, 3 (1873), pp. 316–35.

Rosenwein, B.H., *Emotional Communities in the Early Middle Ages* (Ithaca, NY: Cornell University Press, 2006).

Said, E.W., *Orientalismo: l'immagine europea dell'Oriente* (Milan: Feltrinelli, 2015).

Schettini, L., *Il gioco delle parti: travestimenti e paure sociali tra Otto e Novecento* (Florence: Le Monnier, 2011).

Schields, C., and Herzog, D. (eds.), *The Routledge Companion to Sexuality and Colonialism* (New York: Routledge, 2021).

Schrader, P., 'Fears and Fantasies: German Sexual Science and Its Research on African Sexualities, 1890–1930', *Sexualities*, 23 (2020), 127–45.

Stoler, A.L., *Race and the Education of Desire: Foucault's History of Sexuality and the Colonial Order of Things* (Durham, NC: Duke University Press, 1995).

Tasca, L., 'Il "senatore erotico". Sesso e matrimonio nell'antropologia di Paolo Mantegazza', in B.P.F. Wanrooij (ed.), *La mediazione matrimoniale in Italia e in Europa tra Otto e Novecento. Il terzo (in)comodo* (Rome: Storia e Letteratura, 2004), pp. 295–322.

Waters, C., 'Sexology', in M. Houlbrook and H. Cocks (eds.), *Palgrave Advances in the Modern History of Sexuality* (Basingstoke: Palgrave Macmillan, 2006), pp. 41–63.

Westermarck, E., *The History of Human Marriage* (London: Macmillan, 1891).

Chapter 9

Writing the man of politeness: the hidden importance of shame in eighteenth-century masculinity

Michael Rowland

As an object of focus for historians of emotion, shame is perhaps best represented by Peter N. Stearns's book *Shame: A Brief History* (2017), which divides the West's relationship to shame into 'pre-modern' and 'modern' halves, with the hinge being somewhere in the middle of the eighteenth century.[1] His argument is that shame's grip on Western societies begins to lessen with the increased individualism produced by the Enlightenment. It is not possible, Stearns claims, to use shame as a social corrective through punishments such as the stocks or pillory when communities in urbanizing areas, which increasingly set the moral tone of European and North American cultures, are composed of mutual strangers.[2] The Enlightenment view of the individual 'no longer defined by individual sin, capable of improvement through rational education, deserving protection for key rights such as freedom of religion and of expression' promoted personal privacy and dignity. This emphasis prized these two aspects of human experience in new ways from pre-modern ages, and once prized were less vulnerable to subversion by public shaming rituals which asserted community norms.[3]

This does not mean that shame ceased to play a formative role in individual and collective identity formation in this period. Instead, as I argue in this chapter, the very mechanisms by which eighteenth-century Britain began to move away from public shaming towards privacy and dignity in fact provided new routes for shame's influence.

Stearns brings attention to the lack of critical work on shame at this historical juncture: 'the exploration of this new attachment to self has not ... been applied directly to shame'.[4] The parameters of Stearns's examination of pre-modern shame are based primarily on evidence of shaming punishments listed in official records, saying that there is little available evidence for 'daily emotional experience and relevant family practice' in these eras.[5] With the advent of a mass culture of writing (published or otherwise) in the eighteenth century, however, this changes and the historian of emotion can and should draw upon this wealth of evidence and pay particular attention to its literary qualities. This is because shame and shaming take a literary turn in the eighteenth century, a claim I will develop here.

To clarify what I mean by this, I wish to make two interventions here, one literary-historical and the other methodological. First, the literary-historical. The literary public sphere, mass-disseminated and privately consumed, developed subtle methods for shaming that were available to those living in this historical moment. These were all the more effective because, as critics from Jürgen Habermas to Michael Warner have argued, authority was displaced from court, church and traditional sources of hierarchical power and instead diffused through the pens and printing presses of those participating in polite society.[6] Shame came from one's peers through the public sphere rather than a distant source of power or public shaming ritual, and in a period of profound social change and anxiety, this amplified the private power of the literary public. I focus here, then, on how these literary evocations of shame worked to shape polite masculine identity in the first half of the century.

My second, methodological, intervention has implications for the field of emotions history. I wish to advocate for the utility of affect studies in the history of emotions. In order to account for the subtleties of emotion in the lived experience of historic periods, we must allow our analysis to be responsive to literary works as historical records. The rich colours of a medieval church, the smell of the early modern London street and the insistent pull of certain words and turns of phrase for contemporary readers of an eighteenth-century periodical; the phenomenological experience of these to a contemporary individual or community is no less a record of what happened at a given historical moment than, say, parish records. It is through using the tools of affect studies that we can approach an understanding of how these moments were experienced by those living through them.

A literary history of emotions?

The history of emotions as a field of study has crystallized as individual projects by founding historians have begun to collectively set the boundaries and characteristics of what is now a field in its own right.[7] There are a few ideas that can be considered central, chiefly that emotions, how they are named, described and even felt, have histories because emotion is culturally and socially constructed. This means that anger, fear, happiness and any other emotion for that matter are not hardwired or essentialized but shaped by particular cultures and societies at particular times, and no single emotion has persisted unchanged since time immemorial. Indeed, some emotions may have been brought into existence by particular historical circumstances.[8] These insights have been derived in part from disciplines outside of history, especially anthropology and neuroscience.[9] Recent advances in the sciences have suggested that brain plasticity and epigenetics might provide biological evidence for the impact of external influence on the human capacity to feel and express certain emotions.[10]

I wish to posit the usefulness of literary critical analysis as a tool to capture the idiosyncrasies of lived experience in history, and how these idiosyncrasies might develop into the kinds of systems and practices that historical study generally relies upon for analysis. To do this, we might incorporate approaches more commonly found in literary studies: close reading, critical theoretical analysis and a focus on affect as a medium for thinking through phenomenological experience. This last is less favoured by historians of emotion at present, while literary analysis has adopted affect theory as a key lens for discussing the emotions. Emotions history as a field has tended to be suspicious of affect because its roots in affect theory's biological emphasis seem, in contrast to newer ideas around brain plasticity, to disavow the role of cultural and historical change in shaping how actors express and understand emotion. Affect theory derives largely from the work of psychologist Silvan Tomkins in his long project published as *Affect, Imagery, Consciousness* (1962, 1991). Tomkins's core claim, that there are only nine affects, most hardwired from birth, and from which emotional experiences are formed, has been critiqued for being both narrow and poorly evidenced. Ruth Leys has critiqued affect theorists deriving their ideas from Tomkins, for example Brian Massumi, for formulating an analysis which essentially refuses intentionalism – the ability of humans to choose – in favour of an unscientific reading of human emotional experience as determinist.[11] Despite this, it has had some considerable impact in different disciplines, including psychology and the humanities, especially in literary and cultural studies. Leys finds this remarkable, contending that its anti-intentionalism implies 'such a radical separation between affect and reason as to make disagreement about meaning, or ideological dispute, irrelevant to cultural analysis'.[12]

What Leys seems to suggest is that without intentionalism, there can be no analysis. While I agree that denying intentionality altogether would be a reductive move, I don't believe that thinking affectively inevitably ends with the breakdown of analysis. In contrast, paying close attention to affect may enrich analysis further, allowing us to hypothesize about lived experience by including the *un*intentional along with the intentional to complicate our readings in productive ways. Rob Boddice presents a trenchant rebuttal of affect theory's use in historical analysis, observing that 'when scholars in the humanities bow down before certain influences from neurobiology', the result is 'throwaway analyses that beg more questions than they provide answers'.[13] Paul Ekman's application of affect theory is of particular focus in Boddice's critique, and while his characterization of Ekman's use of Tomkins is accurate in identifying its essentializing claims, there are other ways of using Tomkins that avoid Ekman's over-determined approach.[14] The work of Eve Sedgwick in the late 1990s up until her death in 2009 interprets Tomkins through literary readings of often historical literary texts.[15] It is through her work that Tomkins's true value as something akin to a philosopher of affect, rather than the architect of a viable psychological model, is established. It becomes clear that Tomkins's model of affect is open-ended: it should not, as Ekman does, be used to judge definitively whether an actor is lying or to construct a gallery of standardized facial expressions. Rather, as Sedgwick notes, what his work offers is a series of hypotheses and theories about how affect might be experienced and expressed in different people in different places and at different times. His insistence that 'an affect theory is a simplified and powerful summary of a larger set of affect experiences' demonstrates the role of experience – that is, the interaction with environment, culture and society – that leads to an individual actor developing affect theories which they then use to navigate feeling.[16]

Take the affect in which I am especially interested, shame. Tomkins insists that this is a social emotion, a learned feeling, and one that is therefore shaped by cultural context. Despite Tomkins expressing his ideas in language including 'feedback', 'general image', 'mechanism' and even the seemingly damning term 'innate', the real value of his thinking is to be found in its flexibility and capacity for accommodating an unending range of possibilities for emotional expression: 'Whatever one is excited by, enjoys, fears, hates, is ashamed of, is contemptuous of, or is distressed by is an object of value, positive or negative. Value hierarchies result from value conflicts wherein the same object is both loved and hated, both exciting and shaming, both distressing and enjoyable.'[17] Throughout his work, Tomkins emphasizes that affect is analogue, not digital: all affects can plug into, coincide or coexist with, amplify or decrease any other affect. Thus, for Tomkins, interest in being a successful member of society would heighten the shame an actor might feel at their perceived failure to attain that goal. However, this will be modified, enhanced or characterized by a whole range of factors, including the historical moment in which that actor lives, the society in which the actor imagines themselves to be living and affect theories that actor might hold about what constitutes success for a person such as they understand themselves to be and what attainment of or failure to attain that success should feel like. These factors are all responsive to the historical moment, the sensing environment in which the actor lives their lives. I focus here on eighteenth-century Britain and the methods used by literary culture, broadly conceived, of the time to create a set of affect theories around success in fitting the ideal of polite masculinity. Key to this investigation is the role of shame in these literary texts, both as a rhetorical tool and as an affect that dwells in the very texts themselves. How do these texts explicitly shame their male readers for their efforts to attain polite masculine ideals? How do the texts themselves betray shame through being self-conscious with regards to message and form?

To be clear, then, using affect is about recognizing the importance and value of embodiment and sensation to the experience of emotion. I follow Melissa Gregg and Gregory Seigworth's description of affect as arising 'in the midst of *in-between-ness*: in the capacities to act and be acted upon'.[18] Affect can address issues of feeling and emotion, but more properly describes the ways in which sensing bodies are exposed to, and receptive of, '*force*, or *forces of encounter*', for example the ways emotional energy can ripple through a crowd in response to an event, or through a body at the touch of a lover, or the sight of something disturbing. Affect is useful as a concept because of its readiness to recognize and make room for the strange and unexpected ways that individual bodies and their environments – physical, social, intellectual – connect and impact on one another. This is vital if we wish to understand how Rosenwein's communities, or Reddy's regimes, work on a phenomenological level. Sara Ahmed, whose work has appealed to historians of emotion while also being deeply invested in affect studies, argues that emotions should be understood through how contact with those objects which elicit a feeling response is encountered and evaluated.[19] Affect allows us to see 'an ethico-aesthetics of a body's capacity for becoming sensitive to the "manner" of a world', as Gregg and Seigworth describe it. In the context of this essay, it helps us to be more aware of how polite discourse as an encountered and evaluated object has an impact on individual men and vice versa. It also collapses some of the barriers created by the gap of time and resists the imperative to believe too absolutely that the past is a foreign country. As Boddice observes, 'there is an "empathy wall" between us and the past. It is not insurmountable, however. We can learn to "see" in the ways past actors saw'.[20] In other words, affect calls attention to the ways in which emotion is an embodied experience; felt in the body as much as understood in the mind, affect demonstrates how human experience, and its historicity, is mediated through the body's capacity to be porous to and for the world in which it moves. Far more than just 'unnamed' emotion, affect is the state of receptivity to sensation and perception: the way the body and mind respond to touch, glimpse and tone, and in turn impress themselves upon the world.

How can this be accounted for historically, when our subjects belong to emotional regimes perhaps very different from our own? Some historians have begun to work towards this by paying attention to what historical accounts of the body and embodied emotions can tell us. The exploration of embodied gendered experience in history is a vibrant field, as demonstrated by the work of Joanne Begiato, Katie Barclay and Karen Harvey, among others. Begiato observes that 'gender is not only performed, it is inhabited through one's body'.[21] Elsewhere, she demonstrates this through the changing notions of sailors' bodies, what they can or should do, and what they can be used for, in the eighteenth and nineteenth centuries. Tears in particular show the sailor's capacity for feeling, and the increased capacity of sailors in the lower ranks to cry meaningful tears demonstrates a democratization of the types of bodies that could be used to represent the emotional regime.[22] Katie Barclay finds masculine embodied emotion used to influence the legal process in nineteenth-century Irish courtrooms. In her investigation, she finds a largely homosocial space in which men tell one another stories, drawing on 'wider cultural discourses including literature and folklore, and different spatial and rhetorical strategies ... to help bring meaning to the disparate events of everyday experience'.[23] Men in the period used narrativity and embodiment alongside one another to impress themselves upon the world; in the courtroom 'displays of emotion were used as evidence of character'.[24] Barclay identifies the body's capacity to receive impressions from the world as core to eighteenth-century understandings of character:

> According to eighteenth-century science, the body interpreted the world through the senses, judging experience through the levels of pain or pleasure produced. When placed into a sophisticated moral

value system, emotion became a central mechanism by which the body interpreted right or wrong.[25]

It is Karen Harvey who points most directly to the relationship between gender, embodiment and affect when she aims at studying 'the lived, embodied experience of gender'.[26] She has suggested combining the material experience of the historian with documentary evidence to aim at a more complete analysis.[27] Like affect theory, this approach relies on the commonality of bodily experience between the historian and their subjects in order to draw insights that would otherwise be impossible due to time's flattening-out effect. While Begiato finds this too ambitious, preferring to aim at representation based on the historical record, I find Harvey's invitation an intriguing one.[28] While Harvey herself does not explicitly invoke affect, the methodologies she gestures towards certainly lead us in affect's direction. We can further our understanding of a historical period if we make the turn to affect, in particular by casting our eye over the literary mode's privileged capacity for the expression of embodied experience, as I shall now begin to do.

Shame and eighteenth-century polite masculinity

My focus in this chapter is mostly on writing from the first half of the eighteenth century, at a point at which the emotional community of politeness is emerging.[29] This means that the moral and emotional values of the community are still volatile; as we will see, all sorts of perceived infractions are debated with a surprising degree of ferocity through the technique of literary form. I focus here on periodical and letter-writing, but of course this is the great age of Augustan satire, with Pope, Swift and others regularly deploying shame to subdue the commercial and artistic aspirations of others. The discursive foundations of polite culture are foregrounded, ironically, by virtue of their being debated in print, their presence on paper seeming to make them less unassailable than emotional communities formed over time without literacy as their primary mode. This instability was not lost on the men who attempted to write into being an ideal of masculinity for themselves and their peers, as we shall see as we turn now to an exploration of their work.

For Anthony Ashley Cooper, Third Earl of Shaftesbury, the ideal mental, emotional and physical state for a man to exist in was one of equilibrium. In his body of writing, completed in the first decade of the eighteenth century, he attempts to develop a 'sensitivity to the "manner" of a world' now often called 'politeness'. Eighteenth-century politeness might be defined as '"the art of pleasing in company," or, in a contemporary definition, "a dextrous management of our Words and Actions, whereby we make other People have better Opinions of us and themselves".[30] Already we can see an alertness to the community-building pressure of words and actions on others that affect emphasizes in identity formation. For Shaftesbury, as for other architects of polite culture, politeness was about the relationship between internal thought and feeling and external behaviour and action. His later work *The Moralists* (1711) foregrounds feeling and its relation to manhood in philosophical dialogue that turns repeatedly to shame. He points out the paradox in which politeness must function if polite masculinity's ideals are to be attained: 'will he who cries shame refuse to acknowledge any in his turn?'[31] He considers shame in relation to personal conviction in conflict with popular opinion. He sees the aim of a polite man's life to be secure enough in his private and public conscience that he is 'free from the reproach of shame or guilt'.[32] Until then, the polite man must ensure politeness functions as a social tool (here by crying shame against those who threaten it) while ensuring in turn that he utilizes shame on himself. Shame, for Shaftesbury and his followers, operates in polite writing by and about men in order to improve both self and society.

It is perhaps not a surprise that Shaftesbury uses the philosophical conversation as the structure on which to build his ideals of politeness. The conversation in *The Moralists* between two virtually identical men, Philocles and Theocles, who are cyphers of philosophical ideals but male nonetheless, is a dualistic construction that enables the basis of a community to flourish. Early eighteenth-century polite culture was structured around communities: male friendships such as that of Shaftesbury's characters, along with those of Mr Spectator and his friends; the coffee-house culture of consumption and clubbability; religious sects. Most were reflected in and formed by writing in print, bought or shared between friends. All communities have emotional hallmarks, as Barbara Rosenwein has taught us, which might be new but might also be composed of aspects of older communities.[33] Polite male culture takes the anger and pride of honour-based homosocial emotional communities and begins to replace them with the shame of communities invested in what Dror Wahrman, borrowing a phrase from Sarah Knott, calls the 'socially-turned self'. Shaftesbury demands that a polite man both cry shame against others and acknowledge the necessity of feeling his own. He is a creature of a society which, as Adam Smith and David Hume both later recognize, demands the individual incorporate society's expectations in his own self-image.[34]

Contemporaries of Shaftesbury understood this need to internalize the external. The century's most famous periodical, *The Spectator*, references this act in its title, and the name of its fictional protagonist, Mr Spectator. This character records what he sees using his own emotional community made up of characters based on eighteenth-century urban types such as the Whig man of business Sir Andrew Freeport and the aging libertine relic Will Honeycomb, demonstrating the changing values of masculinity in doing so: Honeycomb, the representative of the older Restoration emotional community of indulgence, is safely married off in the course of the periodical's three-year span. This narrative, such as it is, is always subjugated to the chief purpose of *The Spectator*, which is to provide observational vignettes that not only describe and reflect the tastes and values of the time but also set the boundaries and crystallize what it means to be polite. J.G.A. Pocock famously saw politeness as the 'active civilizing agent' which helped transform a new, mistrusted commercial phenomenon into a powerful and influential system of sociability.[35] The emotional community of writers like Shaftesbury and the authors of *The Spectator*, Joseph Addison and Richard Steele, were attempting to forge an emergent collection of emotional values and styles into what Rob Boddice, borrowing from Lorraine Daston, calls a 'moral economy', a peculiarly Smithian term which nicely references both the moral and commercial imperatives of the masculinity under examination here.[36]

To see the subtle formation of this moral economy playing out in print, we need look no further than a contribution by Steele to *The Spectator* of Thursday 23 August 1711. It takes as its subject 'Men of Wit and Pleasure'. The piece is a meditation on the affective consequences of 'Wenching, Liveliness and Vice'. Steele's argument is made not from a censorious angle of emotional correction but from a nuanced analysis of personal, private shame. Starting with general comments on how 'Men of Wit and Pleasure' both shock reason and tickle the imagination, and how these men are 'in every Body's Mouth that spends any Time in Conversation' (no. 151, II: 93), his writing then takes a different turn:

> Pleasure, when it is a Man's chief Purpose, disappoints it self; and the constant Application to it palls the Faculty of enjoying it, tho' it leaves the Sense of our Inability for that we wish, with a Disrelish of every thing else. Thus the intermediate Seasons of the Man of Pleasure are more heavy than one would impose upon the vilest Criminal.[37]

What is instantly striking about this passage is the level of empathy. Far from condemning the 'Man of Pleasure', Steele uses the self-proclaimed non-partisan voice of Mr Spectator to place his reader adjacent to the suffering coxcomb. This sensation of walking side by side with a man one is supposed to condemn is heightened as we are presented with the sight of him at his darkest:

> Take him when he is awaked too soon after a Debauch, or disappointed in following a worthless Woman without Truth, and there is no Man living whose Being is such a Weight or Vexation as his is. He is an utter Stranger to the pleasing Reflections in the Evening of a well-spent Day, or the Gladness of Heart or Quickness of Spirit in the Morning after profound Sleep or indolent Slumbers. He is not to be at Ease any longer than he can keep Reason and good Sense without his Curtains; otherwise he will be haunted with the Reflection, that he could not believe such a one the Woman that upon Trial he found her. What has he got by his Conquest, but to think meanly of her for whom a Day or two before he had the highest Honour? and of himself for, perhaps, wronging the Man whom of all Men living he himself would least willingly have injured?[38]

The affective proximity the reader might feel to the man supposedly being decried is striking. We are with him at his most vulnerable moment, when he awakes beleaguered by a hangover and regretting last night's behaviour. Steele is appealing here to the experiences of his contemporary readers, urban men of polite society. His prose leaves open the possibility that his reader may well see himself in the description and feel shame as he begins to wonder whether or not the piece condemns him. The passage uses shame to create a surprising emotional community, one where bad feeling can be used to move towards a desirable identity. This is achieved through the peculiar ability of writing to bring public morality into the private emotional world of the reader. It is through the suggestive capacity of literature that Steele begins to assert the expectations of an emotional community, and through the affective response of the reader that we as historians can begin to parse this historically situated community for ourselves.

Literary uses of shame

Something that remains difficult to parse is where, if anywhere, there is a shift between the emotional community of a few periodical writers and their readers and what William Reddy has called an emotional regime which sets the tone for wider society.[39] In many ways, this is a fruitless effort, both because to draw too sharp a distinction between an emotional 'community' and a 'regime' leads to over-simplification and because it

WRITING THE MAN OF POLITENESS   227

erases what is central to emotions history and to affect: communities and regimes are always in flux, always incorporating remnants of old orders and the outriders of new ones. Despite the shift in power and influence in British society, politeness still imposed hierarchies remarkably similar to those of older orders, especially those related to the notion of hierarchy itself. In other areas, other values gained greater emphasis. One of these areas was masculine self-presentation, especially in relation to effeminacy. Prior to this period, the spectacular male body, especially that of the king, was a locus of desire in a way that was rejected in later eras, as Thomas A. King has demonstrated.[40] As Philip Carter defines it, effeminacy in the eighteenth century did not carry the overt suggestion of queer sexualities that it later would, but instead an over-investment in luxury and the performance of manners which spectacularized the male body to an unacceptable extent. This, he argues, threatened not just the integrity of individual manhood but also that of the nation state: 'attachment to the fashionable world denoted an unacceptable dependence in individual men who collectively as citizens sacrificed their nation's political independence to absolutism'.[41] As Matthew McCormack has outlined, independence became one of the defining markers of virtuous action especially in the political sphere.[42] To be trustworthy, and to have one's nation's and society's best interests at heart, a man had to be independent of influence from others, whether that be financial or social. Effeminate men, known by a range of names including dandies, beaux, fops and macaronis, were perceived to be slavishly dependent on fashion and a conduit of decadence especially from France, with whom Britain was at war for most of the eighteenth century.

I turn again to *The Spectator* for an example of the ways shame was deployed to place the effeminate man beyond the reach of politeness. In one of Joseph Addison's more lurid entries, Mr Spectator recounts a dream, during which he observes the dissection of a beau's head. Mr Spectator finds himself gazing upon a brain 'stuffed with invisible Billetdoux, Love-Letters ... and other Trumpery of the same Nature'.[43] The organ is filled entirely with the symbols of excess, including snuff and sonnets. The beau's brains are partly composed of liquids such as quicksilver for venereal disease, orange water as scent and 'Froth'. In abundance, we find fabric and textiles, including 'Ribbons, Lace and Embroidery, wrought together in a most curious Piece of Network'.[44] A spongy substance, meanwhile, is discovered to be composed of 'Nonsense' (572).[45] Addison's piece is fascinating for several reasons. Firstly, its appropriation of the language of science brings into sharp relief the inadequacies of the beau. Mr Spectator and his fellows are men of science; they inspect, probe and discover truth. Meanwhile, the beau is not just led astray by excess; by nightmarish mutation, he is composed of it. Becoming an object of inspection and invasion by other men denaturalizes – or even unmans – him even further; he is displayed, sliced open, poked at, sniffed at and preserved by a team of men who clearly believe themselves to be his moral superiors. This is highlighted by Addison's reference to the unused 'Elevator' muscle, apparently needed to 'turn the Eye towards Heaven'.[46] Writing brings the unacceptable body too close for comfort, initiating disgust and the shame of recognition in those men given to fashionable pursuits. To feel that one might be a beau or a fop, and that others might have seen that in you without your realizing it, leaves one exposed, vulnerable and ashamed. The most popular periodical of the century's key message for its male readers, then, was to warn them that excess of corporeality, whether in dress and deportment as for the fop or drinking and sex as for the man of pleasure (and in truth the two were often linked or commensurate types), would lead to shame, as these were threats to the polite ideals of masculinity in the newly commercial world of early eighteenth-century Britain.

Writing the male body: shame in Lord Chesterfield's letters

In 'The Mass Public and the Mass Subject', Michael Warner describes a moment in which we, as individuals, 'adopt the attitude of the public subject, marking to ourselves its nonidentity with ourselves'.[47] Simultaneously, we are both subjective individuals and the subjective public. Adopting the attitude of the public subject involves an affective shift. We are, in this moment, absorbed into an imagined body known as 'the public' and are thus in intimate contact with unidentifiable, indefinably numerous others. The community of consumption that mass print culture allowed for meant that even if one spent the majority of one's time behind a shield of one's own making – as of course Addison does with Mr Spectator – one was still strongly aware of the ideas and opinions of others. This was a virtual community with very real effects on its members. It became increasingly important to individuals at this time to know what those they had never met thought and felt about given topics. That means that nothing the architects of politeness such as Shaftesbury, Addison and Steele could write could make them immune to the same process of normalizing via shame to which they subjected the fops and men of pleasure they wrote about.

As the century wore on, the emotional community of polite masculinity began to adapt and to become more overtly responsive to the importance of the male body and its affective and political potential. We see this when we turn to the private letters of Lord Chesterfield to his son, Philip Stanhope. In one of his most striking one-liners, amidst a variety of advice on manners, Chesterfield tells his son, 'My object is to have you fit to live; which, if you are not, I do not desire that you should live at all.'[48] Harsh as it may sound, this sentence underlines the importance men of the eighteenth century placed on the ability to deploy politeness. Chesterfield's son was illegitimate, heightening the importance of the visible display of manners further as he lacked birthright. The failure to embody polite masculinity indicated a shameful failure to be a man and could present a significant threat to Stanhope's future social and economic wellbeing. However, it also offered unprecedented opportunities to a man in his position. It is for this reason that Chesterfield's letters to Stanhope, which make up the bulk of his published correspondence, are so heavily preoccupied with the latter's social education. Chesterfield was a strong believer, *avant la lettre*, in the socially turned self, and his letters are thick with exhortations to Stanhope to turn towards society, not just mentally but bodily too. He emphasizes the importance of the dancing master – often a figure treated contemptuously by 'men of sense' – as teaching important lessons for polite society: 'Do you mind your dancing while your dancing-master is with you? ... Remember, that the graceful motion of the arms, the giving your hand, and the putting-on and pulling-off your hat genteelly, are the material parts of a gentleman's dancing.'[49]

This strikes a different tone from Addison, despite both having strong investment in the polite commercial world. The attention paid to the masculine body and how it conducts itself demonstrates Chesterfield's understanding of the ways in which surface was believed to communicate depth in shorthand: 'The world is taken by the outside of things', he observes in a later letter.[50] Chesterfield frequently refers to 'polish' and 'shine' as desirable effects that his son must achieve through practice, rather than evidence of shameful falsity as they are for Addison: 'My plan for you, from the beginning, has been to make you shine equally in the learned and the polite world.'[51] However, Stanhope sometimes fell short of Chesterfield's expectations, and the response could often make quite explicit use of parental and societal shaming strategies. In a letter of 22 September 1749, sent from London and addressed to Stanhope, at that point in Verona, Chesterfield chastises his son for careless dining habits:

> I know no one thing more offensive to a company, than that inattention and *distraction*. It is showing them the utmost contempt; and people never forgive contempt. No man is *distrait* with the man he fears, or the women he loves; which is a proof that every man can get the better of that *distraction*, when he thinks it worth his while

to do so ... For my part, I would rather be in company with a dead man than an absent one.[52]

The language is theatrically overstated, but hardly unrepresentative of writing about masculine behaviour in the period. Chesterfield alludes to social death through permanently withheld forgiveness, and the image of the dead man as preferable company to a gauche Stanhope. Bad manners were an insensitivity to the manner of the world, as affect theorists might have it. As with effeminacy, part of the threat presented by poor manners was that politeness required others not to make one aware of where one had crossed the line. The great lengths Chesterfield goes to in these letters to educate Stanhope are therefore readable as an attempt to rescue him from this horrifying fate. He frequently uses the language of paternal care to frame the repeated advice on behaviour in company and cites his age and greater experience as reasons to be taken seriously. He makes use of proxies in Europe to act as his eyes and ears while Stanhope is out of the country; indeed, the above example is based on reports by Sir Charles Williams, at this point envoy to Saxony, who otherwise speaks of Stanhope's 'character and learning' in glowing terms.[53] This dispersed surveillance allows Chesterfield to continually assert his authority, not just as a father but also as an arbiter of politeness. He understands the polite world, and the letters work to reiterate this fact. As Ann C. Dean notes: 'The letters repeatedly describe the earl as part of an audience for his son's performance, an audience imagined as an extension of the group one might find in any drawing room where "good company" is assembled. He writes ... in a rhetorically constructed and strategic relation to a late-eighteenth-century social imaginary.'[54] We might also call this an emotional community. Shame becomes not just easy but also appropriate to deploy from this position of unassailable rightness. It is perversely admirable, then, that Stanhope continues to act *distrait* even when he knows his social failings will get back to his father, communicated by the very men he is required to pass his time with.

What Chesterfield demonstrates through his use of shame in the letters is what Silvan Tomkins recognizes two centuries later, namely that shame is both a measure and condition of civilization.[55] One should be appropriately ashamed of one's social transgressions as this is what prevents the breakdown of society; people are hindered from indulging their own selfish desires by what might blandly be called 'consideration for others', but as several eighteenth-century thinkers recognized might be more accurately called a fear of the social consequences of this behaviour.[56] These experiences are the extreme end of what Gregg and Seigworth call 'forces of encounter': sociability and civilization felt as pressure on the individual. Although shame was more explicitly applied to women in the eighteenth century, through misogynistic ideas of female sexual and social behaviour, a male discourse of shame, as I have shown here, did exist. Much of this comes via the responsibility men expected themselves and others to bear to a society of, generally speaking, other men. This homosociality is no better demonstrated than by Chesterfield's assertion of the separateness of masculine experience from feminine: 'as women are a considerable, or at least a pretty numerous part of the company; and as their suffrages go a great way towards establishing a man's character in a fashionable part of the world (which is of great importance to the fortune and figure he proposes to make in it), it is necessary to please them'.[57] In other words, although women were important enough to please, this importance rested entirely on their function in men's identity construction. Rarely does Chesterfield assume commonality between men and women; men, therefore, are alone among themselves in society.

Throughout the letters, Chesterfield contextualizes his advice to Stanhope in terms of gender. Much discussion of politeness and morality in eighteenth-century discourse uses the universal masculine 'man' to stand in for society as a whole, while still describing a social world that was, in practice, a male one. Chesterfield's letters consider politeness in its relationship to a gendered world where the masculine and feminine are the two poles. In this, he is typical of a period that saw the rise in understandings of the social world being divided into two discrete genders with differing but mutually compatible motivations and goals.[58] This shifted the emphasis and responsibilities for certain characteristics onto one or other of the two genders, with the body being an interesting case in point. Emphasis on the female body as an object of spectacularization had always existed, but this was redoubled in the eighteenth century, while the male body began to retreat from view behind the privileging of the male mind and its capacity for reason. *The Spectator* enacts this through Mr Spectator, whose position as the unassailable arbiter of politeness is crafted in part from his absence-in-presence, his ghost-like lack of corporeality and evaluative gaze.[59] Chesterfield's letters demonstrate that while this disembodiment of masculinity may have been an ideal, the reality was more complex. People have bodies, and no matter how they are biologically configured, those bodies can provide both opportunities and barriers in the way they move through the world. Chesterfield's close attention to how Stanhope behaved at the table, on how he entered a room, how he moved through space, all undermine the idea that the male body was not still the object of spectacle. Of course, everyone, male or female, was always watching everyone else, especially in this period of hypervisualization.[60] Chesterfield is remarkably – and characteristically – candid in the letters in terms of how male embodiment and its subsequent inevitable and necessary self-consciousness should work. He encourages Stanhope to observe other men and model his own dress on those he calls 'men of sense': 'A man of sense carefully avoids any particular character in his dress; he is accurately clean for his own sake; but all the rest is for other people's.'[61] This consideration for others is standard fare in polite discourse, but for Chesterfield it is vital because of the advantage it ultimately brings the individual in his worldly business.

Chesterfield finds remarkably little shame in performing politeness as a man. Unlike Addison, he is mostly unfazed by effeminacy, observing at one point to Stanhope that 'I would rather have you a fop than a sloven' (158).[62] He champions what he calls '*une certaine douceur*', which he defines as 'not so easily described as felt ... a complaisance, a flexibility, but not a servility of manners; an air of softness in the countenance, gesture and expression', all feminine traits which, in a man, could attract the suspicion of effeminacy but are nonetheless absolutely essential for Chesterfield, especially in the handling of difficult people or those you need to refuse.[63] His concept of masculinity is largely unaffected by the effeminacy panic of the time or the ongoing concerns over the state of that emblem of British brute strength, the army, which at several points in the period was perceived as weakened by apathy, dissipation and even sodomy.[64] What he is offended by is the opposite of effeminacy: distracted or inattentive behaviour in public, a careless approach to the presentation of the self and vulgarity. He also disapproves as we have seen of 'absence', the man who may be physically present in company but does not participate. For Ann C. Dean, politeness in Chesterfield is always an active principle, one that engages with society in an ultimately self-promoting mode: 'By guiding Stanhope's behaviour and circulating him among various audiences, the earl was in a sense publishing his son.'[65] In doing so, he is able to insert himself, as Stanhope's author-father, into the polite conversation and company of Europe while remaining himself at a distance. This is the only kind of absence Chesterfield deems acceptable, but with it comes anxiety. Stanhope's tendency for distracted or absent behaviour means that the message he gives out about his father always threatens to undermine the older man's reputation. This is why the same advice is repeated over and over in the letters, and why, when anxiety gets the better of Chesterfield, he resorts to shame.

Conclusion

It is clear that eighteenth-century male writers had the capacity to use shame to develop and maintain the ideals of polite masculinity.

Effeminacy was a powerful and lurid weapon to shame men out of seemingly impolite attachments to fashion above manly sense and reason, as Addison's beau passage demonstrates. Effeminophobia was merely the most visible when it came to coercive strategies for defining acceptable masculinity. Chesterfield's letters demonstrate the importance of the socially turned self and the successful negotiation of a world of sociability in which every gaze was a critical, evaluative one. Errors in judgement of manners could mean social death, and so Chesterfield's advice, ranging from the philosophical to the exasperated, attempted to imply the shame of this failure in a variety of ways. That these men made use of linguistic craft and the emerging literary forms of the eighteenth century, in particular the periodical, is not merely evidence of language's generalized ability to exert force on those who encounter its fracturing multiplicity of meaning, but also demonstrates the peculiar susceptibility of masculine self-understanding at this historical moment to affective suggestion.

Polite culture was a community with unstable but developing norms, but rising emphasis on individualism complicated its coherence as a recognizable group. Addison and Steele's character Mr Spectator writes eloquently and passes judgement on social practice, but as the fop episode discussed above demonstrates, neither he nor his friends always behave with decorum or restraint. Rather it is style, specifically Addison's and Steele's writing styles, that provides the paradigm for the polite self, further highlighting that polite masculinity is a discursive, even literary, construction. It is unsurprising, then, that these texts make use of shame to provide stability through evocative and emotive descriptions of transgressions, the fop being the most obvious. This shaming betrays the anxieties of its authors, however, with the threat of the fop's appealing performativity undermining their work to use him as a figure of shame. Chesterfield's rehabilitation of foppishness to some extent in his letters to his son, where attractive dress, manners and deportment become a key political tool, seems to confirm these fears. An emotional community based on writing is ultimately too likely to be reshaped by rhetorical and literary style.

Notes

1. Peter N. Stearns, *Shame: A Brief History* (Urbana, IL: University of Illinois Press, 2017), p. 13.

2. Stearns, *Shame*, p. 63.

3. Stearns, *Shame*, p. 71.

4. Stearns, *Shame*, p. 71.

5. Stearns, *Shame*, p. 18.

6. Jürgen Habermas, *The Structural Transformation of the Public Sphere* (Cambridge: Polity Press, 1989); Michael Warner, 'The Mass Public and the Mass Subject', in Craig Calhoun (ed.), *Habermas and the Public Sphere* (Cambridge, MA: MIT Press, 1992), pp. 377–401.

7. This is demonstrated by the increase of 'textbooks' summarizing and laying out the past, present and future of the field, for example Jan Plamper's *The History of Emotions: An Introduction* (Oxford: Oxford University Press, 2015), Barbara Rosenwein and Riccardo Cristiani's *What Is the History of Emotions?* (Cambridge: Polity Press, 2017) and Rob Boddice's *The History of Emotions* (Manchester: Manchester University Press, 2018).

8. In particular, Tiffany Watt Smith's work on schadenfreude argues for specific historical and cultural origins for this emotion. See Watt Smith, *Schadenfreude: The Joy of Another's Misfortune* (London: Profile, 2018).

9. William Reddy's *The Navigation of Feeling* (2001) is one of the earlier books to devote considerable space to the ways in which these two disciplines conceive of emotion and how this might inform a historical case study, in Reddy's case late eighteenth- and early nineteenth-century France. Reddy makes the case for how anthropology's efforts to decentre its Western universalism have demonstrated how differently emotions can be expressed and valued in different cultures.

10. See Boddice, *History of Emotions* (*passim*), for a useful example of how these new areas of research are influencing emotions history.

11. Ruth Leys, 'The Turn to Affect: A Critique', *Critical Inquiry*, 37, 3 (spring 2011), 434–72.

12. Leys, 'The Turn to Affect', p. 472.

13. Boddice, *History of Emotions*, p. 112.

14. See Boddice, *History of Emotions*, pp. 111–20. Ekman has successfully packaged affect theory's insights reductively enough to sell products such as the 'Facial Action Coding System', a way of reading emotions through combinations of facial movements: www.paulekman.com/facial-action-coding-system (accessed 23 February 2023).

15. Sedgwick begins to draw on Tomkins in earnest after her co-editing of *Shame and Its Sisters: A Silvan Tomkins Reader* (edited with Adam Frank; Durham, NC: Duke University Press, 1995). Her subsequent works foreground or demonstrate the influence of Tomkins: *A Dialogue on Love* (Boston, MA: Beacon Press, 1999), *Touching Feeling* (Durham, NC: Duke University Press, 2003) and *The Weather in Proust* (Durham, NC: Duke University Press, 2011).

16. Silvan Tomkins, *Shame and Its Sisters: A Silvan Tomkins Reader*, Eve Sedgwick and Adam Frank (eds.) (Durham, NC: Duke University Press, 1995), p. 121.

17. Tomkins, *Shame and Its Sisters*, p. 68.

18. Melissa Gregg and Gregory J. Seigworth, (eds.), *The Affect Theory Reader* (Durham, NC: Duke University Press, 2010), p. 1.

19. Summarized by Boddice, *History of Emotions*, p. 183.

20. Boddice, *History of Emotions*, p. 131.

21. Joanne Begiato, 'Between Poise and Power: Embodied Manliness in Eighteenth- and Nineteenth-Century British Culture', *Transactions of the Royal Historical Society*, 6, 26 (2016), 125–47.

22. Begiato, 'Tears and the Manly Sailor in England, 1760–1860', *Journal for Maritime Research*, 17, 2 (2015), 117–33.

23. Katie Barclay, *Men on Trial: Performing Emotion, Embodiment and Identity in Ireland 1800–1845* (Manchester: Manchester University Press, 2018), p. 3.

24. Barclay, *Men on Trial*, p. 94.

25. Barclay, *Men on Trial*, p. 113.

26. Karen Harvey, 'Men of Parts: Masculine Embodiment and the Male Leg in Eighteenth-Century England', *Journal of British Studies*, 54 (October 2015), 797–821.

27. Harvey, 'Craftsmen in Common: Objects, Skills and Masculinity in the Eighteenth and Nineteenth Centuries', in Hannah Greig, Jane Hamlett and Leonie Hannan (eds.), *Gender and Material Culture in Britain since 1600* (London: Palgrave, 2016), p. 83.

28. Begiato, 'Between Poise and Power', p. 130.

29. I am defining this emerging community by following Barbara Rosenwein's definition of an emotional community, namely as 'groups – usually but not always social groups – that have their own particular values, modes of feeling, and ways to express those feelings ... They ... share important norms concerning the emotions that they value and deplore and the modes of expressing them'. See Rosenwein, *Generations of Feeling: A History of Emotions, 600–1700* (Cambridge: Cambridge University Press, 2016), p. 3.

30. Lawrence Klein, *Shaftesbury and the Culture of Politeness: Moral Discourse and Cultural Politics in Early Eighteenth-Century England* (Cambridge: Cambridge University Press, 1994), p. 3.

31. Shaftesbury, *The Moralists*, in Lawrence E. Klein (ed.), *Characteristics of Men, Manners, Opinions, Times* (Cambridge: Cambridge University Press, 1999), p. 328.

32. Shaftesbury, *The Moralists*, p. 334.

33. Rosenwein, *Generations of Feeling*, p. 9.

34. Of course, many emotional communities in various periods of European history have asked their members to do this. It is no coincidence, however, that it is the so-called 'Enlightenment' that produces a moral philosophy like that of the Scottish Enlightenment type, summed up by Smith's concept of the impartial spectator: a 'man within' who plays the role of societal expectation, fully amalgamated into the sensing, thinking and feeling body. See Smith, *The Theory of Moral Sentiments*, Ryan Patrick Hanley (ed.) (London: Penguin Classics, 2009), p. 159.

35. J.G.A. Pocock, *Virtue, Commerce and History* (Cambridge: Cambridge University Press, 1985), p. 236.

36. Boddice, *The History of Emotions*, p. 195.

37. Richard Steele, *The Spectator*, no. 151, II, ed. Donald Bond (Oxford: Oxford University Press, 1965), p. 94.

38. Steele, *The Spectator*, no. 151, II, p. 94.

39. Reddy defines an emotional regime as 'a normative order for emotions' which can be general to a society or political state or specific to certain institutions, such as 'armies, schools, priesthoods'. The key defining factor here seems to be that emotional regimes are inherently power-orientated, regulatory and perhaps hierarchical. See Reddy, *Navigation of Feeling*, pp. 124–5.

40. See Thomas A. King, 'Gender and Modernity: Male Looks and the Performance of Public Pleasures'. in Laura J. Rosenthal and Mita Choudhury (eds.), *Monstrous Dreams of Reason: Body, Self, and Other in the Enlightenment* (Lewisburg, PA: Bucknell University Press, 2002), pp. 25–44.

41. Philip Carter, 'An "Effeminate" or "Efficient" Nation? Masculinity in Eighteenth-Century Social Documentary', *Textual Practice*, 11, 3 (1997), 433.

42. See Matthew McCormack, *The Independent Man: Citizenship and Gender Politics in Georgian England* (Manchester: Manchester University Press, 2005).

43. Addison, *The Spectator*, no. 275, II, p. 571.

44. Addison, *The Spectator*, p. 571.

45. Addison, *The Spectator*, p. 572.

46. Addison, *The Spectator*, pp. 572–3.

47. Warner, 'The Mass Public and the Mass Subject', p. 377.

48. Lord Chesterfield, *Lord Chesterfield's Letters*, David Roberts (ed.) (Oxford: Oxford World's Classics, 2008), p. 63.

49. Lord Chesterfield, *Lord Chesterfield's Letters*, p. 99.

50. Lord Chesterfield, *Lord Chesterfield's Letters*, p. 185.

51. Lord Chesterfield, *Lord Chesterfield's Letters*, p. 159.

52. Lord Chesterfield, *Lord Chesterfield's Letters*, p. 155, emphasis original.

53. Lord Chesterfield, *Lord Chesterfield's Letters*, p. 154.

54. Ann C. Dean, 'Authorship, Print, and Public in Chesterfield's Letters to His Son', *SEL Studies in English Literature 1500–1900*, 45, 3 (2005), 694.

55. Tomkins, *Shame and Its Sisters*, p. 121.

56. For example, Smith discusses shame and remorse as the consequence of social transgression in *The Theory of Moral Sentiments*, pp. 100–102.

57. Lord Chesterfield, *Lord Chesterfield's Letters*, p. 91.

58. See Tim Hitchcock and Michele Cohen (eds.), *English Masculinities 1660–1800* (Harlow: Longman, 1999).

59. See Manushag N. Powell, '"See No Evil, Hear No Evil, Speak No Evil": Spectation and the Eighteenth-Century Public Sphere', *Eighteenth Century Studies*, 45, 2 (2012), 255–77.

60. There is perhaps too much emphasis in modern criticism on the Enlightenment's supposed obsession with the visual and ocular as a rational tool for evaluating the external world, but it is undeniable that many theorists and commentators of the time did make frequent use of the visual, from Addison's discussion of the imagination in *The Spectator* (p. 144) to Smith's society of surveillance in *The Theory of Moral Sentiments*. A useful discussion of ocular culture in the eighteenth century is still Peter de Bolla's *The Education of the Eye*, but more recent work by historians like William Tullett in emphasizing the other senses has helped to improve our understanding of the eighteenth-century sensorium. See William Tullett, *Smell in Eighteenth-Century England: A Social Sense* (Oxford: Oxford University Press, 2019).

61. Lord Chesterfield, *Lord Chesterfield's Letters*, p. 128.

62. Lord Chesterfield, *Lord Chesterfield's Letters*, p. 158.

63. Lord Chesterfield, *Lord Chesterfield's Letters*, p. 217.

64. See Carter, 'An "Effeminate" or "Efficient" Nation?', pp. 429–43.

65. Ann C. Dean, 'Authorship, Print, and Public in Chesterfield's Letters to His Son', p. 696.

References

Joseph Addison and Richard Steele, *The Spectator*, ed. by Donald Bond (Oxford: Oxford University Press, 1965).

Katie Barclay, *Men on Trial: Performing Emotion, Embodiment and Identity in Ireland 1800–1845* (Manchester: Manchester University Press, 2018).

Joanne Begiato, 'Tears and the Manly Sailor in England, 1760–1860', *Journal for Maritime Research*, 17, 2 (2015), 117–33.

——, 'Between Poise and Power: Embodied Manliness in Eighteenth- and Nineteenth-Century British Culture'. *Transactions of the Royal Historical Society*, 6, 26 (2016), 125–47.

Rob Boddice, *The History of Emotions* (Manchester: Manchester University Press, 2018).

Philip Carter, 'An "Effeminate" or "Efficient" Nation? Masculinity in Eighteenth-Century Social Documentary', *Textual Practice*, 11, 3 (1997), 429–43.

——, 'Men about Town: Representations of Foppery and Masculinity in Early Eighteenth-Century Urban Society', in Hannah Barker and Elaine Chalus (eds.), *Gender in Eighteenth-Century England: Roles, Representations and Responsibilities* (Harlow: Longman, 1997), pp. 31–57.

Lord Chesterfield, *Lord Chesterfield's Letters*, ed. by David Roberts (Oxford: Oxford World's Classics, 2008).

Anthony Ashley Cooper, Third Earl of Shaftesbury, *Characteristics of Men, Manners, Opinions, Times*, ed. by Lawrence E. Klein (Cambridge: Cambridge University Press, 1999).

Ann C. Dean, 'Authorship, Print, and Public in Chesterfield's Letters to His Son', *SEL Studies in English Literature 1500–1900*, 45, 3 (2005), 691–706.

Peter De Bolla, *The Education of the Eye: Painting, Landscape and Architecture in Eighteenth-Century Britain* (Stanford, CA: Stanford University Press, 2003).

Melissa Gregg and Gregory J. Seigworth, eds., *The Affect Theory Reader* (Durham, NC: Duke University Press, 2010).

Jurgen Habermas, *The Structural Transformation of the Public Sphere* (Cambridge: Polity Press, 1989).

Karen Harvey, 'Men of Parts: Masculine Embodiment and the Male Leg in Eighteenth-Century England', *Journal of British Studies*, 54 (October 2015), 797–821.

——, 'Craftsmen in Common: Objects, Skills and Masculinity in the Eighteenth and Nineteenth Centuries', in Hannah Greig, Jane Hamlett and Leonie Hannan (eds.), *Gender and Material Culture in Britain since 1600* (London: Palgrave, 2016), p. 83.

Tim Hitchcock and Michele Cohen, eds., *English Masculinities 1660–1800* (Harlow: Longman, 1999).

Thomas A. King, 'Gender and Modernity: Male Looks and the Performance of Public Pleasures'. in Laura J. Rosenthal and Mita Choudhury (eds.), *Monstrous Dreams of Reason: Body, Self, and Other in the Enlightenment* (Lewisburg, PA: Bucknell University Press, 2002), pp. 25–44.

Lawrence Klein, *Shaftesbury and the Culture of Politeness: Moral Discourse and Cultural Politics in Early Eighteenth-Century England* (Cambridge: Cambridge University Press, 1994).

Ruth Leys, 'The Turn to Affect: A Critique', *Critical Inquiry*, 37, 3 (2011), 434–72.

Matthew McCormack, *The Independent Man: Citizenship and Gender Politics in Georgian England* (Manchester: Manchester University Press, 2005).

Jan Plamper, *The History of Emotions: An Introduction* (Oxford: Oxford University Press, 2015).

J.G.A. Pocock, *Virtue, Commerce and History* (Cambridge: Cambridge University Press, 1985).

Manushag N. Powell, '"See No Evil, Hear No Evil, Speak No Evil": Spectation and the Eighteenth-Century Public Sphere', *Eighteenth Century Studies*, 45, 2 (2012), 255–77.

William M. Reddy, *The Navigation of Feeling: A Framework for the History of Emotions* (Cambridge: Cambridge University Press, 2001).

Barbara Rosenwein, *Generations of Feeling: A History of Emotions, 600–1700* (Cambridge: Cambridge University Press, 2016).

Barbara Rosenwein and Riccardo Cristiani, *What Is the History of the Emotions?* (Cambridge: Polity Press, 2017).

Eve Sedgwick, *A Dialogue on Love* (Boston, MA: Beacon Press, 1999).

——, *Touching Feeling* (Durham, NC: Duke University Press, 2003).

——, *The Weather in Proust* (Durham, NC: Duke University Press, 2011).

Adam Smith, *The Theory of Moral Sentiments*, ed. by Ryan Patrick Hanley (London: Penguin Classics, 2009).

Peter N. Stearns, *Shame: A Brief History* (Urbana, IL: University of Illinois Press, 2017).

Silvan Tomkins, *Shame and Its Sisters: A Silvan Tomkins Reader*, ed. by Eve Sedgwick and Adam Frank (Durham, NC: Duke University Press, 1995).

William Tullett, *Smell in Eighteenth-Century England: A Social Sense* (Oxford: Oxford University Press, 2019).

Michael Warner, 'The Mass Public and the Mass Subject', in Craig Calhoun (ed.), *Habermas and the Public Sphere* (Cambridge, MA: MIT Press, 1992), pp. 377–401.

Tiffany Watt Smith, *Schadenfreude: The Joy of Another's Misfortune* (London: Profile, 2018).

Chapter 10

'At nature's mighty feast there is no vacant cover for him': suicide, masculine shame and the language of burden in nineteenth-century Britain

Lyndsay Galpin

Introduction

In the wake of the 2008 financial crash, the UK witnessed a steady rise in suicide rates, but male suicide rates in particular became a matter of public concern in 2013, when suicides amongst men hit their highest in just over a decade. While the most recent report on suicide statistics, produced in 2018, indicates that the male suicide rate is now at its lowest in thirty years, the peak of 2013 ignited popular debate over the state of modern masculinity, raising concerns that expectations of masculinity are damaging men's mental health.[1] This public discourse has blamed a rigid model of masculinity – which puts pressure on men to perform, succeed and remain strong and emotionally reticent – for damaging men's health and pushing them to the edge. Journalists, charities and sociologists feel that this emphasis on male success and strength leaves little space for men to open up about personal and emotional struggles for fear of being branded as weak, and campaigns such as the Campaign Against Living Miserably (CALM) have attempted to 'challenge male stereotypes and encourage positive behavioural change and help-seeking behaviour'.[2] This is something scholars from a variety of fields have been doing since the 1980s, when Raewyn Connell first introduced the analytic frame of 'hegemonic masculinity', used to distinguish a dominant societal ideal that suppresses marginalized masculinities from everyday practice.[3] Turning focus to the nineteenth century, scholars such as James Eli Adams, John Tosh and more recently Holly Furneaux and Joanne Begiato have done much to demonstrate that the traditional model of masculinity is not a true representation of nineteenth-century masculine experience.[4]

This current 'crisis of masculinity' has a long history. While the twentieth century saw a steady drop in male suicide rates (with the exception of peaks during the Great Depression, the 1950s and the 1980s), the 1990s saw them return to levels not seen since the nineteenth century.[5] Then, as now, men killed themselves three to four times more frequently than women, and many of our contemporary conceptions of masculinity as outlined above can be traced back to this same period. Yet, men have largely been left out of historical studies of suicide, which have either primarily focused on the apparent feminization of suicide in the nineteenth century or constitute broad statistical or geographical studies lacking deeper analyses of gender.[6] When Olive Anderson published one of the first historical studies of suicide, *Suicide in Victorian and Edwardian England* (1987), she acknowledged that undertaking separate histories of men's and women's suicides provides 'hints on the changing significance in Victorian and Edwardian England of being male or female'.[7] However, few historians have continued where Anderson left off, and suicide, particularly men's suicide, continues to be an under-researched field within history.

Informed by Anderson's approach and using suicide as a lens upon Victorian society, here I turn to the narratives and stories that were told about male suicide as sites of historical enquiry, which reveal the expectations and pressures of masculinity upon the individual in the nineteenth century. These stories of suicide and suicidal motive, as told through the coroner's courts and retold in newspapers about real deaths and their motives, offered explanations and made judgements about behaviours deemed unusual or unacceptable. As Kali Israel has recognized, stories are more than just windows into the past; they 'do' history through the way in which 'they organise perception and delineate possible ways of thinking, acting and being'.[8] These sources have allowed me to move beyond the archetypes of nineteenth-century masculinities upon which previous histories have relied and towards a more nuanced study of the experiences of 'everyday' men. What becomes clear in these narratives of suicide is that, despite the hegemonic ideal of the male breadwinner being largely unattainable for many working-class families, it was still a powerful ideology of respectability, and having work was central to a man's identity.

The stories included here are of the overbearing pressures of hegemonic masculinity, often exacerbated by unemployment or financial strife, and the resultant feelings of shame, guilt and failure engendered by the rampant individualism of the nineteenth century. This individualism, championed by those such as Thomas Malthus and Samuel Smiles, was enshrined in the New Poor Law system of 1834, which sought to emphasize that financial security 'was an individual obligation in the natural order of the economic market'. This new system aimed to lessen the 'burden' of poor relief for the parish and ratepayers by reducing the scope of outdoor relief and requiring the able-bodied poor to enter the workhouse in order to receive it. Workhouse conditions were purposely harsh in order to deter parishioners from resorting to state welfare; families were separated and lodged in crowded dormitories; inmates were put to useless work like picking oakum and made to wear the workhouse uniform. Entering the workhouse, as David Englander highlights, was seen as 'a public admission of personal and moral failure'.[9] This cultural climate measured masculinity and men's worth by their productivity and utilized a language of burden in discourses of unemployment and poverty, a language still present in contemporary debates around austerity and suicide.[10]

As a social emotion, shame was key in enforcing these utilitarian principles, even on those who found themselves unemployed through no fault of their own. Shame, as Jennifer Biddle discusses, is a learned emotion, and these suicide narratives provide a stark demonstration of this fact.[11] Not only is this shame taught and learned through the language of burden used in utilitarian discourses of poverty, but the shame of unemployment was acted out again and again in the pages of the press, in showing suicide as a rational response to such hardship. As Kali Israel notes, 'people enact as well as write the stories they inherit',[12] and so, in turning to look at these narratives of poverty and suicide, we see how the shame of unemployment and poverty was learned and reinforced. But these stories also reveal the ways in which suicides were politicized through the adoption of melodramatic narratives, or used in calls for social reform, offering an alternative language with which to highlight the suffering of the poor and alleviate these feelings of shame and moral failure.

A Malthusian framework for suicide: utilitarianism, individualism and the language of burden

In his 1798 *Essay on the Principle of Population*, Thomas Malthus raised concerns over a population that appeared to be growing at an unsustainable rate and criticized the Poor Laws for encouraging the working classes to produce families beyond their ability to provide for them. Malthus's conceptual conflation of population and labour and his idea of surplus population, both of which are central themes throughout his essay, are key to reading the narratives of these suicides.[13] The implication of his essay was that only those who were useful to society were deserving of financial aid, and that this was to be given as benevolent *charity* rather than being a human *right*. In the controversial 'Nature's mighty feast' passage, which was removed in later editions,[14] Malthus wrote:

> Man who is born into a world already possessed, if he cannot get subsistence from his parents on whom he has a just demand, and if the society do not want his labour, has no claim of *right* to the smallest portion of food, and, in fact, has no business to be where he is. At nature's mighty feast there is no vacant cover for him. She tells him to be gone, and will quickly execute her own orders, if he do [sic] not work upon the compassion of some of her guests.[15]

In Malthus's theory, nature executes her orders through 'positive checks' on population: disease, famine, war and other causes of premature death. He also identified 'preventative checks' which he considered to be a form of moral restraint, such as delaying marriage and having children.[16]

Although Malthus never wrote explicitly on the issue of suicide, his principles pervade the welfare provision of the New Poor Law and offer a framework through which to interpret suicide as a response to unemployment. In a utilitarian context, those who committed suicide because they were unable to find unemployment can be considered part of the surplus population: those whose labour society does not appear to need or want. While at 'Nature's mighty feast' nature executes her own orders, the suicide obeys these orders and carries them out himself. Here, suicide can be seen as another Malthusian 'check' on population.

The best-known example of such suicide is that of Jude Fawley's son, Little Father Time, who kills himself after having murdered his two siblings in Thomas Hardy's *Jude the Obscure* (1895). The episode is described by Gillian Beer as a 'late-Malthusian tragedy'[17] and the note left by Father Time, 'Done because we are too menny',[18] explicitly frames the suicide in Malthusian terms. Father Time's actions operate as a 'positive check' on the family's population where the 'preventative check' – in this case, moral restraint and celibacy – has failed. The Malthusian sentiment is recognizable even to readers who are only 'passingly familiar' with Malthus's work.[19] The incident comes after a failed search for lodgings with his adoptive mother, Sue Bridehead, because 'Every householder looked askance at such a woman and child inquiring for accommodation.'[20] As well as being a demonstration of the suicidal implications of Malthusian sentiment, the

'AT NATURE'S MIGHTY FEAST THERE IS NO VACANT COVER FOR HIM'   243

incident also brings the social and contagious aspects of shame into sharp relief, which Biddle suggests is particularly felt between parent and child.[21] As an extension of the parent, Father Time feels his part in the shame of their situation, and takes on the guilt of his involvement in that.

This narrative was more than just a fictional plot; many real suicides had felt themselves to be an unnecessary burden upon families by the time *Jude the Obscure* was published. When Walter Swallow, who had been out of work for four months, cut his throat in 1886, his letter revealed that he felt he 'were only a burden to my mother', with whom he had been living.[22] Similarly, a note left by John Joseph Perkins after his suicide on 8 September 1891 explained how he could not 'be a burden' on his family any longer. He believed that they would 'get along better' without him, as he had been suffering from crippling pains in his limbs, which prevented him from working and left him and his children entirely dependent on the earnings of the woman with whom they had been living for eleven years.[23] Others felt the burden they would incur on the wider population by depending on the parish in times of unemployment. William Lenny, who was seventy-two and had been a farmer in Romford, died by suicide after coming into serious pecuniary difficulties. The *Chelmsford Chronicle* reported that, as his circumstances became more embarrassed, he had had to borrow 'various sums of money' from his neighbours, and 'after being reduced to great distress' he 'determined to commit suicide, rather than become a burden to the parish, which must have been the result had he survived'.[24] In this rhetoric of burden, people's worth was measured in terms of productivity and their ability to contribute to society.

Malthus's views on the right of the people to subsistence reinforced the notion that an individual's value is intrinsically linked to their labour power. In his view, the laws of nature did not allow for a universal right to subsist because nature was unable to provide unlimited resources. Refuting Thomas Paine's *Rights of Man* (1791), Malthus declared that 'there is one right which man has generally been thought to possess, which I am confident he neither does nor can possess, *a right to subsistence when his labour will not fairly purchase it*'.[25] When those without labour power claimed from the Poor Laws, they were directly or indirectly interfering with their neighbours' rights to live. This point is made by implication in a passage analogizing the right to subsist to the right to live indefinitely: 'Undoubtedly he had then, and has still, a good right to live a hundred years, nay a thousand, *if he can*, without interfering with the right of others to live; but the affair in both cases is principally an affair of power, not of right.'[26] What this makes clear is that power was also linked to labour; those without labour had no power and no right to claim from the state. As Gregory Claeys neatly summarizes the argument: 'No "right to charity" consequently existed, separate from the ability and willingness of the poor to make a contribution to common produce.'[27] The suicides in this chapter, according to Malthus, would have had no right to subsistence because of their state of unemployment; unable to find employment, suicide became their last perceived option.

These sentiments were even used by those wishing to defend their right to choose death in light of religious arguments against suicide, which often emphasized each individual's duty to their neighbour and the potential utility that a suicide denied society.[28] David Hume's essay *On Suicide*, published posthumously in 1777, defended the right to suicide along such utilitarian and Malthusian grounds:

> suppose that it is no longer in my power to promote the interest of society; suppose that I am a burden to it; suppose that my life hinders some person from being much more useful to society. In such cases, my resignation of life must not only be innocent, but laudable.[29]

According to this rationale, those unable to find work would be justified in, or even lauded for, dying by suicide if they required subsistence without being able to contribute in return. In such circumstances, suicide might even become a moral duty. This was the belief of Thomas Owen Bonser, a proponent of Malthus's work and the author of a paper defending suicide. In his paper *The Right to Die* (1885), he maintained that 'in many cases it is justifiable, or even a moral duty, to retire from life' and challenged the religious notion that life, in itself, is sacred.[30] Echoing Malthus, he wrote that nothing in nature was cheaper or incurred more waste than life, and that the rate of population growth far exceeded any increase in the provision of sustenance. Bonser concluded that 'the places at the board of life are quite insufficient for the number brought in. The superfluous lives come simply to be eliminated'.[31] In accordance with this rationale, those who were found to be superfluous were morally justified, if not morally *obliged*, to choose suicide. In utilitarian terms, unemployment constituted a justifiable reason for suicide.

These narratives of suicide suggest that many were unable to reconcile this contradiction between the work ethic that Smiles described as 'that honest and upright performance of individual duty, which is the glory of manly character' and the inability to find work that suggested that his labour was not needed, that there was 'no room' for him.[32] In these stories suicide becomes an emotional performance of poverty and the masculine shame engendered by the language used to describe it acted out again and again in the pages of the press. In understanding suicide as an emotional performance, I am drawing on Monique Scheer's use of practice theory in understanding emotions as embodied. Practice theory, as Scheer points out, is concerned with social scripts of acceptable behaviour, through which community expectations 'are implicated through learned habits of feeling'.[33] Through the repetition of these stories of suicide and discourses of poverty as shameful, the self-inflicted death becomes an appropriate response to poverty and an embodied practice of shame.

An alternative form of knowing: reclaiming respectability through melodramatic narratives

Based on the ideal of the male breadwinner, work has been seen as a central component of masculine identity, both as a signifier of masculine status and as a site of masculine identity formation. Having work meant a man would be able (ideally) to support himself and even provide for a family. Of course, this was not always the case, and for the many who lived on the borderlands of poverty, it was an impossibility. For the working-class man, (un)employment could be a constant source of anguish. Reports of working-class suicides often detailed the length of time workers had been without employment, which for some was as long as eight years.[34] For many, though, even just a few weeks was enough to plunge the family into dire straits. Sixty-two-year-old George Saville had been a foreman for the Midland Railway, but for the month before his suicide he had found himself without work and with no prospects of finding any. After just one month of unemployment Saville and his wife were destitute and their furniture was seized and sold, causing Saville to 'become gloomy and desponding'. The article in the *Sheffield and Rotherham Independent* signed off by declaring that, 'It is generally stated in … the neighbourhood that the deceased committed suicide because of being in want; but as he had only been out of work a month his condition could hardly have been that of absolute want.'[35] Implicitly, the apparent ignorance of the emotional and material experience of poverty reflects Samuel Smiles's expectation that the respectable and honest working man would possess sufficient savings to protect himself and his family in hard times.

A second report of Saville's suicide in the same paper also pointed to a history of drinking, acknowledging that although recently he had not been drinking heavily, he 'used to drink a great deal'.[36] This comment acted as a clear moral judgement in line with Smilesian ethics, which saw alcohol as an irresponsible use of money. Saville's history of drinking makes the suggestion that he was guilty of an excessive and frivolous misuse of money during a time when expectations of respectable working-class masculinity encompassed saving and frugality. A lack of such forward thinking inevitably led to failure.[37] The use and misuse of money was a topic to which Samuel Smiles devoted an entire chapter in his 1859 work *Self-Help*. Smiles lamented 'the readiness with which so many are accustomed to eat up and drink up their earnings as they go'. Men who failed to provide a safety net for themselves and their households in times of unemployment, sickness or death lacked self-respect, as well as respect from their neighbours, independence and manly character. The failure to live honestly within his means also meant that 'he must necessarily be living dishonestly upon the means of somebody else'. The comment on past drinking habits here served to admonish Saville for his failure to live up to expectations of respectable masculinity. Saville had expected to get fresh employment a few days prior to his suicide, but this had fallen through and served the final blow to his character. The article concluded that 'There was nothing to throw light upon the reason for the deceased laying violent hands upon himself', yet the narrative clearly indicated that lack of work, and its consequent poverty, had been the cause of his suicide. This failure to acknowledge the narrative of unemployment and poverty as a viable motive to suicide served to reinforce the individualistic principles that blamed poverty on individual moral failing. The jury reached an open verdict of suicide, with no evidence accounting for his state of mind at the time.[38]

While such heavy moral judgement was common in the stories told about working-class men's suicides, depositions and reports could also invoke melodramatic narrative devices to bring attention to the blameless suffering experienced by the poorest in society. By invoking the images of families broken up, men's tireless searches for work or the sacrifices made for families, these narratives make use of key plot devices of melodrama to tell their stories. As David Mayer describes it, melodrama is

> a theatrical or literary response to a world where things are seen to go wrong, where ideas of secular and divine justice and recompense are not always met, where suffering is not always acknowledged, and where the explanations for wrong, injustice, and suffering are not altogether understandable. Melodrama provided emotional answers to a world where explanations of why there is pain and chaos and discord are flawed or deeply and logically inconsistent.[39]

The melodramatic mode was not only confined to literature and the stage but permeated wider culture, acting as a tool for expression, understanding and meaning-making. As Rohan McWilliam argues, it also shaped journalism, which used the 'language and categories of the stage' to make sense of events and scandals.[40] In an age when unemployment was structural and cyclical, the melodramatic mode in suicide narratives offered reassurance that those in dire straits were not suffering on account of their own moral failings. Instead, as Martha Vicinus suggests, melodrama made the moral visible through the passive suffering of virtuous characters.[41] Many of the stories told about suicide and unemployment emphasized the good character of those at the heart of these domestic tragedies, telling of their tireless searches for work, their hardworking nature when employment could be found and the personal sacrifices they made so that their children might not go without. J. Challiner, who had suffered constitutional fits that prevented him from working and died by suicide in 1845, was described as bearing 'a very good character';[42] George William Short, who died by suicide in 1879, had been unemployed for nearly nine months but 'had tried to get work every day' without success;[43] and George William Lock had 'striven hard to earn a livelihood'.[44] The stories of Challiner and Short both attest to the shame of their situations. Challiner wrote in his suicide note that he was 'ashamed to be beholden' to his friends, while Short had told his wife that he was 'ashamed of walking about the streets'.

While these narratives did not necessarily offer clear answers as to why poverty happened, they went some way towards showing others that it was not necessarily through any fault of their own – for being lazy, or wasteful with money, as Smilesian doctrine might suggest. Melodrama, as Vicinus argues, appeals to those who feel powerless, 'who feel that their lives are without order and that events they cannot control can destroy or save them',[45] and, as McWilliam suggested, it could offer 'a form of psychic healing by dramatizing anxieties such as the fear of not being able to pay the rent'.[46] Reports of suicide could provide evidence of the blameless suffering which often went unacknowledged in the nineteenth-century climate of individualism. The melodramatic narrative, then, served to politicize working-class suicides by acknowledging that the suffering which the Poor Law system blamed on individual failure was often unaccountable, and offered an alternative form of knowledge to Malthusianism, utilitarianism and individualism.[47]

Where these narratives differed from stage melodrama is in the absence of a clear, identifiable villain. While traditionally the villain of melodrama was an embodied representation of a larger problem projected onto a middle-class figure, the villain in journalistic suicide narratives was more often the abstract external force itself, such as capitalism, the competitive individualism it engendered or the structural nature of unemployment, all of which threatened domestic peace.[48] This threat to domesticity was a key part in evoking sympathy in melodrama, and the most alarming manifestation of this threat to domestic peace was the murder of an entire family by the father who should have protected them. On Sunday 10

March 1895, *Reynolds's Newspaper* reported just such a tragedy.[49] Frank Taylor awoke at an early hour on Thursday March 7 and proceeded to cut the throats of his wife and six of their children before taking his own life in the same manner. The eldest boy, only fourteen, survived his father's attempt at murder and rushed to his neighbours to raise an alarm. The police were sent for and arrived almost immediately. Upon entering the house, the scene was described as 'having the appearance more of a slaughter-house than a human habitation, the furniture and walls being splashed with blood, while pools of it lay upon the floor'.[50]

In the reports that followed, Frank Taylor was praised as a 'kind father', an 'affectionate husband', 'hard working but very unfortunate' and a 'steady, industrious man'.[51] But despite being 'active and willing to work',[52] he had been unemployed since Christmas and the family had been 'plunged into distress'. They subsisted on what they could grow in their allotment but had to rely on the penny dinners provided at the local church and the charity of clergymen.[53] Taylor had recently found some work at Tooting Junction, and the papers reported that as soon as he had been paid he 'stocked the larder and purchased boots for some of the children'. Unfortunately, only a week after resuming work he was taken ill with influenza, once again throwing him out of work. The day before the tragedy occurred, he returned to work and, although not fully recovered, witnesses and the jury believed there was no reason to suspect that his illness had affected his mind.[54]

This was a sensational case that garnered national attention and was laced with the trappings of domestic melodrama, through the detailing of the household, family circumstances, the threat to domesticity unemployment posed and even the narrative flow of events. It was the kind of narrative repeatedly attributed to men who killed themselves while out of work and appealed to the rhetoric of hegemonic masculinity and readers' domestic sensibilities. Taylor was clearly framed as a devoted, hardworking and industrious family man, seeking employment when he could find none, which, combined with his sober habits, made the family part of the 'deserving poor' who qualified for the sympathy of the public.

Although domesticity has predominantly been associated with the middle-class idea of 'separate spheres', it occupied a central place in working-class rhetoric. As Anna Clark has shown, Chartists used images of domesticity in their political rhetoric, drawing on melodramatic plots that shifted the blame of poverty and domestic misery from the immorality of the working-class individual to 'the aristocratic libertine, symbolizing capitalism and corruption'.[55] For working-class readers, this domestic tragedy would have been equally distressing. As a patriarchal figure, it should have been Taylor's duty to protect and care for his family, not be the one to destroy it, and the fact that the tragedy took place inside the home is significant in this way. The sanctity of the home occupied an important part of the ideological space of the home as a sanctuary away from the outside world of competition and business. In her work on domestic violence, Shani D'Cruze has discussed how domestic murders that took place in the home threatened the middle-class ideology of the home as a safe haven.[56] While D'Cruze talks more explicitly about the *middle-class* home, it is equally applicable to the working-class one: Taylor was represented as possessing characteristics lauded as respectable across all classes – family devotion, industriousness and sobriety – and thus the murder within the working-class home appears just as threatening to the ideological conception of domesticity. The description of the Taylor residence gives a vivid illustration of this: 'The bedding in the front room was saturated with blood, and the apartment was bespattered with it in all directions';[57] Mrs Taylor's 'thumbs were nearly cut off'[58] and:

> More revolting still was the sight of six children lying lifeless, four of them upon the floor, and two of them, both girls, hanging over the side of the bed with their heads nearly severed from their bodies. It was only too apparent that the little victims had put forth all their feeble strength to resist the furious onslaught of their murderer, and had died struggling hard against dreadful odds.[59]

Viewed in the context of domestic melodrama, although Taylor was not turned into the melodramatic villain, he represented the wider social issues threatening working-class domesticity. Low wages and the precarious nature of many working-class jobs – which were often vulnerable to the changing nature of industry or the weather – meant that unemployment threatened not just a man's masculinity but the welfare of the entire household. According to the melodramatic narrative, it was unemployment, and by implication individualistic capitalist society, that killed the Taylor family.

Moreover, the way Taylor's story was marked by distinct periods of employment, unemployment, sickness and health reflects the pacing of melodramatic performances. Juliet John describes 'the emotional economy of melodrama' as 'best figured in a series of waves',[60] alternating, literally, between music and pictures, music and speech, but also between movement and stasis.[61] To this we can also add calm and crisis. The Taylor case, for example, alternated between relative calm and security and moments of crisis. We learn that Taylor had been a hard worker when in work, but thrown out of work the family was plunged into crisis; Taylor again found work but was again thrown into a crisis when he contracted influenza. He returned to work despite not having fully recovered, and

'Death before the workhouse': suicide and masculine shame

Despite these attempts to relieve the blame of poverty from the working classes, the sense of shame that surrounded the experience of poverty was felt keenly. Vivienne Richmond's study of working-class clothing has shown how important appearances (cleanliness and clothing) were in creating and maintaining respectability. The Sunday best, for example, was held up as the 'sartorial barometer' of respectability, and those without might even keep themselves and their children inside all day long for fear of disgrace.[62] It was better to not be seen at all than to be seen to be without. With his first new wages, the papers reported how, in addition to stocking the larder, Frank Taylor had immediately bought new boots for some of the children, shining boots being a 'blazon of family respectability'.[63] Richmond's evidence of the unwillingness of families to be seen without the right clothing could also shed light on a comment made in some reports that Taylor had been summoned and fined for failing to regularly send his children to school.[64] If the children had had few changes of clothes, or their clothing was ragged and dirty, it is feasible that Taylor's neglect to send his children to school was in fact an evasion of shame. This, again, attests to Biddle's suggestion that shame was keenly felt between parent and child, when the latter acts as representative or an extension of the former.[65] In this way, ensuring the children were respectably dressed (or keeping them out of the public eye if they were not) was an important protector against the shame of poverty. The clothing which bore the most shame, however, was the workhouse uniform.

The workhouse and its uniform acted as part of a ritual of public shaming, which aimed to regulate moral behaviour.[66] The workhouse coat was seen as a 'slothful, degrading badge'[67] and shattered any ambition of respectability, stripped men of their civil rights, broke up families and cast shame over generations to come.[68] Even more, in the context of Smilesian self-help and Malthusian utility, the workhouse engendered feelings of individual moral failure. So shameful was this Victorian institution that headlines such as 'Death before the Workhouse' were not uncommon in narratives of men's suicides.[69] The suicide of Benjamin Klimcke, a watchcase polisher from Coventry, gained national attention and was used to comment on the 'false pride' of the working classes, the workhouse system and the distress and suffering that pervaded in Coventry at the time.[70]

Klimcke had been out of work for six months before taking his own life and had been surviving on only bread. According to the letter he left on the table in his sitting room, Klimcke had become 'almost wild through no work' and seeing no prospects of finding employment in the near future, he wrote, 'I prefer death to the workhouse.'[71] Twelve out of the fifteen papers reporting Benjamin Klimcke's suicide added the following paragraph to the end of their reports:

> It adds a touch to the pathos of the story to learn on the authority of Alderman Worwood that Klimcke, who was a member of a local 'Early Morning Class,' would have been relieved had he made his case known. Some feeling of false pride had restrained him from telling his sorrows to the outside world.[72]

But dependence on parish relief was antithetical to working-class respectability, and above all to masculinity. A letter to the editor of *Reynolds's Newspaper*, decrying the Poor Laws and the Charity Organization Society, used Klimcke's suicide to highlight the degradation that accompanied entry into the workhouse and call for reform. The author lambasted 'the gentlemen of the Charity Organization Society' for failing to understand why the working classes refused to apply for relief. The anonymous author outlined how 'before he could do that he would have to conquer that curious pride which makes decent and honest men shirk the workhouse'; this aversion to the workhouse was a result of the simple fact that 'the workhouse is a badge of disgrace' and branded them as paupers.[73] As Claudia Klaver has noted, there was an important distinction between pauper and labourer. 'Pauperism', Klaver points out, 'entailed laziness, drunkenness, and thriftlessness.'[74] This distinction engaged with the individualistic and utilitarian conflation of labour and morality where independence represented a high moral character and dependence was a sign of immorality. For the working man, the workhouse was a profound symbol of masculine shame as it represented the loss of independence that was an important marker of manhood and masculinity.[75]

Conclusion

While the workhouses of the nineteenth century have long disappeared, stories of suicide from poverty, unemployment and overwork have not. However, with strict media guidelines on the reporting of suicides, the social causes of suicide have been obfuscated.[76] In recent years, suicidological work has attempted to highlight the impact of government policies on increasing suicide rates and to challenge the pathologization and internalization of suicide which distances it from 'other cultural meanings' and wider social causes.[77] Looking at economic crises throughout the twentieth century to the present day, David Stuckler and Sanjay Basu have demonstrated how austerity measures have a direct impact on suicide rates across the world, while China Mills has drawn on reports of suicides directly linked to the UK government's austerity measures and benefit cuts to demonstrate how benefit claimants are made to feel they are a burden by 'neoliberal market logic'.[78] This was a familiar feeling to the working-class men of the nineteenth century who, after losing employment, being unable to support their families and refusing to degrade themselves and their families by submitting to the workhouse, chose to take their own lives. These stories of hardship were picked up and amplified by radical papers such as *Reynolds's* who utilized melodramatic tropes to provide recognition to the blameless suffering that many experienced.

The liberalism of the nineteenth century embraced utilitarian measures of value which conflated moral worth with labour power, while Tory paternalism reconceptualized the helping of the poor as a benevolent act of charity rather than a moral obligation. This was also the ethos of the individualism captured in Samuel Smiles's *Self-Help*, which placed responsibility for one's situation on the individual.[79] As Peter Mandler has highlighted, the elites came to see free markets 'as Providentially-designed mechanisms for the cultivation of true morality', which, he notes, Boyd Hilton has attributed to Evangelical influences that placed faith in a 'natural order' to 'discipline the weak and punish the vicious'.[80] As a result, the unemployed, who were unable to make a contribution to general utility, were deemed to be less worthy of help, idling rather than working, a burden on the state and parish.

Although these suicide narratives were mediated by editors and journalists, the fact that inquest proceedings were often printed verbatim offered a way for the working classes to regain some control over their identities. By recounting the tireless searches and miles walked by many in desperate attempts to find work, and the recognizable appeals made to symbols of respectability, the narratives help to challenge the idea espoused by Thomas Malthus and Samuel Smiles that the unproductive were immoral. The melodramatic language and motifs found in the reports also offered a way to acknowledge and understand the suffering experienced by these working-class men that might otherwise go unacknowledged; they allowed them to see that they were suffering through no fault of their own but were rather victims of the changing social and economic landscape.

Notes

1. E. Scowcroft and C. Simms, *Suicide Statistics Report 2018* (Samaritans, December 2018), p. 11.

2. 'What Is CALM?', *Campaign against Living Miserably*, www.thecalmzone.net/what-we-do; D. Lester, J.F. Gunn III and P. Quinnett (eds.), *Suicide in Men: How Men Differ from Women in Expressing Their Distress* (Springfield, IL: Charles C. Thomas, 2014); D. Coleman, M.S. Kaplan and J.T. Casey, 'The Social Nature of Male Suicide: A New Analytic Model', *International Journal of Men's Health*, 10 (2011), 240–52.

3. R.W. Connell, *Gender and Power: Society, the Person, and Sexual Politics* (Stanford, CA: Stanford University Press, 1987); R.W. Connell, *Masculinities* (Cambridge: Cambridge University Press, 1995).

4. J.E. Adams, *Dandies and Desert Saints: Styles of Victorian Masculinity* (Ithaca, NY: Cornell University Press, 1995); J. Tosh, *Manliness and Masculinities in Nineteenth-Century Britain: Essays on Gender, Family, and Empire*, Women and Men in History vol. 1 (Harlow: Routledge, 2005); H. Furneaux, *Military Men of Feeling: Emotion, Touch, and Masculinity in the Crimean War* (Oxford: Oxford University Press, 2016); J. Begiato, 'Between Poise and Power: Embodied Manliness in Eighteenth- and Nineteenth-Century British Culture', *Transactions of the Royal Historical Society*, 26 (2016), 125–47.

5. K. Thomas and D. Gunnell, 'Suicide in England and Wales 1861–2007: A Time-Trends Analysis', *International Journal of Epidemiology*, 39 (2010), 1464–75 at pp. 1467, 1474.

6. For example, B.T. Gates, *Victorian Suicide: Mad Crimes and Sad Histories* (Princeton, NJ: Princeton University Press, 1988); Margaret Higonnet, 'Suicide: Representations of the Feminine in the Nineteenth Century', *Poetics Today*, 6 (1985), 103–18; O. Anderson, *Suicide in Victorian and Edwardian England* (Oxford: Oxford University Press, 1987); V. Bailey, *This Rash Act: Suicide across the Life Cycle in the Victorian City* (Stanford, CA: Stanford University Press, 1998); R. Houston, 'Fact, Truth, and the Limits of Sympathy: Newspaper Reporting of Suicide in the North of England, circa 1750–1830', *Studies in the Literary Imagination*, 44 (2011), 93–108.

7. Anderson, *Suicide in Victorian and Edwardian England*, pp. 44–5.

8. K. Israel, *Names and Stories: Emilia Dilke and Victorian Culture* (New York: Oxford University Press, 1999), p. 14.

9. D. Englander, *Poverty and Poor Law Reform in Britain: From Chadwick to Booth, 1834–1914* (London: Routledge, 1998), pp. 38, 44 (quotes on p. 44).

10. C. Mills, '"Dead People Don't Claim": A Psychopolitical Autopsy of UK Austerity Suicides', *Critical Social Policy*, 38 (2017), 302–22.

11. J. Biddle, 'Shame', in J. Harding and E.D. Pribram (eds.), *Emotions: A Cultural Studies Reader*, vol. 1 (London: Routledge, 2009), p. 115.

12. Israel, *Names and Stories*, p. 14.

13. B. Shenton, 'Suicide and Surplus People/Value', *Identities*, 18 (2011), 63–8 at p. 64.

14. G. Claeys, 'Malthus and Godwin: Rights, Utility and Productivity', in R.J. Mayhew (ed.), *New Perspectives on Malthus* (Cambridge: Cambridge University Press, 2016), p. 66.

15. Thomas Malthus, *An Essay on the Principle of Population: Or. A View of Its Past and Present Effects on Human Happiness* (London: J. Johnson, 1803), p. 53.

16. Malthus, *An Essay on the Principle of Population*, pp. 15–21.

17. G. Beer, *Darwin's Plots: Evolutionary Narrative in Darwin, George Eliot, and Nineteenth-Century Fiction*, vol. 2 (Cambridge: Cambridge University Press, 2000), p. 240.

18. T. Hardy, *Jude the Obscure* (London: Oxford World's Classics, 1998), p. 336.

19. E. Steinlight, 'Hardy's Unnecessary Lives: The Novel as Surplus', *Novel: A Forum on Fiction*, 47 (2014), 224–41 at p. 224.

20. Hardy, *Jude the Obscure*, pp. 332–3.

21. Biddle, 'Shame', p. 116.

22. 'Attempted Suicide in Sheffield', *Sheffield and Rotherham Independent*, 2 August 1886, p. 3.

23. 'A Suicide's Letter', *Huddersfield Daily Chronicle*, 10 September 1891, p. 4.

24. 'Melancholy Suicide', *Chelmsford Chronicle*, 23 April 1858, p. 3.

25. Malthus, *Principle of Population*, p. 306 (emphasis added).

26. Malthus, *Principle of Population*, p. 307.

27. Claeys, 'Malthus and Godwyn', p. 68.

28. For example, Sydney Smith, 'On Suicide', in *Two Volumes of Sermons*, vol. 2 (London: T. Cadell and W. Davies, 1809), p. 11; George Gregory, *A Sermon on Suicide* (London: J. Nichols; sold by C. Dilly, Messrs. F. and C. Rivington, J. Johnson and J. Hookham, 1797), pp. 12–13.

29. D. Hume, 'Essay I. On Suicide', in *Essays on Suicide and the Immortality of the Soul* (Basel: Printed for the Editor of the Collection of English Classics, 1799), p. 12.

30. T.O. Bonser, *The Right to Die* (London: Freethought Publishing Company, 1885), p. 3.

31. Bonser, *The Right to Die*, p. 7.

32. S. Smiles, *Self-Help: With Illustrations of Character, Conduct, and Perseverance* (London: John Murray, 1868), p. xi.

33. M. Scheer, 'Are Emotions a Kind of Practice (And Is That What Makes Them Have a History)? A Bourdieuian Approach to Understanding Emotion', *History and Theory*, 51 (2012), 193–220 at pp. 202, 216.

34. 'Double Murder and Suicide', *Belfast News-Letter*, 22 January 1895, p. 5.

35. 'The Distress in Brightside', *Sheffield and Rotherham Independent*, 19 January 1878, p. 3.

36. 'The Suicide at Brightside', *Sheffield and Rotherham Independent*, 26 January 1878, p. 12.

37. Smiles, *Self-Help*, pp. 291–7.

38. 'The Suicide at Brightside', *Sheffield Independent*.

39. D. Mayer, 'Encountering Melodrama', in K. Powell (ed.), *The Cambridge Companion to Victorian and Edwardian Theatre* (Cambridge: Cambridge University Press, 2004), p. 148.

40. R. McWilliam, 'Melodrama', in P.K. Gilbert (ed.), *A Companion to Sensation Fiction*, Blackwell Companions to Literature and Culture, 75 (Malden, MA: Wiley-Blackwell, 2011), p. 59.

41. M. Vicinus, '"Helpless and Unfriended": Nineteenth-Century Domestic Melodrama', *New Literary History*, 13 (1981), 127–43 at p. 137.

42. 'Shocking Case of Suicide', *Berrow's Worcester Journal*, 14 August 1845, p. 4.

43. 'Distressing Suicide through Want of Work at Neepsend', *Sheffield and Rotherham Independent*, 2 June 1879, p. 3.

44. 'Suicide through Poverty', *North-Eastern Daily Gazette*, 3 November 1886, p. 4.

45. Vicinus, '"Helpless and Unfriended"', pp. 131–2.

46. R. McWilliam, 'Melodrama and the Historians', *Radical History Review*, 78 (2000), 57–84 at p. 72.

47. McWilliam, 'Melodrama and the Historians', p. 74.

48. Mayer, 'Encountering Melodrama', p. 151; K. Leaver, 'Victorian Melodrama and the Performance of Poverty', *Victorian Literature and Culture*, 27 (1999), 443–56 at p. 444.

49. 'A Tooting Horror', *Reynolds's Newspaper*, 10 March 1895, p. 1.

50. 'Terrible Tragedy in London', *Liverpool Mercury*, 8 March 1895, p. 5.

51. 'Terrible Tragedy in London', *Liverpool Mercury*; 'Terrible Tragedy in London', *Northern Whig*, 8 March 1895, p. 5; 'Terrible Tragedy in London', *Yorkshire Herald*, 8 March 1895, p. 5; 'The Tooting Tragedy', *Liverpool Mercury*, 11 March 1895, p. 5.

52. 'Murder of a Wife and Six Children', *The Standard*, 8 March 1895, p. 3.

53. 'Terrible Tragedy in London', *Liverpool Mercury*.

54. 'Murder of a Wife and Six Children', *The Standard*; 'Terrible Tragedy in London', *Liverpool Mercury*.

55. A. Clark, 'The Rhetoric of Chartist Domesticity: Gender, Language, and Class in the 1830s and 1840s', *Journal of British Studies*, 33 (1992), 62–88 at pp. 62–4; Kristen Leaver also identifies a shift from the upper-class villain to a middle-class one. See Leaver, 'Victorian Melodrama', p. 444.

56. S. D'Cruze, 'The Eloquent Corpse: Gender, Probity, and Bodily Integrity in Victorian Domestic Murder', in J. Rowbotham and K. Stevenson (eds.), *Criminal Conversations: Victorian Crimes, Social Panic, and Moral Outrage* (Columbus, OH: Ohio State University Press, 2005), p. 181.

57. 'Terrible Tragedy in London', *Yorkshire Herald*.

58. 'The Murders at Tooting', *The Standard*, 11 March 1895, p. 2.

59. 'Terrible Tragedy in London', *Yorkshire Herald*.

60. Juliet John, quoted in C. Williams, 'Melodrama', in K. Flint (ed.), *The Cambridge History of Victorian Literature* (Cambridge: Cambridge University Press, 2012), p. 193.

61. Williams, 'Melodrama', p. 193.

62. V. Richmond, *Clothing the Poor in Nineteenth-Century England* (Cambridge: Cambridge University Press, 2013), pp. 132–3.

63. R. Roberts, *The Classic Slum: Salford Life in the First Quarter of the Century* (Manchester: Manchester University Press, 1971), p. 23.

64. 'The Tooting Tragedy', *The Globe*, 8 March 1895, p. 7.

65. Biddle, 'Shame', p. 116.

66. D. Nash and A. Kilday, *Cultures of Shame: Exploring Crime and Morality in Britain 1600–1900* (Basingstoke: Springer, 2010), pp. 4–11; M. Doolittle, 'Fatherhood and Family Shame: Masculinity, Welfare and the Workhouse in Late Nineteenth-Century England', in L. Delap, B. Griffin and A. Wills (eds.), *The Politics of Domestic Authority in Britain since 1800* (Basingstoke: Springer, 2009), p. 87; P. Fox, *Class Fictions: Shame and Resistance in the British Working-Class Novel, 1890–1945* (Durham, NC: Duke University Press, 1994), p. 15.

67. Quoted in Richmond, *Clothing the Poor*, p. 274.

68. Doolittle, 'Fatherhood and Family Shame', p. 96.

69. For example, 'Distressing Suicide in a Workhouse' *Morning Post*, 7 May 1841, p. 2; 'Suicide in the Work-House', *Yorkshire Gazette*, 23 June 1821, p. 3; 'Death before the Workhouse', *North-Eastern Daily Gazette*, 27 August 1892, p. 2; 'Death before the Workhouse', *South Wales Daily News*, 30 March 1899, p. 8; 'Death before the Workhouse', *Gloucester Citizen*, 26 January 1895, p. 4.

70. 'A Victim of Free Trade', *Lincolnshire Chronicle*, 24 November 1893, p. 6; 'Death Rather than the Workhouse', *Reynolds's Newspaper*, 26 November 1893, p. 2.

71. 'Starvation and Suicide', *Yorkshire Evening Post*, 22 November 1893, p. 3; 'Death Better than the Workhouse', *Dundee Evening Telegraph*, 23 November 1893, p. 2; 'A Pathetic Story of Depression', *Nuneaton Advertiser*, 25 November 1893, p. 2.

72. 'Starvation and Suicide', *Huddersfield Chronicle*.

73. 'Death Rather than the Workhouse', *Reynolds's Newspaper*.

74. C.C. Klaver, *A/Moral Economics: Classical Political Economy and Cultural Authority in Nineteenth-Century England* (Columbus, OH: Ohio State University Press, 2003), p. 114.

75. Doolittle, 'Fatherhood and Family Shame', pp. 88–90; J. Bailey, '"A Very Sensible Man": Imagining Fatherhood in England c.1750–1830', *History*, 95 (2010), 267–92 at p. 291.

76. The World Health Organization discourages framing suicide as a 'constructive solution to problems'. WHO, *Preventing Suicide: A Resource for Media Professionals* (Geneva: WHO, 2017), p. 6. Earlier editions of these guidelines more explicitly discourage depicting suicide as a method of coping with personal problems, such as financial trouble or relationship breakdown. WHO, *Preventing Suicide: A Resource for Media Professionals* (Geneva: WHO, 2008), p. 7; WHO, *Preventing Suicide: A Resource for Media Professionals* (Geneva: WHO, 2000), pp. 7–8.

77. See particularly chapter 3 of I. Marsh, *Suicide: Foucault, History and Truth* (Cambridge: Cambridge University Press, 2010), quote on p. 47.

78. Mills, 'Dead People Don't Claim', p. 317.

79. Smiles, *Self-Help*, pp. ix, 6–7.

80. P. Mandler (ed.), *Liberty and Authority in Victorian Britain* (Oxford: Oxford University Press, 2006), pp. 5, 9.

References

Adams, J.E., *Dandies and Desert Saints: Styles of Victorian Masculinity* (Ithaca, NY: Cornell University Press, 1995).

Anderson, O., *Suicide in Victorian and Edwardian England* (Oxford: Oxford University Press, 1987).

Bailey, J., '"A Very Sensible Man": Imagining Fatherhood in England c.1750–1830', *History*, 95 (2010), 267–92.

Bailey, V., *This Rash Act: Suicide across the Life Cycle in the Victorian City* (Stanford, CA: Stanford University Press, 1998).

Beer, G., *Darwin's Plots: Evolutionary Narrative in Darwin, George Eliot, and Nineteenth-Century Fiction*, vol. 2 (Cambridge: Cambridge University Press, 2000).

Begiato, J., 'Between Poise and Power: Embodied Manliness in Eighteenth- and Nineteenth-Century British Culture', *Transactions of the Royal Historical Society*, 26 (2016), 125–47.

Biddle, J., 'Shame', in J. Harding and E.D. Pribram (eds.), *Emotions: A Cultural Studies Reader*, vol. 1 (London: Routledge, 2009).

Bonser, T.O., *The Right to Die* (London: Freethought Publishing Company, 1885).

Claeys, G., 'Malthus and Godwin: Rights, Utility and Productivity', in R.J. Mayhew (ed.), *New Perspectives on Malthus* (Cambridge: Cambridge University Press, 2016).

Clark, A., 'The Rhetoric of Chartist Domesticity: Gender, Language, and Class in the 1830s and 1840s', *Journal of British Studies*, 31 (1992), 62–88.

Coleman, D., Kaplan, M.S. and Casey, J.T., 'The Social Nature of Male Suicide: A New Analytic Model', *International Journal of Men's Health*, 10 (2011), 240–52.

Connell, R., *Gender and Power: Society, the Person, and Sexual Politics* (Stanford, CA: Stanford University Press, 1987).

Connell, R.W., *Masculinities* (Cambridge: Cambridge University Press, 1995).

D'Cruze, S., 'The Eloquent Corpse: Gender, Probity, and Bodily Integrity in Victorian Domestic Murder', in J. Rowbotham and K. Stevenson (eds.), *Criminal Conversations: Victorian Crimes, Social Panic, and Moral Outrage* (Columbus, OH: Ohio State University Press, 2005).

Doolittle, M., 'Fatherhood and Family Shame: Masculinity, Welfare and the Workhouse in Late Nineteenth-Century England', in L. Delap, B. Griffin and A. Wills (eds.), *The Politics of Domestic Authority in Britain since 1800* (Basingstoke: Springer, 2009).

Englander, D., *Poverty and Poor Law Reform in Britain: From Chadwick to Booth, 1834–1914* (London: Routledge, 1998).

Fox, P., *Class Fictions: Shame and Resistance in the British Working-Class Novel, 1890–1945* (Durham, NC: Duke University Press, 1994).

Furneaux, H., *Military Men of Feeling: Emotion, Touch, and Masculinity in the Crimean War* (Oxford: Oxford University Press, 2016).

Gates, B.T., *Victorian Suicide: Mad Crimes and Sad Histories* (Princeton, NJ: Princeton University Press, 1988).

Gregory, G., *A Sermon on Suicide* (London: J. Nichols; sold by C. Dilly, Messrs. F. and C. Rivington, J. Johnson and J. Hookham, 1797).

Hardy, T., *Jude the Obscure* (London: Oxford World's Classics, 1998).

Higonnet, M., 'Suicide: Representations of the Feminine in the Nineteenth Century', *Poetics Today*, 6 (1985), 103–18.

Houston, R., 'Fact, Truth, and the Limits of Sympathy: Newspaper Reporting of Suicide in the North of England, circa 1750–1830', *Studies in the Literary Imagination*, 44 (2011), 93–108.

Hume, D., 'Essay I. On Suicide', in *Essays on Suicide and the Immortality of the Soul* (Basel: Printed for the Editor of the Collection of English Classics, 1799).

Israel, K., *Names and Stories: Emilia Dilke and Victorian Culture* (New York: Oxford University Press, 1999).

Klaver, C.C., *A/Moral Economics: Classical Political Economy and Cultural Authority in Nineteenth-Century England* (Columbus, OH: Ohio State University Press, 2003).

Leaver, K., 'Victorian Melodrama and the Performance of Poverty', *Victorian Literature and Culture*, 27 (1999), 443–56.

Lester, D., Gunn III, J.F. and Quinnett, P. (eds.), *Suicide in Men: How Men Differ from Women in Expressing Their Distress* (Springfield, IL: Charles C. Thomas, 2014).

Malthus, T., *An Essay on the Principle of Population: Or, A View of Its Past and Present Effects on Human Happiness* (London: J. Johnson, 1803).

Mandler, P. (ed.), *Liberty and Authority in Victorian Britain* (Oxford: Oxford University Press, 2006).

Marsh, I., *Suicide: Foucault, History and Truth* (Cambridge: Cambridge University Press, 2010).

Mayer, D., 'Encountering Melodrama', in K. Powell (ed.), *The Cambridge Companion to Victorian and Edwardian Theatre* (Cambridge: Cambridge University Press, 2004).

McWilliam, R., 'Melodrama and the Historians', *Radical History Review*, 78 (2000), 57–84.

——, 'Melodrama', in P.K. Gilbert (ed.), *A Companion to Sensation Fiction*, 75 (Malden, MA: John Wiley, 2011).

Mills, C., '"Dead People Don't Claim": A Psychopolitical Autopsy of UK Austerity Suicides', *Critical Social Policy*, 38 (2017), 302–22.

Nash, N., and Kilday, A., *Cultures of Shame: Exploring Crime and Morality in Britain 1600–1900* (Basingstoke: Springer, 2010).

Richmond, V., *Clothing the Poor in Nineteenth-Century England* (Cambridge: Cambridge University Press, 2013).

Roberts, R., *The Classic Slum: Salford Life in the First Quarter of the Century* (Manchester: Manchester University Press, 1971).

Scheer, M., 'Are Emotions a Kind of Practice (And Is That What Makes Them Have a History)? A Bourdieuian Approach to Understanding Emotion', *History and Theory*, 51 (2012), 193–220.

Scowcroft, E., and Simms, C., *Suicide Statistics Report 2018* (Samaritans, December 2018).

Shenton, B., 'Suicide and Surplus People/Value', *Identities*, 18 (2011), 63–8.

Smiles, S., *Self-Help: With Illustrations of Character, Conduct, and Perseverance* (London: John Murray, 1868).

Smith, S., 'On Suicide', in *Two Volumes of Sermons*, vol. 2 (London: T. Cadell and W. Davies, 1809).

Steinlight, E., 'Hardy's Unnecessary Lives: The Novel as Surplus', *Novel: A Forum on Fiction*, 47 (2014), 224–41.

Thomas, K., and Gunnell D., 'Suicide in England and Wales 1861–2007: A Time-Trends Analysis', *International Journal of Epidemiology*, 39 (2010), 1464–75.

Tosh, J., *Manliness and Masculinities in Nineteenth-Century Britain: Essays on Gender, Family, and Empire*, vol. 1 (Harlow: Routledge, 2005).

Vicinus, M., '"Helpless and Unfriended": Nineteenth-Century Domestic Melodrama', *New Literary History*, 13 (1981), 127–43.

'What Is CALM?', *Campaign Against Living Miserably*, www.thecalmzone .net/what-we-do (accessed 15 June 2023).

WHO, *Preventing Suicide: A Resource for Media Professionals* (Geneva: WHO, 2000).

——, *Preventing Suicide: A Resource for Media Professionals* (Geneva: WHO, 2008).

——, *Preventing Suicide: A Resource for Media Professionals* (Geneva: WHO, 2017).

Williams, C., 'Melodrama', in K. Flint (ed.), *The Cambridge History of Victorian Literature*, The New Cambridge History of English Literature (Cambridge: Cambridge University Press, 2012).

Chapter 11

'Sadistic, grinning rifle-women': gender, emotions and politics in representations of militant leftist women

Hannah Proctor

Terrorist girls, wild furies, unnatural daughters, crazed outlaws, gun broads, megaeras, amazons, furies, viragoes, jackals, hecates, mad-women. Hybrid creatures, drunken Bacchantes, hysterical Messalinas, devils, infernal witches, unhuman creatures from the netherworld, whore proletarians, shameless slatterns, moral monstrosities. Erotic women, unfeeling women, vulgar women. These are just some of the terms I scrawled in my notebook while taking notes to write this essay.[1] This list, plucked from a range of texts written in the nineteenth and twentieth centuries pertaining to women associated with left-wing political move-ments, gives a sense of the often mythical and historical analogies that have been resorted to when describing forms of political violence commit-ted by modern women. Paradoxically, when political upheavals threaten to disturb the prevailing social order and the traditional gender relations associated with it, commentators hoping to uphold existing norms seem to reach for long-established, even ancient, archetypes of deviant womanhood. This tension between the historically specific and the transhistorical runs through my discussion.

This chapter will explore representations not only of impassioned female subjects but also of impassioned and politicized female subjects. It will talk about the figure of the politically militant left-wing woman, both in reality and fantasy. And it will attempt to probe the critical implications of the negative affects associated with such subjects. My approach is associative in form – ranging over time and space – and more interested in theoretical than historical claims. It is a tentative attempt to think about the gendered emotions associated with left-wing woman militants in different movements and moments in order to probe the relationships between gender, emotion and political violence.[2] Usually I work as a historian of the psy disciplines but although the question of pathologization is relevant to these discussions, it remains in the background. Instead, I'm going to experiment by trying to think about iconography, archetypes and stereotypes employed by the right and how right-wing anxieties about Communist revolution have taken the form of a militant woman.

Preamble: naming the world

In her 2017 essay 'On Liking Women', published in *n +1*, Angela Long Chu writes of first encountering and later teaching Valerie Solanas's excoriating attack on patriarchy, *The SCUM Manifesto*, published a year before Solanas infamously attempted to kill the artist Andy Warhol in 1968 (the acronym SCUM stands for Society for Cutting Up Men). Chu underlines that in Solanas's text 'politics begins with an aesthetic judgement'.[3] For Solanas, 'Life under male supremacy isn't oppressive, exploitative, or unjust: it's just fucking boring.'[4] Chu contends that

> male and female are essentially *styles* for [Solanas], rival aesthetic schools distinguishable by their respective adjectival palettes. Men are timid, guilty, dependent, mindless, passive, animalistic, insecure, cowardly, envious, vain, frivolous, and weak. Women are strong, dynamic, decisive, assertive, cerebral, independent, self-confident, nasty, violent, selfish, freewheeling, thrill-seeking, and arrogant. Above all, women are cool and groovy.[5]

Solanas inverted the traditional adjectival ordering here and subverts not only the traditional gendering of emotions but also the gender binary itself in the process; the nouns 'woman' and 'man' come to take on new meanings.

Although I began by presenting a litany composed mostly of nouns, emotions and dispositions are often ascribed to people through adjectives, as Chu outlines in Solanas's text. And gendered emotions often appear in pairs, mimicking the gender binary, but even if the binary is being subverted as in *The SCUM Manifesto*, it is only very occasionally abandoned altogether. In *Autobiography of Red* (1998) Anne Carson asks:

What is an adjective? Nouns name the world. Verbs activate the names. Adjectives come from somewhere else. The word adjective (*epitheton* in Greek) is itself an adjective meaning 'placed on top', 'added', 'appended', 'imported', 'foreign'. Adjectives seem fairly innocent additions but look again. These small imported mechanisms are in charge of attaching everything in the world to its place in particularity. They are the latches of being.

... In the world of the Homeric epic, for example, being is stable and particularity is set fast in tradition. When Homer mentions blood, blood is *black*. When women appear, women are *neat-ankled* or *glancing*. Gods' laughter is *unquenchable*. Human knees are *quick*. The sea is *unwearying* ... Homer's epithets are a fixed diction with which Homer fastens every substance in the world to its aptest attribute and holds them in place for epic consumption.[6]

How, Carson asks, would it be possible to release being so 'all the substances of the world float up'? This is more than a linguistic question. Carson claims that though Stesichoros was born into the code, into the stable constellation of descriptions established by Homer, he somehow managed to prise the world open. He undid, for example, the tradition of attaching adjectives of whoredom to Helen of Troy: 'When Stesichoros unlatched her epithet from Helen there flowed out such a light as may have blinded him for a moment.'[7]

I'm beginning with these digressive examples not because I'm particularly interested in the relationship between nouns and adjectives or even in language per se but because I'm interested in how language, as one among many social practices, participates in giving things the appearance of fixity. I'm interested in how the historical comes to appear natural, how diction and representations come to appear fixed and substance with it. Obviously this pertains to gender itself – not only to nouns but also to substances (i.e. to embodied subjects interpellated and interpellating in a social world). Ascribing and re-ascribing particular emotions to particular genders is part of the process whereby a distinction between men and women (and not only between the masculine and the feminine) is consolidated – ideas adhere to people but eventually seem to inhere in them and this can in turn participate in consolidating structural inequalities by making them appear as though they are grounded in nature. If, as Chu claims in her discussion of Solanas, 'politics begins with an aesthetic judgment', it is worth remembering that 'aesthetics was born ... as a discourse of the body'.[8] I will mostly be considering aesthetic judgements about gender in this essay, but although these judgements may not always have described actual acts of violence by actual women, they nonetheless had actual violent effects, even if sometimes these were subtle, dispersed and difficult to trace. I wanted to try reading the relationship of adjective to noun, as Carson describes it, as somehow analogous to the relationship of emotion to gender; perhaps unlatching one might help unlatch the other. Would it be possible to unleash a light so blinding that it might not only illuminate the rigid historically established associations between emotions and genders but also burn them to the ground? Perhaps, but perhaps it would involve doing more than simply flipping the binary as Solanas does in *The SCUM Manifesto*.

Violent mutilations

On the night of 30 September 1965 six generals of the Indonesian army were killed by army officers in a coup attempt. Although the circumstances of the coup remain contested, the murders were blamed on the Communist Party of Indonesia (PKI) and this was used as a pretext for a brutal purge. Members of the PKI and trade unions, as well as ethnic Chinese people and many with tenuous rumoured connections to the left or their family members, were killed in massacres orchestrated by the military and carried out with the participation of various youth militia groups. It has been estimated that at least half a million people were killed and many more were brutally tortured and incarcerated without trial in prisons and camps. The coup brought Major-General Suharto to power, after which a constructed counter-narrative of the events circulated in propaganda and in schools, while discussions of the events that deviated from these official state-sanctioned accounts were forbidden. The killers were celebrated as heroes. The threat of reemergent Communism was kept discursively alive.[9] Even after Suharto's fall in 1998, the Indonesian state never officially acknowledged the atrocities. Crocodile Hole, the place from which the corpses of the generals were exhumed, is still today the site of a giant monument and accompanying museum memorializing their deaths and was the site for the Suharto regime's more significant state rituals. Built in 1969, the Sacred Pancasila Monument includes giant statues of the seven generals with nearby friezes depicting PKI activists committing the murders and dumping the bodies, while scantily clad women frolic around them.[10]

In the aftermath of the coup, lurid stories began to spread about the involvement of members of the Indonesian Women's Movement (Gerwani) – an organization that had been involved in campaigns to promote education and literacy, help improve women's working conditions, oppose polygamy and provide childcare – in the kidnapping and murder of the generals. Gruesome sexualized images and narratives of torture, genital mutilation and orgies were circulated in the military-controlled media, described by historian John Roosa as an 'absurd fabrication by psychological warfare experts'.[11] Increasingly graphic depictions of sadistic acts allegedly performed by Communist women circulated via propaganda, emphasizing their rapacious prurience and lack of religious beliefs. These misogynistic demonizing myths of sexual excess among Communist women also contributed to the backlash against suspected Communists more generally, and specifically fuelled sexualized violence against women and girls on a huge scale, many of whom were raped or sexually assaulted during interrogation proceedings, which were described by their perpetrators as acts of vengeance.[12] Imaginary violence both concealed and begat concrete violence. The entanglement of gender and politics in the image of the Gerwani women indicates how naturalized assumptions about gender roles can entangle with naturalized assumptions about the organization of society. Fears relating to the denaturalization of the former can be mobilized to stir up fears relating to the destabilization of the latter. Fantasy can become a kind of weapon; wild imaginings with no counterpart in empirical reality can then lead to concrete actions.

The fantastical image of depraved Gerwani women, who functioned as a kind of metonym for the threat of Communism more broadly, recalls a historically and geographically distant example in which imaginary violent and licentious working-class women became a cipher for political anxieties: the *pétroleuses*, women rumoured to have lit fires across Paris during the last days of the Paris Commune of 1871.[13] As in Indonesia in the wake of the coup, soon after the bloody repression of the Paris Commune, the French state began to obliterate its popular memory through strict censorship; counter-revolutionary counter-narratives of recent history were soon established. The effacement of history involved not only obscuring the memory and shared experience of actual events but also constructed alternative accounts in their place to stir up and cement anti-Communard feeling. The figure of the *pétroleuse*, like the figure of the Gerwani woman, was a key protagonist in these fabricated accounts. The process of suppression was also a process of invention, with new versions of events emerging that were based not in fact but in fantasy. Public memory may depart from private memories but it also shapes how people perceive the world around them. Fantasy and imagination can have a utopian dimension, evincing the possibility of imagining things otherwise, but it can also be enlisted for repressive ends, erecting images that blot out real experiences. In these moments social movements composed of oppressed and exploited people sought to create a more equal society but were crushed by the right.

The imagined threat to the status quo in both cases took the form of a militant woman whose (non)existence was used to justify real violence. The militant, sexually rapacious left-wing woman seemed to represent the ultimate threat to the existing social order. Do the emotions associated with or experienced by militant leftist women conform to gender stereotypes or transgress them? Does the figure of the politically violent woman threaten to explode the gender binary altogether or does it entrench it? Is the image and reality of the politically violent woman itself a product of patriarchal violence?

Unruly women

My starting point for this essay and the main sources of the litany I began with were two secondary accounts of fantastical representations of militant proletarian left-wing women that I happened to read around the same time: Gay L. Gullickson's *Unruly Women of Paris: Images of the Commune* (1996) which discusses the figure of the *pétroleuses* and *Male Fantasies* by Klaus Theweleit (whose first volume was first published in German in 1977), a short sub-section of the first volume of which is devoted to fantastical descriptions of Communist women written by German Freikorps officers in the aftermath of the First World War. Both works concern images of women divorced from reality that reveal more about the right-wing masculine fantasies and anxieties of those who created them than they do about the experiences of actual women (left-wing or otherwise). These fantastical figures share some common tropes – the gendered emotions associated with them, the entanglement of the sexual and the political they embody, their relation to mythic or historical women and their relation to allegory.

From 18 March to 28 May 1871 a socialist and revolutionary government ruled Paris before being brutally defeated by the French army in what became known as 'bloody week'. Ordinary working women played a prominent role in the Paris Commune. Women from a range of professions – seamstresses, waistcoat makers, sewing machine operators, dressmakers, linen drapers, bootstitchers, hatmakers, laundresses, cardboard makers, embroiderers, braidmakers, tie makers, schoolteachers, perfume makers, jewellery makers, goldpolishers, bookbinders – joined the Union des Femmes and participated in campaigns for fairer wages and shorter working hours. Women also took an active role in defending the Commune – aside from the famous leaders and orators associated with it (including Elisabeth Dmitreff, Andre Leo, Louise Michel and Paule Mink), many women sewed sandbags for the barricades, assembled weapons, distributed clothing and tended to the wounded. Some women took up arms, as Edith Thomas notes: 'With their chassepot rifles, their revolvers, their cartridge cases, their red sashes, and their fantastic Zouave, naval or infantry uniforms, they were a target of caricaturists; a woman wearing trousers was a scandal in itself.'[14]

The figure of the *pétroleuse*, however, seems to have been largely imaginary. She appears in caricatures in the bourgeois press, hair streaming, eyes blazing like the fires behind her – clutching a can of petrol – usually old and haggard and in tattered clothing. Gullickson notes that visual representations of the figure of the *pétroleuse* tended to picture her as older and less sexually alluring than in written accounts, where she tends to be younger and more seductive. If fires were deliberately lit in Paris just before the Commune's defeat, there is no evidence to suggest that the arsonists were primarily women – no women were convicted of arson in the Commune's aftermath – but 'Enemies of the Commune' accused women of setting fire to Paris. Eight thousand *pétroleuses* were said to exist – with a squad in every quarter, with its own female sergeants and commanders. Places were said to have been marked with an acronym to indicate that they were 'good for burning' (*bon pour bruler*). According to Gullickson: 'Every poor woman was a suspect. Even more so if she carried a shopping basket or a bottle: she was a pétroleuse, and [in some cases] was executed on the spot to the furious cries of the mob.'[15] Later she noted that wild rumours circulated 'about petroleum eggs equipped with nitroglycerine primers, and about balloons carrying incendiary material'.[16] Increasingly florid and hysterical newspaper stories were printed that were not only improbable but impossible – like one account of a charred skeleton still fully clothed with a pipe in her mouth.

Drunk, left-wing, working class, promiscuous – characteristics associated with the *pétroleuses* – are echoed in descriptions of militant leftist women encountered in Klaus Theweleit's *Male Fantasies*. Focusing on diaries and letters written by members of the Freikorps, German paramilitary groups of the First World War and veterans who fought against the newly created Weimar Republic between 1918 and 1923 (many of whom went on to become Nazis), Theweleit explores the relationship between sexuality and politics, asking 'why, under certain conditions, desiring-production can turn into murdering-production'.[17] The first chapter of the first volume focuses on the way these 'soldier males' spoke about women, investigating the relationship between misogyny and far-right ideology. The Freikorps officers, he discovers, don't talk much about their wives. 'Woman' is an ideal; actual wives or fiancées are 'objects of convenience', 'marginal figures ... child-bearers; silent supporters'.[18] A soldier's

268 HANNAH PROCTOR

'princess' is often forsaken for the sake of the Fatherland: 'Love of women and love of country are at opposite poles', he observes.[19]

The two short sections of volume 1 that I'm most interested in are called 'Woman as Aggressor' and 'Rifle-Women: The Castrating Woman', which discuss the Freikorps officers' often lurid and fantastical ideas about militant working-class women. As in the case of the real women of the Commune and of the actual Gerwani members in Indonesia, Theweleit emphasizes the stark contrast between the imaginary figure of militant sexualized leftist woman and the reality of Red Army nurses. Woman as aggressor is a sexualized but monstrous proletarian figure – 'a fantastic being who swears, shrieks, spits, scratches, farts, bites, pounces, tears to shreds; who is slovenly wind-whipped, hissing-red, indecent'.[20] Such women figure as 'agents of destruction'.[21] Violence, class and lasciviousness are linked, and proletarian women are also often assumed to be Communists, sex workers and Jews (though his tendency to view fascism as misogyny has ambiguous implications for his understanding of anti-semitism and racism, a point I will return to in my concluding section).

A racialized aspect was also, incidentally, present in representations of *pétroleuses*: Silvia Federici includes a caricature of a *pétroleuse* in her discussion of early modern witch trials in *Caliban and the Witch*, situating it in a tradition that 'Africanizes' the figure of the witch.[22] In an earlier passage Federici writes that long after the witch hunts had ceased

> the specter of the witches continued to haunt the imagination of the ruling class. In 1871, the Parisian bourgeoisie instinctively returned to it to demonize the female Communards, accusing them of wanting to set Paris aflame. There can be little doubt, in fact, that the models for the lurid tales and images used by the bourgeois press to create the myth of the pétroleuses were drawn from the repertoire of the witchhunt ... Hundreds of women were thus summarily executed, while the press vilified them in the papers. Like the witch, the pétroleuse was depicted as an older woman with a wild, savage look and uncombed hair.[23]

Theweleit's anachronistic use of illustration – the text is interspersed with an array of images including advertising from the Third Reich, election campaign posters from the German Democratic Republic in the 1970s, late nineteenth-century English paintings, movie stills from the Golden Age of Hollywood and medieval engravings – suggests that the figure he is describing is similarly not specific to the historical and cultural moment but a kind of archetype. However, as Federici discusses, archetypes can also be reclaimed and repurposed, referring to the WITCH network of feminist groups involved in the US Women's Liberation Movement, and citing a flyer from New York in the late 1960s that declared: 'Witches have always been women who dared to be courageous, aggressive, intelligent, non-conformists, curious, independent, sexually liberated, revolutionary.'[24] A French socialist feminist journal from the same period called itself *Les Pétroleuses*.

Theweleit is clear that sexual and political anxieties are intertwined. 'The fantasized proletarian woman'[25] is often armed; she may be one of the 'sadistic, grinning rifle-women' of the Red Army'[26] or a 'bestial foe [who] has desecrated defenceless wounded men'.[27] 'Just like waitresses, bar-maids, cleaning women, prostitutes, dancers, and circus performers the rifle-women are given only first names.'[28] Theweleit cites a passage – almost dream-like in its vivid surrealism – in which a Sparticist woman is depicted 'hair flying, packing pistols, and riding shaggy horses [presenting] an image of terrifying sexual potency'.[29]

'The sexuality of the proletarian woman/gun slinging whore/commu-nist is out to castrate and shred men to pieces',[30] Theweleit declares. One account describes a woman who proclaims: 'we want guns, grenades, rev-olution!' and is represented as drunk and lascivious, her stained silk dressing gown a symbol of her seductive yet dangerous moral depravity. 'Shred them to pieces and pulverize them with dynamite', one of these threatening but wholly imaginary female revolutionaries declares, which Theweleit reads as an anxiety the author has about the leftist woman's desire to annihilate all men on the right.[31] In Nazi propaganda the image of the First World War Red Army rifle woman resurfaced and was presented as if it had posed a real threat – take this example from a 1935 primer:

> It is well-known that there were rifle-women behind the Red lines who were under orders to stop the troops from falling back, or if the retreat could not be stopped, to shoot at their own people. The rifle-women were the sort of cruel furies only Bolshevism could devise. While the heart of one of the men of the Red Guard might be moved to pity at the sight of suffering innocents, those women were bes-tialised and devoid of all human feeling.[32]

Here, the woman becomes not only a figure who transgresses traditional gender roles; she is situated outside humanity as such. She isn't simply masculine but becomes animalistic. Her emotions are not just 'wrong' or unnatural ones for women to express; they're not even recognizably human. Accusations of base animality were also hurled at Communard women. The judge at the trial of four women accused of incendiary behav-iour described their actions as an onslaught of civilization and called the women 'unworthy creatures who seem to have taken it on themselves to become an opprobrium to their sex, and to repudiate the great and magnificent role of women in society'.[33] The judge also made an explicit link between criminality and the Commune's pursuit of education for women and calls for the emancipation of women. But how, Gullickson asks (and the questions could equally be applied to the context Theweleit discusses), 'did the political threat posed by the Commune [and by Communism] come to be represented by a hideous and fierce but sexually compelling female figure? ... Why was the political threat of the Commune [or Communism] represented as a fury, a hideous, powerful, avenging, mad, sexually compelling woman?'[34] Gullickson argues that various anxieties met in the figure of the *pétroleuse* which demonstrate the entanglement of political and gendered anxieties:

> The *pétroleuse* threatened to overturn the entire social order. She not only challenged male authority by leaving her home and acting in the public sphere, but she also attacked property, the source of the bourgeois male's sense of importance, burned down the home in which she was supposed to take care of her children, and corrupted her children by encouraging them to aid her in this deed. She was the evil mother, capable of killing her children, controlling men, and destroying their power base. This was what any man could expect to happen if women escaped the bonds of civilization and the home and were allowed to 'give rein to their very worst instincts.' They would 'desex' themselves and destroy society.[35]

To repeat what I have already observed about the function of images of Gerwani members in propaganda in the aftermath of the coup: the entanglement of gender and politics indicates how naturalized assumptions about gender were entangled with naturalized assumptions about the organization of society; denaturalizing one could thus call into question the legitimacy of the other.

Everything flows

Gullickson seems to read the relationship of the political and the gendered in the figure of the *pétroleuse* as running in parallel – the woman as a metaphor for revolution – but I would argue that they are more closely intertwined: the transgression of traditional gender roles the *pétroleuse* embodied was tied to the political claims of the Commune which included calls for the emancipation of women. Revolution was the ultimate social threat, and it took the form of an unruly, proletarian, sexualized and politicized woman who threatened to rupture the existing structures of the world. Although an exaggerated and extreme figure with no direct counterpart in reality, I would nonetheless argue that the image of the *pétroleuse* exists as a metonym rather than a metaphor for revolution. This relationship between the imagined woman and the feared revolution, I would argue, also holds for the function of images of murderous and sexualized Gerwani women in Indonesia.

The *pétroleuse* could also be understood as an allegorical counterpart to Liberty, Justice, Marianne or various other female figures used to symbolized the French nation. Although similarly remote from actual women, who were unlikely to experience liberty or justice themselves, these virtuous, calm and beautiful figures of social harmony stand in stark contrast to the wild figure of the *pétroleuse*. As Marina Warner discusses in *Monuments and Maidens: The Allegory of the Female Form* (1985):

> The allegorical female body either wears armour, emblematic of its wholeness and impregnability ... or it proclaims its virtues by abandoning protective coverings, to announce it has no need of them. By exposing vulnerable flesh as if it were not so, and especially by uncovering the breast, softest and most womanly part of woman, as if it were invulnerable, the semi-clad female figure expresses strength and freedom.[36]

The Commune's own images explicitly employed this iconography. The allegorical figure of the Commune was often dressed in red, with a Phrygian cap and with her breast uncovered. Although both the allegorical Liberty and the fictional *pétroleuse* of the bourgeois imagination were often represented in a state of partial undress, and both were represented as strong and militant, the differences were stark. Gullickson discusses a reactionary caricature explicitly parodying the allegory of the Commune by rendering her as a *pétroleuse*. In this image her exposed flesh is explicitly fleshy rather than having an almost stone-like smoothness in the sense described by Warner – her figure is old and sagging, her nipple clearly visible, indicating she has been divested of the pure, desexualized quality identified by Warner. Far from whole and impregnable, the satirical image is of an unconfined, uncontrolled and uncontrollable body. The representation of emotion is key: the face is not serene, strong and impassive but wild-eyed and full of rage, not muscular and steady but saggy and out of control.

Warner's insistence on the whole and impregnable ideal allegorical figure is reminiscent of Theweleit's discussion of the ideal of nationalism to which Communism (and Communism-as-woman) posed a threat. Liquidity is central to Theweleit's argument. He sees flowing everywhere in the documents produced by the Freikorps officers. The Bolshevik masses flow and surge like 'floods, torrents, raging water'.[37] Here are some characteristic verbs: inundate, engulf, pour, flow, swallow up, stream, gush, rage, flood, boil, bubble, seethe, whirl. The officers abhor everything that gushes and rushes, particularly the 'Red floods' of Bolshevism. Revolution figures as liquification. And the right-wing men want to dam it all up, to contain it, to bring it to a halt. They proclaim '[d]eath to all that flows'.[38] This leads Theweleit to Freud's limitless oceanic feeling and then to the surging qualities of libidinal desire (as described in Deleuze and Guattari's *Anti-Oedipus*, which was published shortly before his book and from which he drew much inspiration) and so to the experience of boundlessness and release of tension associated with orgasm. Theweleit distinguishes his understanding of ego development from Freud's, rejecting an account focused on the Oedipus complex in favour of an argument emphasizing instead the discipline of the body associated with military drills and parades: a bounded, homogeneous, synchronized mass entity emerges. These Freikorps men are repressed, terrified of sexual abandon, and this fear is linked to their fear of women (which is in turn, as he discusses in detail in *Male Fantasies*' second volume, linked to a fear of the mass). The only time they let themselves dissipate is in a deathly confrontation with a male enemy with whom they identify: 'he melts into the blood of a man of his own kind. His ecstasy takes the form of a "blackout": perception of an end to the torment of existence as a man for whom some form of coupling is indispensable, yet who never experiences the flowing of pleasure'.[39] Death takes the place of sex.

Women in the sources Theweleit analyses are also associated with everything that flows; they have permeable boundaries and threaten the boundaries of others. He veers off from his historical documents towards the end of the first volume of *Male Fantasies* to discuss mythic and literary representations of woman and takes a detour via ancient and early modern European history. The suggestion is that gender stereotypes are, if not exactly transhistorical, then at the very least extremely long-standing and resistant to change. The image that he is concerned with excavating is of

> woman-in-the-water; woman as water, as a stormy, cavorting, cooling ocean, a raging stream, a waterfall; as a limitless body of water that ships pass through, with tributaries, pools, surfs, and deltas; woman as the enticing (or perilous) deep, as a cup of bubbling body fluids; the vagina as a wave, as foam.[40]

The final sections of the chapter discuss dirt and contamination and it is here that he returns to his primary sources and to the explicitly anti-Communist political content with which the chapter began. Headings include: 'The Mire', 'The Morass', 'Slime', 'Pulp', 'Shit' and 'Rain'.

'SADISTIC, GRINNING RIFLE-WOMEN'   273

Images of national decay are linked to descriptions of menstruating sex workers.[41] Men of the right characterized the left as filthy and saw leftist bodies as insufficiently contained: they ooze excrement and pus and menstrual blood, weep 'secretions from the different orifices of the lower body'.[42] Freikorps men will only consent to transcend boundaries by blacking out or in death; they 'couple' with themselves in combat and their 'own struggle for survival [becomes] a direct onslaught on femininity'.[43] It is not only that militant leftist women were associated with particular mythological figures (which the list I began with made clear) but that these accounts reveal long-standing associations between women, liquidity and dirt more generally.

One or several women?

The weapon-wielding woman who threatens to shred men to pieces is simultaneously the antithesis and epitome of the feminine. Theweleit reads the woman as aggressor in terms of castration anxiety. The women in the narratives he discusses pull weapons from beneath their clothing and cut off protruding body parts. He insists that the imagined threat is not vaginal but phallic: 'we are dealing with the fantasy of a threatening penis'.[44] But these men only assign penises to certain types of women: violent leftist women. As such, he claims: 'The men experience "communism" as a *direct* assault on their *genitals*.'[45] The threat these women pose is more than just castration; it is total annihilation understood in political terms. Within the space of a few paragraphs, however, Theweleit connects the specific image of a politically violent woman with a phallic weapon with erotic woman in general; both figures are examples of 'nature perverted'[46] and both also seem to respond to anxieties about the changing social status of women understood as a transgression of the natural order. Women don't need to be Communists with a penis-gun to threaten men after all. Indeed, elsewhere Theweleit notes the preponderance of the trope in the Freikorps corpus that 'Women are all the same.'[47]

If the image of the militant leftist woman confounds nature, takes on masculine attributes and defies feminine norms, she is also then in some sense the epitome of the feminine. She both defies and defines womanhood; she is a kind of hyperbolic vision of woman. She is an abject woman, though in some sense all women are understood as abject. She is a madwoman, though in some sense all women are understood as mad. She is excessively 'woman', but women as such are excess. Amanda Third notes of the figure of the female terrorist in *Gender and the Political* that she is both '*hyperterrorist* (and therefore not properly feminine) and simultaneously *hyperfeminine* (and therefore not properly terrorist but nonetheless highly dangerous)'.[48] She may violate nature by being violent, overtly sexual, non-reproductive or a bad mother, yet attributes understood as naturally feminine (even if viewed negatively) – such as excess, abjection, irrationality and heightened emotion – are also applied to her, while a man who commits an act of political violence tends to be viewed as a rational actor even by those who condemn his actions; he is understood as acting according to his principles or class interests. This was also evident in the Communard trials: men on trial were viewed as criminal, the women as simply pathological.

Violent women versus violence against women

In Theweleit's sources ideas of women are often paired with representations of violence. Women are rendered 'cold and dead' in these men's descriptions (and are sometimes literally murdered); they become 'inanimate objects'.[49] Women are both desired and feared; they might be asexual and nurturing (a maternal nurse) or erotic and threatening (a sex worker) but these two types of imagined woman must both be 'rendered lifeless';[50] the first through objectification, the second through physical violence: 'it is the aliveness of the real that threatens these men'.[51] Threatening women are killed and mutilated. In death they acquire an erotic aspect. He writes: 'The "red roses" of her sex *only* blossom from the wounds on her dead, deformed, opened-up body.'[52] These dead objects can then take on new forms:

> Reality, robbed of its independent life, is shaped anew, kneaded into large, englobing blocks that will serve as the building material for a larger vista, a monumental world of the future: the Third Reich. In constructions of this kind, with their massive exteriors and solid forms, everything has its proper place and determinate value.[53]

If the liquidity of sexualized woman threatens the solid structures and boundaries of the man and of the masculine nation, then here the suggestion is that if controlled and harnessed, those same liquids – blood and pus and vaginal discharge – can become the basis for a new solid world. It is all a question of power and domination.

Yet the critique levelled at Theweleit by West German critics and particularly by feminists when his book was published was that because he only examined male fantasies about women, he also reduced women to an image, thus excluding the experiences of real women from his analysis. His strange image of 'englobing blocks'[54] says nothing about actual violence against actual women, neither direct physical nor sexual violence nor the numerous slow violences of patriarchal oppression. What is the relationship between a fantastical image of violent woman and the reality of violence against women? He castigates right-wing men for objectifying women but is only interested in how this phenomenon relates to fascistic ideology more generally. Here violence becomes strangely abstract: the objectification of woman is merely a stepping-stone on the way to a particular fascistic conception of the nation. He is not interested in restoring real women to their place in this history or in asking about their experiences and fantasies. As a generally sympathetic reviewer, Lutz Niethammer, noted (in a piece that was translated into English in the *History Workshop Journal* in the late 1970s): 'he says that men and women ought always to be considered in relation to each other – but then goes ahead and investigates only men, and their image of women. Women as people in their own right are barely present in his work; they are there as hypothetical constructs.'[55]

In *Sex after Fascism* (2007) Dagmar Herzog argues that Theweleit's book should be understood in relation to the historical context in which it was written. In the context, that is, of the aftermath of the 'sexual revolution' and during the women's liberation movement. Written in the disenchanted aftermath of the student and worker's movements of 1968, when many on the left began to question their previous insistence on the entanglement of the personal with the political, 'Theweleit's book', Herzog argues, 'was in its own way an effort to recapitulate and retrieve much of 1968's original impetus and to reestablish a strength of connection between sexuality, leftist politics, and the Nazi past that had started to become frayed'.[56] The book was a huge success, a 'blockbuster'. Despite criticisms by women at the time, Herzog claims that 'Theweleit's message to the heterosexual men of his own generation was that they should not resist feminism'.[57] Theweleit is constantly warning men on the left not to succumb to the misogynistic fear of sexual abandonment that he associated with proto-fascist masculinity. He is anxious that all men are proto-fascists or that being a misogynist might not be the preserve of men on the right at all. Although unlike Herzog, Niethammer made fun of Theweleit for insisting he was somehow immune to misogyny:

> he's a man himself – but of quite a different sort: he is concerned about *Berufsverbot* and doesn't give a damn about academic achievements. He looks out on romantic bourgeois house-tops (not a modern roof to be seen from his window), but he has a very trendy pin-board on his wall. He lives in comradely solidarity with a

working woman, he helps with the childcare, he's a man of the left, he admires the women's movement, he's gentle.[58]

Despite her insistence on reading Theweleit in historical context, absent from Herzog's account of *Male Fantasies* is any discussion of how his characterization of militant leftist women chimed with representations of West German woman militants at the very moment his book emerged in public (though she does discuss the Red Army Faction (RAF) earlier in the chapter). The year 1977, when Theweleit's books were first published, was also the year in which the militant activities of the RAF peaked in West Germany. Over 50 per cent of the group were women, a fact to which the mainstream press paid a lot of attention. Amanda Third claims that during the 1960s and 1970s the female terrorist was assumed to be a feminist, and the emphasis on the participation of women in militant activist groups and the demonization of those women was tied to a more general backlash against feminism: terrorism was defined as a symptom of excessive emancipation.

In the mainstream West German press, women's acts of political violence were framed as either self-motivated (performed to impress a dominant male lover) or pathological; the political motivations behind their actions could thus be dismissed. Patrizia Melzer, discussing left-wing feminist grassroots publications, argued that:

> The de-politicization of violent acts committed by women – the reduction of such acts to self-serving and pathological motives – reflects society's inability to conceptualize women as independent thinkers. It further allows those in power to deny that they are dealing with a political opponent by characterizing female militants as randomly crazy women ... The overall image that 'women who resist are crazy' results in a psycho-pathologizing of militant women that 'completely deflects from their political motives'.[59]

Women's motivations were assumed to be emotional rather than intellectual (two realms it was further assumed must be kept firmly apart) and their political actions could thus be dismissed.

Women in the RAF had a real existence apart from the press's representations of them and they mostly emerged from the same movements in which Theweleit had been involved. As was common among Western radicals of the period, the RAF drew inspiration from distant revolutionary movements across the world. They were allied with armed struggles in Palestine and had connections with Irish Republicans, but in some of their expressions of solidarity with oppressed racialized women in distant countries, such as Vietnam, China, Cuba and Guatemala, another gap between image and reality opens up, as Quinn Slobodian discusses: 'West German feminists often lionized the multi-tasking "guerrilla mother" who could incorporate the multiple demands of political struggle effortlessly, including those coded both masculine and feminine.'[60]

In Western Europe and North America, the spirit of universalism and internationalism that underpinned emancipatory movements that erupted in 1968 also became central to the women's liberation movement and could tip into false equivalencies that ignored differences of race, nationality and class and that was often founded, particularly in the case of China, on ignorance about lived experiences of the women they sought to emulate. This could result in what Judy Tzu-Chun Wu, in her work on internationalist North American radicals, has termed 'radical orientalism'.[61] In contrast to the fantastical right-wing representations of militant left-wing women this essay has discussed thus far, these representations tended to romanticize and idealize rather than demonize, but they were similarly inaccurate projections based on essentializing assumptions. Like the right-wing representations of violent working-class women, West German militant women's ideas about 'Third World' woman revolutionaries reveal far more about the former than the latter. To cite Wu again, they produced 'projections to more clearly define themselves'.[62]

(Not) all men

Theweleit's thesis is premised on a connection between hatred of women and violent nationalism but he can't quite rid himself of the anxiety that there is nothing exceptional about the misogyny of the (proto-)fascist men he discusses. Just as the weapon-wielding Communist woman soon collapses into woman as such, so the right-wing ideologue collapses into all men. Theweleit poses an uneasy question: 'Is there a true *boundary* separating "fascists" from "nonfascist" men? ... Or is it true, as many feminists claim, that fascism is simply the norm for males living under capitalist-patriarchal conditions?'[63] He argues that current conditions are already a form of fascism, not latent or potential but actual:

> We need to understand and combat fascism not because so many fell victim to it, not because it stands in the way of the triumph of socialism, not even because it might return again; but primarily because, as a form of reality production that is constantly present and possible under determinate conditions, it can, and does, become our production. The crudest examples of this are to be seen in the relations that have been the focus of this first chapter, male–female relations, which are also relations of production.[64]

This is a clear echo of Deleuze and Guattari's *Anti-Oedipus* again and of Michel Foucault's famous questions posed in the preface to that book:

> How does one keep from being fascist, even (especially) when one believes oneself to be a revolutionary militant? How do we rid our speech and our acts, our hearts and our pleasures, of fascism? How do we ferret out the fascism that is ingrained in our behaviour?[65]

Yet it seems a shortcoming in his analysis that different forms of hatred, violence and oppression all get collapsed into one another so easily. What exactly does he think fascism is?

Just because a man with professed 'progressive' views might also be a misogynist does not mean that his misogyny is identical to that expressed by someone on the far right, nor does the misogyny of either have a straightforward connection to racism or other forms of hatred (of which he makes no mention in the passage cited above). Is he saying that 'male–female relations' are analogous to fascism, are fascism or produce fascism? The possible implications are bemusing. Do fascist women simply not exist? Are all men white? Are all white men white supremacists? How can a different reality be produced? Is reality itself founded in fantasy? Despite their anti-fascist, anti-colonial and anti-racist commitments, white West German radical women themselves elided differences between themselves and women of colour from countries in the Global South, which risks downplaying forms of oppression that racialized women face. In Theweleit's case, conflating violent misogyny with fascism risks downplaying the specificities of *both* forms of violence and risks producing just another kind of 'englobing block' into which actual people (and actual struggles against interconnected but distinct forms of oppression) disappear. Perhaps this is also symptomatic of analyses that focus on images of people rather than their lived realities. Destroying the tropes and caricatures, unlatching the epithets, would involve beginning elsewhere.

Epilogue

Although in some ways it remains frustratingly stuck in a dichotomous understanding of gendered emotions and dispositions, and understands gender difference as being tied to particular activities traditionally performed by women, an anonymous text by a leftist woman proximate to the armed struggle in Italy in the 1970s called 'Pushed by the Violence of Our Desires ...' associates an approach to politics that begins from the concrete rather than the abstract with women. The author asks: 'Are men and women driven differently to take up arms in order to change the world?'[66]

The answer given is that women have a relationship to the 'concrete and fantastic' while men have a relationship to the 'abstract and rational'.[67] She argues that even if individuals resist these binaries, they are still shaped by them. She suggests that woman's relationship to politics is shaped through socially reproductive labour – 'at home we wash, iron, clean up, cook'[68] – arguing that through these small-scale ongoing indispensable daily actions performed by women their 'ant-like concreteness' is paired with a 'grasshopper-like imagination'[69] – the dimension of fantasy. Unlike men who operate with grand teleological visions of social transformation, women's relation to politics emerges from their concrete experiences. This can drive women to armed struggle – as they want to concretely transform their daily lives – we 'are driven by the violence of our dreams'.[70] Although it seems unhelpful to maintain the notion of distinctly and essentially feminine attributes this text insists on, perhaps an 'ant-like concreteness' paired with a 'grasshopper-like imagination' would be a useful alternative to an approach that attempts to understand the concrete by beginning from fantasy.[71] This would involve dispensing with an analysis of male fantasies and instead starting from women's lives and their attempts to imagine ways of transforming their lives.

Notes

1. This chapter is based on a paper given at the conference 'Gendered Emotions in History' held at Sheffield University in June 2018.

2. This essay continues some of the thoughts I tried to articulate in 'Ulrike Meinhof's Brain/Charlotte Corday's Skull: Gender, Matter and Meaning', in M. Timonen and J. Wilkstrom (eds.), *Objects of Feminism* (Helsinki: The Academy of Fine Arts Helsinki, 2017) and 'Woman on the Edge: History, Temporality, Sisterhood and Political Militancy in Marge Piercy's Vida and Margarethe von Trotta's *Die bleierne Zeit*', *Another Gaze*, 3 (2019).

3. A.L. Chu, 'On Liking Women', *n+1*, 30 (2017), https://nplusonemag.com/issue-30 /essays/on-liking-women (accessed 27 June 2023).

4. Chu, 'On Liking Women'.

5. Chu, 'On Liking Women'.

6. A. Carson, *Autobiography of Red: A Novel in Verse* (London: Alfred A. Knopf, 1998, 2010), p. 4.

7. Carson, *Autobiography of Red*, p. 5.

8. T. Eagleton, 'Aesthetics and Politics in Edmund Burke', *History Workshop Journal*, 28 (1989), 53–62 at p. 53.

9. See A. Vickers, 'Where Are the Bodies: The Haunting of Indonesia', *The Public Historian*, 32 (2010), 45–58 (which also provides a useful overview of the existing literature on the massacres of 1965–6) and M.S. Zurbuchen, 'History, Memory, and the "1965 Incident" in Indonesia', *Asian Survey*, 42 (2002), 564–81.

10. J. Roosa, *Pretext for Mass Murder: The September 30th Movement and Suharto's Coup d'état in Indonesia* (Madison, WI: University of Wisconsin Press, 2006), p. 10.

11. Roosa, *Pretext for Mass Murder*, p. 40.

12. A. Pohlman, 'The Spectre of Communist Women, Sexual Violence and Citizenship in Indonesia', *Sexualities*, 20 (2017), 196–211. See also K.E. McGregor and V. Hearman, 'Challenges of Political Rehabilitation in Post-New Order Indonesia: The Case of Gerwani (the Indonesian Women's Movement)', *South East Asia Research*, 15 (2007), 355–84.

13. S. Wieringa, *Sexual Politics in Indonesia* (New York: Springer, 2002).

14. E. Thomas, *The Women Incendiaries*, trans. J. Atkinson (London: Secker & Warburg, 1967), p. 121.

15. G.L. Gullickson, *Unruly Women of Paris: Images of the Commune* (Ithaca, NY: Cornell University Press, 1996), pp. 135–6.

16. Gullickson, *Unruly Women of Paris*, p. 140.

17. K. Theweleit, *Male Fantasies, vol. 1: Women, Floods, Bodies, History*, trans. S. Conway with E. Carter and C. Turner (Minneapolis, MN: University of Minnesota Press, 1987), p. 220.

18. Theweleit, *Male Fantasies*, pp. 16, 18.

19. Theweleit, *Male Fantasies*, p. 30.

20. Theweleit, *Male Fantasies*, p. 67.

21. Theweleit, *Male Fantasies*, p. 63.

22. Although the kinds of metaphors Federici discusses abounded in accounts by their political adversaries and Communards were likened in the press to 'savages'

and 'barbarians' when surviving Communards were sent into exile to the colonial archipelago New Caledonia, they were intended to act as a 'civilizing' influence on the indigenous Kanak population, reforming themselves through participation in the settler colonial project, and did often identify more strongly with the French state than with Kanak insurgents who they viewed as 'primitive'. See A. Bullard, *Exile to Paradise: Savagery and Civilization in Paris and the South Pacific, 1790–1900* (Stanford, CA: Stanford University Press, 2001).

23. S. Federici, *Caliban and the Witch: Women, the Body and Primitive Accumulation* (New York: Autonomedia, 2014), p. 206.

24. Federici, *Caliban and the Witch*, p. 206.

25. Theweleit, *Male Fantasies*, p. 70.

26. Theweleit, *Male Fantasies*, p. 74.

27. Theweleit, *Male Fantasies*, p. 74.

28. Theweleit, *Male Fantasies*, p. 74.

29. Theweleit, *Male Fantasies*, p. 73.

30. Theweleit, *Male Fantasies*, p. 76.

31. Theweleit, *Male Fantasies*, p. 76.

32. Theweleit, *Male Fantasies*, p. 76.

33. Quoted in Thomas, *The Women Incendiaries*, p. 151.

34. Gullickson, *Unruly Women of Paris*, p. 260.

35. Gullickson, *Unruly Women of Paris*, p. 260.

36. M. Warner, *Monuments and Maidens: The Allegory of the Female Form* (Oakley, CA: University of California Press, 2001), p. 277.

37. Theweleit, *Male Fantasies*, p. 230.

38. Theweleit, *Male Fantasies*, p. 230. However, the impulse to stop the flow paradoxically creates it in the form of blood: 'Red is female flesh wallowing in its blood; a reeking mass, severed from the man. Red is a mouth dripping blood – now beaten.' Theweleit, *Male Fantasies, vol. 2 Male Bodies: Psychoanalysing the White Terror*, trans. E. Carter and C. Turner (Minneapolis, MN: University of Minnesota Press, 1989), p. 283.

39. Theweleit, *Male Fantasies, vol. 2*, p. 276.

40. Theweleit, *Male Fantasies*, p. 283.

41. Theweleit, *Male Fantasies*, p. 392.

42. Theweleit, *Male Fantasies*, p. 407.

43. Theweleit, *Male Fantasies, vol. 2*, p. 279.

44. Theweleit, *Male Fantasies*, p. 72.

45. Theweleit, *Male Fantasies*, p. 74.

46. Theweleit, *Male Fantasies*, p. 79.

47. Theweleit, *Male Fantasies, vol. 2*, p. 274.

48. A. Third, *Gender and the Political: Deconstructing the Female Terrorist* (New York: Springer, 2014), p. 1.

49. Theweleit, *Male Fantasies*, pp. 35, 41 (and again on p. 51).

50. Theweleit, *Male Fantasies*, p. 183.

51. Theweleit, *Male Fantasies*, p. 217.

52. Theweleit, *Male Fantasies*, p. 196.

53. Theweleit, *Male Fantasies*, p. 218.

54. Theweleit, *Male Fantasies*, p. 218.

55. L. Niethammer, 'Male Fantasies: An Argument for and with an Important New Study in History and Psychoanalysis', *History Workshop Journal*, 7 (1979), 176–86 at p. 181.

56. D. Herzog, *Sex after Fascism: Memory and Morality in Twentieth-Century Germany* (Princeton, NJ: Princeton University Press, 2007), p. 221.

57. Herzog, *Sex after Fascism*, p. 242.

58. Niethammer, 'Male Fantasies', p. 181.

59. P. Melzer, '"Death in the Shape of a Young Girl": Feminist Responses to Media Representations of Women Terrorists during the "German Autumn" of 1977', *International Feminist Journal of Politics*, 11 (2009), 35–62 at p. 49. See also C. Scribner, *After the Red Army Faction: Gender, Culture and Militancy* (New York: Columbia University Press, 2015).

60. Q. Slobodian, 'Guerilla Mothers and Distant Doubles: West German Feminists Look at China and Vietnam, 1968–1982', *Zeithistorische Forschungen/Studies in Contemporary History*, 12 (2015), 39–65 at p. 59. See also J.R. Hosek, 'Subaltern Nationalism and the West Berlin Anti-Authoritarians', *German Politics and Society*, 26, 1 (2008), 57–81.

61. J.T. Wu, *Radicals on the Road: Internationalism, Orientalism, and Feminism during the Vietnam Era* (Ithaca, NY: Cornell University Press, 2013), p. 4 (the term is introduced here but used throughout the book).

62. Wu, *Radicals on the Road*, p. 138.

63. Theweleit, *Male Fantasies*, p. 27.

64. Theweleit, *Male Fantasies*, p. 221.

65. M. Foucault, 'Preface' to Deleuze and Guattari, *Anti-Oedipus: Capitalism and Schizophrenia*, trans. R. Hurley, M. Seem and H.R. Lane (Minneapolis, MN: University of Minnesota Press, 2003), pp. xi–xiv, xiii.

66. Thanks to Sophie Jones for suggesting this text to me. Anonymous, 'Pushed by the Violence of Our Desires ...', in P. Bono and S. Kemp (eds.), *Italian Feminist Thought: A Reader* (Oxford: Blackwell, 1991), pp. 303–8, 303.

67. Anon., 'Pushed', p. 304.

68. Anon., 'Pushed', p. 304.

69. Anon., 'Pushed', p. 305.

70. Anon., 'Pushed', p. 307.

71. Anon., 'Pushed', p. 308.

References

Anonymous, 'Pushed by the Violence of our Desires ...', in P. Bono and S. Kemp (eds.), *Italian Feminist Thought: A Reader* (Oxford: Blackwell, 1991), pp. 303–8.

Bullard, A., *Exile to Paradise: Savagery and Civilization in Paris and the South Pacific, 1790–1900* (Stanford, CA: Stanford University Press, 2001).

Carson, A., *Autobiography of Red: A Novel in Verse* (London: Alfred A. Knopf, 1998, 2010).

Chu, A.L., 'On Liking Women', *n +1*, 30 (2017), https://nplusonemag.com/issue-30/essays/on-liking-women (accessed 27 June 2023).

Eagleton, T., 'Aesthetics and Politics in Edmund Burke', *History Workshop Journal*, 28 (1989), 53–62.

Federici, S., *Caliban and the Witch: Women, the Body and Primitive Accumulation* (New York: Autonomedia, 2014).

Foucault, M., 'Preface' to Deleuze and Guattari, *Anti-Oedipus: Capitalism and Schizophrenia*, trans. R. Hurley, M. Seem and H.R. Lane (Minneapolis, MN: University of Minnesota Press, 2003), pp. xi–xiv.

Gullickson, G.L., *Unruly Women of Paris: Images of the Commune* (Ithaca, NY: Cornell University Press, 1996).

Herzog, D., *Sex after Fascism: Memory and Morality in Twentieth-Century Germany* (Princeton, NJ: Princeton University Press, 2007).

Hosek, J.R., 'Subaltern Nationalism and the West Berlin Anti-Authoritarians', *German Politics and Society*, 26, 1 (2008), 57–81.

McGregor, K.E., and Hearman, V., 'Challenges of Political Rehabilitation in Post-New Order Indonesia: The Case of Gerwani (the Indonesian Women's Movement)', *South East Asia Research*, 15 (2007), 355–84.

Melzer, P., '"Death in the Shape of a Young Girl": Feminist Responses to Media Representations of Women Terrorists during the "German Autumn" of 1977', *International Feminist Journal of Politics*, 11 (2009), 35–62.

Ngai, S., *Ugly Feelings* (Cambridge, MA: Harvard University Press, 2005).

Niethammer, L., 'Male Fantasies: An Argument for and with an Important New Study in History and Psychoanalysis', *History Workshop Journal*, 7 (1979), 176–86.

Pohlman, A., 'The Spectre of Communist Women, Sexual Violence and Citizenship in Indonesia', *Sexualities*, 20 (2017), 196–211.

Roosa, J., *Pretext for Mass Murder: The September 30th Movement and Suharto's Coup d'état in Indonesia* (Madison, WI: University of Wisconsin Press, 2006).

Scribner, C., *After the Red Army Faction: Gender, Culture and Militancy* (New York: Columbia University Press, 2015).

Slobodian, Q., 'Guerilla Mothers and Distant Doubles: West German Feminists Look at China and Vietnam, 1968–1982', *Zeithistorische Forschungen/Studies in Contemporary History*, 12 (2015), 39–65.

Theweleit, K., *Male Fantasies, vol. 1: Women, Floods, Bodies, History*, trans. S. Conway with E. Carter and C. Turner (Minneapolis, MN: University of Minnesota Press, 1987).

——, *Male Fantasies, vol. 2: Male Bodies – Psychoanalysing the White Terror*, trans. E. Carter and C. Turner (Minneapolis, MN: University of Minnesota Press, 1989).

Third, A., *Gender and the Political: Deconstructing the Female Terrorist* (New York: Springer, 2014).

Thomas, E., *The Women Incendiaries*, trans. J. Atkinson (London: Secker & Warburg, 1967).

Vickers, A., 'Where Are the Bodies: The Haunting of Indonesia', *The Public Historian*, 32, (2010).

Warner, M., *Monuments and Maidens: The Allegory of the Female Form* (Oakley, CA: University of California Press, 2001).

Wieringa, S., *Sexual Politics in Indonesia* (New York: Springer, 2002).

Wu, J.T., *Radicals on the Road: Internationalism, Orientalism, and Feminism during the Vietnam Era* (Ithaca, NY: Cornell University Press, 2013).

Zurbuchen, M.S., 'History, Memory, and the "1965 Incident" in Indonesia', *Asian Survey*, 42 (2002), 564–81.

Index

A

absence, 34, 38, 42, 44, 132, 231–2, 247
activism, 5, 6, 9, 12, 13, 14, 32, 56–69, 149, 264, 276
activists. *See* activism
Addison, Joseph, 225, 227, 228, 229, 233
affect, 34, 42, 60, 77, 121, 181, 196–9, 218–23, 233, 262
  affective relationships, 8, 9, 154, 159, 196, 225–6
  theory, 16, 219–20, 230
affection, 1, 82, 85, 88, 95, 133–4, 151, 177, 195, 198, 199, 207, 248
Africa, 3, 13, 15, 148–9, 172, 174, 204
  African people, 15, 121–6, 128, 129, 130–37, 145–59, 203
agency, 34, 44, 86, 136, 201
Anderson, Olive, 240
anthropology, 12, 196–7, 200–209, 218
  evolutionary anthropology, 197, 201, 203, 204, 205, 207, 208
anxiety, 42, 208, 218, 232–3, 247, 262–6, 269, 270, 273, 277
  ideological, 35
  psychological, 81
  racial, 121–2, 127, 130–32, 137
authority, 11, 32, 34, 56, 80, 135, 218, 230, 251, 270
autobiography. *See* life-writing

B

belonging, 13–15, 44, 83, 148, 158–9, 222
bisexuality, 5, 9, 13, 56–65, 67–9
blackness, 148–50, 155
'Black Peril', 131, 151
Boddice, Rob, 10, 171, 220, 222, 225
body, 12, 14, 32, 81–2, 199, 221, 222–3, 227–9, 231, 263, 271–4
  odour, 148–50
Bolshevik, 31–3, 35, 42, 44, 271
  Bolshevism, 269, 272
boundaries, 10, 12, 32, 34, 63, 105, 219, 225,
  gendered, 38, 60, 97, 108, 174, 272–4
  racial, 15, 121–2, 126, 128, 134, 146–7, 151–3, 158, 203
Britain, 16–17, 95, 100, 105, 106, 107, 109, 123, 132
  eighteenth-century, 217, 221, 227–8
  See also hospital, British

C

capitalism, 15, 32, 37, 85, 106, 107, 247–8, 249, 277
  colonial,15
care, 39–40, 43, 55, 56, 81, 88, 103, 108, 172, 175
  childcare, 35–7, 40, 98, 108, 199, 264, 270, 276
  healthcare, 122
  paternal, 230, 248
childbirth, 35, 38, 39, 267,
childhood, 40, 132–3, 145, 147, 153
children, 31–2, 36–8, 40–45, 56, 98, 127–34,136, 152–3, 195, 199, 242–3, 247–50, 270
  grandchildren, 104, 152, 155, 157
China, 3, 13, 14, 77, 78, 82, 84, 86, 87, 88, 90
  People's Republic of China, 13, 78, 87
Chinese People's Voluntary Force (CVPF), 78, 80, 81, 82, 83, 84, 85
cinema. *See* film
civility, 149, 156, 176–7, 196, 203, 205, 225
civilization, 198, 201, 204, 230, 269, 270
  civilizing, 176–7, 203, 225
Civil War, 33, 34, 41, 42, 148
class, 32, 57, 88–90, 95, 122, 124, 130, 132, 136, 137, 145, 146, 149, 150, 153–7, 174, 180, 249, 268, 274, 277
  feeling, 77, 78
  identity, 32, 122, 128, 129, 146, 252
  middle, 132, 150, 153, 155, 157, 174, 247–8, 249
  struggle, 79, 88, 89
  working, 96, 103, 109, 121–4, 129, 132, 146, 148, 240–42, 245–52, 265–8, 277
collectivism, 5, 9, 14, 32, 33, 34, 35, 42, 43, 45, 77, 82, 84, 85
colonialism, 9, 10, 15–16, 85, 121–2, 145–7, 170–72, 175, 196, 202–5
  colonial discourse, 16, 148, 150, 156, 196
  colonial science, 16, 202, 203, 206
  Italian, 16, 196, 204–5, 206
  post-colonial. *See* post-colonial
  settler, 9, 13, 122, 149, 155
community, 4, 7, 8, 12–13, 15, 16, 42, 55, 57, 59, 61–6, 83, 86, 96–8, 101–9, 122, 124, 127, 131, 132, 136, 158, 176
  emotional. *See* emotion
  LGBTQ+. *See* LGBTQ+
  norms, 108, 147, 217, 233, 245
conflict, 4, 37, 40, 43, 77, 85, 88, 89, 220, 224

285

286 INDEX

D

darkness, 31, 32, 38, 39, 41, 81, 178, 226
Darwin, Charles, 197, 200–201, 202, 207, 208
depression, 1, 82, 126
Depression, the, 123, 129, 132–3, 134–5, 240
diary. *See* life-writing
digital space. *See* space
discourse, 10, 68, 146, 207, 209, 222, 239, 241, 245, 263
  colonial. *See* colonialism
  gendered, 2, 14, 56–7, 59
  polite, 221, 232
  public, 56, 63–4, 104, 231
  scientific, 195, 196, 197, 203, 205
  of smell, 148, 149, 150, 151, 155, 156, 158
  Soviet, 33, 35, 37, 44, 56
discrimination, 57, 59, 63, 150
disgust, 105, 145–6, 147, 148, 151, 153, 154, 155, 156, 158, 228
divorce, 32, 197, 198, 206

E

education, 4–5, 58, 65–8, 122, 124, 128–9, 153, 180, 203, 229–30
  and culture, 79, 87, 217
  gender and schooling, 36, 39–40, 43–4
  women's, 264, 270
effeminacy, 125, 227, 230, 232–3
eighteenth century, 7, 11, 16, 195, 202, 217–33
emancipation, 32, 38, 41–2, 270, 276, 277
embodiment, 6–8, 10, 15–16, 33–4, 41, 81, 86–8, 146–7, 153, 221–3, 228–9, 231–2, 245, 247, 263, 266, 270
emotion
  agency. *See* agency
  behaviour, 6, 10, 65, 96, 100, 224
  bond, 13–14, 33, 36, 38, 45, 89, 95, 98, 128, 132–3, 146–7, 151, 158, 195, 198, 204–6
  capital, 57, 58–9, 61, 62, 63, 64, 67, 69
  community, 10–14, 16, 32, 34, 38, 55, 58, 61, 63–9, 96, 107, 109, 146, 152–4, 158, 199, 221, 223–8, 230, 233
  conflict. *See* conflict
  control. *See* emotion, regulation
  distance, 1, 15, 125, 137, 148, 232
  expectation, 10, 14, 32–3
  experience, 7–8, 15–16, 58–9, 97, 99, 107, 218–19, 221, 245
  expression, 6, 7, 10, 58–60, 65, 122–4, 127, 136, 146, 200–201, 204, 220
  emotionality, 2, 13, 33, 40, 63, 201
  history, 6, 7, 17, 218, 219, 222, 227
  labour, 5, 155

language, 15, 146, 154
norms, 4, 7, 9, 12, 14, 15, 136, 146, 147, 153, 157, 158
paradigm, 16, 195, 196, 197, 199, 202, 208, 209
performance, 6–9, 11–12, 14, 33, 37, 58, 67, 84, 89, 121, 134, 136, 232–3, 239, 244, 249–50
practice, 10, 11, 12, 58, 67, 68, 171, 177, 179, 180, 244–5
regime, 9, 10, 22, 222, 226–7
regulation 7, 9–11, 15, 17, 38, 58–60, 63, 67, 85, 97, 108, 122–3, 146, 151–2, 157–8, 225, 250
response, 6–7, 10, 44, 62, 131–2, 145–8, 155–7, 199, 221, 226, 242, 245–6
rhetoric. *See* rhetoric
spaces. *See* spaces
strategy, 9, 121, 122, 146, 148, 152, 229
style, 8, 33, 225
vocabulary, 6, 8, 9, 14, 33
work, 43, 146, 155
empathy, 65, 67, 105, 106, 124, 131, 222, 225, 226
empire, 9, 14, 16, 172, 196
  British Empire, 14, 121, 127, 171, 175, 180, 181
  imperialism, 16, 85, 89, 121, 124, 176
  Italian Empire, 16, 203–4
  Russian Empire, 39
environment, 1, 4, 8, 13, 15, 57, 68, 98, 147, 158, 171–2, 178, 181, 220, 221
essentialization, 32, 121
  of emotions, 3, 151, 219–20
  of gender, 32–3, 36, 38, 66, 277
eugenics, 130, 201–2
Europe, 2, 3, 4, 7, 8, 100
  cultures, 8, 17, 35, 195, 196, 198, 217, 232
  people, 4, 15–16, 17, 123, 126, 129–30, 135, 148, 150–51, 202–5
  powers, 2, 4, 149, 204
experience, 11, 33, 41, 88, 89, 90, 154, 157, 177–81, 195, 203, 230, 231
  activist, 61, 62, 65, 66, 67
  bodily, 222–3, 245, 250
  emotional. *See* emotions
  histories of, 15
  lived, 81–2, 136, 218–20, 277–9
  of pleasure, 198, 272
  sensory, 149
  of solidarity, 96, 97, 98–9, 107
  of war, 80–81, 82, 83, 85

F

failure, 56, 84, 105, 121, 132, 137, 151, 170, 221, 229, 233, 241, 246, 247, 250

family, 56, 102–9, 125, 126, 177–80, 218, 240–50, 252, 264
  economy, 97–9
  interracial, 152–4
  nuclear, 33, 36–7, 132, 195, 198–9
  providing for, 129–32
  transnational, 89
fashion, 227, 228, 231, 233
fatherhood, 97, 104, 126, 133, 134, 230, 232, 247–8
fear, 1, 4, 97, 100–101, 107–8, 121, 219, 230, 239, 247, 250, 272, 275
  history of, 7, 10
  racial, 125, 127, 134, 136, 145–7, 151–5, 203
femininity, 36, 60, 85, 98–9, 103–4, 108, 124, 136–7, 174, 231–2, 263, 273–4, 277, 279
feminism, 4, 14, 55–62, 64–8, 79, 88, 268–9, 274–7
film, 14, 37–8, 39, 42, 62–3, 78–90, 96, 102
First World War, 123, 263, 267, 269
folk tradition, 35, 39, 89, 222
France, 1, 265, 266, 269, 271
Freikorps, 17, 266, 267–8, 271, 272, 273

G

gender
  equality, 4, 32, 43, 55–6, 59, 65
  identity, 11, 15, 32, 55, 57, 65, 124, 218, 245
  relations, 35, 43, 44, 261
  roles, 6, 13, 14, 17, 55–6, 103–4, 108, 131–3, 265, 269, 270
generation, 11, 35, 38, 39, 40, 43, 45, 201, 202, 275
grief, 1, 14, 33, 37, 38–9, 40, 42, 43–4

H

Heroic Sons and Daughters (1964), 14, 78, 79, 83, 84, 87, 88, 89, 90
heteronormativity, 56, 57, 63, 64, 97
hierarchy, 4, 10, 15, 64, 145, 153, 155, 197, 201, 218, 220, 227
  of cultures or civilizations, 39, 201
  of love, 199, 205–6
  racial, 123, 135, 136, 137, 145, 155, 205, 206
homosexuality, 55, 56, 207
hospital, 15, 169–72, 173, 174, 175–80, 181
  British, 175, 180, 181

I

identity, 5, 11, 56, 62, 68, 122, 131, 134, 149, 206, 226, 228, 240, 252
  class. See class

collective, 10, 11, 124, 217
construction, 9–10, 39, 44, 58, 64, 231
formation, 224, 245
gender. See gender
individual, 10, 39, 65, 88, 196, 217
racial, 122, 124, 129, 131, 134, 146, 147
social, 10, 39, 44
imperial. See empire
inclusion, 32, 63, 105, 171, 181
India, 3, 13, 15, 171, 174, 175, 177, 180, 181, 204
interiority, 14, 79, 88
intermediality, 7, 11, 12, 14, 57, 78, 85–6, 90, 222
intimacy, 15, 59, 77, 128, 145–8, 150–55, 158, 171, 196, 228,
Italy, 13, 16, 202, 204, 278
  post-unification, 197–8, 203

J

joy, 32, 82, 126, 129

K

Kenya, 13, 15, 121, 146–50, 152–8
Korean War 14, 77–81, 83–90
Krest'ianka journal, 34, 41, 42
Kruspakaia, Nadezhda Konstantinovna, 32, 39, 41, 42, 43

L

labour, 5, 8, 32, 35, 37, 40, 55, 57, 88, 96–100, 106–8, 122–37, 155, 173, 242–4, 251–2, 279
  domestic, 37, 40, 55. See also servant
  emotional. See emotion
landscape, 1–2, 17, 32, 44–5, 82–3, 174, 252
language, 1–4, 17, 33, 66, 220, 227, 230, 233, 239–43, 245–52, 263
  emotive, 4, 15,146–8, 154, 158
  gendered, 10
  inclusive, 63
  knowledge of, 135, 154–6
  visual, 79, 81, 84, 87
legitimacy, 14, 33, 35, 37, 43, 78, 136, 146–51, 155–8, 205, 208, 229, 270
Lenin, Vladimir Ilich, 32, 42
letters, 14, 16, 33–4, 44–5, 136, 170, 199, 227–33, 267
  letter-writing, 34, 38, 44, 223
LGBTQ+, 56, 58
  communities, 57, 60–61, 62, 63, 64, 66
  rights, 55, 56–7, 60, 62
liberation, 39, 67, 268, 275, 277
life-writing, 42, 80, 122, 132, 133, 201, 262. See also letters, letter-writing

literary analysis, 217–23
Liverpool, 5, 9, 13, 95–109
loneliness, 125–8, 137
Lord Chesterfield, 229–32
love, 1, 6, 16, 62, 65, 77, 85, 95, 99, 220,
    227, 229, 232, 268
  familial love, 132–3, 152–4, 170
  maternal love, 35–8, 42–5
  perfect love, 199
  romantic love, 195–9, 201, 205,
    207, 208
lyricism, 14, 78–9

M

Malthus, Thomas, 13, 241, 242, 243, 244,
    247, 250, 252
Mantegazza, Paolo, 16, 197, 198–200,
    203–4, 204–8
  Archivio per l'antropologia e l'etnologia
    (1893), 207
  Fisiologia dell'amore (1873), 200, 201,
    202, 206
  Gli amori degli uomini (1885),
    204, 206
marriage, 31, 152, 195, 197, 197–8, 202,
    205–6
masculinity, 124–5, 224, 225, 227, 230, 231,
    239, 240
  hegemonic, 239–40, 241
  polite, 221, 224, 228, 229, 232–3, 233
materiality, 16, 34, 38, 44, 133, 151,
    171, 179
media, 3–4, 56, 57, 60–65, 68, 78, 79, 85,
    90, 135, 239, 246, 251, 252, 265
  digital, 57, 60, 64. *See also* film; space,
    digital
  print, 14, 31–5, 41–2, 54, 96, 106, 122,
    124, 126–7, 136, 218–19, 240–41,
    244–51, 267–9, 276
  social. *See* social media
mediation, 11–14, 56–7, 90
melodrama, 84, 241, 245, 246–7, 248,
    249–50, 252
metaphor, 1–2, 11–12, 39, 270–71
misogyny, 3, 5, 17, 41, 44, 231, 265, 267–8,
    275–8
mission, 15, 155, 169–81, 202
mobilization, 8–9, 37, 42–5, 78, 86–7,
    102, 128, 131, 154, 265
monogamy, 206–8
morality, 98, 201, 205, 217, 226, 228, 231,
    241, 248, 251–2
  moral economy, 32, 225
  sexual, 197, 201, 203, 207
motherhood, 14, 33, 34–5, 35–7, 38–9, 40,
    42–3, 55–6, 126, 128, 133

N

narrative, 42, 45, 58, 61, 80, 86, 88–9,
    96, 108, 170, 225, 240–41, 243–52,
    264–5, 273
nation, 2, 4, 17, 78, 86–7, 90, 146, 197,
    198, 204, 208, 227, 271, 274, 275
  national identity, 82, 86, 89, 124, 208,
    272, 277
  nationalism, 78, 82, 83, 87, 89, 271, 277
  statehood, 2, 197, 227
networks, 57–60, 105, 227, 268
nineteenth century, 12–13, 16, 171–5, 181,
    196–200, 202–8, 222, 240–41, 251–2,
    261, 268

O

obshchestvennitsa, 36, 37
oral history, 15, 96, 147

P

Paris Commune, 17, 265–6
party
  Bolshevik, 31, 32, 38, 41, 42
  Chinese Communist Party, 78
  Communist Party of Indonesia, 264
  Rhodesian Labour Party, 122, 126
paternity, 198, 230
patriarchy, 2, 6, 36, 57, 88, 248, 262, 266,
    275, 277
patriotism, 82, 83, 197, 198
peasantry, 31, 35, 41
People's Republic of China (PRC).
    See China
performance, 6–9, 11–12, 14, 33, 58, 79,
    82, 84–6, 126, 134, 136, 227, 230, 233
  of gender, 222, 230, 232
periodicals, 16, 223, 225–8, 233
pétroleuses, 17, 265–71
philosophy, 68, 172
politeness, 224, 227, 230, 231, 232
polygamy, 197, 205–8
Poor Laws, 241, 242, 243, 247, 251
population, 4, 6, 16, 35, 122, 129, 155, 158,
    200, 202–5, 241–4
post-colonial, 13, 15, 146, 148, 150,
    153–5, 157–8
poverty, 15, 17, 44, 55, 122, 130–36, 145,
    241, 245–6, 248–51
press. *See* media, print
pride, 42, 97–105, 107–8, 122, 124, 127–31,
    134, 136–7, 224, 250–51
primitive, 196, 197, 202, 203, 205,
    206, 208
protest, 9, 57, 68
Protestant, 170, 172
psychology, 12, 32, 200, 207, 219

public sphere, 14, 68, 199, 218, 228, 270
  literary, 218
purdah, 15, 171–2, 177–81

Q

queer, 56, 64
  sexualities, 227

R

race, 8–9, 17, 122, 136–7, 153, 157, 197–8,
    200, 205–7, 277
  construction of, 8–9, 149–50
racialization, 9–10, 13, 15, 146, 152, 205,
    268, 276, 278
  of labour, 126, 136, 149, 155–6
racism, 9, 126, 145, 149, 203, 205, 206,
    268, 278
railways, 15, 122–3, 125–32, 245
religion, 6, 32, 39, 68, 97, 169, 179–80,
    205, 217, 224, 244, 265
  Christianity, 155, 177
  Hinduism, 177, 179
  Islam, 177
  Judaism, 68
resistance, 4, 9–11, 78, 123
respectability, politics of, 11, 124, 126,
    128–30, 134, 240, 250–52
revolution, 40–41
  revolutionary struggle, 37
  October Revolution, 31, 40, 42, 43
rhetoric, 3–4, 57, 64–7, 198, 221–2, 230,
    233, 243, 248
Rhodesia (Southern), 13, 15, 121–6, 131–2,
    146–7, 149
romantic love. *See* love
Rosenwein, Barbara, 6, 8, 12, 96, 123, 146,
    221, 224
Russia, 41, 55, 56–7, 58, 61, 64, 67–8
  Russian, 1, 39, 62, 66
  Russian Federation, 3, 4, 13, 55, 56–7,
    58, 68

S

scientific language, 66, 195, 197, 200, 203,
    227
selfhood, 3, 6, 10, 11, 33, 34, 224, 233
senses, 15, 147–8, 158, 198, 222
sensory knowledge, 15, 147, 150
servant, 133–4, 149, 155
settler colonialism. *See* colonialism
sexual difference, 10, 33, 173
sexuality, 2–3, 5–6, 8–10, 13, 55–6, 58,
    64, 146, 151–3, 155, 158, 195–208, 267,
    269, 277
  sexual minorities, 56
  sexual behaviour, 200, 202–4

sexual reproduction, 35, 152, 200
sexual science, 16, 195, 196, 197, 199,
    200–202, 208
sexual selection, 201–2, 207–8
sex work, 131, 268, 269, 273–4
shame, 7, 16, 105–7, 124, 126, 129–31,
    136–7, 203, 217, 220–29, 231–3, 261
  of poverty, 122, 131–4, 241, 243–5, 247,
    250–51
Shanggan Ridge, 14, 78–81, 84, 87–8
smell, 145–50, 153, 154–5, 157, 158, 218
Smiles, Samuel, 241, 244–5, 247, 250, 252
sociability, 225, 230, 233
social
  construction, 5, 7, 9, 11, 196, 208
  reproduction, 7, 129, 151
socialism, 38, 43, 79, 277
  socialist construction, 32, 33, 37, 42
social media, 14, 57, 58, 59–60, 64, 65,
    66, 67, 68
  Facebook, 59, 60–61, 62
  Instagram, 59, 60
  Telegram messenger, 59, 61
  vkontakte.com, 59, 61, 62
solidarity, 9, 13–14, 37, 95–100, 102–3,
    105–9, 126, 275–6
Soviet Union, 3, 13, 31, 34, 36, 43, 55
space
  digital, 5, 14, 57–60, 63–4, 69
  emotional, 58
  liminal, 34, 44, 154
  public, 149, 179
  urban, 68, 85, 136, 180
The Spectator, 225, 227, 231
Steele, Richard, 225, 226, 228, 233
stories, 59, 79–80, 96, 222, 240–41, 244–7,
    251–2, 264, 267
strike action, 13, 37, 96, 99–100, 123
subjectivity, 6, 11, 77, 87, 96, 147
suicide, 16, 40, 42–5, 239–47, 250–52
  suicide rates, 239, 240
  suicidology, 240, 251–2
sweat, 148–50, 155

T

Theweleit, Klaus, 17, 266–78
Tomkins, Silvan, 219, 220
  Affect, Imagery, Consciousness (1962,
    1991), 219
trade union, 95–6, 98, 100, 105–7, 109,
    122–8, 130–31, 134, 136, 264
transformation, 38, 41, 59, 77, 98, 196,
    279
transgender, 9, 13, 56–61, 63–9
transition, 56, 64–8
transphobia, 9, 65–7

290 INDEX

trans women, 57, 58,
twentieth century, 95, 98, 108, 123, 149,
171–3, 204, 207, 240, 252, 261
two-line struggle, 14, 79

U

unemployment, 13, 123, 130–31, 135,
241–9, 251
United States of America, 4, 13, 78, 106, 149
utilitarianism, 241–2, 244, 247, 251–2

V

violence, 10, 17, 56, 123, 135, 137, 246, 249,
263–8, 274–9
political, 261–2, 274, 276
sexual, 4, 275

W

Weimar Germany, 17, 267
Westermarck, Edward, 207, 208,
209
The History of Human Marriage
(1893), 207
whiteness, 9, 15, 68, 126, 129, 146–7,
151, 158
witches, 10, 11, 261, 268, 269
workhouse, 241, 250–52

Z

Zambia, 13, 15, 145–6, 148, 153, 155–6,
158
Zhenotdel, 41, 44
Zimbabwe, 13

Printed in the USA
CPSIA information can be obtained
at www.ICGtesting.com
LVHW060531160224
771887LV00001B/3